# THE NATURE OF INTERNATIONAL LAW

Jurisprudence has up until recently largely neglected international law as a subject of philosophizing. *The Nature of International Law* tries to offset this deficiency, by providing a comprehensive explanatory account of international law. It does so within an analytical tradition, albeit within the one which departs from the nowadays dominant method of the metaphysically driven conceptual analysis. Instead, it adopts the prototype theory of concepts, which is directed toward determining typical features constitutive of the nature of international law. The book's central finding is that those features are: normativity, institutionalization, coercive guaranteeing, and justice-aptness. Since typical features are context sensitive, their specificities at the international level are further elucidated. The book, finally, challenges the often raised claim that fragmentation is international law's unique feature, by demonstrating that international institutional actors, particularly adjudicative ones, largely perceive themselves as officials of a unified legal order.

Miodrag A. Jovanović is Full Professor in Jurisprudence, Faculty of Law, University of Belgrade. His areas of interest are jurisprudence, philosophy of international law, legal theory of collective rights, political theory of multiculturalism, federalism, and the legal and political nature of the EU. He is a fellow of the Alexander von Humboldt Foundation and the 2016 Brandon Fellow of the Lauterpacht Centre for International Law, University of Cambridge. He has previously published *Collective Rights – A Legal Theory* (Cambridge University Press, 2012).

# ASIL STUDIES IN INTERNATIONAL LEGAL THEORY



The purpose of the ASIL Studies in International Legal Theory series is to clarify and improve the theoretical foundations of international law. Too often the progressive development and implementation of international law has foundered on confusion about first principles. This series raises the level of public and scholarly discussion about the structure and purposes of the world legal order and how best to achieve global justice through law.

This series grows out of the International Legal Theory project of the American Society of International Law. The ASIL Studies in International Legal Theory series deepens this conversation by publishing scholarly monographs and edited volumes of essays considering subjects in international legal theory.

*Books in the Series*

*The Nature of International Law*
Miodrag A. Jovanović

*Reexamining Customary International Law*
Edited by Brian D. Lepard

*Theoretical Boundaries of Armed Conflict and Human Rights*
Edited by Jens David Ohlin

*Human Rights in Emergencies*
Edited by Evan J. Criddle

*The Theory of Self-Determination*
Edited by Fernando R. Tesón

*Negotiating State and Non-State Law: Global and Local Legal Pluralism*
Edited by Michael A. Helfand

*Normative Pluralism and International Law: Exploring Global Governance*
Jan Klabbers and Touko Piipaerinen

*Jus Post Bellum and Transitional Justice*
Edited by Larry May and Elizabeth Edenberg

*The Future of International Law: Global Government*
Joel P. Trachtman

*Morality, Jus Post Bellum, and International Law*
Edited by Larry May and Andrew T. Forcehimes

*Parochialism, Cosmopolitanism, and the Foundations of International Law*
Edited by Mortimer Sellers

*Global Justice and International Economic Law: Opportunities and Prospects*
Edited by Chios Carmody, Frank J. Garcia, and John Linarelli

*The Role of Ethics in International Law*
Edited by Donald Earl Childress III

*The New Global Law*
Rafael Domingo

*Customary International Law: A New Theory with Practical Applications*
Brian D. Lepard

*International Criminal Law and Philosophy*
Edited by Larry May and Zachary Hoskins

# The Nature of International Law

MIODRAG A. JOVANOVIĆ
University of Belgrade

CAMBRIDGE
UNIVERSITY PRESS

CAMBRIDGE
UNIVERSITY PRESS

Shaftesbury Road, Cambridge CB2 8EA, United Kingdom

One Liberty Plaza, 20th Floor, New York, NY 10006, USA

477 Williamstown Road, Port Melbourne, VIC 3207, Australia

314–321, 3rd Floor, Plot 3, Splendor Forum, Jasola District Centre, New Delhi – 110025, India

103 Penang Road, #05–06/07, Visioncrest Commercial, Singapore 238467

Cambridge University Press is part of Cambridge University Press & Assessment, a department of the University of Cambridge.

We share the University's mission to contribute to society through the pursuit of education, learning and research at the highest international levels of excellence.

www.cambridge.org
Information on this title: www.cambridge.org/9781108461382

DOI: 10.1017/9781108608060



First published 2019
First paperback edition 2026

*A catalogue record for this publication is available from the British Library*

ISBN 978-1-108-47333-0 Hardback
ISBN 978-1-108-46138-2 Paperback

To my parents

# Contents

# Contents

# Acknowledgments

I have been dealing for quite some time with topics falling within the ambit of the philosophy of international law. As a visiting scholar I have been giving lectures on these topics at the University of Geosciences (Wuhan), Lucernaiuris Institute (University of Lucerne), the University of Katowice, and the Institute of the Foundations of Law (University of Graz). At various international conferences I have presented several papers of that sort: "Interpretation in International Law and International Rule of Law," at the 2012 annual conference of the Serbian IVR Section "Courts, Interpretation, the Rule of Law"; "Revisiting the Concept of International Law – Methodological Aspects," at the 2013 conference "Methodology of Legal Theory," University of Zagreb; "Dworkin on International Law: Not Much of a Legacy?," at the 2014 conference "The Legacy of Ronald Dworkin," McMaster University, Hamilton; "Theorizing 'Unidentified Normative Objects' of the Global Regulatory Regimes," at the 2015 conference "Unity and Diversity of Global Administrative Regimes," Centre for Research in Public Law, University of Lisbon; and "Is Legality like Virginity? An Essay on the Normativity of International Law," at the 2015 World Congress of Philosophy of Law and Social Philosophy (IVR), Washington, at the 2015 annual conference of the Serbian IVR section, Belgrade, as well as at the 2015 conference "Validity and Public Trust," University of Groningen. Some of the papers have been published in the meantime and they served as a starting point for discussions in this book (references to those works are scattered throughout the book).

In the process of book writing I have especially benefited from a June–July 2014 research stay at the Max Planck Institute for Comparative Public Law and International Law, where I conducted research on the topic "Revisiting the Concept of International Law – Philosophical Foundations." I finalized this research, under a slightly revised name – "The Concept of International Law Revisited – A Jurisprudential Inquiry" – in the period of July–September 2017 at the Lauterpacht Centre for International Law, as the 2016 Brandon Research Fellow. I was there provided with a setting in which I had everything I needed for good quality research. For this, special thanks go to Karen Fachechi and Anita Rutherford. On more than one occasion I also had fruitful conversations with collaborators and other research scholars of the Centre. This is particularly true of discussions with members of the so-called Kitchen Consensus group – Julia Kapelańska-Pręgowska, Rossana Deplano, Justyna Chrzanowska, Enrico Milano, and Guo Ran.

I am most thankful to friends and colleagues who were willing to sacrifice their time and help me by reading, and commenting on, parts of this book: Ken Himma, Brian Bix, Veronica Rodriguez-Blanco, Marko Milanović, Vladimir Đerić, Tatjana Papić, Bojana Čučković, and Marko Novaković. I owe special gratitude to my dear friends from the Law Faculty, University of Belgrade, Bojan Spaić and Goran Dajović. Not only did they provide me with intellectually stimulating talks, but their ideas in many respects directed the course of this book, in particular its methodological orientation toward the prototype theory of concepts. Last, but not least, I once again enjoyed cooperating with the CUP editorial team, led by Finola O'Sullivan and Tom Randall.

***In Belgrade, 31 July 2018***

# Introduction

This is a treatise on the philosophy of international law. Hence, its successes or failures should be measured primarily by the yardsticks of legal philosophy. Still, its purpose, as in the case of any other work in the area of jurisprudence, is to cast some new light on the legal practice – in this case the international one – and to offer to those working in this practice a fresh perspective on the issues with which they deal on a daily basis. In doing so, legal philosophers are not there "to act as backroom boffins for the law industry." That is, theirs is not "to lay on new ideas or arguments for lawyers any more than philosophers of art are there to provide new ideas or materials for artists."[1] Theirs is to "see legal problems . . . as different problems from those that appear on the face of the law."[2] In that respect, this book aspires to persuade international legal practitioners that it is meaningful to take a deep gaze at old problems with new eyes.

This aspiration is far from warranted though. International scholars are not necessarily keen to employ a jurisprudential perspective. Take Brownlie's words from his *General Course to the Hague Academy of International Law*: "In spite of considerable exposure to theory, and some experience in teaching jurisprudence, my ultimate position has been that . . . theory produces no real benefits and frequently obscures the more interesting questions."[3] It is mainly legal philosophers' fault for the fact that this statement could, until recently, be taken as representative enough of the overall attitude of the international scholarship. With the notable exception of Kelsen, whose legal philosophy is not always easily digestible even for those working in the field, no other

[1] John Gardner, "Why Study Jurisprudence?" (2006) *The Inner Temple Yearbook 2006/2007*: 6, at https://www.dropbox.com/s/rz9l4n8nlgzk7yv/whystudyjurisprudence.pdf?dl=0

[2] *Ibid*, 7.

[3] Ian Brownlie, "International Law at the Fiftieth Anniversary of the United Nations," The Rule of Law in International Affairs: International Law at the Fiftieth Anniversary of the United Nations (The Hague: Martinus Nijhoff Publishers, 1998), 30.

prominent contemporary legal philosopher was ready to seriously engage with the subject matter of international law. Worse still, those who decided to grapple with the topic, including the one who "was credited with having more or less reinvented the philosophy of law" in the Anglo-American world – Herbert Hart,[4] did so without much enthusiasm for the subject of inquiry. Hart opens *The Concept of Law* with a remark that "only a relatively small and unimportant part of the most famous and controversial theories of law" are focused on the topic of international law,[5] as if he wanted to convey the message to all those who will become his followers – "Don't waste your time on these topics."[6]

Although the situation has improved recently, jurisprudence is still in need of more systematic philosophical accounts of international law. This book offers one such account. It proceeds from a cursory excursion into philosophizing about international law (Chapter 1). This historical journey reveals how the interest in law beyond the state (*polis*) was born with the natural law doctrine and its idea that certain legal rules are of universal validity. Throughout the centuries, this philosophical doctrine has played a dominant role in formulating theoretical background for the study of international law. However, this philosophical landscape has slowly started to change with the rise of nineteenth-century legal positivism. While it became the dominant force in the German international legal discourse (*Staatswillenspositivismus*), the British school of analytical jurisprudence "found no room for a law beyond sovereignty."[7] The subsequent influence of the analytical school of thought was reflected in the fact that most jurisprudential dealings with international law, including Hart's, did not go far beyond the "ontological" question of whether international law is "true" law, thereby reinforcing skepticism of the pioneers, Bentham and Austin.

One may concede to Franck's famous dictum that we have by now entered the "post-ontological era"[8] without denying the necessity of a more thorough study of both conceptual and normative issues about international law. While

4 Nicola Lacey, *A Life of H.L.A. Hart: The Nightmare and the Noble Dream* (Oxford: Oxford University Press, 2004), 1.

5 Herbert Hart, *The Concept of Law* (With an Introduction by Leslie Green, 3rd ed.) (Oxford: Clarendon Press, 2012), 4.

6 Jeremy Waldron, "International Law: 'A Relatively Small and Unimportant' Part of Jurisprudence?,'" in Luís Duarte d'Almeida, James Edwards, and Andrea Dolcetti (eds.), *Reading HLA Hart's 'The Concept of Law'* (Oxford: Hart Publishing, 2013), 210.

7 Martti Koskenniemi, *The Gentle Civilizer of Nations – The Rise and Fall of International Law 1870–1960* (Cambridge: Cambridge University Press, 2001), 34.

8 Thomas M. Franck, *Fairness in International Law and Institutions* (Oxford: Clarendon Press, 1995), 6.

the latter might indeed be "the most pressing" ones,[9] the former are far from being jurisprudentially settled. The conceptual question concerning the nature of international law, which is the subject of this book, requires first and foremost laying down an adequate methodological approach. While it is undisputable that some sort of analytical work is needed, it is far more questionable whether such work can be provided by the now dominant method of the metaphysically driven conceptual analysis. It is directed toward finding essential, a priori, and necessary features that are present in each instance falling under the given concept. The aim of Chapter 2 is to show that the mentioned methodology does not live up to its expectations. First, it has been rightly accused, primarily by socio-legal scholars, of being unable to strike the right balance between an empirical step and the analytical work. Conceptual analysis is guilty of either arbitrarily or selectively reporting about instances of a social practice to which competent users of language attach the word "law," which, in the next step, becomes the ground for metaphysical claims about necessary, i.e., universal features of law.[10] Secondly, conceptual analysts regularly employ the terminology of "borderline cases" (international law is often classified in such a way), despite the fact that it is incompatible with one of the central premises of this method, namely, that all the instances satisfying necessary conditions are equally good examples of the category membership. This leads to the final problem. To the extent that the conceptual analysis in its pre-analytical step has to rely on intuitive categorization judgments, it is limited by our ordinary representation of concepts. However, this method seems to be premised on psychological assumptions that are contrary to recent experimental findings in the field of cognitive psychology. Experiments have demonstrated that we take category (concept) to be "a representation of an array of features clustered around some sort of prototype."[11]

The analytical work in this book, undertaken within the prototype theory of concepts, boils down to an explanatory elucidation of law. Law is conceived in its most abstract sense as a "genre," that is, as "a type of human activity"[12] that is in some respects distinguishable from other social practices. This elucidation leads to the formulation of the concept of law, understood as a representation of a group of features clustered around some prototype case. In proceeding

9 Samantha Besson and John Tasioulas, "Introduction," in Samantha Besson and John Tasioulas (eds.), *The Philosophy of International Law* (Oxford: Oxford University Press, 2010), 4.

10 In that respect, "[t]his method is circular." Brian Tamanaha, A *Realistic Theory of Law* (Cambridge: Cambridge University Press, 2017), 71–72.

11 William M. Ramsey, *Representation Reconsidered* (Cambridge: Cambridge University Press, 2007), 10.

12 As noted by Ehrenberg, "[w]hen general jurisprudents offer theories of law, they are trying to account for this general type of activity." Kenneth M. Ehrenberg, *The Functions of Law* (Oxford: Oxford University Press, 2016), 18.

from the idea that our pre-analytical samples of law have to account for various social contexts, including the one beyond the state, in which the concept-word is used to denote this complex human practice, Chapter 3 comes up with a preliminary finding: A social practice is typically judged as falling within the category of "law" if it consists of rules purporting to coordinate behavior of actors and to settle their disputes (*normativity*); if it at least possesses institutions in charge of judging whether those rules were violated (*institutionality*); if the rules in question are guaranteed, normally through some form of coercive mechanisms (*[coercive] guaranteeing*); and if the rules are, overall, apt for inspection and appraisal in light of justice (*justice-aptness*). These typical features, which vary depending on contexts (e.g., municipal v. international level; simple v. modern society), are further elaborated in the remainder of the book.

It is a widely held belief of contemporary legal philosophers that the key for law's distinctiveness is its normativity. Chapter 4 challenges this claim, by distinguishing between the two *how* questions of normativity. The first *how* question calls for the epistemological perspective. It is concerned with finding out how to ascertain a norm, and more specifically a legal norm. It relies on Kelsen's understanding of "validity" as a specific norm's "existence," which is determinable due to the doctrine of formal sources of law. This question is, then, investigated in the specific setting at the international level, where the following problems are discussed: how to ascertain a valid international legal norm and differentiate it from a mere act of will; how to ascertain a valid customary legal rule; how to ascertain what is a *jus cogens* rule; how to ascertain what is an *erga omnes* obligation; and, finally, how to ascertain invalidity of an international rule based on its inefficacy (*desuetudo*).

The second *how* question endorses the perspective of practical rationality. It tries to elucidate how norms in general and legal norms in particular provide us with reasons for action. According to the traditional wisdom, legal norms pre-empt and exclude all the conflicting reasons that norm-subjects might have for the contrary behavior, that is, they are "binding," i.e., "non-optional." It is argued that this view raises unsolvable paradoxes of "intentionality" (Rodriguez-Blanco) and "practical authority" (Hurd) and, thus, has to be abandoned. The undertaken analysis leads to a rather unorthodox conclusion that *there is nothing special about the normativity of law*. Law's normative force competes with the normative force of other normative orders, and its capacity to be authoritative for its norm-subjects, that is, to generate the sense of obligation, cannot be attributed to some special sort of normativity, but to combined effects of law's typical features. Such an understanding of law's capacity to provide us reasons for action opens the room for gradation of legal normativity, which is of particular importance for the perennial topics of international legal scholarship – relative normativity of international law and soft law.

Chapter 5 discusses international law as an institutionalized and (coercively) guaranteed order. In providing a short genealogy of institutionalization of the international order, which largely rests on horizontality of international law and the balance of power, this chapter reveals specificities regarding law-making and law-applying institutions at the international level. In the legal order in which states are key subjects of law-making, through the processes of treaty and customary rule making, it is questionable to what extent various non-state institutional actors are assuming this role as well. Having in mind the relevance of the United Nations as the global institutional structure, the chapter addresses this issue, by putting particular emphasis on the law-making capacities of the UN Security Council and General Assembly.

Since institutionalization of a normative order implies primarily institutionalization of judgment, the second section of the chapter deals with the process of judicialization of the international legal order. Not only we have been witnessing in last decades a rapid multiplication of new international courts and tribunals, but their functioning also has raised the question of whether these institutions at times go beyond the law-applying role and actively contribute to international law-making. It is claimed that the answer to this question largely depends on the understanding of judicial interpretation, as well as on the precedential nature of various international adjudicative regimes.

The final section of this chapter is dedicated to the role of coercion in guaranteeing the order with the lack of centralized enforcement agencies. After showing that even at the municipal level, where such agencies normally exist, law's coerciveness implies neither that it necessarily threatens the infliction of "evil and pain" (Austin), nor that the enforcement mechanism relies in the first place on the use of physical force, it is argued, alongside Hathaway and Shapiro, that the primary model of international coercive guaranteeing is "external outcasting." It is "outcasting," because it "involves denying the disobedient the benefits of social cooperation and membership." It is "external" because it is "frequently carried out by those outside the regime."[13]

Chapter 6 deals with law's justice-aptness. Both law-making and law-application are in the function of coordinating behavior of norm-subjects and settling their disputes. These functions are conducted through the

[13] Oona Hathaway and Scott J. Shapiro, "Outcasting: Enforcement in Domestic and International Law" (2011) 121 *The Yale Law Journal* 2: 258.

allocation of certain benefits and burdens in the form of rights and obligations, as well as through remedying harms stemming from the wrongful behavior of norm-subjects. Therefore, "[i]n view of the function of law in creating and enforcing obligations, it necessarily makes sense to ask whether law is just." Justice-aptness "applies as much to the substance of law as it does to its administration and procedures."[14] Proceeding from Aristotle's classical distinction between distributive and corrective justice, this chapter explores to what extent international law can be appraised in these terms.

The closing Chapter 7 discusses "fragmentation" as a possible distinctive feature of international law. First, it discharges Hart's well-known argument that, due to its institutional deficiencies and the lack of a unifying "rule of recognition," international legal rules "resemble that simple form of social structure" that can be "contrast[ed] with a developed legal system."[15] In the next step, it is shown that what at first seemed to be the International Law Commission's incredibly negative portrayal of international law in terms of its "fragmentation," turned eventually into a more positive picture of a legal order that has at its disposal a wealth of interpretative devices for the solution of normative conflicts between mushrooming specialized international legal regimes. However, since these techniques are not self-applicable, it is of crucial importance that the adjudicative bodies of different specialized regimes use them in such a way *"as if"* international law is a coherent and unified system of rules. The chapter closes with the argument that there are plenty of indicators that various international adjudicative bodies adopt the adequate *"as if"* lens and depict themselves as officials of a unified international legal order.

The final introductory caveat is of the methodological nature. It is important to bear in mind that, unlike scientists, legal philosophers are not in the position to forge the concept of law, thereby completely revising the complex social reality they are studying. Thus, a jurisprudential inquiry into the nature of law is always "partly responsive to our normal notions, and partly [it is] a stipulative regimentation of these notions."[16] By being such, no jurisprudential account can claim to be *the correct* depiction of the nature of law. In that respect, Finnis's comments on the title of Hart's *The Concept of Law* come to mind. Finnis says that "despite the definite article ('the') ... [t]he book does

14 Leslie Green, "Positivism and the Inseparability of Law and Morals" (2008) 83 *New York University Law Review* 4: 1050.

15 Hart, *The Concept of Law*, 214.

16 Joseph Raz, "Can There Be a Theory of Law?," in Martin P. Golding and William A. Edmundson (eds.), *The Blackwell Guide to the Philosophy of Law and Legal Theory* (Oxford: Blackwell Publishing, 2005), 326.

not for a moment try to establish that there exists . . . a concept of law which is entitled to be called 'the' concept of law." Instead, Hart's treatise seeks "to arrive at an 'improved understanding,' a *better concept*, of law." Finnis concludes that "Hart might more accurately, if less elegantly, have called his book A *New and Improved Concept of Law*."[17] Without any pretension of drawing an analogy with the most influential twentieth-century jurisprudential treatise, I am using Finnis's reminder merely to emphasize that the definite article in the title of this book should be similarly understood as an attempt to provide *a new and improved explanatory account of international law*.

[17] John Finnis, *Philosophy of Law: Collected Essays Volume IV* (Oxford: Oxford University Press, 2011), 107.

# 1

# International Law as a Subject Matter of Legal Philosophy – A Brief Historical Overview

Any talk about law regulating relations between different states is, conceptually speaking, based on a set of empirical conditions.[1] As Bederman has stated, "[I]nternational law is impossible without a system of multiple States, each conscious of its own sovereignty and the choice between relations being premised on order or on anarchy."[2] Now, one may object that this statement already employs some concepts, like "system," "state," "sovereignty," or "anarchy," which are not only theoretically controversial, but can also be considered as products of a certain era. In order to meet this challenge, it seems possible to rephrase this statement in a more neutral fashion, as follows: International law talk is impossible without a world of multiple political communities, each conscious of the idea that it should be ruled from the inside rather than from the outside, and of the choice between rule-based or rule-less relations among them. When put this way, it becomes clear that such conditions existed in antiquity. This still does not warrant extending the discussion of international law back to ancient times because everything hinges upon our prior understanding of "international law." Nonetheless, there are authors who claim that talking about international law made sense even in antiquity. They tend to support this argument by demonstrating that even in the ancient Near East[3] there was "a common *idea* or *tradition*" that

1 Verdross speaks of "sociological fundamentals of international law." Alfred Verdross, *Völkerrecht (unter Mitarbeit von Karl Zemanek* (4th ed.) (Vienna: Springer, 1959), 5.

2 David J. Bederman, *International Law in Antiquity* (Cambridge: Cambridge University Press, 2001), 7.

3 Bederman's study is confined to "(1) the ancient Near East including the periods subsuming the Sumerian city-States, the great empires of Egypt, Babylon, Assyria and the Hittites (1400–1150 BCE), and a later, brief period focusing on the nations of Israel and their Syrian neighbors (966–700 BCE); (2) the Greek city-States from 500–338 BCE; and (3) the wider Mediterranean during the period of Roman contact with Carthage, Macedon, Ptolemaic

international relations were to be grounded in some basic rules that are nowadays regarded as norms of international law.[4]

## 1 EARLY THEORIZING ABOUT LAW BEYOND THE STATE – ANCIENT GREECE AND ROME

With far less controversy, it is possible to argue that the philosophical treatment of law can hardly be traced before ancient Greece.[5] There, we find a distinctive tradition of thinking about law beyond the state (*polis*) that very much resembles contemporary concepts of universal human rights and *jus cogens*.[6] As noted by Gagarin and Woodruff, "[a] concept of universal law, applying to all peoples … is well attested for the classical period."[7] In that respect, one may argue that the current distinction between international and municipal law displays some similarities with the Greek differentiation between natural and positive law, insofar as this division was, inter alia, structured around the criterion of the territorial sphere of validity of the two sets of legal rules. Aristotle was the first one to draw this distinction. He writes in the *Rhetoric* that there are two kinds of laws, "particular" (*idios*) and "common" (*koinos*). While the former are "those established by each people in reference to themselves," the latter are "those based upon nature." Natural law is equivalent to natural justice, that is, to "a general idea of just and unjust in accordance with nature."[8] Apart from the criterion of territorial validity,

Egypt, and the Seleucid Empire (358–168 BCE)." *Ibid*, 2. A more recent study, by Altman, focuses on the ancient Near East, but extends the time span of the research to the period 2500–330 BCE. Amnon Altman, *Tracing the Earliest Recorded Concepts of International Law – The Ancient Near East (2500–330 BCE)* (Boston: Martinus Nijhoff, 2012).

4 Following Maine, Bederman qualifies the ancient law of nations as "a primitive legal system." Bederman, *International Law in Antiquity*, 6. Altman deliberately avoids discussing the question whether anything resembling "an international legal order" existed in the ancient Near East. Altman, *Tracing the Earliest Recorded Concepts of International Law*, xxv. One of the pivotal studies in this area speaks of "the international relations of antiquity." Amos S. Hershey, "The History of International Relations during Antiquity and the Middle Ages" (1911) 5 *American Journal of International Law* 4:901.

5 Speaking about possible Near Eastern antecedents of the Greek legal philosophy, Fred D. Miller Jr. concludes "that even when Greek laws and legal concepts resembled their predecessors', this does not prove influence." Fred D. Miller Jr., "Near Eastern Antecedents of Western Legal Thought," in Fred D. Miller, Jr. and Carrie-Ann Biondi (eds.), *A Treatise of Legal Philosophy and General Jurisprudence* Vol. 6 – *A History of the Philosophy of Law from the Ancient Greeks to the Scholastics* (Heidelberg: Springer, 2007), 5.

6 *See, infra* pp. 109–123.

7 Michael Gagarin and Paul Woodruff, "Early Greek Legal Thought," in Miller and Biondi (eds.), *A Treatise of Legal Philosophy and General Jurisprudence* Vol. 6, 31.

8 Aristotle, *Rhetoric* (translated by John Henry Freese) (New York: William Heinemann and G. P. Putnam's Sons, 1926), I, xiii, 2.

natural and positive law could be also distinguished with respect to the temporal sphere of validity. Whereas natural law "is ever constant and never changes," particular laws "often vary."[9]

Interestingly enough, in none of his political and ethical works does Aristotle speak again of "natural law." Instead, he introduces the distinction between "natural" (*physikon*) and "legal" (*nomikon*) i.e., positive law "justice." Natural justice has universal force, whereas positive law justice is conventionally established for this or that political community.[10] Commentators note that in *Nicomachean Ethics*, Aristotle contradicts what he writes in the *Rhetoric*, by raising "an objection against the possibility of natural justice."[11] Despite apparent inconsistencies,[12] Aristotle's work laid down foundations for the subsequent doctrines of natural law,[13] which are more boldly connected to the idea of law beyond the state.

Such was the philosophy of Stoicism,[14] which not only marked the turn from ancient natural law to Middle Age/Christian natural law,[15] but also shifted the focus of the investigation from *polis* to *cosmopolis*. Stoics argued that "the cosmos is, as it were, a polis, because the cosmos is put in perfect order by law, which is right reason."[16] This teaching was very influential throughout the Greco-Roman world, partly because it was apt to provide a philosophical account of the rise of empires, particularly the Roman empire. Despite the fact that Romans were exposed to different Greek philosophical traditions, natural law, especially in Cicero's works, has continued to develop

9 *Ibid*, I, xv, 3–9.

10 Aristotle, *Nicomachean Ethics* (translated, with an interpretative essay, notes, and glossary by Robert C. Bartlett and Susan D. Collins) (Chicago: University of Chicago Press, 2011), Book V, Ch. 7, 1134b20, 104.

11 Fred D. Miller, Jr., "Aristotle's Philosophy of Law," in Miller and Biondi (eds.), *A Treatise of Legal Philosophy and General Jurisprudence* Vol. 6, 96.

12 For more detail, *see ibid*, 94–99.

13 This is particularly true of the *Rhetoric*, which "offers a coherent account of natural law with noteworthy similarities to the later natural law tradition." *Ibid*, 95.

14 One of the reasons for claiming that Aristotle made a crucial contribution to the foundation of the natural law doctrine has exactly to do "with the impact which his ideas had, or may plausibly be thought to have had, on the thinking of the Stoic thinkers who came after him." Tony Burns, *Aristotle and Natural Law* (London: Continuum International Publishing, 2011), 175.

15 Arthur Kaufmann, "Problemgeschichte der Rechtsphilosophie," in Arthur Kaufmann, Winfried Hassemer, and Ulfried Neumann (eds.), *Einführung in Rechtsphhilosophie und Rechtstheorie der Gegenwart* (Heidelberg: C. F. Müller Verlag, 2004), 38.

16 Pauline Kleingeld and Eric Brown, "Cosmopolitanism," in Edward N. Zalta (ed.), The Stanford Encyclopedia of Philosophy (Fall 2013 ed.), at http://plato.stanford.edu/archives/fall2013/entries/cosmopolitanism/.

under the influence of Stoicism.[17] Furthermore, Cicero takes this philosophy "and develops it more concretely in connection with politics than the Stoics before him had done."[18] But most important, his thought "had the unique gift of perfectly combining Natural Law theory with Cosmopolitan Humanism."[19]

## 2 NATURAL LAW THEORY AND THE BIRTH OF INTERNATIONAL LEGAL SCHOLARSHIP – GROTIUS, PUFENDORF, AND HOBBES

Cicero's interpretation of Stoicism was a significant source of inspiration for Grotius's treatise *De Iure Belli ac Pacis*, which is considered one of the cornerstones of the newly emerging field of international legal studies. To begin with, Grotius follows Cicero in taking famous Carneades's critique of justice[20] as the starting point for his defense of the law of nations. Grotius believes that Carneades is the perfect "spokesman" for the philosophical voices denying natural law and justice and that refuting Carneades's arguments would "win acceptance for [his] project."[21] Grotius dismisses Carneades's claim that humans are by nature impelled to pursue their own interest, which leads to the conclusion that there cannot be one, universal natural law. Instead, Grotius contends, "the source of *ius*, properly so called" can be found in the "unique" feature of the human nature – his "desire for society [*appetitus societatis*]" although "not a community of any kind, but one

17 See Dirk Baltzly, "Stoicism," in Zalta (ed.), The Stanford Encyclopedia of Philosophy (Fall 2010 ed.), at http://plato.stanford.edu/entries/stoicism/.

18 Marcia Colish, *The Stoic Tradition from Antiquity to the Early Middle Ages: Stoicism in Classical Latin Literature* (Leiden: Brill Publishers, 1985), 91. It would be fair to say that this transition toward political aspects had already taken place within the Greek Stoicism. Roderick T. Long, "Hellenistic Philosophers of Law," in Miller and Biondi (eds.), A *Treatise of Legal Philosophy and General Jurisprudence Vol.* 6, 127ff.

19 Fernando Llano Alonso, "Cosmopolitanism and Natural Law in Cicero," in Francisco José Contreras (ed.), *The Threads of Natural Law – Unravelling a Philosophical Tradition* (Heidelberg: Springer, 2013), 33. Take Cicero's words from *De Legibus*: "[T]here is one equal manner of life, shared by all people; and finally, that all people are bound by a sort of natural goodwill and benevolence as well as by the bond of justice." Cicero, *On the Laws*, in *On the Commonwealth and On the Laws* (edited by James E. G. Zetzel) (Cambridge: Cambridge University Press, 1999), Book I, 35.

20 There were two Carneades's speeches in the Roman Senate – the first one was affirmative, while the second defamatory. For a reconstruction of Carneades's argumentation, *see* Gisela Striker, *Essays on Hellenistic Epistemology and Ethics* (Cambridge: Cambridge University Press, 1996), 263ff. For Cicero's criticism of Carneades's speech, *see* Cicero, *On the Commonwealth*, Book III, 8ff.

21 Hugo Grotius, *The Rights of War and Peace* (edited and with an introduction by Richard Tuck) (Indianapolis: Liberty Fund, 2005); and Hugo Grotius, *Prolegomena to the first edition of De Iure Belli ac Pacis* (1625), 1746.

at peace, and with a rational order [*pro sui intellectus modo ordinatae*]."[22] Human sociability and rational nature are, thus, true foundations of law, and its principles would be available to us even if we were to suppose the most blasphemous idea imaginable – that there is no God.[23] All this does not imply that *utilitas* is irrelevant for our discussion about law. On the contrary, "anyone who prescribes laws for other people usually does so with a view to increasing utility" and what counts for the laws of each state counts also for "the law of nations."[24] Therefore, Carneades was clearly wrong to consider justice irrational, because just as it is not irrational for a citizen to obey the law even though this would require foregoing some personal benefit, "so a nation is not irrational if it does not pursue its own interest at the expense of the common laws of nations." The rationale is the same in both cases: "[A] citizen who breaks the civil law for the sake of some immediate interest will thereby undermine his own and his descendants' permanent interests, and a nation which violates the laws of nature and nations will have renounced its right [*rescindit munimenta*] subsequently to live in peace."[25]

The relationship between the emerging international legal scholarship and the natural law doctrine was further supported by the writings of two other seventeenth-century contemporaries, Samuel von Pufendorf and Thomas Hobbes. Pufendorf was a scrupulous follower of the "noble discipline of natural law" whose founder was, according to him, "the incomparable Hugo Grotius."[26] Like the Dutch philosopher, Pufendorf grounded his natural law teaching in the principle of "peaceful sociability."[27] And in the same manner, he considered natural law to be distinguishable from positive law in both territorial and temporal scope. That is, natural law is "*universal* and *perpetual*: the former, in regard that it binds the whole body of human race, the latter, because it is not subject to change, which is the disadvantage of positive laws."[28] Finally, when it comes to the law of nations, Pufendorf argues that it is exclusively of the natural-law kind, insofar as there is no "voluntary or positive law of nations, properly invested with a true and legal force."[29]

22 *Ibid*, 1747.
23 *Ibid*, 1748.
24 *Ibid*, 1749–1750.
25 *Ibid*, 1750.
26 Quoted from Michael Seidler, "Pufendorf's Moral and Political Philosophy," in Zalta (ed.), The Stanford Encyclopedia of Philosophy (Winter 2015 ed.), at http://plato.stanford.edu/archives/win2015/entries/pufendorf-moral.
27 Samuel von Pufendorf, *Of the Law of Nature and Nations* (translated by Basil Kennett) (London: J. Walthoe et. al., 1729), Book II, Ch. 3, 15.
28 *Ibid*, Book II, Ch. 3, 1.
29 *Ibid*, Book II, Ch. 3, 23.

In this respect, Pufendorf follows in Hobbes's footsteps.[30] Despite commonly being considered the forerunner of modern Anglo-American jurisprudence,[31] Hobbes's "major source of reflection on the relations between states came from the natural law tradition."[32] At first glance, one is inclined to conclude that Hobbes "shut himself off from all possibility of understanding the nature of international law" by defining law as a command of the sovereign.[33] In the absence of an international sovereign, no (positive) international law could be conceived. On the other hand, Hobbes does speak of "the law of nations," explicitly stating that this law "and the law of nature is the same thing."[34] Even though the laws of nature i.e., "dictates of reason," are not laws *stricto sensu*, some authors, nonetheless, offer a more charitable reading of Hobbes, according to which not only that these laws in the inter-commonwealths' state of nature have to be more effective than those between humans, but also that some more concrete rules and obligations of international conduct could be logically derived from them.[35]

Despite apparent differences between these three authors on fundamental issues regarding the nature of the law of nations,[36] in certain basic commitments

[30] Some scholars argue that Hobbes's influence on Pufendorf can be also found in the framing of his central concept of *socialitas*. *See* Fiammetta Palladini, "Pufendorf Disciple of Hobbes: The Nature of Man and the State of Nature: The doctrine of Socialitas" (2008) 34 *History of European Ideas* 1: 26–60.

[31] Robert S. Summers, "The New Analytical Jurist" (1966) 41 *New York University Law Review*: 862.

[32] That is, from "the tradition of moral theology strongly influenced by Christianity." Glen Newey, *Routledge Philosophy Guidebook to Hobbes and Leviathan* (New York: Routledge, 2008), 160. For a more thorough elucidation of Hobbes's complex view of natural law, *see, e.g.*, Ross Harrison, "The Equal Extent of Natural and Civil Law," in David Dyzenhaus and Thomas Poole (eds.), *Hobbes and The Law* (Cambridge: Cambridge University Press, 2012), 22–38.

[33] Alexander Passerin d'Entreves, *The Notion of the State – An Introduction to Political Theory* (Oxford: Clarendon Press, 1967), 111.

[34] He further specifies that "the same law that dictateth to men that have no civil government what they ought to do, and what to avoid in regard of one another, dictateth the same to Commonwealths." Thomas Hobbes, *Leviathan* (London: Andrew Crooke, 1651), 217–218. Electronic version available at socserv.mcmaster.ca/econ/ugcm/3ll3/hobbes/Leviathan.pdf.

[35] Akashi speaks of the principle of equality of sovereign states, the right to self-preservation and self-defense, the principle of nonintervention in domestic matters of other states, as well as a set of principles arising from a more general duty of "escaping from the state of war and accomplishing peace" such as "the inviolability of legates, the recognition of the force of treaties (*pacta sunt servanda*), the acceptance of the *compromis* and award of arbitration and so on." Kinji Akashi, "Hobbes' Relevance to the Modern Law of Nations" (2000) 2 *Journal of the History of International Law* 2: 213–214.

[36] For more detail, *see* Richard Tuck, *The Rights of War and Peace – Political Thought and the International Order from Grotius to Kant* (Oxford: Oxford University Press, 1999)

they "were all part of one enterprise, and must be read together."[37] In employing the vocabulary of natural law, they sounded "in part like philosophers, in part like lawyers" and while heavily relying on "the idioms of mathematics and natural sciences" these authors "were able to speak persuasively about the role of the new territorial entities in providing security and, in due course, welfare to their populations."[38] Although the natural law doctrine has largely served as the background philosophy of the bourgeoning international legal scholarship, the end of the eighteenth century signified the turn "to a novel technical idiom about treaties, diplomacy and war as key parts of distinctly 'modern' inter-sovereign relations."[39] Unlike Pufendorf, who excluded bilateral and multilateral treaties from the category of "the law of nations,"[40] both Wolff and Vattel recognized the existence of "customary" and "stipulative law" as forms of a "particular" law of nations. Together with "voluntary law" – which concerns "all the alterations which the rigour of the natural law must be made to undergo in the affairs of nations"[41] – they form "the positive law of nations." This conventional law "takes its origin from the will of nations."[42]

## 3 THE GERMAN PUBLIC LAW TURN

A fundamental distancing from the traditional natural law approach to the law of nations came, however, with the newly emerged German public law tradition.[43] Yet, this tradition itself was divergent. Its philosophical aspects were developed along the lines of Kant's moral philosophy and *Rechtslehre* teaching. Kant criticized Grotius, Pufendorf, and Vattel for being "sorry comforters" because "their philosophically or diplomatically formulated codes do not and cannot have the slightest *legal* force, since states as such

37 Benedict Kingsbury and Benjamin Straumann, "State of Nature versus Commercial Sociability as the Basis of International Law: Reflections on the Roman Foundations and Current Interpretations of the International Political and Legal Thought of Grotius, Hobbes, and Pufendorf," in Besson and Tasioulas (eds.), *The Philosophy of International Law*, 35.

38 Martti Koskenniemi, "Into Positivism: Georg Friedrich von Martens (1756–1821) and Modern International Law" (2008) 15 *Constellations* 2: 189.

39 *Ibid*, 190.

40 Pufendorf, *Of the Law of Nature and Nations*, Book II, Ch. 3, 23.

41 Emmerich de Vattel, *The Law of Nations; Or Principles of the Law of Nature Applied to the Conduct and Affairs of Nations and Sovereigns* (Philadelphia: T. & J. W. Johnson Law Booksellers, 1844), xii.

42 Christian Wolff, *Jus Gentium Methodo Scientifica Pertractatum, Vol. II* (translated by Joseph H. Drake) (Oxford: Clarendon Press, 1934), 19.

43 Koskenniemi, "Into Positivism: Georg Friedrich von Martens (1756–1821) and Modern International Law," 191.

are not subject to a common external constraint."[44] Such an "external constraint" can come only through the "*formal institutionalization*" of a legal-political order on the global scale.[45] As is well known, Kant argued in favor of a special form of league of states, called "a *pacific federation* (*foedus pacificum*)," whose ultimate objective would be to secure the freedom of its members.[46] Without such *status iuridicus* one can sensibly speak only of "private rights" of states, as in the state of nature. The necessary "publicness criterion" can be satisfied solely through "some sort of contract" between the free states establishing the federation. However, unlike the compact through which an individual state originates, this contract "must not be based on coercive laws" but should take the form of "a state of *permanent and free association*."[47]

German public international law scholarship, on the other hand, has been developed without causing an immediate and sharp discontinuity with the natural law classics in the field. Hence, Pütter and Achenwall's 1750 textbook *Elementa juris naturae*,[48] which laid out the principles of *ius publicum universale* and *ius gentium universale*, was an instance of "successful combination of a vocabulary of philosophical politics (i.e., natural law) with pragmatic studies on the government of modern states."[49] The same is true of Georg Friedrich von Martens. Although he is often considered the forefather of international legal positivism,[50] von Martens has not outright repudiated the natural law teaching of his predecessors. On the contrary, his elaboration of

44 Immanuel Kant, "Perpetual Peace: A Philosophical Sketch," in *Political Writings* (Cambridge: Cambridge University Press, 1991), 103.

45 *Ibid*, 98.

46 *Ibid*, 104.

47 *Ibid*, 127 (all emphasis in the original). "Perhaps Kant's approach to rules of international law is best understood as akin to his approach to rules of equity in domestic law ... Equity, Kant argues, is a 'right in a *wider* sense (*ius latium*), in which there is no law by which an authorization to use coercion can be determined': it 'admits a right without coercion.'" Amanda Perreau-Saussine, "Immanuel Kant on International Law," in Besson and Tasioulas (eds.), *The Philosophy of International Law*, 60.

48 Johann Stephan Pütter and Gottfried Achenwall, *Anfangsgründe des Naturrechts (Elementa juris naturae)* (edited by Jan Schröder) (Frankfurt: Insel Verlag, 1995).

49 Koskenniemi, "Into Positivism: Georg Friedrich von Martens (1756–1821) and Modern International Law," 193.

50 His treatises *Versuch über die Existenz eines positiven europäischen Völkerrechts und den Nutzen dieser Wissenschaft* (1789) and *Einleitung in das positive Europäische Völkerrecht auf Verträge und Herkommen gegründet* (1796) laid the foundations of the European public law (*Droit public de l'Europe*). Dietrich Rauschning, "Georg Friedrich von Martens (1756–1821) Lehrer des praktischen Europäischen Völkerrechts und der Diplomatie zu Göttingen," in Fritz Loos (ed.), *Rechtswissenschaft in Göttingen: Göttinger Juristen aus 250 Jahren* (Göttingen: Vandenhoeck & Ruprecht, 1987), 135.

the natural law doctrine "is respectful and frequent." Nevertheless, "there is a down-to-earth character in his writing that gives it a more contemporary or 'modern' feel" than the works of his forerunners. And yet, this is "rather a matter of style" than a full-fledged "philosophical argument."[51] Unlike Pufendorf and Vattel, who argued that a detailed discussion of particular bilateral and multilateral treaties belongs to the disciplinary province of history,[52] von Martens' contribution to international legal scholarship consisted in large part of an extensive collection of treaties, declarations, and other international acts, which were all compiled in his *Recueil de Trait´es*. Von Martens's insistence on the historical and empirical approach was coupled with "an endless series of classifications, divisions and subdivisions of each subject-matter to its component parts" whereby the raw data of the international legal world was thoroughly systematized.[53]

## 4 CLASSICAL ANALYTICAL JURISPRUDENCE: THE RISE OF SKEPTICISM TOWARD INTERNATIONAL LAW

In this respect, von Martens's work might be seen as paving the way for a subsequent positivist-oriented international legal scholarship.[54] In terms of methodological inclinations toward empiricism and systematization, von Martens' writings were a clear precursor of the philosophically grounded Anglo-American school of analytical jurisprudence, whose key figures were Bentham and Austin.[55] A fundamental tenet of this school of thought was, however, the explicit rejection of the "nonsensical" language of natural law and natural rights.[56] Of the two, Bentham was far more interested in

[51] Koskenniemi, "Into Positivism: Georg Friedrich von Martens (1756–1821) and Modern International Law," 196.

[52] Vattel, *The Law of Nations*, xiii. Cf. Pufendorf, *Of the Law of Nature and Nations*, Book II, Ch. 3, 23.

[53] Koskenniemi, "Into Positivism: Georg Friedrich von Martens (1756–1821) and Modern International Law," 197.

[54] As noted by Bernstorf, "decidedly anti-naturalist approaches increasingly dominated the German scholarly scene over the course of [the nineteenth] century." Jochen von Bernstorf, "German Intellectual Historical Origins of International Legal Positivism," in Jörg Kammerhofer and Jean D'Aspremont (eds.), *International Legal Positivism in a Post-Modern World* (Cambridge: Cambridge University Press, 2014), 51.

[55] In German scholarship, the nineteenth century is also identified as the period of the birth of legal theory as an independent and autonomous discipline. *See*, Annette Brockmöller, *Die Entstehung der Rechtstheorie im 19. Jahrhundert in Deutschland* (Baden-Baden: Nomos, 1997).

[56] According to Bentham, the "terrorist language" of the natural law theory was to be contrasted with "the language of reason and plain sense." Jeremy Bentham, "Anarchical Fallacies," in Sir John Bowring (ed.), *The Works of Jeremy Bentham*, Vol. 2 (Edinburgh: William Tait, 1843),

international law and politics.[57] Moreover, he is known, among other things, for coining the neologism "international." In differentiating between five criteria for the further division of various branches of expository and censorial jurisprudence,[58] Bentham identifies one criterion as the *political quality* of the persons whose conduct laws undertake to regulate.[59] These may be considered either as members of the same state, or as members of different states. Yet, only "the mutual transactions between sovereigns, as such" can be considered "the subject of that branch of jurisprudence which may be properly and exclusively termed *international*." Despite being clear about the province of one such jurisprudential discipline, Bentham was cautious whether its subject really existed, writing, "With what degree of propriety rules for the conduct of persons of this description can come under the appellation of *laws*, is a question that must rest till the nature of the thing called *a law* shall have been more particularly unfolded."[60] Nevertheless, his subsequent writings and reformatory projects along the utilitarian lines as applied in international relations[61] can be read as "strong suggestions that Bentham, for himself, was at least sometimes satisfied that there was enough to international law that was lawlike to let one call it law."[62]

501. Austin similarly qualified the natural law theory's stance that "human laws which conflict with the Divine law are not binding, that is to say, are not laws" as "stark nonsense." John Austin, *The Province of Jurisprudence Determined* (edited by Wilfrid E. Rumble) (Cambridge: Cambridge University Press, 1995), 158.

57 Due to Bentham's extensive discussions about decolonization and his involvement in various constitutional projects around the globe, the Central American reformer José del Valle hailed him in 1826 as the "legislator of the world" (*Legislador del mundo*). On Bentham's critique of colonial rule, *see* Jennifer Pitts, *A Turn to Empire. The Rise of Imperial Liberalism in Britain and France* (Princeton: Princeton University Press, 2005), Ch. 4. Cf. David R. Armitage, "Globalizing Jeremy Bentham" (2011) 32 *History of Political Thought* 1: 63–82.

58 Whereas "expository jurisprudence" is the investigation of what the law is, "censorial jurisprudence" is the investigation of whether the existing law ought to be in line with a certain assumed standard. Jeremy Bentham, *An Introduction to the Principles of Morals and Legislation (1780/1789)* (Kitchener: Batoche Books, 2000), 234. Cf. Jeremy Bentham, *A Fragment on Government (with an introduction by F. C. Montague)* (Oxford: Clarendon Press, 1891), 99.

59 For the other four criteria, see Bentham, *An Introduction to the Principles of Morals and Legislation*, 234–238.

60 *Ibid*, 236.

61 Bentham's most important essays on this subject were collected by John Bowring and his co-editor Richard Smith under the title "Principles of International Law." In the first essay regarding the objects of international law, Bentham applied the principle of utility, arguing that "the end that a disinterested legislator upon international law would propose to himself, would therefore be the greatest happiness of all nations taken together." *The Works of Jeremy Bentham, Vol. 2*, 538.

62 M. W. Janis, "Jeremy Bentham and the Fashioning of 'International Law'" (1984) 78 *American Journal of International Law* 2: 412.

Despite having some doubts about the "legality" of international law, Bentham was far less skeptical than his successor Austin. In further developing the project of legal positivism, one of Austin's key preoccupations was to thwart the common tendency among legal philosophers to "confound positive law with the science of legislation and positive morality with deontology." The distinction between that which is from that which ought to be was for him so "simple and glaring" that it seemed "idle to insist upon it."[63] In this respect Austin greatly admired von Martens who, unlike Grotius and Pufendorf, "has seized this distinction with a firm grasp" and "has distinguished the rules which ought to be received in the intercourse of nations, or which would be received if they conformed to an assumed standard of whatever kind, from those which *are* so received."[64] In Austin's opinion, von Martens was the first international legal scholar who "endeavoured to collect from the practice of civilized communities what are the rules actually recognized and acted upon by them, and gave to these rules the name of positive international law."[65] Despite all this, Austin did not share von Marten's belief that these rules of conduct could be properly classified as "law."[66] Instead, he famously argued that "the law of nations" should be classified as "positive morality rather than positive law."[67] More precisely, in his taxonomy of laws, properly and improperly so called, international law belonged to the class of rules that were "closely analogous to human laws."[68]

## 5 TWENTIETH-CENTURY LEGAL POSITIVISM ON INTERNATIONAL LAW

With the two successive twentieth-century attempts of establishing global international legal order, one would expect philosophy of international law to boost its disciplinary credibility. However, by that time jurisprudence was dominated by the philosophical tradition of legal positivism,[69] and both

63 Austin, *The Province of Jurisprudence Determined*, 157.
64 *Ibid*, 160.
65 *Ibid.*
66 Von Martens defined "positive international law" as "the aggregate of the rights and obligations established among the nations of Europe (or the majority of them), whether by particular but uniform treaties, by tacit convention, or by custom." Georg Friedrich Martens, *Summary of the Law of Nations, Founded on the Treaties and Customs of the Modern Nations of Europe* (translated by William Cobbett) (Philadelphia: Thomas Bradford, 1795), 4–5.
67 Austin, *The Province of Jurisprudence Determined*, 219.
68 *Ibid*, 20.
69 On the other hand, "the dominance of positivism in the international legal scholarship of the twentieth century was never as absolute as in many domestic legal traditions, and both positivism and naturalism continued to be influential." (Jörg Kammerhofer and Jean

"classical and post-classical" representatives of this school of thought "have made it difficult for public international law to pass as a legal system."[70] Nevertheless, the two most important and influential legal philosophers of that era – Kelsen and Hart – did try to elucidate international law, as they were both of the opinion that "no legal theory may be considered satisfactory without encompassing the awkward position of international law within the legal field."[71] The former, however, admittedly devoted far more space to international law as the subject matter of jurisprudence. At this point, I will briefly summarize Kelsen's and Hart's stances on the "legality" of international law, because throughout the book their arguments, as well as disagreements, will be used as useful points of reference for our discussion.[72]

### a) *Kelsen: International Law as a "True" Law*

Despite a general tendency of his Pure Theory of Law toward scientism,[73] Kelsen opens one of his central treatises in international law with the claim that "[a]ny attempt to define a concept must proceed from a certain usage of

D'Aspremont, "Introduction – The Future of International Legal Positivism," in Kammerhofer and D'Aspremont (eds.), *International Legal Positivism in a Post-Modern World*, 12) In his 1925 essay, Lauterpacht argued that the "renascence of natural law" was not of the old style – "it is rather the modern 'natural law with changing contents,' 'the sense of right,' 'the social solidarity,' the 'engineering' law in terms of promoting the ends of the international society." (Hersch Lauterpacht, "Westlake and Present Day International Law" (1925) 15 *Economica*: 315) The growth of legal realism and the influence of social sciences "led a number of international lawyers towards a more pragmatic, sociological approach." (Richard Collins, "Classical Legal Positivism in International Law Revisited," in Kammerhofer and D'Aspremont [eds.], *International Legal Positivism in a Post-Modern World*, 27) Pound's role was, in that respect, important. For his view on international law, *see*, Roscoe Pound, "Philosophical Theory and International Law," in *Bibliotheca Visseriana dissertationum ius internationale illustrantium* Vol. 1 (Leiden: E. J. Brill, 1923). For a contribution of Scandinavian legal realism, *see*, Alf Ross, A *Textbook of International Law – General Part* (London: Longmans, Green & Co., 1947).

70 Alexander Somek, "Beyond Kelsen and Hart," in Kammerhofer and D'Aspremont (eds.), *International Legal Positivism in a Post-Modern World*, 152.

71 Francois Rigaux, "Hans Kelsen on International Law" (1998) 9 *European Journal of International Law* 2: 325.

72 As noted by Giudice, who also proceeds from the Kelsen-Hart debate, "This point of departure seems to me to be justified as it represents the most sophisticated analytical disagreement about the nature of international law, even if over forty years old now." Michael Giudice, 'Hart and Kelsen on International Law', in Leslie Green and Brian Leiter (eds.), Oxford Studies in Philosophy of Law, Vol. 2 (Oxford: Oxford University Press, 2013), 150.

73 Zolo notes that "the premises Kelsen takes have their roots in general epistemology." Danilo Zolo, "Hans Kelsen: International Peace through International Law" (1998) 9 *European Journal of International Law* 2: 307. See in more detail in Mónica García-Salmones Rovira, *The Project of Positivism in International Law* (Oxford: Oxford

language, from the usual meaning of the word by which we intend to designate the concept."[74] However, contra Austin, this remark is not intended to highlight the potentially dubious status of international law as an instance of law in the respective linguistic practice. Kelsen actually asks whether there is some defining character of "law" as such, thereby instantly indicating that what counts for law in general counts for international law as well. Accordingly, not only does jurisprudence operate with a unified subject of its study; it is itself a unified discipline, whose methodological toolkit is equally applicable to various branches of law, including international law.[75]

Consequently, Kelsen's ultimate test for the "legality" of international law boils down to determining whether it can be said to possess this distinctive criterion – easily traceable at the municipal level – of being a "coercive order," i.e., of being "the social technique which consists in bringing about the desired social conduct of men through the threat of a measure of coercion which is to be applied in case of contrary conduct."[76] Hence, international law would be law "in the true sense of the term" if "it is, in principle, possible to interpret the employment of force directed by one state against another either as sanction or as delict."[77] Since, legally speaking, a conduct of the state can be qualified as delict only if the state responsible for this conduct is subjected to sanction, the inquiry ultimately depends upon the possibility of tracing international sanctions. Kelsen eventually takes reprisals and just (meaning: legal) war to be specific sanctions of international law. The reliance on measures of self-help testifies to the fact that international law is a relatively decentralized form of coercive order,[78] which is, at the same time, the most important distinguishing feature of international law in comparison to the national one. And only in this limited sense could one draw an analogy between some primitive law and the evolving international legal regime.[79] Yet, Kelsen believed that this analogy would gradually become obsolete with the process of the centralization of international law, which "is steadily increasing

University Press, 2013), especially chapter 4, "The Scientific Method of International Law: Kelsen." I will return to this methodological inclination of Kelsen's theory in Chapter 2.

74 Hans Kelsen, *Principles of International Law* (New York: Rinehart & Company Inc., 1952), 3.

75 An earliest account is provided in Hans Kelsen, *Das Problem der Souveränität und die Theorie des Völkerrechts* (Tübingen: J. C. B. Mohr [P. Siebeck], 1920).

76 Hans Kelsen, *General Theory of Law and State* (with a new introduction by A. Javier Treviño) (New Brunswick: Transaction Publishers, 2006), 19.

77 Kelsen, *Principles of International Law*, 18.

78 The state authorized to undertake reprisals "may be considered to be acting as an organ of the international community constituted by international law." *Ibid*, 25.

79 *Ibid*, 16.

by the establishment of international organizations instituting international tribunals and international executive agencies."[80]

### b) Hart: International Law as a "Primitive" Law

Hart enters the chapter on the nature of international law by connecting it to the previously developed argument in favor of a broader concept of law, which would include morally iniquitous rules as "legal." He justifies this argument by contending that the rival approach would not only be inconsistent "with so much usage," but it would "not advance or clarify either theoretical inquiries or moral deliberation."[81] The case is quite the opposite with international law. Despite the fact that this phrase has been in usage for more than 150 years, the absence of a set of state-like institutions – a global legislature, courts with compulsory jurisdiction, and a system of centralized sanctions – "[has] inspired misgivings" among legal philosophers. Hart, thus, concludes that the question whether international law is really law "can hardly be put aside."[82]

After dismissing those attempts of refuting the "legality" of international law that proceed from the sanction-based theory and the principle of the sovereign will of states,[83] Hart tries to elucidate the nature of international law by drawing analogies with other "borderline cases"[84] that possess "only some of the normally concomitant characteristics" of the central concept of law.[85] The central concept takes the form of a mature legal system, insofar as it is the union of primary and secondary rules.[86] Some simpler forms of social structure, which lack this systemic feature, are not fully devoid of "legality," but they are, nonetheless, to be treated as borderline cases. In that respect, international law resembles "in its form" a primitive regime of primary rules.[87]

At this point, Hart launches a harsh criticism of Kelsen's view that there is and has to be the "basic norm" of international law. Since "basic norm" has the same function in Kelsen's theory as the "rule of recognition" in Hart's – to connect all the rules into a single system by being the ultimate standard of their validity – Hart reiterates his charge that international law does not have this critical feature of a fully developed legal system. Despite the fact that it does

80 *Ibid*, 403.
81 Hart, *The Concept of Law*, 214.
82 *Ibid*, 214.
83 *Ibid*, 216–226.
84 *Ibid*, 16.
85 *Ibid*, 15.
86 *Ibid*, Chapter V.
87 *Ibid*, 227.

have rules, in particular primary rules, "[s]uch rules do not form a system but a mere set," because we lack "a way of demonstrating the validity of individual rules by reference to some ultimate rule of the system." This implies that "we must wait and see whether a rule gets accepted as a rule or not; in a system with a basic rule of recognition we can say before a rule is actually made, that it *will* be valid *if* it conforms to the requirements of the rule of recognition."[88]

For Hart, this was a plain fact of international life. And since in his comparison between municipal and international law he was "concerned with what exists in fact,"[89] Hart could not justify Kelsen's insistence on the "basic norm" at the international level. In fact, he characterized this effort as "comic:" "It is as if we were to insist that a naked savage *must* really be dressed in some invisible variety of modern dress."[90] He particularly criticized the putative content of that norm, which according to Kelsen should state as follows: "States should behave as they have customarily behaved." In Hart's words, such a formulation "is a mere useless reduplication of the fact that a set of rules are accepted by states as binding rules."[91]

Hart's dismissal of Kelsen's approach stems, however, from the fundamentally different methodological orientations of their theories. These differences profoundly shaped and affected their ultimate views on the nature of international law.[92] Hart eventually argued that the most one could say was that there existed analogies in terms "of function and content" between municipal and international law. Those concerning function "emerge most clearly when we reflect on the ways in which international law differs from morality," whereas "[t]he analogies of content consist in the range of principles, concepts, and methods which are common to both municipal and international law, and make the lawyers' technique freely transferable from the one to the other."[93]

## 6 REVIVED JURISPRUDENTIAL INTEREST IN INTERNATIONAL LAW

Unlike Kelsen and Hart, most contemporary legal philosophers have developed their theoretical accounts of law without paying much attention to

88 *Ibid*, 235.
89 *Ibid*, 233.
90 *Ibid*, 236.
91 *Ibid*, 236.
92 Kelsen is interested in determining under what conditions is legal cognition possible. Basic norm is an a priori condition of legal knowledge. Hart is interested in doing descriptive sociology. I will return to this problem in Chapter 2.
93 Hart, *The Concept of Law*, 237.

international legal rules. Hence, these scholars leave us with the open question whether their tacit assumption is that international law can be elucidated with the same meta-theoretical toolkit as the one developed for municipal law, or they simply hold that the primary, if not the exclusive, task of legal theory is to address the nature of municipal law. If the former is the case, then it is upon the authors themselves or by their disciples to explicitly demonstrate how adequate their theories are for the exposition of international law. It seems, however, that more often the latter is the case. Take Raz's stance from a 1971 article on the identity of legal systems. He says that in elucidating the nature of municipal legal systems, it may turn out that they "are not unique, that all their essential features are shared by, say, international law . . . If this is indeed so, well and good." Nevertheless, "it is not a requirement of adequacy of a legal theory that it should be so or indeed that it should not be so. It is, however, a criterion of adequacy that the theory will successfully illuminate the nature of municipal systems."[94] Some four decades later, the global legal landscape, determined by the relation between municipal and international law, has changed so dramatically that Raz was forced to admit that "exclusive concentration on state law was, it now turns out, never justified, and is even less justified today." In particular,

> we need to rethink the relations of state-law to other legal systems, as the scope both of the authority and of the sovereignty of states has diminished and is likely to diminish still further, and the ways states integrate within the emerging international law is going to confront us with practical and theoretical problems."[95]

International legal scholars' stance regarding the philosophical treatment of international law constitutes the other side of the story. They often have displayed an ambivalent position toward this issue. On the one hand, they have criticized legal philosophers for dealing with a topic with which they are not familiar. On the other hand, they tended to demonstrate a certain contempt for excessive theorizing in the field of international law. One of the authorities in the field, Ian Brownlie, is paradigmatic of both of these trends. In an article dedicated mostly to the criticism of Hart, he says:

94 Joseph Raz, "The Identity of Legal Systems," in *The Authority of Law – Essays on Law and Morality* (Oxford: Oxford University Press, 1979), 105.

95 Joseph Raz, "Why the State?" (2014) Legal Studies Research Paper Series, Paper No. 2014–38: 22. available at ssrn.com/abstract=2339522. For a critical exploration of the applicability of Raz's theory of legal system on non-state law, *see, e.g.*, Jennifer W. Primmer, "Beyond the Law-State: The Adequacy of Raz's Account of Legal Systems in Explaining Intra-State and Supra-State Legality" (2015) 28 *Ratio Juris* 1: 149–158.

> The legal philosophers, with few exceptions, are unacquainted with international law. Certainly they lack knowledge of its practical applications. Thus there is much theorizing, usually on the basis of testing the law of nations against criteria which are thought to be characteristic of domestic legal systems, and not enough examination of the vast array of evidence of the actual role of international law, both in the routine stewardship of State affairs and also in more strenuous political circumstances.[96]

And yet, we are witnessing a revived interest of international scholars in the philosophical treatment of international law. This trend demonstrates the need for revisiting classical jurisprudential accounts of international law in light of the complex structure of the current international legal order.

### *a) International Law and Contemporary Theories in the Positivist Tradition*

Waldron not long ago said that "[t]he neglect of international law in modern analytical jurisprudence is nothing short of scandalous."[97] Although, in his words, this situation "is beginning to change ... there is still no leadership in this regard from Hart's most prominent followers."[98] Not only has international law been largely neglected by newly developing legal theories in the positivist tradition, but to the extent that this subject matter has been tackled, it has been mostly in relation to Kelsen's and Hart's writings. It seems, however, that international scholars more readily claim that Kelsen's ideas and insights can still be used profitably for the elucidation of international law than is the case with Hart's theory.[99] This conviction stems from a widely acknowledged fact that Kelsen was "the only great legal theorist to have placed international law and its relations with domestic law at the centre of his considerations."[100]

96 Ian Brownlie, "The Reality and Efficacy of International Law" (1981) 51 *British Yearbook of International Law*: 8.

97 Jeremy Waldron, "Hart and the Principle of Legality," in Matthew H. Kramer et. al. (eds.), *The Legacy of H.L.A. Hart: Legal, Political, and Moral Philosophy* (Oxford: Oxford University Press, 2008), 69.

98 Waldron, "International Law: 'A Relatively Small and Unimportant' Part of Jurisprudence?," 211.

99 *See, e.g.*, Jörg Kammerhofer, "The Benefits of the Pure Theory of Law for International Lawyers, or: What use is Kelsenian Theory?" (2006) 12 *International Legal Theory*: 5–54. Alexander Somek, "Kelsen Lives" (2007) 18 *European Journal of International Law* 3: 409–451. Jochen von Bernstorff, *The Public International Law Theory of Hans Kelsen: Believing in Universal Law* (translated by Thomas Dunlap) (Cambridge: Cambridge University Press, 2010).

100 Charles Leben, "Hans Kelsen and the Advancement of International Law" (1998) 9 *European Journal of International Law* 2: 287.

Hence, his theory is celebrated, among other things, for paving the way for the dominant contemporary view that international law can encompass every aspect of human life. What used to be a shocking argument when advanced by Kelsen – that international law can regulate virtually any aspect of human life[101] – has increasingly become a common place in international law textbooks.[102] However, Kelsen's treatment of international law on an equal footing with municipal law has, according to critics, its downsides. The major objection concerns his "insistence on grounding the legal character of international law on recourse to physical force, on the pattern of violent retribution (*Vergeltung, talio, vendetta*), borrowed from primitive communities of a remote past."[103] According to Rigaux, international law does not rely as much on sheer physical force as it does on some other mechanisms, such as, for instance, the denial of membership to disobedient states.[104] Therefore, this is not a most adequate path for defending the "legality" of international law.[105]

Hart's contribution to the philosophy of international law was, from the outset, received far less enthusiastically.[106] While Kelsen readily acknowledged the "truly legal" nature of international law, his case was vulnerable owing to the "statist" approach, not fully suitable for the international realm. Hart's theory faced a somewhat reverse challenge – its initial "statist" perspective seemed to obstruct him from treating international law as an instance of "true law."[107] Hence, Brownlie charges Hart's theory with "*a priorism* and over-simplification," insofar as he proceeds from legal systems of "modern states" as "clear standard cases" that are then contrasted with "doubtful cases" of primitive and international law. In this respect, Hart's elucidation of the concept of law resembles "a search for a species of butterfly which, it is believed, has certain characteristics, though it has not yet been found." Those "noticed

101 "Every matter that is, or can be, regulated by national law is open to regulation by international law as well." Kelsen, *Principles of International Law*, 406.

102 Take, for example, the title of one of the chapters of Shaw's *International Law* – "The expanding legal scope of international concern." It depicts a trend of contemporary international law to extend "to include individuals, groups and international organisations, both private and public, within its scope." Malcolm N. Shaw, *International Law* (6th ed.) (Cambridge: Cambridge University Press, 2008), 45.

103 Rigaux, "Hans Kelsen on International Law," 337.

104 *Ibid*, 338.

105 I will address the problem of coercion in international law in more detail in Chapter 5.

106 For an early criticism, *see*, D'Amato, "The Neo-Positivist Concept of International Law," 321–324.

107 Some authors argue that Hart's treatment of international law is in some important respects similar to that of Austin, from whose general theory of law he wanted to depart. *See*, Jason A. Beckett, "The Hartian Tradition in International Law" (2008) *The Journal Jurisprudence*: 51–83. *Cf.* Waldron, "Hart and the Principle of Legality," 68.

during the search are ignored as not corresponding to the model searched for." When, finally, "a butterfly is found which for a while is thought to correspond to the model then others noticed are *ex hypothesi* of no account."[108]

On this reading, Hart's approach fails for not being grounded in the relevant empirical evidence, at least not that related to the treatment of international law.[109] This is certainly a grave accusation, particularly for the author who tried to distance himself from Kelsen's apriorism, by emphasizing more than once that "the question to be faced is one of fact." For Hart, this meant that any inquiry into the nature of international law should proceed from the question: "What is the actual character of the rules as they function in the relations between states?"[110]

Waldron's criticisms of Hart's chapter on international law are structured along a different line of argumentation. Waldron praises Hart for initially providing us with some important insights regarding the nature of sovereignty and the role of sanctions in the international order.[111] Yet, once the reader starts expecting Hart to cast some original light on the institutional aspect of international law, he proceeds "as though his interest in the subject has just run out. His arguments become careless and their application thoughtless in regard to law in this area."[112] Thus, Waldron's main objection is that Hart's methodological and conceptual apparatus, developed initially for a municipal legal system, could have been more consistently applied in the international realm as well. This would, consequently, have forced Hart to acknowledge the truly legal nature of international law.

Instead, Hart argues that in the absence of a state-like institutional apparatus, international law could at best be said to resemble primitive law. However, if the key distinction between primitive law and a more developed legal system concerns the ability of the latter to meet the challenges of uncertainty, of the static character of the social rules, and of the inefficiency of the enforcement mechanisms,[113] "than there is no compelling reason why an international legal order needs to resemble the domestic legal order in *form*." What, then, is required is to assess the nature of the international legal order "on the basis of whether it contains rules and mechanisms which perform the three *functions*

108 Brownlie, "The Reality and Efficacy of International Law," 6.

109 *Ibid.*

110 Hart, *The Concept of Law*, 236.

111 Waldron, "International Law: 'A Relatively Small and Unimportant' Part of Jurisprudence?," 211–213.

112 *Ibid*, 213. Hence, Waldron speaks of "[t]he real harm [which] lies in the opportunity costs of Hart's negligence." Namely, "[w]hat we miss is what might have been done" in Hart's more sophisticated treatment of the subject matter. *Ibid*, 222.

113 Hart, *The Concept of Law*, 91ff.

which Hart deems necessary for the existence of a legal system." In case it does, "there are no grounds to deny international law the status of a legal system."[114]

Contemporary scholars working in the positivist tradition[115] seem to agree that accounting for the complexity of the contemporary international law requires moving beyond Kelsen and Hart.[116] And yet, while they are trying to distance themselves from classical international legal positivism, they are not into "a project for the renewal, vindication or revolution of positivist thought."[117] Working along the lines of "a few recurring 'theses'" and "paradigms" of legal positivism,[118] they are primarily interested in "a theoretical refinement"[119] of the positivist approach in international law, leaving it purposefully in a state of flux.[120]

### b) International Law and Contemporary Theories of Legal Non-positivism

One of the immediate replies to Hart's exposition of international law entailed the argument that his "attempt to apply a positivist Occam's razor to morality or natural law in international law may lead to considerable distortion in its interpretation."[121] Having in mind the aforementioned historical interconnectedness of international law and the natural law theory, one would expect this theoretical camp to provide some more comprehensive theoretical accounts of this body of rules. However, no influential author writing in the natural law theory tradition offered such a theory.[122] One of the reasons for

114 Mehrdad Payandeh, "The Concept of International Law in the Jurisprudence of H.L.A. Hart" (2010) 21 *European Journal of International Law* 4: 981.

115 A group of them was gathered in a volume on the present-day international legal positivism *See*, Kammerhofer and D'Aspremont (eds.), *International Legal Positivism in a Post-Modern World.*

116 Somek has recently argued for "shifting the perspective from the legal positivist's understanding of law *qua* special type of product to law *qua* special type of relationship," which can help refram[e] "the foundational challenge." Somek, "Beyond Kelsen and Hart," 153.

117 Kammerhofer and D'Aspremont, "Introduction – The Future of International Legal Positivism," 7.

118 These would be: "the separation, autonomy and social or conventional theses," "the necessity for formal law-ascertainment, the political and creative character of interpretation, the idea of autonomy or the possibility of a critique of law." *Ibid*, 14.

119 *Ibid*, 8.

120 *Ibid*, 14.

121 Anthony D'Amato, "The Neo-Positivist Concept of International Law" (1965) 59 *American Journal of International Law*: 324.

122 One of the most elaborated accounts of international law, which is grounded in Finnis's idea that the legal scientist has to adopt the "practically reasonable perspective," comes from Capps, who is an international scholar, albeit with a strong theoretical background. He argues "that international law is a type of law that attempts to constitute the conditions by which human agents can have dignity in a particular field of human conduct: the relations between

such state of affairs might be found in the fact that contemporary natural law theorists have not much in common with their forerunners, insofar as they are inclined to carve out their substantive and methodological positions partly in response to arguments of the opposing camp. Since legal positivists have largely determined the outline and terms of the jurisprudential debate, and international law was not ranked high on their list of priorities, natural law theorists also refrained from entering into this domain. In addition, rejoinders to the key tenets of contemporary legal positivism are so manifold and diverse that all of them can hardly be subsumed under the label of natural law theory. For that reason, all contemporary theories departing from legal positivism are more often assembled under the umbrella term of "legal non-positivism."[123]

Probably the most prominent theory of legal non-positivism not belonging to the traditional camp of natural law theory is that of Ronald Dworkin. Çali has noticed that Dworkin's interpretativism is one of the contemporary theories of law that "has been received with indifference by theorists of international law." She attributes this indifference to the fact that "Dworkin is yet another legal philosopher who has not offered a full-length treatment of international law."[124] It transpired, however, that Dworkin's last piece in legal philosophy, which was posthumously published, concerned exactly the subject matter of international law.[125] This came as no small surprise for both followers and critics of his work, having in mind how little Dworkin had previously dwelt on this topic. For instance, in his penultimate book *Justice for Hedgehogs*,[126] which is characterized as "the great synthesis" of his work,[127] the very phrase "international law" was explicitly mentioned three times, and only in relation to the discussion about the nature of human rights. However,

states." Patrick Capps, *Human Dignity and the Foundations of International Law* (Oxford: Hart Publishing, 2009), 103.

[123] Alexy distinguishes between *exclusive non-positivism* (the strongest form of the *lex inuista non est lex*-type of legal non-positivism); *super-inclusive non-positivism* (which maintains that legal validity is in no way affected by moral defects of legal rules); and *inclusive non-positivism* (which holds that moral defects undermine legal validity only in the cases of extreme injustice of legal rules). Robert Alexy, "Law, Morality, and the Existence of Human Rights" (2012) 25 *Ratio Juris* 1: 2–14.

[124] In spite of that, Çali advances "an argument for the relevance of interpretivism to the theoretical and normative debates about international law and its central claim that law is an interpretive concept." Başak Çali, "On Interpretativism and International Law" (2009)20 *European Journal of International Law* 3: 805–806.

[125] Ronald Dworkin, "A New Philosophy for International Law" (2013) 41 *Philosophy and Public Affairs* 1: 2–30.

[126] Ronald Dworkin, *Justice for Hedgehogs* (Cambridge, Mass.: The Belknap Press of Harvard University Press, 2011)

[127] Jeremy Waldron, "Ronald Dworkin: An Appreciation" (2013) Public Law and Legal Theory Research Paper Series – Working Paper No. 13–39: 2.

already Dworkin's treatment of this special international legal regime[128] demonstrated potential inherent tensions within a theoretical project that was once famously labeled as "parochial"[129] – a designation that Dworkin was apparently ready to accept to a certain extent.[130]

Dworkin's theory of human rights was grounded in a conception of dignity which, in his view, has the status of a universal, objective, and absolute moral truth. In "A Philosophy for International Law," he takes a further step, by grounding all international law in his master ethical conception of the unity of value. He dismisses "the self-limiting consent of sovereign nations . . . [as] the basic ground of international law,"[131] which is allegedly the common starting point of all legal positivists' accounts in this field.[132] Instead, he finds "the true moral basis of international law" in the "general obligation of each state to improve its political legitimacy," which also "includes an obligation to try to improve the overall international system."[133] The unmitigated system of Westphalian state sovereignty is detrimental for citizens of particular states in the following ways: states may violate basic human rights of their citizens; they may fail to intervene and help citizens of other states who are subjected to systematic and gross violations of their basic rights; and they are discouraged from cooperating internationally, which lack of cooperation often exposes their citizens to large economic, health, or environmental disasters; finally, this system makes impossible the improvement of the democratic legitimacy of particular states, which consists in "some genuine, even if minimal and indirect" role of citizens in the enactment and administration of their government's policies.[134] Thus, Dworkin suggests the principle of "mitigation," which is the "most general structural principle and interpretive background

128 He already had elaborated on this topic more thoroughly in Ronald Dworkin, *Is Democracy Possible Here? Principles for a New Political Debate* (Princeton, N.J.: Princeton University Press, 2006), chapter 2.

129 Raz, "Can There Be a Theory of Law?," 332.

130 Ronald Dworkin, *Justice in Robes* (Cambridge, Mass.: The Belknap Press of Harvard University Press, 2006), 231.

131 Dworkin, "A New Philosophy for International Law," 10.

132 This mischaracterizes at least one well known positivist account of international law, that of Kelsen. Furthermore, contemporary scholars, whom Dworkin explicitly mentions as trying to construct a doctrinal account from the Hartian version of positivism, such as Besson, are explicitly opposed to the idea that the authority of international law *tout court* could be justified solely by invoking the principle of state consent. *See*, Samantha Besson, "Sovereignty, International Law and Democracy" (2011) 22 *European Journal of International Law* 2: 373–387.

133 Dworkin, "A New Philosophy for International Law," 17.

134 *Ibid*, 17–18.

of international law." However, it has to be supplemented with the further principle of "salience," which states as follows:

> If a significant number of states, encompassing a significant population, has developed an agreed code of practice, either by treaty or by other form of coordination, then other states have at least a prima facie duty to subscribe to that practice as well, with the important proviso that this duty holds only if a more general practice to that effect, expanded in that way, would improve the legitimacy of the subscribing state and the international order as a whole.[135]

Not only is this a theory about the grounds of international law, but it is also an interpretative strategy for this body of law, which relies on the idea that the goals resulting from the mitigation of the Westphalian model have to be understood in such a way as to make them mutually compatible.[136]

Dworkin's new philosophy for international law shares all the important features of his latest stage of philosophizing about municipal law: It is an attempt to treat law as a distinct part of what morality requires in the international realm;[137] it is a normative theory of an interpretative concept;[138] it provides an interpretative strategy for the theory of adjudication;[139] and it proves its superiority over the Hartian "sociological" account, by using "hard cases" that involve interpretive doctrinal questions (e.g., the NATO intervention in Kosovo).[140]

Dworkin's piece has, as expected, attracted high interest in the community of legal philosophers. Some authors emphasize the novel aspects of this approach and compare it with a view about international law that one might have expected Dworkin to offer on the basis of his theory of state law.[141] Some criticize his outright rejection of state consent as the ground of international law's legitimacy and argue that, taken in the narrow sense, this consent can play an important role in a morally defensible international system.[142] Some authors argue that this theoretical proposal is profoundly futuristic, insofar as it

135 *Ibid*, 19.
136 *Ibid*, 22.
137 *Ibid*, 13.
138 *Ibid*, 11.
139 *Ibid*, 22.
140 *Ibid*, 5.
141 Eric J. Scarffe, "'A New Philosophy for International Law' and Dworkin's Political Realism" (2016) 29 *Canadian Journal of Law & Jurisprudence* 1: 191–213.
142 Thomas Christiano, "Ronald Dworkin, State Consent, and Progressive Cosmopolitanism," in Wil Waluchow and Stefan Sciaraffa (eds.), *The Legacy of Ronald Dworkin* (Oxford: Oxford University Press, 2016), 49–70.

is no more about the claim that "law as it is" needs to be assessed in light of "law as it ought to be," according to some inherent standards of political morality of the given political community, but in light of some law that might develop sometime in the distant future.[143] There are those who argue that Dworkin's proposal may not only be unrealistic, but harmful as well, because, if taken seriously by the international community, it may result in states being less willing to negotiate deep international agreements in the future.[144] Finally, there are some more optimistic views, which take Dworkin's founding principles of mitigation and salience to provide a sound moral foundation for international law.[145]

143 Miodrag Jovanović, "Dworkin on International Law: Not Much of a Legacy?" (2015) 28 *Canadian Journal of Law & Jurisprudence* 2: 443–460.

144 Adam S. Chilton, "A Reply to Dworkin's New Theory of International Law" (2013) 80 *The University of Chicago Law Review Dialogue*: 105–115.

145 Thomas Bustamante, "Revisiting Dworkin's Philosophy of International Law: Could the Hedgehog Have Done It Any Other Way?" (2017) 30 *Canadian Journal of Law & Jurisprudence* 2: 259–285.

# 2

# In Search of the Nature of (International) Law – Methodological Postulates

As Chapter 1 demonstrates, philosophizing about law started long before the emergence of classical analytical jurisprudence, but its forefathers – Bentham and Austin – are praised by the vast majority of jurisprudents for establishing methodological parameters for the study of law that were devoid of distracting influences of other branches of philosophy and theology. Dan Priel has recently argued that, despite debatable connections between scientific, i.e., logical positivism and legal positivism,[1] this jurisprudential tradition can be accurately labeled as "positivist" legal positivism, owing primarily to its methodological orientation toward *scientism*. According to this methodological stance, "knowledge should be attained by following scientific *methods* and *goals*, especially those of the natural sciences. A central aim of the scientific method is to provide an objective description and explanation of phenomena in the world."[2] In that respect, the aforementioned early legal positivists, as well as some of their twentieth-century successors, such as Ross and Kelsen, were largely concerned with the self-reflective, meta-philosophical task of

[1] It is a well-documented fact that the emergence of the school of logical (empirical) positivism (the so-called Vienna Circle) has not only contributed to the development of analytical philosophy, but that it was decisive in the grounding of the Pure Theory of Law. *See* Rudolf Carnap, Hans Hahn, and Otto Neurath (eds.) *Logischer Empirismus – der Wiener Kreis. Ausgewählte Texte mit einer Einleitung* (München: Fink, 1975) On relations between the Vienna Circle and the Pure Theory of Law, see Clemens Jabloner and Friedrich Stadler (eds.), *Logischer Empirismus und Reine Rechtslehre – Beziehungen zwischen dem Wiener Kreis und der Hans Kelsen-Schule* (Wien: Springer, 2001). Cf. Peter Langford, Ian Bryan, and John McGarry, "Introduction: Kelsen, Legal Science and Positive Law," in Peter Langford, Ian Bryan, and John McGarry (eds.), *Kelsenian Legal Science and the Nature of Law* (Cham: Springer, 2017), 1–19.

[2] Dan Priel, "Jurisprudence Between Science and the Humanities" (2012) 4 *Washington University Jurisprudence Review*: 279. The other features of the "positivist" legal positivism are: materialism, anti-historicism, and a minimal role for the analysis of language in explanation. *Ibid*, 279–280.

determining what it means to philosophize about law. For them, this question boiled down to the problem of elucidation of the scientific nature of legal inquiry.[3] The scientific rigor of the newly emerging jurisprudence was commonly demonstrated in opposition to what they envisaged as the "metaphysical," i.e., anti-empirical speculation of the natural law theory.[4]

The mid-twentieth century legal positivists largely abandoned the overall methodological inclination of the former camp, by substituting external observation for internal understanding. According to this newly emerged view, "[s]ince there is no way of 'translating' reasons for action to causal description, any attempt to offer a scientific account of human action is bound to fail."[5] Hence, Raz dismisses Kelsen's scientism as "clearly fallacious." Methods have to be adjusted to the subject of study, and if it "cannot be studied 'scientifically' then its study should not strive to be scientific."[6] Instead, Hart's "internal point of view"[7] has become the new paradigm in legal positivists' approach.[8] This by no means implies that this strand of legal positivism has given up scientific objectives of neutrality, objectivity, and accuracy. Therefore, it would be fair to conclude that "Hart sought to occupy a methodological halfway house that would avoid the pitfalls of (scientific, M. J.) positivism but which was, he thought, rigorous enough to provide an objective description of reality."[9]

3 As noted by Bulygin, Kelsen's "concern was to shape a model of a legal science that would satisfy the requirements of this programme of a positivistic science, and to provide methodological foundations and conceptual tools for such an enterprise." Eugenio Bulygin, "An Antinomy in Kelsen's Pure Theory of Law," in Stanley L Paulson and Bonnie Litschewski Paulson (eds.), *Normativity and Norms – Critical Perspectives on Kelsenian Themes* (Oxford: Clarendon Press, 1998), 301.

4 Alf Ross, *On Law and Justice* (Berkeley: University of California Press, 1959), 25. *Cf.* Hans Kelsen, "Naturrechtslehre und Rechtspositivismus" in Friedrich Koja (ed.), *Hans Kelsen oder Die Reinheit der Rehtslehre* (Vienna: Böhlau Verlag 1988), 231.

5 The other features of this "anti-positivist" legal positivism are holism, historicism, and a central role for the analysis of language in the explanation of human action. Priel associates this stance with Hart, Raz, and their followers. Priel, "Jurisprudence Between Science and the Humanities," 280–281.

6 Joseph Raz, "The Purity of the Pure Theory," in *The Authority of Law – Essays on Law and Morality* (2nd ed.) (Oxford: Oxford University Press, 2009), 297. Similar critical attitudes toward "scientism" (*Scientismus*) can be found in contemporary German legal philosophy. *See, e.g.*, Arthur Kaufmann, "Rechtsphilosophie, Rechtstheorie, Rechtsdogmatik," in Arthur Kaufmann, Winfried Hassemer, Ulfried Neumann (eds.), *Einführung in Rechtsphilosophie und Rechtstheorie der Gegenwart* (Heidelberg: C.F. Müller Verlag, 2004), 7.

7 Hart, *The Concept of Law*, 89ff.

8 *See, e.g.*, the symposium on "the internal point of view" in *Fordham Law Review*, Vol. 75, No. 3, 2006.

9 Priel, "Jurisprudence Between Science and the Humanities," 316–317.

Although divided on the question of whether jurisprudence, methodologically speaking, falls within the ambit of the sciences or humanities, scholars from the positivist tradition are in unison in discarding methods of evaluation and normative justification commonly associated with the natural law theory. Yet, again, there is a lack of consensus when it comes to the potential role of empirical (sociological) method in a jurisprudential treatment of law. On the one hand, Hart famously remarked that his theory can be also read as "an essay in descriptive sociology,"[10] whereas Kelsen was determined to avoid the "syncretism in method" by clearly distinguishing between sociological jurisprudence and the Pure Theory of Law.[11]

These hesitations in the positivist camp, finally, influence another important meta-philosophical question[12] regarding applicable *criteria of success* of a theory of law. What, if anything, can serve as such criteria?[13] It seems hardly disputable that criteria of success are, first and foremost, determined by the self-proclaimed characterization and classification of the given jurisprudential approach. Hence, all those jurisprudential accounts that conceive of themselves as belonging to the *positivist* tradition would have to be assessed against some presumably uncontroversial standards of legal positivism.[14] The same

10 Hart, *The Concept of Law*, vi.

11 Hans Kelsen, "The Pure Theory of Law and Analytical Jurisprudence" (1941) 55 *Harvard Law Review* 1: 52. This dilemma eventually affects a much broader issue as to whether there is *the* methodology of jurisprudence. Kelsen forcefully advanced the positive response, by distinguishing between the Pure Theory of Law, sociological jurisprudence, and legal politics. Hans Kelsen, *Pure Theory of Law* (translation by Max Knight) (Berkeley: University of California Press, 1967) 1. On the other hand, Hart says: "I do not regard analytical jurisprudence as exclusive of other forms of jurisprudence. There is room, of course, for other approaches." Herbert Hart, "Analytical Jurisprudence in Mid-twentieth Century: A Reply to Professor Bodeheimer" (1957) 105 *University of Pennsylvania Law Review*: 974. Green is even more explicit when contending that "[n]o legal philosopher can be *only* a legal positivist" (emphasis in the original). Leslie Green, "Legal Positivism," in Edward N. Zalta (ed.), *The Stanford Encyclopedia of Philosophy* (Spring 2018 ed.), at https://plato.stanford.edu/archives/spr2018/entries/legal-positivism/

12 The province of metaphilosophy of law concerns generally the problem of the adequate methodological approach to answering the question, "'What is law?' (or its concept)." Paweł Banaś, "The Philosophy of Legal Philosophy: An Introduction," in Paweł Banaś, Adam Dyrda, and Tomasz Gizbert-Studnicki (eds.), *Metaphilosophy of Law* (Oxford: Hart Publishing, 2016), 1.

13 Dickson is interested exactly in offering "a schematic account" of what she takes to be "the criteria of success of a legal theory." Julie Dickson, *Evaluation and Legal Theory* (Oxford: Hart Publishing, 2001), 15.

14 "[T]here is nothing philosophical to say about 'legal positivists' as a group unless there is some distinctive proposition or set of propositions that was advanced or assumed by all of them." John Gardner, "Legal Positivism: 5½ Myths" (2001) 46 *The American Journal of Jurisprudence* 1: 199.

would apply to all jurisprudential inquiries that characterize themselves as *analytical*. However, just as there are meaningful debates about what it means for a theory of law to be positivist in nature,[15] there are also significant disagreements as to what amounts to an "analytical" approach in jurisprudence. This question is not only of relevance for the present study, which strives to deliver an explanatory and analytic account of international law, but of broader importance, because even the most prominent representatives of the natural law theory also tend to stress that their inquiries cannot be completed without the help of the "analytical" approach.[16] In the course of elucidating distinctive conceptions of an "analytical" approach in jurisprudence I hope to demonstrate its intricate relation with the empirical method. In doing so, I will scrutinize arguments coming from the "third branch of jurisprudence,"[17] which generally pulls in the direction of the "naturalization" of jurisprudence and the overall skepticism toward the method of conceptual analysis.[18] By the end of the chapter, these two methodological approaches should be put in a more sustainable relation within the proposed *prototype theory of concepts*.

## 1 GRASPING "ANALYTICAL" IN THE ANALYTICAL APPROACH

This book is most certainly not the adequate place for dealing with all the intricate problems surrounding analytical method in philosophy. The fact that it is fairly dominant in the contemporary philosophy might suggest that there is

15 Starting from one such proposition – the so-called separability thesis – I tried to investigate whether there can be a successful legal positivist account that is not in some way grounded in the meta-ethical stance of moral relativism. Miodrag Jovanović, "Is Legal Positivism Tenable Beyond Moral Relativism" (2015) 9 *Problema – Anuario de Filosofia y Teoría del Derecho*: 193–252.

16 *See, e.g.*, Mark C. Murphy, "Two Unhappy Dilemmas for Natural Law Jurisprudence" (2015) 60 *The American Journal of Jurisprudence* 2: 121–141. Robert Alexy, "On the Concept and the Nature of Law" (2008)21 *Ratio Juris* 3: 281–299. Even though Finnis argues that "[a] sound theory of natural law is one that explicitly . . . undertakes a critique of practical viewpoints," he also notes that such an undertaking is in need "of the assistance of descriptive and analytical social science." John Finnis, *Natural Law and Natural Rights* (Oxford: Oxford University Press, 2011), 18, 19.

17 This is the label Tamanaha uses to denote both traditional schools of historical and sociological jurisprudence and legal realism, as well as new proponents of socio-legal studies, who all heavily rely on the empirical method in studying law. Tamanaha, A *Realistic Theory of Law*, chapter I.

18 In his seminal work on this topic, Leiter argues in favor of a Quine-inspired naturalism, which is skeptical about the analytical approach and takes philosophy to be continuous with empirical science. Brian Leiter, *Naturalizing Jurisprudence: Essays on American Legal Realism and Naturalism in Legal Philosophy* (Oxford: Oxford University Press, 2007).

a consensus with respect to what that method amounts to. However, "this is far from clear," because throughout its history analysis "has been understood and practised in many different ways."[19] In focusing on the development of modern analytical philosophy, Williamson has noticed that "a species of philosophy with so much anti-metaphysics in its gene pool"[20] has in the last decades witnessed "the growth and flourishing of boldly speculative metaphysics" within its tradition.[21]

This transformation is hardly unnoticeable within the analytical tradition in legal philosophy. It already had been demonstrated that, irrespective of different philosophical backgrounds, all jurisprudents within the camp of "positivist" legal positivism understood their disciplinary approach as sharply contrasted with "metaphysical speculation" that has led natural law theorists to hold some "nonsensical" positions. Hence, while grounding his Pure Theory of Law in the philosophical foundations of the Vienna Circle, Kelsen at the same time argued that his "orientation is much the same as that of so-called analytical jurisprudence," which he associated with Austin. What, according to Kelsen, united both jurisprudential approaches despite some apparent differences was exactly the method of "analysis."[22]

In a 1966 article on the new wave of Anglo-American analytical jurisprudence, Summers tried to identify what differentiated it in comparison with the classical school of thought. Despite obvious mutual differences within this new generation of analytical scholars,[23] he argued that their work "is broader in scope, more sophisticated in methodology, less doctrinaire and positivistic, and more likely to be of practical utility."[24] Although new analytical jurisprudents are "performing a wider variety of analytical activities," the chief of them is, nonetheless, reserved for "conceptual analysis," i.e., "analysis of the existing

19 Michael Beaney, "Analysis," in Zalta (ed.), *The Stanford Encyclopedia of Philosophy* (Summer 2016 ed.) at https://plato.stanford.edu/archives/sum2016/entries/analysis/

20 Apart from the already mentioned Vienna Circle of logical positivists, "[a]nother main strand in the development of the analytic tradition, ordinary language philosophy, tended to be almost equally suspicious of the ways in which metaphysicians made free with ordinary words, far from the everyday contexts of use on which their meaning was supposed to depend." Timothy Williamson, "How Did We Get Here From There? The Transformation of Analytic Philosophy" (2014) 27 *Belgrade Philosophical Annual*: 7.

21 *Ibid.*

22 Kelsen, "The Pure Theory of Law and Analytical Jurisprudence," 54.

23 Summers mentions Hart, Williams, and Hughes as British representatives; and Dworkin, Fried, Morris, and Wasserstrom as American representatives, of this new wave. He stresses that "[t]hey form a school only in the limited sense that a major part of the work of each is analytical in nature," from which it "should not be concluded that they have no interest in sociological or evaluative inquiries." Summers, "The *New* Analytical Jurist," 864.

24 *Ibid*, 863.

conceptual framework of and about law."[25] This method is of crucial importance because "clarity and insight are important."[26] Conceptual analysis, according to Summers, goes beyond linguistic analysis, insofar as the "[t]he relevant subject matter consists of concepts or ideas currently used by either laymen or professionals in dealing with law." Furthermore, this is not "a single activity," but "a family of related activities," including "breaking down concepts, differentiating related concepts, correlating and/or unifying related concepts, classifying them in some way, and charting their implications – their 'logical bearings.'"[27] Finally, the end result of the employed method should be "a better understanding of some important domain within our conceptual scheme."[28]

Let us now contrast Summers's reconstruction of the analytical approach of mid-1960s analytical jurisprudents with a dominant understanding of conceptual analysis, as spelled out by some of the most prominent contemporary legal philosophers. Raz takes conceptual analysis to be the prime philosophical method, which, when applied to the field of jurisprudence, amounts to the explanation of the nature of law. Consequently, a theory of law "consists of necessary truths, for only necessary truths about the law reveal the nature of law." When we talk of the "nature of law," we "refer to those of the law's characteristics which are of the essence of law, which make law what it is."[29] Dickson follows in Raz's footsteps when arguing that "analytical jurisprudence is concerned with accurately and adequately explaining the nature of law."[30] Hence, "only necessarily true propositions about law will be capable of explaining the nature of law."[31] Spaak says that "the analysis of a concept aims to establish an analytically true equivalence between *analysandum* (that which is to be analyzed) and *analysans* (that which does the analyzing)." In that respect, "the task of the analyst is to find properties that are individually

25 The other activities within the broader analytical approach are: "construction of new conceptual frameworks with accompanying terminologies; rational justification of institutions and practices, existing and proposed; and 'purposive implication' – tracing out what the acceptance of social purposes 'implies' in terms of social arrangements and social ordering." *Ibid*, 865–866.

26 *Ibid*, 866.

27 *Ibid*, 867.

28 *Ibid*, 868.

29 Raz, "Can There Be a Theory of Law?," 328. On the non-positivist side of the spectrum, Alexy notes in a similar fashion that the question on the nature of law may be substituted with the one on the necessary properties of law. Alexy, "On the Concept and the Nature of Law," 290.

30 And, again, when she speaks of "the nature of law," she refers "to those essential properties which a given set of phenomena must exhibit in order to be law." Dickson, *Evaluation and Legal Theory*, 17.

31 *Ibid*, 18.

necessary and jointly sufficient for X to qualify as law, and that the type of necessity involved is that of conceptual."[32]

Finally, here is Himma's lengthy passage, which more boldly emphasizes the metaphysical – Frank Jackson's style[33] – character of conceptual analysis:

> [C]onceptual analysis of law is intended to tell us something about the nature or essence of law; that is to say, it is supposed to tell us something about not just all existing legal systems, but all conceptually possible legal systems. Thus conceived, a conceptual analysis of law consists in a set of conceptually (or metaphysically) necessary truths and thus constitutes a piece of metaphysical theorizing . . . The project of analyzing the content of legal concepts is the project of exploring the metaphysics of law, explicating its nature in terms of claims that are necessarily true – the hallmark of metaphysical inquiry. The metaphysical character of conceptual analysis, traditionally conceived, is logically connected to the view that the epistemology of conceptual analysis is *a priori* in character.[34]

That conceptual analysis aims at metaphysically necessary truths is confirmed in Green's statement that "the features necessary to law are those found not only in all existing and historical legal systems, but in all possible ones – or all humanly possible ones – and those are numberless and unobservable."[35] This, finally, implies that such determined metaphysical truths about the concept of law are of universal validity. In Raz's words, "our inquiry is universal in that it explores the nature of law, wherever it is to be found."[36]

## 2 CHALLENGES TO THE CONCEPTUAL ANALYSIS

This metaphysical turn in understanding the method of conceptual analysis[37] has recently come under serious attack both from inside and outside the camp of analytical jurisprudence. All the important features of this methodological

32 Torben Spaak, "Schauer's Anti-Essentialism" (2016) 29 *Ratio Juris* 2: 188.

33 Jackson argues against differentiating between conceptual and metaphysical necessity (truth). Frank Jackson, *From Metaphysics to Ethics – A Defence of Conceptual Analysis* (Oxford: Clarendon Press, 1998), 67ff.

34 Kenneth Einar Himma, "Conceptual Jurisprudence: An Introduction to Conceptual Analysis and Methodology in Legal Theory" (2015) 26 *Revus*: 83.

35 Leslie Green, "The Morality in Law," in Duarte d'Almeida, Edwards, and Dolcetti (eds.), *Reading HLA Hart's The Concept of Law*, 199.

36 Raz, "Can There Be a Theory of Law?," 332. Dickson affirms this stance by saying that the objects of the study of conceptual analysis are those features of law "which law, at any time, and in any place, must exhibit." Dickson, *Evaluation and Legal Theory*, 18.

37 Whenever in the remainder of the text I refer to "conceptual analysis" without further qualification, this should be understood as the metaphysically-driven version of analysis.

approach – *essentialism*, *necessarianism*,[38] *apriorism*, and *universalism* – are challenged. In what follows, I will make a brief survey of these criticisms.

The argument against essentialism boils down to the claim that law does not in fact possess any essential properties. According to Dickson, this sort of criticism invites one who fosters it to expose "the inability" of theories of law relying on the method of conceptual analysis to detect and explicate such essential features, and not merely to claim "that such theories are wrong, or question-begging, in their attempt to do so."[39] However, this is hardly the point of the anti-essentialist argument. A claim denying that law possesses any essential properties need not focus on showing "inabilities" of some theory to find them, because even if a theory is unable to complete its task, this still does not imply that law does not have essential properties. Therefore, anyone fostering the aforementioned claim would primarily focus on what it means for a feature to be "essential." For instance, if this is a feature without which the given phenomenon would be stripped of its "identity,"[40] would it, then, be correct to assume that an "essential" feature is unalterable?

This is exactly what Tamanaha has in mind when noting that all legal philosophers pursuing the project of essentialism "are caught on the horns of the same paradox owing to the fact that concepts and social institutions vary and change over time."[41] Raz avoids addressing directly the question of whether law's essential features are unchangeable. At first he calls it "a misconceived question," since what matters is whether law does possess such features.[42] Then he considers it unanswerable, in the same way as is Jeremiah's question: "Can the Ethiopian change his skin or the leopard his spots?" (Jeremiah 13:23) Namely, it is not clear whether it is implied that such change would be conceptually, i.e., metaphysically inconceivable or just factually impossible.[43]

Chiassoni's attack comes from within the camp of analytical jurisprudence. He fosters an accusation that essentialist jurisprudence "constitutes a very serious threat to philosophical progress in jurisprudence," insofar as it

38 I am using this label here in a philosophically non-traditional way, not to designate some form of crude determinism, but a method of analysis that is focused on determining conceptual, i.e., metaphysical necessities.

39 *Ibid*, 19.

40 "Things are what they are, have an identity, because of the properties that they have." Joseph Raz, "Theory and Concepts: Responding to Alexy and Bulygin," in *Una Discusion Sobre la Teoria del Derecho* (Madrid: Marcial Pons, 2007) (in Spanish) English version is available at josephnraz.googlepages.com/TheoryandConcepts-finalversion.pdf, 7.

41 Tamanaha, A *Realistic Theory of Law*, 68.

42 Raz, "Can There Be a Theory of Law?," 328.

43 *Ibid*, 329.

represents "the return to a pre-analytical theory of concepts."[44] In particular, the essentialist jurisprudence is "mistaken for it overlooks the stipulated nature of theoretical concepts." That is, it "is misleading, for it suggests legal theory to be an enterprise that can *discover* what, in fact, cannot be the simple output of a discovery."[45] Hence, while Tamanaha implies that essentialists are interested in the nature of the object the concept of which is the concept of law, and that their project is bound to fail since the object of their study changes over time, Chiassoni charges essentialists with trying to discover the essential features of the concept of law, which is a futile enterprise since that concept is a "theoretical," that is, "stipulated" one.

So, do conceptual analysts search for essential features of a particular social practice called law or for essential features of the very concept of law? Raz is, again, inconclusive when presented with this dilemma. He asks: "Is it not our aim to study the nature of law, rather than our culture and its concept of law?" His quick answer is baffling: "Yes and no. We aim to improve our understanding of the nature of law. The law is a type of social institution, the type which is picked up – designated – by the concept of law. Hence in improving our understanding of the nature of law we assume an understanding of the concept of law, and improve it."[46] Unlike Chiassoni, Raz believes that the concept of law is not a stipulated, that is, theoretical concept, because it is not "introduced by academics," and, as such, is not "part of the scholarly apparatus of any learned discipline." Rather, the concept of law "is a concept entrenched in our society's self-understanding."[47]

This somewhat confusing language, which certainly does not contribute to analytical clarity,[48] is a direct implication of the widely held belief of conceptual analysts themselves that the method they are undertaking "*is* connected with lived experience in some ways," which inevitably raises the question – "a surprisingly difficult one" – of what is the nature of that connection.[49] Apart from objects and concepts, conceptual analysts most often deal with words or phrases that we use in our daily linguistic practice when referring to the object (understood as the relevant set of traceable

44 Pierluigi Chiassoni, "Supporting The Force of Law: A Few Complementary Arguments Against Essentialist Jurisprudence," in Christoph Bezemek and Nicoletta Ladavac (eds.), *The Force of Law Reaffirmed – Frederick Schauer Meets the Critics* (Cham: Springer, 2016), 69.

45 *Ibid*, 66.

46 Raz, "Can There Be a Theory of Law?," 331.

47 *Ibid*. At some other place Raz repeats that "the concept of law is not a product of the theory of law." Joseph Raz, "Two Views of the Nature of the Theory of Law: A Partial Comparison" (1998) 4 *Legal Theory* 3: 281.

48 Tamanaha, *A Realistic Theory of Law*, 61.

49 Brian H. Bix, "Raz on Necessity" (2003) 22 *Law and Philosophy* 6: 546.

features) we are trying to conceptualize.[50] The relation between these elements is intricate to say the least. Raz, for instance, says: "Concepts are placed between the world, aspects of which they are concepts of, and words or phrases, which express them (the concepts) and are used to talk about those aspects of the world."[51] Himma, for his part, observes that "the contents of our concepts are highly responsive to the linguistic practices involving the associated words because we cannot share an understanding of how to use a word without sharing a grasp of the core content of a concept."[52]

One way of trying to debunk the project of conceptual analysis is to advance the famous "semantic sting" criticism, according to which conceptual analysis is not more than a "semantic theory of law,"[53] and the method of "glorified lexicography."[54] Although the claim that conceptual analysis boils down to linguistic analysis is largely considered in the contemporary jurisprudence as misconceived,[55] the argument still has some bite due to the fact that conceptual analysts tend to follow Jackson's dictum that this method should be taken in its "modest" version.[56] Insofar as "modest" conceptual analysis "is explicitly grounded in contingent social practices like those that define the language of the community, conceptual truths are necessary *relative to that set of particular commitments*." Put differently, conceptual analysts "impose a certain metaphysical structure on the world through conceptual commitments that arise out of social practices we construct."[57]

This is where criticism of necessarianism comes into play. For conceptual analysists, "a concept is a summary representation of some sets of things in terms of conditions that are singly necessary and jointly sufficient for determining member-

50 Sometimes, there are no doubts as to whether words and phrases, as well as concepts, are inventions of the given discipline. For instance, there are numerous legal concepts and corresponding concept-words (e.g., "impeachment") or phrases (e.g., "piercing the corporate veil") that are products of the legal community (theory and doctrine), and not creations of everyday linguistic practice.

51 Raz, "Can There be a Theory of Law?," 325.

52 Himma, "Conceptual Jurisprudence," 68.

53 Ronald Dworkin, *Law's Empire* (Cambridge, Mass.: Harvard University Press, 1986), 31–44.

54 Brian Leiter, "Beyond the Hart/Dworkin Debate: The Methodology Problem in Jurisprudence" (2003) 48 *American Journal of Jurisprudence* 1: 45.

55 Nonetheless, Marmor has recently argued, along Dworkinian lines, that conceptual analysis is not more than a linguistic inquiry of the meaning of words in the given context. Andrei Marmor, "Farewell to Conceptual Analysis (in Jurisprudence)," in Wil Waluchow and Stefan Sciaraffa (eds.), *Philosophical Foundations to the Nature of Law* (Oxford: Oxford University Press, 2013), 209–229.

56 Jackson, *From Metaphysics to Ethics – A Defence of Conceptual Analysis*, 42ff.

57 Himma, "Conceptual Jurisprudence," 83, fn. 15. (emphasis in the original)

ship in that set."[58] Consequently, a "complete mastery of a concept" exists with one's "knowledge and understanding of all the necessary features of the objects to which it applies."[59] Thus, conceptual analysis is interested in explicating the nature of law "in terms of claims that are necessarily true," which is, as Himma reminds us, "the hallmark of metaphysical inquiry."[60] But how are we to square this ambition with "a necessity relative to a society and a time or a 'way of life'"?[61] If conceptual analysts are indeed to follow the "modest" approach interested in necessities that are conditional upon observable contingent sociolinguistic practices, does this, then, lead to the conclusion that "conceptual jurisprudence is a sociological enterprise in everything but name"?[62]

At this point, the criticism goes further. If in searching for the alleged necessary features the conceptual analyst "must defer to the way the world is,"[63] in what sense can such propositions be said to be a priori, that is, justified independent of our experience? Faced with this challenge, Giudice argues that "if we are to hang on to necessity claims in analytical legal theory, many of such claims are best understood as *a posteriori* necessity claims."[64] It may certainly be so, but this then contradicts Kant's classical distinction, according to which only a priori propositions are logically necessary, while a posteriori ones are logically contingent. Put differently, the category of *a posteriori analytical* propositions was considered by Kant as patently self-contradictory.[65] One way out of this conundrum would be to argue, alongside with Kripke, that there are a posteriori necessary truths,[66] which are of a non-analytical nature.[67] However, Giudice thinks that such necessary truths could be of use exactly to "analytical legal theorists."[68] It seems, however,

58 Birger Hjørland, "Concept Theory" (2009) 60 *Journal of the American Society for Information Science and Technology* 8: 1520–1521.

59 Raz, "Can There be a Theory of Law?," 326.

60 Himma, "Conceptual Jurisprudence," 83.

61 Bix, "Raz on Necessity," 556.

62 Dan Priel, "The Misguided Search for the Nature of Law" (2015) *Osgoode Legal Studies Research Paper* No. 34/2015: 41. available at https://ssrn.com/abstract=2642461

63 Bix, "Raz on Necessity," 543, fn. 24.

64 Michael Giudice, *Understanding the Nature of Law: A Case for Constructive Conceptual Explanation* (Cheltenham: Edward Elgar Publishing, 2015), 93.

65 Immanuel Kant, *Kritik der reinen Vernunft* (Hamburg: Felix Mainer, 1956), 45ff.

66 "Any necessary truth, whether a priori or a posteriori, could not have turned out otherwise. In the case of some necessary a posteriori truths, however, we can say that under appropriate qualitatively identical evidential situations, an appropriate corresponding qualitative statement might have been false." Saul A. Kripke, *Naming and Necessity* (Cambridge, Mass.: Harvard University Press, 1980), 142.

67 Giudice explicitly acknowledges Kripke's stance. Giudice, *Understanding the Nature of Law*, 92.

68 Giudice says that "the next step for analytical legal theorists wishing to defend necessity claims in legal theory [is] to show how *a posteriori* necessity arguments regarding natural kinds (or identities) can be extended to social kinds or practices such as law." *Ibid*, 102.

that reconciling *analytical* propositions with *a posteriori necessity* requires much more, namely, deferring to Quine's rejection of the strong distinction between analytic and synthetic propositions.[69] And this is what Jackson himself does to a certain extent when saying that "the modest role we are giving conceptual analysis allows us to agree in practice with, while dissenting in theory from, W. V. Quine's famous critique."[70]

All this has a final bearing on criticizing metaphysical universalism of conceptual analysis. As demonstrated, Raz believes that the theory of law grounded on the method of conceptual analysis "is universal for it consists of claims about the nature of all law, and of all legal systems … wherever they may be, and whatever they might be."[71] Being interested in "the universal and invariant truth," which holds in all possible worlds, legal philosophers' object of study is "the timeless necessity of all this contingency," which surrounds the phenomenon of law.[72]

However, the "in-all-possible-worlds" condition has recently become a bone of contention among analytical jurisprudents. It permeates the ongoing dispute regarding the question whether coercion is a necessary or contingent feature of the concept of law. Raz was the first one to use the counter-factual example of the "society of angels," in order to claim that a legal system without coercion is conceptually, i.e., metaphysically conceivable.[73] Green follows in his footsteps. He says that while "[w]e all know that even a 'society of angels' would need rules, if only to help them coordinate their altruistic activities,"[74] such system of rules, given the angels' celestial nature, need not be coercive. This leads Green to conclude that "it is a feature of our concept of law that it is *coercive if necessary*, though not necessarily coercive."[75]

The "angels" argument was already used by Fuller in his explication of eight requirements of law's "inner morality." In commenting on the widespread belief that the need for legal rules "arises wholly out of man's selfish, quarrelsome, and

69 Willard Van Orman Quine, "Two Dogmas of Empiricism" (1951) 60 *The Philosophical Review* 1: 20–43.

70 Jackson, *From Metaphysics to Ethics – A Defence of Conceptual Analysis*, 44. At one point Jackson is even more specific: "[I]n practice, the role I am recommending for conceptual analysis will often be very like the role Quine gives the notion of paraphrase." *Ibid*, 46. He, nonetheless, has a lot to say about theoretical disagreement with Quine. *Ibid*, 53ff.

71 Joseph Raz, "On the Nature of Law," in *Between Authority and Interpretation – On the Theory of Law and Practical Reason* (Oxford: Oxford University Press, 2009), 91.

72 John Gardner, *Law as a Leap of Faith* (Oxford: Oxford University Press, 2012), 300.

73 Joseph Raz, *Practical Reason and Norms* (2nd ed.) (Oxford: Oxford University Press, 2002), 158–159.

74 Leslie Green, "The Forces of Law: Duty, Coercion and Power" (2016) 29 *Ratio Juris* 2: 165–166.

75 *Ibid*, 167.

disputatious nature," whereas such need would not exist "in a society of angels," Fuller says that this entirely "depends on angels," that is on the way how we imagine them to be.[76] Tamanaha wishes to stress further how arbitrary is this theoretical invention of counter-factual examples. In commenting on Green's assertion that the rule-governed nature of a "society of angels" is something that "we all know,"[77] Tamanaha replies: "To the contrary, we know nothing about a society of angels, which is a fantasy. As such, it is whatever a given theorist projects onto it." Therefore, Green's analytical conclusion that "coercion is not necessary to law is prefigured by his starting assumptions," according to which "angels are like humans (disagreements, conflicting views and desires, etc.), only nicer."[78] In a recent article, Himma pursues the same line of reasoning. He fosters an empirically driven counterclaim that "the society-of-angels argument depends on assumptions about the psychological features of the 'angels' that are simply too far removed from what is possible for us (i.e., human beings) in the conditions in which we live to tell us anything of theoretical significance about our legal concepts."[79] Accordingly, he argues in favor of "coercive enforcement mechanisms" as a "conceptually necessary feature" of law.[80]

## 3 BEYOND THE CONCEPTUAL ANALYSIS? THE PROTOTYPE THEORY OF CONCEPTS AND THE NATURE OF LAW

In reflecting on what has been said so far, as well as on some other important insights from the growing body of literature in the field of metaphilosophy of law, I want now to turn to a related but somewhat different challenge to the conceptual analysis. In focusing on specific features of the method of

76 If we think of them as creatures that can "accomplish their good works without any rules at all," or only with the help of "tacit, informal, and intuitively perceived" rules, then they would need no law. "But, if in order to discharge their celestial functions effectively, angels need 'made' rules, rules brought into existence by some explicit decision, then they need law as law is viewed in these essays." Lon L. Fuller, *The Morality of Law* (revised edition) (New Haven: Yale University Press, 1969), 55–56. In his discussion of "the minimum content of natural law," Hart pictured angels as fully altruistic creatures. With such creatures, "never tempted to harm others, rules requiring forbearances would not be necessary." Hart, *The Concept of Law*, 196.

77 Green does mention Fuller's "angels" argument in order to support this alleged self-evident insight (Green, "The Forces of Law: Duty, Coercion and Power," 166, fn. 2), even though it is clear from the quoted passages from Fuller's work that he does not exclude the possibility of a rule-less society of angels.

78 Tamanaha, *A Realistic Theory of Law*, 65, fn. 53.

79 Kenneth Einar Himma, "Can There Really Be Law in a Society of Angels?" (2016), at https://ssrn.com/abstract=2839942

80 Kenneth Einar Himma, "The Authorization of Coercive Enforcement Mechanisms as a Conceptually Necessary Feature of Law" (2016) 7 *Jurisprudence* 3: 593–626.

conceptual analysis – be it essentialism, necessaritianism, apriorism, or universalism – criticisms tend to overlook a potentially more fundamental challenge with which this project can be faced. If the goal of conceptual analysis of, say, K-hood can be qualified "as the business of saying when something counts as a K,"[81] and this is precisely how virtually all conceptual analysts perceive the task of jurisprudence,[82] then this method of disciplinary approach clearly sets the criteria of its own success. The project of conceptual analysis is, thus, "the project of getting the classification right."[83] It is about "identification and boundary lines." That is, by endorsing this method, "we determine what is inside this category ('law') and what is outside."[84] When put in more detail, under this methodological approach, concepts are required to:

> (1) Be exact, not vague – i.e. have clearly defined boundaries, and (2) Have attributes in common which were the necessary and sufficient conditions for membership in the category . . . (3) All members of a category must be equally good with regard to membership; either they have the necessary common features or they don't.[85]

Consequently, if for whatever reasons this project fails in producing a clear-cut demarcation line between instances of law and non-law, its successfulness can be reasonably questioned.

So, how does the conceptual analysis fare against the self-imposed objective of the neat conceptual differentiation between legal and non-legal phenomena? A preliminary answer would be – not quite well. Let me try, nonetheless, to offer a more elaborate response. If conceptual analysis, as indicated by Jackson, is indeed "concerned to elucidate what governs our classificatory practice,"[86] one may proceed by wondering whether the broader objective itself is problematic. That is, is the goal of conceptual classification really worth pursuing? This is, however, a highly counter-intuitive line of attack, because "[o]ne of the most basic functions of living creatures is to categorize, that is to treat distinguishable objects and events as equivalent. Humans live in

81 Jackson, *From Metaphysics to Ethics – A Defence of Conceptual Analysis*, 46.

82 For instance, Green emphasizes the "counting as" as the main goal of conceptual analysis because it is about "identifying necessary and sufficient conditions." Green, "The Forces of Law: Duty, Coercion and Power," 165.

83 Gardner, *Law as a Leap of Faith*, 279.

84 Brian H. Bix, "Ideals, Practices, and Concepts in Legal Theory," in Jordi Ferrer Beltrán, José Juan Moreso, and Diego M. Papayannis (eds.), *Neutrality and Theory of Law* (Dordrecht: Springer, 2013), 34.

85 Eleanor Rosch, "Reclaiming Concepts," in Rafael Núñez and Walter J. Freeman (eds.), *Reclaiming Cognition: The Primacy of Action, Intention and Emotion* (Thorverton: Imprint Academic, 1999), 64.

86 Jackson, *From Metaphysics to Ethics – A Defence of Conceptual Analysis*, 36.

a categorized world."[87] That being so, we are in need of the categorization studies. But, do we also need concepts? Jackson says, after all, that "[o]ur subject is really the elucidation of the possible situations covered by the words we use to ask our questions." Therefore, "our focus is on getting clear about the cases covered rather than on what does the covering, the word *per se*."[88] Finally, "[w]e mark this," Jackson concludes, "by talking of conceptual analysis rather than word or sentence analysis."[89]

Marmor has recently resurrected the claim that this way of "talking" is actually obfuscating what one is really doing when committing oneself to elucidating or analyzing a concept. He asks, "[I]s there anything else to it than figuring out what the word, in its relevant settings, means in the language in question?" and responds swiftly – "It is difficult to see how it would be different."[90] To illustrate the point, Marmor picks up the example of a fleeing North Korean who has never heard of democracy and when faced in the new setting with this word, he asks about its meaning. After the competent speaker gave the North Korean a correct answer, Marmor wonders if there is anything left for him to grasp the concept – "Is there any point at which you can say, 'You know perfectly well what 'democracy' means, but you have not yet quite grasped the concept?'"[91]

As already indicated, Marmor's is an old argument in the debate. And all the well-known responses seem to me good enough to rebut the claim that, particularly in cases of words denoting complex social practices such as democracy (or law), analysis amounts to detecting surface meanings of those words. Funny enough, Marmor himself has indicated this when making a comment that in the stated example it would be "even more mysterious" to say: "'Well, you may have the concept of democracy, but you do not quite know what the word means'?"[92] If conceptual analysis *equals* linguistic analysis, that is, if "to grasp the concept" *equals* "to know the meaning of the word," how, then, could either of the aforementioned statements be "more mysterious" than the other one? Hence, Marmor's puzzlement could be meaningful only under the assumption that to "grasp the concept" *weighs* in some ways "more" than to merely "know the meaning of the word." And indeed, we do normally expect from competent speakers, particularly those involved in political and academic debates, to know of democracy something beyond the dictionary meaning, according to which,

87 Rosch, "Reclaiming Concepts," 61.
88 Jackson, *From Metaphysics to Ethics – A Defence of Conceptual Analysis*, 33.
89 *Ibid*, 33–34.
90 Marmor, "Farewell to Conceptual Analysis (in Jurisprudence)," 211.
91 *Ibid*.
92 *Ibid*, fn. 5.

this is "[a] system of government by the whole population or all the eligible members of a state, typically through elected representatives."[93] To know nothing else would surely preclude more sophisticated debates about whether, say, former socialist countries, which called themselves "people's democracies," should also be treated as instances of democracy; or, whether a country, like Iran, which does have "elected representatives" in the parliament-like body, also qualifies for the status of democracy, etc.[94] Thus, it seems quite clear that while conceptual analysis "start[s] from something that resembles lexicography, as it is *grounded* in meaning . . . it is considerably more than this."[95] And not only that, Hart has long ago noted that "a philosophical definition or explanatory elucidation [of a concept] is designed not to teach the use to those who are ignorant of it" – like our North Korean friend – "but to explain features which are still puzzling to those who have mastered this use."[96] This is, after all, the only way to explain why political theorists and scientists are continuously producing new works in a, some would say futile, attempt to better "grasp the concept" of democracy.[97]

Accordingly, we do need concepts in order to orient ourselves in the world. As put by Hart, "[t]here is no clarification of concepts which can fail to increase our understanding of the world to which we apply them."[98] Hence, by grasping the concept of law we come to expand our comprehension of the social practice, which competent speakers denote by the distinctive word.[99] To the extent that the concept of law is *not an entirely* "stipulated," i.e., "theoretical" concept, as claimed by Chiassoni,[100] but part of our collective

93 "Democracy," English Oxford Living Dictionaries, https://en.oxforddictionaries.com/definition/democracy.

94 Marmor may reply by saying that he explicitly stressed that "[k]nowing what a word means, and consequently, understanding its concept, admit of degrees." That is, "it makes perfect sense to say that A has a better understanding of the meaning of X than B; or that A's understanding of the concept of X is more complete than that of B." Marmor, "Farewell to Conceptual Analysis (in Jurisprudence)," 212, fn. 7. However, having in mind his unintended distinction between "grasping the concept" and "knowing the meaning of the word," in which the former somehow *weighs* more than the latter, the acknowledgment of "degrees" may be read as a further sign that the distinction between the two is warranted.

95 Himma, "Conceptual Jurisprudence," 70.

96 Hart, "Analytical Jurisprudence in Mid-twentieth Century," 965.

97 Analysis is by no means the dominant, let alone the sole, method of research in this disciplinary field.

98 Hart, "Analytical Jurisprudence in Mid-twentieth Century," 967.

99 Raz, "Can There Be a Theory of Law?," 325.

100 Chiassoni's argument is premised on an even more radical claim that "'law' . . . is a fictitious term referring to a fictitious entity," and, accordingly, the task of essentialist jurisprudents "appears to be [the] weird, ill-conceived, task of nailing down the essential properties of something that does not exist." Chiassoni, "Supporting *The Force of Law*," 70.

self-understanding, daily practices, and lived experience, as argued by Raz, jurisprudence is faced with the fundamental methodological question: *Should our disciplinary categorization of the relevant object of study be in any way responsive to the ways people actually categorize the world in everyday life?* Given the inaptness of linguistic analysis to do the entire job of categorization, this question can be safely read as asking yet again about the proper relation between empirical and analytical methods in grasping the concept of law. In what follows, I want to offer some arguments in favor of *the prototype theory of concepts*, which Schauer has hinted at in his recent work but has not thoroughly worked through. In defending this methodological approach, I also hope to clarify why the conceptual analysis is unsuccessful in achieving its goal of getting the classification right.

### a) *Toward the Prototype Theory of Concepts*

In *The Force of Law*, Schauer argues that "it may still often be more valuable to focus on the typical rather than the necessary features or properties of some category or social phenomenon." For, "[j]ust as we can learn a great deal about birds from the typical but not necessary fact that birds fly … so too might we learn a great deal … from law's typical but not necessary features."[101] As expected, this proposal was harshly criticized by conceptual analysts. Green says: "If jurisprudence needs more attention to contingent, typical, truths about law, then it needs something else too. Before we can know what is typical we need to count. Before we can count we need to know that what counts as what. Counting-as is a matter of identifying necessary and sufficient conditions."[102] This passage aptly summarizes a widely held belief of conceptual analysists that the method of analysis logically precedes the empirical method, insofar as "we cannot study law until we know what we mean by 'law.'"[103]

In response to this criticism, one may notice that before knowing "that what counts as what," we need to start from certain empirical observations about normal and typical, yet theoretically and practically relevant features of phenomena we want to conceptualize. Even authors that defend the priority of analytical method readily admit that "there is also a sense in which the theorist doing conceptual analysis must defer to the way the world is, at least in those cases where the theorist is investigating the nature of an *already-existing* concept,"[104] and one such is the concept of law. Priel remarks that this is exactly the

101 Frederick Schauer, *The Force of Law* (Cambridge, Mass.: Harvard University Press, 2015), 4.
102 Green, "The Forces of Law: Duty, Coercion and Power," 165.
103 Bix, "Raz on Necessity," 542.
104 *Ibid*, 543, fn. 24.

"direction" of jurisprudential inquiries falling within the metaphysically driven project of conceptual analysis. Namely, they tend to proceed "from some samples of law (i.e., pre-theoretically agreed upon examples of things that are law), to a theory that tries to show what the necessary and important features these samples (together with all other laws) have."[105]

It is important, however, to bear in mind that legal philosophers are not in the position of natural scientists. As rightly pointed by Raz, in this disciplinary field we "give scientists a privileged position in forging our concepts." That is, "[w]e take the concept to be whatever it is in the hands of the scientific community working in the area concerned." This cannot be so in the jurisprudential domain, because

> [t]hings are different with social concepts such as gifts, ownership, marriage, law, rights, duties, which are used by all to understand themselves and others, and their position in the world. These concepts are not merely tools of understanding, they are part of what shapes the social world we are trying to understand. *They, the concepts themselves, are what we are trying to understand, and not tools of explanation. If we could change them at will we would be changing the social reality we were trying to understand.*[106]

If the concept of law cannot be fully "revisionist,"[107] that is, if in the process of analytical concept formation legal philosophers are to rely on the ways *how* it is used in our everyday world,[108] then they also need to turn to disciplines that study processes of categorization. Cognitive psychology is one such discipline that deals with the study of the mind as an information processor.[109] Challenges to the analytical approach, which psychology readily accepted from philosophy, came in the 1970s with the work on color categories,[110] but they were quickly extended to other kinds of concepts, including social ones. Taken within

105 Dan Priel, "Jurisprudence and Necessity" (2007) 20 *Canadian Journal of Law and Jurisprudence* 1: 177.

106 Raz, "Theory and Concepts: Responding to Alexy and Bulygin," 10. (emphasis mine)

107 It "cannot be revisionist" due to the fact that the analysis "must be based on observation of linguistic practices and prevailing linguistic intuitions." Marmor, "Farewell to Conceptual Analysis (in Jurisprudence)," 212.

108 Priel says that conceptual analysts can be accused of either arbitrarily or selectively reporting about instances of a social practice to which competent users of language attach the word "law." Priel, "The Misguided Search for the Nature of Law," 20.

109 This is what Schaeur suggests as well. Schauer, *The Force of Law*, 37. Similarly, Priel says that if analytical jurisprudence is willing to work with a more reliable set of empirical data, it would need to "look into the literature in cognitive and social psychology in order to get a sense of what goes on in people's heads." Priel, "The Misguided Search for the Nature of Law," 42.

110 Experimental research leading to the formulation of the prototype theory started with color categories, because they "do not have any obviously analyzable criterial attributes, formal structure, or definite boundaries and they [are] ... cross-culturally agreed upon." Rosch, "Reclaiming Concepts," 65.

Wittgenstein's heuristic framework of "family resemblances,"[111] early experimental works[112] have led to the formulation of "the graded structure/prototype view," according to which "all categories show gradients of membership; that is, subjects easily, rapidly, and meaningfully rate how well a particular item fits their idea or image of the category to which the item belongs."[113] In this approach, "the judged best examples of conceptual categories are called prototypes,"[114] where "best" stands for some "measure of central tendency."[115]

This view is by no means without critics. It is criticized as being "a nonstarter as a mechanism for our categorization capacity."[116] According to Harnad's criticism, "[i]t might explain our typicality judgments – for example, 'Is this a more typical bird than that?' – but being able to make a typicality judgment presupposes being able to categorize; it does not explain it: Before I can say how typical a bird this is, I first need to identify it as a bird!"[117] This line of criticism, however, contradicts Harnad's own claim that "the categorization problem is not determining *what* kinds of things there are, but *how* it is that sensorimotor systems like ourselves manage to detect those kinds that they can and do detect, how they manage to respond differentially to them."[118] Thus, when having a discussion on the terrain of cognitive psychology, the relevant issue is whether "we categorize on the basis of the invariant features that are necessary and sufficient to afford categorization," as claimed by the "classical" view,[119] or we take category (concept) to be "a representation of an

111 Ludwig Wittgenstein, *Philosophical Investigations* (Oxford: Basil Blackwell, 1958[1953]), par. 66–67.

112 *See, e.g.*, Eleanor Rosch and Carolyn B. Mervis, "Family Resemblances: Studies in the Internal Structure of Categories" (1975) 7 *Cognitive Psychology*: 573–605.

113 Rosch emphasizes that "these are not probability judgments but judgments of degree of membership." Rosch, "Reclaiming Concepts," 66.

114 *Ibid*, 67.

115 Daniel N. Osherson and Edward E. Smith, "On the Adequacy of Prototype Theory as the Theory of Concepts" (1981) 9 *Cognition* 1: 35.

116 Steven Harnad, "To Cognize is to Categorize: Cognition is Categorization," in Henry Cohen and Claire Lefebvre (eds.), *Handbook of Categorization in Cognitive Science* (Amsterdam: Elsevier, 2005), 40.

117 *Ibid*, 40–41. In a recent review of Schauer's book, Greenberg repeats this argument: "The fact that people judge typical birds to be birds more quickly than they judge penguins or ostriches to be birds (or that people are much more likely to mention typical birds when asked to name birds) tells us nothing about what it *is* to be a bird, about what makes it the case that a particular object is in fact a bird." Mark Greenberg, "How to Explain Things with Force" (2016) 129 *Harvard Law Review* 7: 1946, fn. 16.

118 Harnad, "To Cognize is to Categorize: Cognition is Categorization," 22. (emphasis in the original)

119 Harnad is explicit that "there is [not] anything the least bit wrong with that 'classical theory.'" *Ibid*, 40.

array of features clustered around some sort of prototype," as argued by the prototype theory.[120] According to the latter view,

> [t]he prototype is an abstracted set of features, and categorization judgments are a function of the number and significance of the features shared between the prototype and the instance in question. If some thing or event and the prototype representation share a sufficient number of salient features, then this gives rise to the intuitive judgment that the thing or event is an instance of the target concept. If the two don't share a sufficient number of features, then the instance is not so judged ... prototypical features are assigned different weights or degrees of salience.[121]

The resulting "consequence of the prototype representation of concepts is that the boundaries between concepts are blurry."[122]

### *b) Psychological Assumptions of Conceptual Analysis*

There is a further obvious problem with Harnad's line of attack. Namely, the "classical" psychological theory of categorization simply cannot avail itself of any "typicality judgments," because it operates with instances that are *equally good* with regard to category membership. That is, all the instances belonging to the category and covered by the concept are there in virtue of possessing features that are deemed necessary and sufficient.[123] And vice versa, all those lacking such features are excluded from the category. To the extent that the conceptual analysis holds to the same, it seems possible to identify some psychological presuppositions of this philosophical approach. According to Ramsey, lurking behind conceptual analysis is "the assumption that our intuitive judgments about categorization and class membership can yield a definition for abstract concepts that (1) takes the form of a small conjunctive set of essential properties and (2) coheres with all relevant intuitions and allows no counterexamples."[124]

120 Ramsey, *Representation Reconsidered*, 10.

121 William M. Ramsey, "Prototypes and Conceptual Analysis" (1992) 11 *Topoi* 1: 64.

122 Anne Peters and Isabella Pagotto, "Soft Law as a New Mode of Governance: A Legal Perspective" (2006) *New Modes of Governance Project*, Paper n. 04°/D11: 12.

123 Harnad labels such features as "invariant sensorimotor features ('affordances')," which can be defined in the following way: "Objects *afford* certain sensorimotor interactions with them. A chair affords sitting upon; flowers afford sorting by color, or by species. These affordances are all invariant features of the sensory input, or of the sensorimotor interaction with the input, and the organism has to be capable of detecting these invariants selectively, that is, of abstracting them and ignoring the rest of the variation." Harnad, "To Cognize is to Categorize: Cognition is Categorization," 31–32.

124 "On this view, it is assumed that we have tacit knowledge of the 'essence' of abstract concepts, that the essence is a small set of necessary and sufficient conditions, and that we can uncover

In their defense, conceptual analysts may argue that putting things this way amounts to confusion between metaphysical and epistemological issues, that is, between "questions about *what* something really is with questions about our ordinary *thoughts about* what it is."[125] This is exactly what Spaak has in mind when criticizing Schauer's anti-essentialism and his reliance on the prototypical approach. Spaak asks rhetorically: "[W]hat does the way people in general think of and with concepts have to do with the existence and properties of concepts and the instances of concepts?"[126] If the metaphysical and epistemological issues can be separated, and Spaak believes that this is possible,[127] then resorting to the prototype view in cognitive psychology is simply "irrelevant" even if its findings are correct.[128]

Ramsey, however, says that if anyone is to blame for forging the linkage between the problems of how things "really" are and the ways we represent them, it is the conceptual analyst. In order to demonstrate this point, he compares the approaches of the natural scientist and the philosopher in "ascertaining definitional features" of their objects of inquiry. The crucial distinction lies in the following. While the scientist's search for "the *types* of defining properties" might be based on intuitions, the actual defining properties (e.g., chemical composition) can in no way be the product of intuitions, but are normally the result of scientific investigations. Hence, "[t]he claim that water is $H_2O$ certainly has no intuitive ring to it."[129] This, in turn, implies that Raz is right when saying that natural scientists are privileged in formulating concepts, precisely because their findings "are not completely dependent upon our intuitive categorization judgments and may transcend our prototype representations for natural kinds in a variety of ways."[130] Most importantly, if

this knowledge by appealing to our intuitive categorization judgments." Ramsey, "Prototypes and Conceptual Analysis," 62.

125 *Ibid*, 66.

126 Spaak, "Schauer's Anti-Essentialism," 196.

127 He argues that "the method of philosophical analysis obviously does not depend on the assumption that people in general do think of and with concepts in terms of necessary and sufficient conditions for their proper application, but on the much weaker assumption that such thinking is *possible*." *Ibid*.

128 And Spaak acknowledges that he is ready to "accept the findings of the cognitive scientists for the purposes of [his] article." *Ibid*.

129 Ramsey, "Prototypes and Conceptual Analysis," 67. Note that this is completely in line with what Jackson has to say when explaining in what sense conceptual analysis is concerned with a priori. Discussing the example of water, he stresses that only the sentence that gives the A-extension of "water" at every world (where A stands for "actual"), "namely 'Water is the watery stuff of our acquaintance,' is a priori," while the sentence that gives the C-extension of "water" at every world (where C stands for "counterfactual"), "namely, 'Water is $H_2O$', is a posteriori." Jackson, *From Metaphysics to Ethics – A Defence of Conceptual Analysis*, 52.

130 Ramsey, "Prototypes and Conceptual Analysis," 67.

a scientific taxonomy goes beyond and corrects our intuitive categorization, say, that whales are fishes, we do not treat our intuitions as counterexamples – in the conceptual analyst's sense of the word – but we normally acknowledge that the science proved us wrong.[131]

In contrast, the philosopher engaged in conceptual analysis operates under a different set of assumptions. When searching for definitional features of its object of research, the philosopher needs to rely on our intuitive categorization judgments. This is what Jackson has in mind when, in proposing the "modest conceptual analysis," he says that "[t]he business of consulting intuitions about possible cases is ... [about] determining *how subjects classify* possibilities."[132] Moreover, if the resulting conceptual findings, given in terms of necessary and sufficient properties, admit of counterexamples, then it is normal to discharge the resulting theory, rather than pre-theoretical intuitions, as defective.[133] Insofar as the conceptual analysis must rely on intuitive categorization judgments as its initial empirical data, it is far more limited by our ordinary representation of concepts than the scientific investigation. The problem with the conceptual analysis is that it seems to be premised on psychological assumptions that are contrary to recent experimental findings in the field of cognitive psychology. Consequently, if the prototype representation is indeed the one that governs everyday categorization judgments, "then it will be such a representation that guides and constrains any search for definitions performed through conceptual analysis."[134]

But what if Spaak rightly assumes that the project of conceptual analysis is built on a weaker assumption that categorization in terms of necessary features is only *possible*, but not necessarily widespread in the everyday classification?[135] Possibility of an advanced categorization would, then, be reserved for those who are "able to articulate [a concept's] conditions of

131 This is, however, not an uncontroversial issue even in the natural sciences. *See, e.g.*, James A. Hampton, "The Role of Similarity in Natural Categorization," in Ulrike Hahn and Michael Ramscar (eds.), *Similarity and Categorization* (Oxford: Oxford University Press, 2001), 13–28.

132 Jackson, *From Metaphysics to Ethics – A Defence of Conceptual Analysis*, 33. (emphasis mine) Hence, he does not discharge the option of conducting "serious opinion polls on people's responses to various cases." *Ibid*, 36.

133 This stems from the fact that "philosophy lacks established procedures for guaranteeing that one has discovered an entity's identity ... There is always the lingering possibility that [philosophers] have pronounced a property to be part of a thing's nature merely because they were not clever or fortunate enough to construct the right counterexample." Scott J. Shapiro, *Legality* (Cambridge, Mass.: The Belknap Press of Harvard University Press, 2011), 18.

134 Ramsey, "Prototypes and Conceptual Analysis," 68.

135 Spaak, "Schauer's Anti-Essentialism," 196.

application" in terms of necessary and sufficient conditions – presumably legal philosophers.[136] Interestingly enough, a cursory look at the literature in conceptual jurisprudence seems to vindicate the finding that operating with "typicality judgments" is "a very robust cognitive phenomenon,"[137] insofar as legal philosophers are apparently not immune to employing them.[138]

Hence, when making remarks on the inquiry of the nature of human beings, which is applicable to all other inquiries of definitional features, Gardner notes that "there is not only the question of which things are included in and which things are excluded from the category at the limits, but also which of those included are members of the category par excellence, and should be used as examples to shed light on the rest."[139] This "par excellence" instance is actually "a paradigm or central case" in virtue of being able to "show how the other cases – including those supposed counter-examples – ought to be."[140] In his exposition of the nature of legal systems, Raz employs the same categorization tools. First, he exposes features of all the "institutionalized systems," arguing that legal systems are "typical examples" of such systems, insofar as they are, in virtue of the "defining features," also "the most important" category members.[141] In the next step, Raz relies on the even more straightforward vocabulary of "typicality judgments" and "graded membership":

> The general traits which mark a system as a legal one are several and each of them admits, in principle, of various degrees. In typical instances of legal systems all these traits are manifested to a very high degree. But it is possible to find systems in which all or some are present only to a lesser degree or in which one or two are absent altogether. It would be arbitrary and pointless to try and fix a precise borderline between normative systems which are legal systems and those which are not. When faced with borderline cases it is best to admit their problematic credentials, to enumerate their similarities and dissimilarities to the typical cases, and leave it at that.[142]

[136] Greenberg says that "[i]n trying to use the psychological research on concepts to support his claims about the nature of phenomena, Schauer makes the common mistake of conflating what a person must know in order to use a concept with what one must know to fully understand the concept or, differently, the nature of the phenomenon." Greenberg, "How to Explain Things with Force," 1946–1947, fn. 16.

[137] Ramsey, "Prototypes and Conceptual Analysis," 62.

[138] This is so despite the fact that, according to the aforementioned psychological assumptions of the conceptual analysis, "one would expect to find all instances of a concept intuitively judged as equally good examples." Ramsey, "Prototypes and Conceptual Analysis," 63.

[139] Gardner, *Law as a Leap of Faith*, 152.

[140] *Ibid.*

[141] Raz, *Practical Reason and Norms*, 149.

[142] *Ibid*, 150.

Bix also argues that "concepts do, and theories should, refer to 'central cases,'" by which one should understand "the large range of the average and the near-average, excluding only the rare instances of extremes of different kinds." When applied to the case of law, "the 'central cases' would arguably be the large range in the statistical middle of instances."[143]

The presented evidence works strongly in favor of the conclusion that if conceptual analysts "search for definitional properties by looking at intuitive categorization judgments," and theirs are also typicality judgments, the resulting theoretical findings "will never go beyond those properties that comprise the ordinary, prototype representation that governs these judgments."[144] This, finally, may explain why conceptual analysts are unable to achieve the objective that they themselves set as the criterion for the success of their theories – to provide a conceptual analysis of law in terms of necessary and sufficient features, which will clearly demarcate instances falling under this category from those that do not.[145]

There is a final line of defense of conceptual analysts. Greenberg says: "The existence of borderline cases of a phenomenon or term presents no obstacle to the existence of necessary and sufficient conditions. Rather, the conditions simply have to themselves be vague in a way that captures the vagueness of the phenomenon or term." He notes that some of the most natural language terms (e.g., human) are of such nature, and "so their conditions of application will be vague."[146] Let us test this claim by returning to Gardner's inquiry into the nature of human beings. He says:

> In explaining what a human being is, it would be profoundly misleading, for example, to present someone in a permanent vegetative state as a first illustration. For she lacks altogether the natural human capacity to respond to reasons . . . If she were not a human being, but literally a vegetable, her lack of rational capacities would not worry us. For it is not part of the nature of a vegetable to be rational.[147]

Following Greenberg's reasoning, one may say that Gardner's analysis leads to the conclusion that "the capacity to be rational" is a necessary feature of the concept of "human being." It, for instance, clearly distinguishes humans from vegetables. However, despite being necessary, it is also vague, insofar as it

[143] Bix, "Ideals, Practices, and Concepts in Legal Theory," 45.

[144] Ramsey, "Prototypes and Conceptual Analysis," 68.

[145] This has led Giudice to state that "disputes about the boundaries of the concept of law are simply irresolvable." Giudice, *Understanding the Nature of Law: A Case for Constructive Conceptual Explanation*, 8.

[146] Greenberg, "How to Explain Things with Force," 1946.

[147] Gardner, *Law as a Leap of Faith*, 149.

leaves room for different interpretations of what it means to be "rational." This, according to Greenberg, would eventually imply that our application of the concept "human" may be vague with respect to some instances. But, is a person in a permanent vegetative state one such instance that testifies to the vagueness of the application of the concept "human"? Hardly so. Irrespective of the fact that we are nowadays expanding our knowledge about the person in such condition,[148] one thing we know for sure – "she lacks altogether the natural human capacity to respond to reasons." Put differently, none of the meaningful interpretations of the vague language phrase "capacity to be rational" can lead to the conclusion that the person in a permanent vegetative state satisfies the given necessary feature for qualifying as a "human being." And yet, we all know that she is a "human being." Just as we all know that having the "capacity to be rational" is a feature of human beings, by which we differentiate humans from plants. It is, however, *one of typical features* of humans, which are all clustered around some case of central tendency. And the prototypical case of "human" is most certainly not the person in a permanent vegetative state.[149] Therefore, Gardner's observation that it would be "profoundly misleading" to take the example of such person as the "first," that is, typical "illustration" of a human being makes sense only under the prototype theory of concepts. Under the view of the conceptual analysis, all the instances satisfying necessary conditions are *equally good illustrations* of the category membership.

### c) *Back to the "Down-to-Earth" Analytical Approach*

After all rebuttal strategies for conceptual analysts are exhausted, there are two possible ways out for them.[150] One would be to try to challenge the prototype accounts of concept representation. A simple denial would obviously not do

148 Take, for example, some new approaches to the question of whether persons in such state are conscious. Nicholas Shea and Tim Bayne, "The Vegetative State and the Science of Consciousness" (2010) 61 *The British Journal for the Philosophy of Science* 3: 459–484.

149 There is no doubt that any experiment in ordinary categorization would confirm this.

150 Actually, there is a third way – to adopt what Jackson labels as the "immodest conceptual analysis," whose role is to determine "the fundamental nature of our world." Jackson, *From Metaphysics to Ethics – A Defence of Conceptual Analysis*, 44. According to Himma, the "immodest" version as applied to law would be an analysis of the content of our concept of law, which "would give us insight into the essential nature of law as it really is *independent of our linguistic practices and conceptual frameworks*." Himma, "Conceptual Jurisprudence," 73. (emphasis in the original) Despite sometimes leaving the impression that they are ready to move in this direction, none of the mainstream conceptual analysts has openly endorsed this approach.

the job,[151] and it would require philosophers to engage in serious empirical research. A more promising way would be "to revise their basic assumptions and expectations about definitions of abstract concepts."[152] This implies sacrificing either the goal of simplicity, emanated in a small conjunctive set of definitional properties, or the assumption that a successful analysis would be the one in which no counterexamples are possible. Ramsey is of the opinion that a more fruitful strategy "might be the one of preserving simplicity and recognizing that we can't capture all intuitive judgments."[153]

Thus, abandoning the metaphysically driven conceptual analysis does not leave us with nothing. It directs us within a proposed prototype theory of concepts toward an analytical work with "a more down-to-earth ambition," the one that both Summers and Chiassoni associate with Hart. Such an analysis is aimed at "'*explanatory elucidation' of the structure of legal phenomena.*"[154] It is still primarily "decompositional" in nature, insofar as it amounts to the process "of breaking something down into its components."[155] In our case, a highly abstract concept of law will have to be broken down in a cluster of less abstract – but nonetheless abstract – typical features. The raw, pre-analytical material with which we have to work is *a complex social practice*, "constituted by the collective behavior, shared beliefs, and social interactions of human beings."[156] However, in striving to complete the analytical work, the legal philosopher is in a much inferior position than the scientist, because "unlike the situation with natural kinds, it is far from clear what *types* of properties would count as more or less 'definitional' for the various abstract concepts,"[157] including law. This is an important reminder, because it further reveals something profound about the nature of both the phenomenon we are investigating and the theoretical work we are undertaking.

First, on the phenomenon. By clearly not being of a natural kind, a complex social practice denoted by the concept-word law can be safely put within a broad category of artifacts, that is, objects that have been "intentionally

151 This seems to be Spaak's strategy when, after acknowledging that he will proceed from what the prototype view in cognitive psychology has to say about our everyday categorization, then simply states that his "own view . . . is that people in general are wrong on this count." Spaak, "Schauer's Anti-Essentialism," 196.

152 Ramsey, "Prototypes and Conceptual Analysis," 68.

153 *Ibid*, 69. In any way, the ultimate decision "will depend a good deal on the sort of work we want our analyses to do for us." *Ibid*, 68.

154 Chiassoni, "Supporting *The Force of Law*," 64. (emphasis in the original)

155 Beaney, "Analysis," at https://plato.stanford.edu/archives/sum2016/entries/analysis/

156 Marmor, "Farewell to Conceptual Analysis (in Jurisprudence)," 217. *Cf*. Finnis, *Natural Law and Natural Rights*, 3.

157 Ramsey, "Prototypes and Conceptual Analysis," 67.

made or produced for a certain purpose."[158] Does admitting that they are dealing with some sort of artifacts deprive legal philosophers of researching into "the nature of" the phenomenon they are studying? And if not, what would be "the nature of" the studied phenomenon if not its necessary and sufficient features to which metaphysically driven conceptual analysts refer? To my mind, "the nature-of-thing" talk does not commit one to some form of metaphysical essentialism, especially when dealing with some form of artifacts. Having in mind the "decompositional" component of the analytical work, this talk is primarily about "constitution," and only secondarily about "identity" of the investigated thing. Although closely related, these are not the same concepts.[159] According to Baker, "[e]ach existing thing is of a primary kind. An entity's primary kind is given by the answer to the Aristotelian question: what is x most fundamentally?"[160] Under this view, "that what something is most fundamentally is often determined by what it can do – its abilities and capacities – rather than by what it is made of." Put differently, "the nature of an artifact lies in its proper function – what it was designed to do, the purpose for which it was produced."[161]

Now, a complex social practice is by no means a simple artifact as is a clock or a pair of scissors. Such a practice, which competent speakers denote by the concept-word law, is an "abstract artifact."[162] Thus, finding a "proper function" of such a practice put before legal philosophers a very demanding, if not

158 Risto Hilpinen, "Artifact," in Zalta (ed.), *The Stanford Encyclopedia of Philosophy* (Winter 2011 ed.), at https://plato.stanford.edu/archives/win2011/entries/artifact/

159 According to Baker, "constitution is a relation that is in some ways similar to identity, but is not actually identity." Lynne Rudder Baker, "The Ontology of Artifacts" (2004) 7 *Philosophical Explorations* 2: 99. The familiar properties of identity are reflexivity (a = a); symmetry (if a = b, then b = a); and transitivity (if a = b and b = c, then a = c). In order to demonstrate the point, Baker uses the example of a brick house. She says that it is "pretheoretically obvious that although the aggregate of bricks constitutes the house, the house does not constitute the aggregate of bricks. It also seems pretheoretically obvious that the house does not constitute itself. So, constitution is neither reflexive nor symmetric. Hence, constitution is not identity." *Ibid*, 100–101.

160 *Ibid*, 100.

161 *Ibid*, 102.

162 Ehrenberg, *The Functions of Law*, 12. This is true of law understood in its most abstract sense as a "genre," that is, as "a type of human activity." At the lower levels of abstraction, we may be investigating what Ehrenberg labels as "prototypes" (e.g., particular legal systems) and "tokens" (e.g., particular legal provisions). *Ibid*, 18. For instance, Burazin is interested in providing an artifact theory of law, where "law" is taken in the sense of the less abstract object, legal system. Luka Burazin, "Can There Be an Artifact Theory of Law?" (2016) 29 *Ratio Juris* 3: 385–401. Ehrenberg is close to this position, when noting that "it is not generally possible to conceive of a law without a legal system of which it is a part. If that conceptual limitation is correct, then the first law could only have come about within the context of the first legal system." Ehrenberg, *The Functions of Law*, 47.

impossible task. Furthermore, since one of the aspects of functions "is that they are value-laden, in that they refer to a benefit that the explanandum brings about through the performance of its function,"[163] it is no wonder that descriptivist theories of law have largely abstained from researching the nature of law in terms of its purported function(s) in order to distance themselves from the natural law theory. However, if part of the jurisprudential agenda consists, as I believe it does, in searching for "the nature of law,"[164] and if the nature of the investigated object, i.e., artifact, appears to be tied to its function, then this seems to clear the path for the elucidation of law in terms of its function(s).

It is generally expected that if we are to determine "the proper function" of an artifact – in this case, law – that it would be the one intentionally assigned to it by its creator. At this point, "the question becomes whether the intention is that of the creator of the genre or the prototype, or of each token," that is, "whether we do so with the original exemplar or genre in mind or with each later token."[165] When jurisprudential account is focused on law as a special type of human activity, the offered functional explanations of law can hardly ever be "complete because they do not explain how law arose in society."[166] But this in no way undermines the theoretical approach centered around law's functionality, because just as no one can grasp the concept of "hospital" without understanding "what hospitals are *for*,"[167] so no one can grasp the concept of law without raising the same theoretical question.

All this eventually takes us to the question of the nature of the theoretical work we are undertaking. It was already emphasized that "law" cannot be entirely a theoretical, that is, stipulated concept, because, unlike natural scientists, legal philosophers are not in the privileged position to forge this concept, and thereby fully revise the complex social reality they are studying. Hence, in order to more fully grasp the concept of law, legal philosophers have to rely on its *conventional* ingredient, that is, on how people in their linguistic practice ordinarily identify law and differentiate it from similar social phenomena.[168] To be sure, conceptual analysts have the point when arguing that in undertaking such an empirical step legal philosophers "must already

[163] *Ibid*, 25.

[164] Hence, the title of this book.

[165] Ehrenberg, *The Functions of Law*, 51.

[166] "The details of the first law are likely . . . shrouded in the mists of prehistory." *Ibid*, 47.

[167] Jeremy Waldron, "Does Law Promise Justice?" (2001) 17 *Georgia State University Law Review* 3: 760.

[168] Chiassoni says that "[c]onventional concepts depend on, and mirror, linguistic practice." Chiassoni, "Supporting *The Force of Law*," 65. Tamanaha speaks of the "conventionalist criterion for the identification of law," which amounts to the step of acknowledging "whatever

know that there is *a common something*" to which the word law and its cognates refer in different social contexts.[169] It seems, thus, that this intricate task of "map[ping] word to idea,"[170] that is, of relating the empirical step with some pre-theoretical, working samples of law, is an inherent feature of the jurisprudential inquiry, which "is partly responsive to our normal notions, and partly a stipulative regimentation of these notions."[171] This, furthermore, implies that an investigation at this highest level of abstractness necessarily yields the following result: the proposed concept of law will *always be a partly theoretical concept*, "one that draws its justification from its adequacy to some previously stipulated purpose."[172] Such theoretical account, by default, cannot claim to be *the correct* conceptualization of law,[173] because it will always carry the stamp of legal philosopher's "stipulative regimentation" (Raz)[174] of raw empirical data.[175] And yet, this implies neither that the offered account is in some way arbitrary,[176] nor that the list of typical features that philosophers identify as constitutive of law is "randomly selected." The depicted features "serve some theoretical purposes, highlighting an aspect of law that calls for theoretical explanation and has some significance for the kind of theory offered."[177]

people identify and treat through their social practices as 'law.'" He stresses that "[t]his formulation is not itself a concept of law." Tamanaha, *A Realistic Theory of Law*, 73.

169 Gardner, *Law as a Leap of Faith*, 298. (emphasis mine)

170 *Ibid.*

171 Raz, "Can There Be a Theory of Law?," 326.

172 Chiassoni, "Supporting The Force of Law," 65.

173 *See, supra* 6–7.

174 In that respect, all the attempts of metaphysically driven conceptual analysists, aimed at correctly depicting the essence of law in terms of necessary and sufficient features for something to count as an instance of law, testify to the fact that "[n]ecessity, essentiality, is, so to speak, in the eye of the beholder." (Chiassoni, "Supporting The Force of Law," 65) Giudice in fact defends one such modified understanding of "pragmatic necessity," "in which theses about law are held to be true if they successfully illuminate some aspect of the social reality of law . . . The pragmatic consideration . . . of making purported necessity claims about law is to emphasize . . . that any supposed counter-example or recalcitrant experience is not really a counter-example or recalcitrant experience at all, but instead an attempt to change the subject or concept." Giudice, *Understanding the Nature of Law*, 108.

175 In Capps's words, "our view of the raw data alters our view of the role of the legal scientist." Capps, *Human Dignity and the Foundations of International Law*, 47.

176 In proposing the method of "constructive conceptual explanation," Giudice emphasizes that "such constructed concepts are not arbitrary, but can be proposed on the basis of argument." Most importantly, "a theorist can argue that certain phenomena ought to be grouped together for the purposes of investigation without settling all the interesting questions about their nature." *Ibid*, Giudice, *Understanding the Nature of Law*, 103.

177 Marmor, "Farewell to Conceptual Analysis (in Jurisprudence)," 225.

However, there is a lingering dilemma. If an explanatory elucidation of the concept of law, understood as a representation of a group of features clustered around some prototype case, is partly of the stipulative nature, does this necessarily turn it into a *subjective* and/or *evaluative* project? For Finnis, it is clear that the differences in various descriptive jurisprudential accounts "derive from differences of opinion, amongst the descriptive theorists, about what is *important* and *significant* in the field of data and experience with which they are all equally and thoroughly familiar."[178] Hence, the crucial methodological question is "[f]rom what viewpoint, and relative to what concerns, are *importance* and *significance* to be assessed?"[179] Finnis' response is that the most important "are the things which, in the judgment of the theorist, make it important from a *practical* viewpoint to have law – the things which it is, therefore, important in practice to 'see to' when ordering human affairs."[180] In relying on Aristotle's concept of "focal analysis,"[181] Finnis labels "the states of affairs referred to by a theoretical concept in its focal meaning the *central case(s)*."[182] Unlike in the prototype approach advanced here, the central case of law would be the one advocated by the person who possesses practical reasonableness. Put differently, "it is central not because it is statistically frequent and 'fits the facts,' but rather because it 'fits reason,' is truly justified."[183]

Does taking this perspective make a jurisprudential account evaluative? According to Finnis, most certainly it does, because it "undertakes a critique of practical viewpoints, in order to distinguish the practically unreasonable from the practically reasonable."[184] Does it make it subjective? No, if you ask Finnis and his followers, because this perspective "claims to be able to identify

178 Finnis, *Natural Law and Natural Rights*, 9.

179 *Ibid.*

180 *Ibid*, 16.

181 Rodriguez-Blanco criticizes Finnis for the mistaken application of Aristotle's notion of central case on the concept of law. In doing so, she proposes a Wittgensteinian understanding of law as "core resemblance," which is in some aspects similar to the one advanced here. Veronica Rodriguez-Blanco, "Is Finnis Wrong? Understanding Normative Jurisprudence" (2007) 13 *Legal Theory* 3–4: 257–283. Finnis addresses this criticism in John Finnis, "Grounds of Law and Legal Theory: A Response" (2007) 13 *Legal Theory* 3–4: 315–344, section I.

182 Finnis says that he prefers "central" to "typical" case, because the latter word "may suggest that the relevant criterion is statistical frequency (whether in human history, or today)." Finnis, *Natural Law and Natural Rights*, 10.

183 Grégoire Webber, "Asking Why in the Study of Human Affairs" (2015) 60 *The American Journal of Jurisprudence* 1: 72.

184 Finnis, *Natural Law and Natural Rights*, 18. Capps follows Finnis's "practically reasonable perspective" in the conceptualization of international law. Capps, *Human Dignity and the Foundations of International Law*, 48.

conditions and principles of practical right-mindedness, of good and proper order among persons, and in individual conduct."[185] If this step implies that a general theory of law has to renounce its descriptive-explanatory objective, so be it, because, then, this is merely "a function of the study of human affairs."[186]

Finnis, thus, sends us the following meta-philosophical dictum: if a jurisprudential account, even the one with the initial analytical ambition, requires from the legal philosopher the aforementioned kind of "decision" as to what in the raw data is worthy of "stipulative regimentation," then ours is necessarily a project of evaluation.[187] This, on the other hand, does not make it subjective, let alone arbitrary, because taking the perspective of practical reasonableness enables the legal philosopher to "identify the truly good reasons for action that are available to any self-directing and self-determining human person."[188] In that respect, making such a step does not violate the requirement of theoretical objectivity.[189]

While legal philosophers may never reach consensus on whether some form of "direct," that is, substantive evaluation is inescapable in jurisprudential work,[190] just as philosophers may never end the dispute as to whether moral objectivism (realism) is a tenable meta-ethical standpoint, the claim that there exist *strong* and *weak* accounts of normative jurisprudence is the subject of far less controversy. Unlike Dworkin, who fosters the former, by claiming that, ultimately, the legal philosopher is advancing her own substantive moral point of view,[191] Finnis purports to offer the latter by praising the soundness of the descriptive-explanatory approach. However, he does not seem to succeed in reconciling this methodological inclination with the practical reasonableness view, without eventually "falling prey to the *strong* version of normative

185 Finnis, *Natural Law and Natural Rights*, 10.

186 Webber, "Asking Why in the Study of Human Affairs," 70.

187 This is so, because "without the evaluations one cannot determine what descriptions are really illuminating and significant." Finnis, *Natural Law and Natural Rights*, 19.

188 Webber, "Asking Why in the Study of Human Affairs," 66.

189 As aptly formulated by Webber, "[t]hose reasons will be mine but I will think them candidates for being yours because – so far as I can judge – they are good reasons for me, you, and anyone else." *Ibid.*

190 According to conceptual analysts, the descriptive-explanatory role of a jurisprudential account may be preserved if the legal philosopher operates only with "indirectly evaluative propositions." One such proposition "of the form 'X is an important feature of the law,' is thus a proposition which attributes some evaluative property to that feature of the law, but which does not entail a directly evaluative proposition that the feature of the law in question is good (or bad)." Dickson, *Evaluation and Legal Theory*, 53. For a contrary view, *see* Finnis, *Natural Law and Natural Rights*, 3.

191 *See, e.g.*, Ronald Dworkin, "Hart's Postscript and the Character of Legal Philosophy" (2004) 24 *Oxford Journal of Legal Studies* 1: 1–37.

jurisprudence,"[192] the one that generates loaded normative debates that are more adequately placed within the ambit of moral and political philosophy.[193] If the overall objective of a jurisprudential account is explanatory elucidation of law – and mine is of such a nature – then, at minimum, such sort of dispute is not to be expected as the direct follow-up of the provided theoretical view.

A final caveat. Apart from relying on constraints dictated by the categorization experiments of cognitive psychology,[194] and from acknowledging that our pre-analytical samples of law have to match the diversity of social contexts in which the concept-word is used to denote a complex human activity,[195] the legal philosopher has also to account for the meta-philosophical aspect of law's functionality. That is, he has to specify what, methodologically speaking, one such approach implies. Ehrenberg's treatise demonstrates that everything hinges upon the pre-stipulated purpose of a jurisprudential inquiry. If it is primarily directed toward a Hartian-style explanatory elucidation of law, then "the least ambitious" approach of "see[ing] the function as explanatorily necessary," without "making any extra claims that performance of those functions are either necessary or sufficient for membership in the class of law"[196] may indeed be the right way to proceed. A potential criticism of this

192 Rodriguez-Blanco, "Is Finnis Wrong? Understanding Normative Jurisprudence," 259. Rodriguez-Blanco tries to offer a rescue strategy for Finnis's theory as a weak normative account.

193 This is merely to acknowledge that certain evaluative claims, even if clothed in the language of the disputed moral objectivism, are far more morally appealing and hardly disputable – for instance, that "knowledge" is an "intrinsic good" (Finnis, *Natural Law and Natural Rights*, 62), while some others – for instance, that "marriage" is also an "intrinsic good" (John Finnis, "Marriage: A Basic and Exigent Good" (2008) 91 *Monist* 3–4: 388–406), lead us directly to the arena of politico-philosophical battles, where someone might as well claim that marriage "does not have a *sui generis* moral status or a transformative moral power." Elizabeth Brake, *Minimizing Marriage – Marriage, Morality, and the Law* (Oxford: Oxford University Press, 2012), 1.

194 "If psychologists' findings are true, it is hard to see how philosophical-style conceptual analysis can be vindicated, and this, ironically, is *especially true of conceptual analysis in its modest guise*." Dan Priel, "Jurisprudence and Psychology," in Maksymilian Del Mar (ed.), *New Waves in Philosophy of Law* (Basingstoke: Palgrave Macmillan, 2011), 83.

195 Twining was among the first ones to raise this criticism. He says that nearly all of the otherwise "vast heritage of Western legal theorizing about law . . . concentrates on the municipal law of sovereign states, mainly those in advanced industrial societies." Hence, this theorizing "is vulnerable to charges of parochialism and ethnocentrism." William Twining, *General Jurisprudence: Understanding Law from a Global Perspective* (Cambridge: Cambridge University Press, 2009), 10. Raz seems to accept this criticism, when noting that "[e]ven if state-law is in some ways the pre-eminent form of law we may find in the course of the inquiry, that by examining it alongside *other forms of law*, our understanding of state-law as well as of law in general changes." Raz, "Why the State?," 1. (emphasis mine)

196 Ehrenberg, *The Functions of Law*, 46.

stance as "too weak to generate a theory of law" might be met with the counterargument that just as pointing to the function of healing would be central for the explanation of hospital, even the one that does not perform its function, so too would the pointing to the law's function serve the important explanatory role.[197] It is crucial, however, to add that a fuller explanation of law's functionality cannot be offered without also saying something about the value(s) supposed to be delivered by law's proper functioning. Just as grasping the concept of hospital requires one to know not only that its function is to heal, but also to do so with the promise of recovering/enhancing the health of its patients, so equally for someone to grasp the concept of law, it would be necessary to know something about the value(s) that is (are) promised by law's proper functioning.

[197] *Ibid.*

# 3

# Typical Features of (International) Law

The preceding Chapter demonstrates that the domain of traditional methodological disputes in jurisprudence needs to be broadened from inquiries concerning "the *way in which* legal philosophy is done" to inquiries "into *what legal philosophy is*: its aims, criteria of success, evidence base, constraints and prospects for progress, and indeed how we should determine and understand its very domain and subject matter."[1] The last mentioned task is in direct relation with the self-imposed criteria of success of a jurisprudential theory. As already indicated, legal philosophers have for quite some time been of the opinion that successfulness of their theories had to be measured against their capacity to "illuminate the nature of municipal systems."[2] A pervasive skepticism of legal philosophers toward "legality" of international law was largely a consequence of this problematic meta-philosophical orientation of treating municipal law as the only proper subject of study.

However, "the state-centric conceptual theories of most analytical legal theorists can be faulted for being narrow or parochial, [because] there is nothing in the nature of conceptual explanation that prevents it from being wider and more general in its scope."[3] Writing in the wake of World War II about the concept of international law, Verdross noted that "every scholar is free to delimit and designate his discipline, as he thinks fit." However, he added that "a delimitation of the object advances knowledge only if it does not

[1] Having this in mind, Dickson thinks that instead of "methodology," "the philosophy of legal philosophy" is a more appropriate name for this meta-theoretical discipline. Julie Dickson, "Ours is a Broad Church: Indirectly Evaluative Legal Philosophy as a Facet of Jurisprudential Inquiry" (2015) 6 *Jurisprudence: An International Journal of Legal and Political Thought* 2: 208.

[2] Raz, "The Identity of Legal Systems," 105.

[3] "General theories of law still need to be general, but this means looking at law as it figures at diverse levels and in diverse places around the world, instead of presuming what law must everywhere be like by comparison to a standard example (most often state law)." Giudice, *Understanding the Nature of Law*, 66.

break connection given to us by experience."[4] Put differently, the scholar's "task [is] to comprehend the legal material in its *totality*."[5] There is a growing consensus among contemporary jurisprudents that leaving aside all the potentially theoretically relevant raw material at the level beyond the state might contribute to the legal theory's failure to account for the totality of a nowadays complex legal experience. Thus, Besson and Tasioulas conclude that "if international law does not fit the criteria of the concept of law used at the domestic level, it may not (only) be a problem for the legality of international law, but (also) for those criteria themselves and hence for a given legal theory."[6] This is, according to Tamanaha, an obvious omission of Hart's theory. Had he "included international law alongside state law within his pre-theoretical data set of what counts as law, he would have modified his theory of secondary rules to accommodate its features, and he would have loosened the systematicity he deemed necessary to law."[7]

In Hart's defense, a raw pre-analytical material at the level beyond the state was presumably far less conclusive then than it is today.[8] Yet, it was obviously persuasive enough for him to treat international law at least as a "borderline case" of law.[9] This shows that while at times referring to "necessary and sufficient" membership conditions,[10] at the most abstract level of conceptual categorization of different normative orders, Hart did employ something akin to the prototype theory of concepts. Take the following passage from the opening chapter:

> [I]t is not a peculiarity of complex terms like "law" and "legal system" that we are forced to recognize both clear standard cases and challengeable borderline cases. It is now a familiar fact (though once too little stressed) that this

4 Alfred von Verdross, "On the Concept of International Law" (1949) 43 *The American Journal of International Law* 3: 436.

5 *Ibid*, 438.

6 Besson and Tasioulas, "Introduction," in Besson and Tasioulas (eds.), *The Philosophy of International Law*, 8.

7 Tamanaha, *A Realistic Theory of Law*, 72.

8 For instance, the Vienna Convention on the Law of Treaties (VCLT) (1155 United Nations, *Treaty Series*, 331), which may be qualified as an international secondary rule of change, was adopted only in 1969. Still, "it is widely accepted that the Convention codified existing customary norms on the subject, many of which had endured for centuries." Waldron, "International Law: 'A Relatively Small and Unimportant' Part of Jurisprudence?," 217.

9 Hart, *The Concept of Law*, 16.

10 Most blatantly, Hart speaks of "two minimum conditions necessary and sufficient for the existence of a legal system." *Ibid*, 116. In that respect, Chiassoni obviously exaggerates when claiming that "*nowhere* . . . Hart presents legal theory as having to do with casting light upon *the necessary*" conditions for something to be included under the concept of law. Chiassoni, "Supporting *The Force of Law*," 64. (emphasis in the original)

> distinction must be made in the case of almost every general term which we use in classifying features of human life and of the world in which we live. Sometimes the difference between the clear, standard case or paradigm for the use of an expression and the questionable cases is only a matter of degree.[11]

The same form of categorization, which can be justified only within the graded structure view, can be found in the work of other legal philosophers of the analytical tradition.[12] Hence, after showing that the analysis in terms of the prototype theory of concepts is a more tenable approach in a jurisprudential inquiry about the nature of law, it is now to be seen what might be depicted as typical features of the central case of law and what is the status of international rules of conduct in this new conceptual scheme.

## 1 THE CENTRAL CASE OF LAW (AS A GENRE)

If a jurisprudential inquiry is taken at the most abstract level – that of law as a "genre" – then its analytical work will necessarily yield equally abstract findings. Not only will the nature of a complex social practice be represented as a cluster of abstract typical features, which are in need of further analysis, but the elucidation of law's functionality will also have to be taken at a highly abstract level of generalization. Let us start, somewhat unconventionally for works interested primarily in explanatory elucidation, with the question about what is law made for in the human world. This will, presumably, enable us to depict the constitutive features of the prototypical, i.e., central, case of law.

As already mentioned, Ehrenberg's recent treatise is one of the most comprehensive studies of law's functionality. After a thorough comparative overview of other scholars' views on this topic, he comes to the conclusion that theoretical problems have arisen "not so much with the function articulated to explain law, but rather with the particular way in which that explanation is fleshed out or the way the theorist understands the relation of law to its function."[13] With respect to the actual functions that are ascribed to law,

[11] Hart, *The Concept of Law*, 4.

[12] Marmor's recently endorsed method of "reduction" has led him to conclude: "Since essential features are neither a priori nor necessary, the possibility of indeterminacy about some cases is not philosophically problematic. I see no reason to deny that what is essential to a social practice is vague, allowing for some borderline cases." Marmor, "Farewell to Conceptual Analysis (in Jurisprudence)," 225. In his discussion of legal systems, Raz has come to the conclusion that "[i]nternational law is a borderline case," insofar as "there are doubts whether it can be regarded as an institutionalized system." Raz, *Practical Reason and Norms*, fn. at 150.

[13] Ehrenberg, *The Functions of Law*, 182.

jurisprudents of different breeds are not so far apart, and most of them argue that law's function is that of "*coordination and dispute settlement.*"[14] Nevertheless, since we are theorizing a rather abstract artifact, there is no reason to "reduce the law's functions to a unitary overarching descriptor,"[15] just as there is the possibility of generalizing by way of enlisting some more specific functions that are normally assigned to law.[16] Finally, it is important to underline that law is supposed to perform its function through a particular mechanism of specifying rights and obligations (deontic powers) of its subjects.[17] In other words, law coordinates social relations and settles disputes through being *normative*, that is, through providing new reasons for action to its subjects. While there is almost a universal assent among jurisprudents that "a central task of legal philosophy is to explain the normative force of propositions of law,"[18] much of the tradition is focused on the nature of legal obligation and tends to neglect the fact that one of the specificities of law might exactly lie in the fact that it confers both public and private powers (rights) to its subjects.[19]

Ehrenberg's analysis of law's functionality falls short of specifying what *value* is to be delivered by the law's successful performance of coordination and dispute settlement. If Ehrenberg were ready to fully employ the previously mentioned analogy with hospital, which he borrows from Waldron, he would have come to conclude, alongside this author, that the key value law is supposed to bring about through regulating social relations is *justice*. Justice is certainly not the only value that could be brought about through legal coordination and dispute settlement – take, for instance, wealth maximization, certainty, or peace. At this preliminary point,[20] it is important to stress that, whatever the value one

[14] *Ibid.* (emphasis mine)

[15] *Ibid*, 186.

[16] Ehrenberg, thus, proceeds by accepting Raz's list of specified functions of law, out of which the "direct" ones – "secured by the law being obeyed and applied" – are more pertinent: "Preventing Undesirable Behaviour and Securing Desirable Behaviour"; "Providing Facilities for Private Arrangements between Individuals"; "The Provision of Services and the Redistribution of Goods"; and "Settling Unregulated Disputes." Raz, "On the Functions of Law," in *The Authority of Law*, 167ff. Ehrenberg rightly notes that the enlisted functions "are themselves instrumental goals serving whatever wider end may be in view of those creating and implementing the law." Yet, this fact alone "does not undermine the explanatory importance of those functions." Ehrenberg, *The Functions of Law*, 188.

[17] *Ibid*, 189.

[18] Hart says that, despite differences in their legal theories, he shares this conviction with Kelsen. Herbert L. A. Hart, "Introduction," in *Essays in Jurisprudence and Philosophy* (Oxford: Clarendon Press, 1983), 18.

[19] Normativity of (international) law is the subject of Chapter 4.

[20] I will return to this problem in Chapter 6.

has in mind, "it is less credible to say that law as such vouches for the goal that is being pursued, more credible that it promises coordination in pursuit of such goal."[21] Put differently, while "law promises a concern for justice, an interest in justice . . . it does not necessarily promise to get justice right."[22] It can simply fail in performing its function properly. This is in the nature of all artifacts, even complex and abstract ones.[23] As pointed out by Baker, "[t]here is no . . . function without the possibility of malfunction."[24]

However, the very possibility of assessing the proper performance of law's coordinating and dispute-settling function in terms of justice reveals another important connection between law and justice. As pointed out by Green, "it necessarily makes sense to ask whether law is just." That is, law is a "*justice-apt*" abstract artifact, insofar as it "is the kind of thing that is *apt* for inspection and appraisal in light of justice."[25] Our language and everyday practice are pervaded with the powerful proofs of law's justice-aptness thus conceived. Even the most elaborate denials of the special connections between law and justice, which expectedly come from voices within legal scholarship,[26] make sense only under the assumption that the perceived connection between the two is so deeply entrenched in all human societies.[27] Think, for instance, of the statement, which is oft invoked by legal positivists but is not uncommon among laypersons as well, that "even unjust law is still law."[28] One can never come across the opposite statement, that "even just law is still law," although the purpose of both

21 Waldron, "Does Law Promise Justice?," 786.

22 *Ibid*, 761.

23 Note that this finding does not necessarily solve the old debate between positivists and natural law theorists as to whether source-based instances of a legal system, be they particular rules or entire legal instruments (e.g., statutes), which gravely fail in providing justice, are for that reason stripped of their "legality." This is an old problem of demarcation that "rarely arise[s] in the ordinary cases, but in the extraordinary ones, where the demands of what seems paradigmatically to be law pull in one direction and the demands of what seem paradigmatically to be moral considerations pull in the other." Brian Leiter, "The Demarcation Problem in Jurisprudence: A New Case for Skepticism" (2011) 31 *Oxford Journal of Legal Studies* 4: 676.

24 Lynne Rudder Baker, "The Metaphysics of Malfunction" (2009) 13 *Techne* 2: 82.

25 This thesis "does not entail that every individual *law* is justice-apt." Green, "Positivism and the Inseparability of Law and Morals," 1050.

26 Waldron quotes O. W. Holmes's words: "I hate justice, which means that I know if a man begins to talk about that, for one reason or another he is shirking thinking in legal terms." Waldron, "Does Law Promise Justice?," 771. One of the most outright rejections of justice from the legal realm is offered in Hans Kelsen, *Was ist Gerechtigkeit?* (Stuttgart: Reclam, 2000).

27 *Cf.* Laura Nader and Andrée Sursock, "Anthropology and Justice," in Ronald L. Cohen (ed.), *Justice – Views from the Social Sciences* (London: Plenum Press, 1986), 205–233.

28 For a positivist stance, *see, e.g.*, Julie Dickson, "Is Bad Law Still Law? Is Bad Law Really Law?," in Maksymilian Del Mar and Zenon Bankowski (eds.), *Law as Institutional Normative Order* (Farnham: Ashgate, 2009), 181.

sentences is presumably the same – to deny that "unjustness" or "justness" of certain norms affect their "legality." The reason why only sentences of the first sort are in usage has exactly to do with the ordinary perception of law's promise of a concern for justice. This can be explained by the fact that "part of the artifactual property itself is that it be useful in producing the belief that the object has a specific sort of usability."[29] In being part of the human world, law generates belief among its subjects that in successfully performing its general function of coordination and dispute settlement it can bring about the value of justice.

Ehrenberg's hesitation to more openly tackle the value-ladenness of law's functionality might stem from his inclination to provide a "neutral" theory of law.[30] However, this seems to be a misplaced worry. On the one hand, the full neutrality can almost never be secured due to the aforementioned fact that the concept of law is always a partly stipulated, that is, theoretical concept. On the other hand, a more robust discussion of law's function-related value(s) need not jeopardize the overall analytical and explanatory ambition of the theory. Hart's analysis of justice's "peculiarly intimate connection with law"[31] aptly demonstrates this point.[32]

Can we infer from all this a stronger claim, which Baker holds true for simple artifacts, that the stipulated law's function of coordination is "a primary-kind property" without which law would no longer exist?[33] Well, everything hinges upon the further analysis of the law's abstract feature of *normativity*. As pointed out by Ehrenberg, "one reason to see the law in terms of its function is so that we can begin an explanation of its normativity."[34] As will be demonstrated in Chapter 4, law's normativity is somewhat shrouded in mystery. But the point

29 Ehrenberg, *The Functions of Law*, 30.

30 Kenneth M. Ehrenberg, "Defending the Possibility of a Neutral Functional Theory of Law" (2009) 29 *Oxford Journal of Legal Studies* 1: 91–113.

31 Hart, *The Concept of Law*, 157.

32 To note this by no means implies that Hart's treatment of justice is not the subject of theoretical controversy. *See, e.g.*, Robert S. Summers, "H. L. A. Hart on Justice" (1962) 59 *Journal of Philosophy*: 497–500. *Cf.* Leslie Green, "The Germ of Justice" (2010) *Oxford Legal Research Paper*, Paper No. 60/2010, at http://ssrn.com/abstract=1703008

33 According to Baker, "a primary-kind property is this: things of a given primary kind cannot survive loss of their primary-kind properties." Baker, "The Ontology of Artifacts," 100. Himma seems to indicate this when saying that if grasping the concept of law requires understanding that "legal systems are capable of guiding behaviour (though they may fail to do so)," then it may be the case that "being capable of performing this function (or something very like it) is one of the existence conditions for law." Kenneth Einar Himma, "Do Philosophy and Sociology Mix? A Non-Essentialist Socio-Legal Positivist Analysis of the Concept of Law" (2004) 24 *Oxford Journal of Legal Studies* 4:732.

34 Ehrenberg, *The Functions of Law*, 3.

is that whatever one endorses as the understanding of law's normativity through which it coordinates social relations, it is perfectly conceivable that this feature might profoundly change in some distant future and that such a modification would still not affect the existence of law. Imagine, for instance, that the majority of legal norms in the future start to coordinate social relations by taking the form of "comply or explain" provisions, which are currently predominant in the area of corporate law and governance, and according to which subjects should comply with the rules or explain why they do not.[35] Such a change might also put some other values at the forefront as more central to law's functionality. In any way, it is hard to see why such profound changes would necessarily result in law's ceasing to exist. This finding is completely in line with a prototype theory, according to which typical features are sensitive to context,[36] as well as with the previously mentioned remark of Ramsey that less ambitious analytical projects have to account for the possibility of some tangible counterexamples.

More importantly, elucidating law in terms of its function "is not to say that anything performing or aiming at the function is law."[37] On the one hand, there are other normative orders, some of which are also concerned with coordinating social relations (e.g., rules of etiquette, customary rules). On the other hand, there are other important features that are typical of law and constitute its nature. One of them is certainly *institutionality*. Law is "a genre of institutionalized abstract artifacts."[38] Now, there are numerous approaches to defining institutions,[39] but according to one fairly broad sociological account, an institution can be defined "as an interlocking double-structure of persons-as-role-holders or office-bearers and the like, and of social practices involving both expressive and practical aims and outcomes."[40] In that respect, many normative

35 *See, e.g.*, Andrew Keay, "Comply or Explain in Corporate Governance Codes: In Need of Greater Regulatory Oversight?" (2014) 34 *Legal Studies* 2: 279–304.

36 In contrast, one of the main alleged virtues of the conceptual analysis "had been that the hypothesized criterial attributes were just what didn't change with context." Rosch, "Reclaiming Concepts," 67.

37 Ehrenberg, *The Functions of Law*, 46.

38 Ehrenberg, *The Functions of Law*, 12.

39 See in more detail in, Seumas Miller, "Social Institutions," in Edward N. Zalta (ed.), *The Stanford Encyclopedia of Philosophy* (Winter 2014 ed.), at https://plato.stanford.edu/archives/win2014/entries/social-institutions/.

40 Rom Harré, *Social Being* (Oxford: Blackwell, 1979), 98. This definition is broad enough to also cover typical institutions of simple societies. It is just important to bear in mind that "practical aims and outcomes" of institutional practices should not be confused with the modern-day ideal of "functional efficiency." Anthropologists have demonstrated that what is "practical" about some institutions of simple societies is that they are "part of a cultural system of meaning," which members use in their daily lives to orient themselves. Many of those institutions, in contrast, cannot be said to be "functionally efficient" in the modern sense of

orders can be said to "contain either norm-creating or norm-applying institutions or both."[41] There is, however, the conceptual primacy of the latter. Namely, an important corollary of the existence of a normative order is that it requires "judgment," insofar as "[b]eing subject to a norm is being liable to judgment by oneself and by others in case one's conduct does not match up to what is required."[42] While this judgment may be personal and autonomous, as, for instance, in the case of one's self-appraisal of obedience of moral norms, it may also be organized. "Institutionalization of judgment is a fundamental feature of the organization of normative orders."[43]

At this point, one may be inclined to generalize further and to argue that the institutionalization of judgment often goes hand in hand with the institutionalization of the process of norm-creation. That is, that the former is typically present whenever there are also institutions that are designated with the role of altering the normative statuses of those subjected to it.[44] However, this need not be so, as the case of law aptly demonstrates. The bulk of research in legal anthropology testifies to the fact that while having some form of the institutionalization of judgment in cases of putative breaches of rules that are deemed legal,[45] a number of simple societies did not know of the institutionalization of norm-creation. Even the rules that were considered legal were created by the society as a whole.[46] Similarly, as legal history teaches us, law in the premodern, medieval times was largely created by the diffuse society, in the form of customary rules.[47]

the word. Christopher Robert Hallpike, *On Primitive Society: And Other Forbidden Topics* (Bloomington: Author House, 2011), 144.

41 Raz, *Practical Reason and Norms*, 123.

42 Neil MacCormick, "Institutional Normative Order: A Conception of Law" (1997) 82 *Cornell Law Review* 5: 1057.

43 *Ibid*, 1058.

44 In discussing law's functionality, Ehrenberg is focused primarily on institutions that create new reasons for action of its subjects. Ehrenberg, *The Functions of Law*, 7.

45 Needless to say, one of the major issues in legal anthropology is how to ascertain which rules in simple societies without norm-creating institutions have the status of legal ones. According to the internal approach, the legal anthropologist relies on the self-characterization of the society under investigation. The opposite, external, approach may proceed from the description of the social life of the simple society, but the investigator may eventually "use a criterion not used by the people themselves to divide the legal from non-legal." Geoffrey MacCormack, "Anthropology and Legal Theory" (1978) *The Juridical Review*:217. In that respect, much like legal philosophers, legal anthropologists are faced with the methodological dilemma concerning the relation between empirical and analytical methods of study.

46 *See, e.g.*, John George Peristiany, "Law," in Edward Evan Evans-Pritchard et al. (eds.), *The Institutions of Primitive Society* (Oxford: Basil Blackwell, 1954), 39–49.

47 "[T]he central problem of the Middle Ages was the creation of the law," insofar as the question was open as to who was entitled to create law. Walter Ullmann, *Law and Politics in the Middle Ages – An Introduction to the Sources of Medieval Political Ideas* (Cambridge: Cambridge University Press, 1975), 29.

It is patently clear that especially the modern-day law, as a normative order, belongs to a narrower subcategory of "institutionalized systems," which knows of both norm-creating and norm-applying institutions. Such normative institutionalized systems "include both norms for guiding individuals and norms setting up institutions for settling at least some categories of disputes."[48] Systematicity implies that such an institutionalized normative order also possesses the quality of being "self-referential," that is, "autopoietic." Systems are autopoietic insofar as their constituent components are reproduced with reference to themselves.[49] In that respect, they are also "functionally differentiated" (from their social environment) and normatively "closed systems" (i.e., autonomous), because all uncertain issues, e.g., what should be the governing norm of the dispute and how it is to be interpreted, are judged in accordance with norms of the system.[50] Law is, however, by no means the only normative system that has managed in the course of social evolution[51] to acquire the status of an autopoietic system.[52] Law's historical rival, in that respect, was a system of religious rules, institutionalized through organized churches.[53]

This takes us to the last important typical feature that we can associate with law. Raz says that "[l]egal systems differ from other institutionalized systems primarily by their relations to other institutionalized systems in force in the same society."[54] The nature of this "relation" is captured in what Raz considers to be three features of legal systems: they are "comprehensive"; they "claim to be supreme"; and they are "open" to norms of other normative orders.[55]

48 Raz, *Practical Reason and Norms*, 141.

49 Gunther Teubner, "Autopoiesis in Law and Society: A Rejoinder to Blankenburg" (1984) 18 *Law & Society Review* 2: 292.

50 Niklas Luhman, *Law as a Social System* (translated by Klaus A. Ziegert) (Oxford: Oxford University Press, 2004), 90.

51 Hart's "genetic-analytic" method, which takes the systematicity of law to be the cure for imperfections of legal rules of "primitive communities," is often charged to be normatively, i.e., non-descriptively, "commending, if not on moral grounds then at any rate on 'other' grounds" this upgrade of law's form and structure. John Gardner, "Why Law Might Emerge: Hart's Problematic Fable" in d'Almeida, Edwards, and Dolcetti (eds.), *Reading HLA Hart's The Concept of Law*, 85. Gardner discusses several possible "ways out" for Hart's theory to escape these criticisms. *Ibid*, 88–90.

52 Referring here to the conceptual tools of Luhmann's and Teubner's "systems theory" does not imply uncritically adopting the entire apparatus of this theory. One of its most controversial aspects is the thesis that the units, which the legal system is composed of, are neither norms nor actions, but "communications." Luhman, *Law as a Social System*, 89ff.

53 *See*, Niklas Luhmann, A *Systems Theory of Religion* (translated by David A. Brenner with Adrian Hermann) (Stanford: Stanford University Press, 2013).

54 Raz, *Practical Reason and Norms*, 149.

55 *Ibid*, 150–154.

According to this picture, it is a conceptual feature of a legal system that it is superior to other normative orders. That is, in a society with a plurality of "judgments" which, with respect to the same behavior, can be conclusively passed within the respective domains of normative orders, the one of the legal norm-applying institution prevails.

Although this appears as a highly intuitive portrayal of virtually all present-day places where law is in interaction with other normative orders, it would be far more correct to say that this is a historical achievement of modern legal systems. There were times and places in which normative orders of dominant religions were as equally "comprehensive," "open," and "supreme" as are present-day legal systems.[56] And MacCormick explains how this, essentially political, conflict of rivalry claims of different normative orders is most commonly resolved:

> Whoever can make a judgment prevail in the last resort, in the sense of its being carried through by force if necessary, and can reliably and predictably enforce such judgments in the general run, has political power; that political power backs, and to a degree reinforces, the authority and prestige of the tribunal whose judgment is enforced, and that of the normative order to which the tribunal self-referentially belongs.[57]

Before jumping to the conclusion that *coerciveness* is a typical feature of law, which made it the superior normative order, let us make several clarificatory remarks. All normative orders are "somehow 'sanctioned' by the specific reaction of the community to conduct of its members corresponding to or at variance with the order." While "conformity to the order is usually connected with the approval of one's fellow men; non-conformity [is] with their disapproval."[58] However, when speaking about different forms of social disapproval,[59] we shall keep in mind subtle differences between *threat, social*

56 Take the example of the Ottoman Empire, in which "Ottoman law was based upon the religious law of Islam." Norman Itzkowitz, *Ottoman Empire and Islamic Tradition* (Chicago: Chicago University Press, 1972), 88. Or, take the ambition of European medieval religious rules to be "comprehensive" by regulating such matters as "usury," that is, money-lending (*see, e.g.*, Elaine S. Tan, "An Empty Shell? Rethinking the Usury Laws in Medieval Europe" (2002) 23 *The Journal of Legal History* 3: 177–196), or dressing and the consumption of various luxuries (the so-called sumptuary rules). *See, e.g.*, Alan Hunt, *Governance of Consumer Passions: A History of Sumptuary Law* (London: Macmillan, 1996).

57 MacCormick, "Institutional Normative Order: A Conception of Law," 1060.

58 Kelsen, *General Theory of Law and State*, 16.

59 I am, thus, leaving aside internal mechanisms of judgment and self-sanctioning, such as compunction, sense of guilt, and remorse, because they may function even in a Robinson Crusoe-type of circumstances. In contrast, law requires society – *Ubi societas, ibi ius*. Hence, when discussing law, we are primarily interested in explaining external, social reactions to undesired behaviors.

*pressure*, and *physical force*. For instance, one may be exposed to instant physical force without even being threatened (e.g., in the case of unexpected violence by a terrorist suicide bomber); one may be threatened to do/refrain from doing something, without being either socially pressured or physically coerced (e.g., in the case of a nonbeliever who is threatened by a local priest with "burning in hell" if he/she does not start visiting the church); and one may be socially pressured to behave in a certain way (e.g., to mourn, by wearing black clothes), even though there is neither the threat that something bad will happen to him/her, nor will physical force be employed in case he/she misbehaves. It is also imaginable that behaving contrary to what is socially required (e.g., playing music loudly during the funeral of victims of a mass murder) may spontaneously lead to the use of physical force by an outraged mob, although no prior threat of that sort existed. Finally, one may be faced with the threat to do something, which is backed up by physical force, but without any social pressure that such thing ought to be done (e.g., in the case of an armed robbery).

Now, different versions of sanction theories of law mainly emphasize threat (Austin)[60] and physical force (Kelsen)[61] as elements of law's coerciveness. Hart, in contrast, acknowledges the importance of social pressure in explaining how legal rules manage to oblige their subjects. He says that "rules are conceived and spoken of as imposing obligations when the general demand for conformity is insistent and the social pressure brought to bear upon those who deviate or threaten to deviate is great." When this social pressure takes the form of physical sanctions, "even though these are neither closely defined nor administered by officials but are left to the community at large, we shall be inclined to classify the rules as a primitive or rudimentary form of law."[62] One may, thus, conclude that much like other normative orders, law is "backed by both strong pressures of opinion, and the regularly confirmed belief that others apply norms that are regarded as common standards for the group in question."[63] However, unlike rival normative orders, law, and most patently state law, "is backed not only by opinion but also by the coercive force of political power."[64] Nevertheless, one should bear in mind two important things. First, the distinctiveness of law as a normative order cannot be entirely

60 Austin, *The Province of Jurisprudence Determined*, 21.

61 Kelsen, *Pure Theory of Law*, 33.

62 Hart, *The Concept of Law*, 86.

63 MacCormick, "Institutional Normative Order: A Conception of Law," 1065.

64 MacCormick, nonetheless, adds that "it is important to remember that the law of the state is not the only law that human beings have." *Ibid*, 1065. Thus, the tendency to equate "law" with "state law" had serious and distortive effects for legal theory. *Ibid*, 1060.

elucidated by overemphasizing coercion as its typical feature. Although, as indicated, the reliance on the use of force of political (state) institutions historically contributed to the present-day superiority of law,[65] it has, nonetheless, "rarely, if ever, succeeded in absolutely eliminating rival orders of one kind or another."[66] In that respect, normativity of law competes with normativity of other functioning orders.[67] And second, coercion, understood narrowly as physical force, is *stricto sensu* only a species of institutional guarantee. Jellinek was right to claim that "a fundamental feature of the concept of law is guarantee, and not coercion, which is only a subspecies of guarantee. Legal norms are not so much coercive, but rather guaranteed norms."[68] And "[t]he guarantees of the state law lie primarily in the organization of the state," that is, in its institutional aspect.[69] Law is, thus, primarily an *institutionally guaranteed* order, and only secondarily a normative order that relies on sheer physical force. Its *(coercive) guaranteeing*, as it will be shown,[70] may take other forms as well.

## 2 TYPICAL FEATURES OF (INTERNATIONAL) LAW – PRELIMINARY FINDING

Having proceeded from the idea that our pre-analytical samples of law have to account for various social contexts in which the concept-word is used to denote this complex human practice, our analytical work, taken within the prototype theory, has led us to the prototypical (central) case of law as a genre, which is an abstracted set of the following features: normativity, institutionalization, (coercive) guaranteeing, and justice-aptness. That is, a social practice is typically judged as falling within the category of "law" if it consists of rules purporting to coordinate the behavior of actors and to settle their disputes; if it possesses at least institutions in charge of judging whether those rules were violated; if the rules in question are guaranteed, normally through some form of coercive mechanisms; and if the rules are, overall, apt for inspection and appraisal in light of justice. These abstract typical features are sensitive to

65 This has led Weber to argue that, in comparison to other normative orders, law "is externally guaranteed by the probability that physical or psychological coercion will be applied by a *staff* of people in order to bring about compliance or avenge violation." Accordingly, he argued that "the concept 'law' will be made to turn on the presence of a staff engaged in enforcement." Max Weber, *Economy and Society – An Outline of Interpretative Sociology*, Vol. 1 (edited by Guenther Roth and Claus Wittich) (Berkeley: University of California Press, 1978), 34.

66 MacCormick, "Institutional Normative Order: A Conception of Law," 1060.

67 I will quickly return to this point.

68 Georg Jellinek, *Allgemeine Staatslehre* (Berlin: Verlag von Julius Springer, 1929), 337.

69 *Ibid*, 336.

70 *See*, Chapter 5.

context, which means that they vary when we compare the law of simple and modern societies, or law at the municipal, international, and global/transnational levels. Finally, since one of the consequences of the prototype theory is that the boundaries between concepts are blurred, law as a genre has not always been easily distinguished from other normative orders. Whereas in certain societal contexts legal rules were sometimes hardly discernable from moral or religious rules, some contemporary global/transnational regulatory regimes, for example, raise doubts as to whether they can be characterized as legal.[71]

[71] *See, e.g.*, Miodrag Jovanović, "Theorizing 'Unidentified Normative Objects' of Global Regulatory Regimes," in Kenneth Einar Himma, Miodrag Jovanović, and Bojan Spaić (eds.), *Unpacking Normativity: Conceptual, Normative, and Descriptive Issues* (Oxford: Hart Publishing, 2018), 227–250.

# 4

# International Law as a Normative Order

Despite the fact that in order to find out something about the nature of law as a genre one needs to analyze it as an abstracted set of the aforementioned typical features, it is not uncommon among contemporary legal philosophers to hold that the key for law's distinctiveness is its normativity. In what follows I will challenge this widely held belief. In order to do so, I will distinguish between the two *how* questions of normativity. While the first one calls for the epistemological perspective, insofar as it is concerned with finding out how to ascertain a norm, and more specifically a legal norm, the second one invites the perspective of practical rationality, insofar as it tries to elucidate how norms in general, and legal norms in particular, provide us with reasons for action. After a more general exposition of each of the two how questions, I will move on to explore the ramifications of the reached conclusions for international law's normativity.

## 1 EPISTEMOLOGICAL PERSPECTIVE – HOW ARE WE TO ASCERTAIN A NORM

I will start this inquiry by asking *how we are to ascertain a normative statement (norm)*.[1] The initial hunch is to rely on the language of the respective statements. However, as is very well known, language may be indicative, but it is often not conclusive of one statement being normative. Alleged descriptive statements may contain a hidden deontic operator, such as in the statement: "The National Assembly of the Republic of Serbia has 250 MPs." One can

[1] Even those who challenge Hume's famous thesis on the gap between "is-statements" and "ought-statements" are ready to argue that, while "not as clear as it might be," this thesis "is at least clear in broad outline: there is a class of statements of fact which is logically distinct from a class of statements of value." John R. Searle, "How to Derive 'Ought' From 'Is'" (1964)73 *The Philosophical Review* 1: 43.

easily discern that this is not a mere descriptive statement by the fact that it is part of a legal document, called the Constitution of the Republic of Serbia, and legal statements – so the common theoretical wisdom goes – are normative in nature.[2] Hence, "[n]ormally, the context clarifies the exact meaning of such utterances. If it does not, it is always proper to require clarification."[3]

The range of normative statements is potentially broader,[4] but jurisprudence is traditionally interested in finding out how to ascertain a special subset of these statements called "norms." In that respect, Kelsen provides us with an important epistemological clarification. He does so by pointing out that the "norm," as "the meaning of an act by which a certain behavior is commanded, permitted, or authorized" has to be "carefully differentiated from the act of will whose meaning the norm is: the norm is an *ought*, but the act of will is an *is*."[5] This, however, does not entirely solve the puzzle. An utterance by a street bully, yelling in my direction – "Do immediately ten push-ups!" also presumably contains a message that the required behavior "ought" to be conducted, just as does the traffic regulation requiring me to stop the vehicle at the red light. At this point, Kelsen introduces a further clarifying distinction between the "subjective" and "objective" meaning of the act of will:

> "Ought" is the subjective meaning of every act of will directed at the behavior of another. But not every such act has also objectively this meaning; and only if the act of will has also the objective meaning of an "ought" is this "ought" called a norm ... That the "ought" is the objective meaning of the act manifests itself in the fact that it is supposed to exist (that the "ought" is valid) even if the will ceases to exist whose subjective meaning it is – if we assume that an individual ought to behave in a certain way even if he does not know of the act whose meaning is that he ought to behave in this way. Then

[2] Raz challenges this view by arguing that not all laws are norms. Joseph Raz, *The Concept of a Legal System: An Introduction to the Theory of Legal System* (2nd ed.) (Oxford: Clarendon Press, 1980), 168–186.

[3] Joseph Raz, *Practical Reason and Norms* (2nd ed.) (Oxford: Oxford University Press, 2002), 84.

[4] Both Kelsen and Raz warn that we should also take into account statements which, although not being norms themselves, are aimed at representing and reconstructing existing norms. Kelsen speaks of "rules of law in a descriptive sense" (Kelsen, "The Pure Theory of Law and Analytical Jurisprudence," 51), while Raz speaks of "detached legal statements," which "simply state what one has reason to do from the legal point of view, namely, what ought to be done if legal norms are valid norms." (Raz, *Practical Reason and Norms*, fn. 3 to ch. 5, 175) For more recent contributions in this area, *see, e.g.*, Svein Eng, "Fusion of Descriptive and Normative Propositions. The Concepts of 'Descriptive Proposition' and 'Normative Proposition' as Concepts of Degree" (2000) 13 *Ratio Juris* 3: 236–260. Luís Duarte D'Almeida, "Legal Statements and Normative Language" (2011) 30 *Law and Philosophy* 2: 167–199.

[5] Kelsen, *Pure Theory of Law*, 5.

> the "ought," as the objective meaning of an act, is a valid norm binding upon the addressee, that is, the individual at whom it is directed.[6]

Thus, only "ought" in the objective sense of the word constitutes a "valid norm." For Kelsen, "validity" is "the specific existence of norms."[7] Consequently, "validity" is what separates proper "norms" from putative power utterances (like the aforementioned one by a street bully). The latter do not possess "objective" meaning of the act of will of an actor uttering a statement directed at the behavior of another.

Without offering here a full-fledged conception of validity of (legal) norms,[8] I want to investigate the claim according to which it is possible to disentangle concepts of a norm's "validity" and "existence," as this might be of particular relevance for international law. One such attempt in the area of law is given by Munzer, who argues that a norm may be valid, yet non-existent, and vice versa. What he implies under the first claim is the situation in which a norm is "enacted by a legally competent authority," and yet there is "a complete failure by officials to apply sanctions or to criticize."[9] In a reverse situation, "a rule might in fact be supported by sanctions and/or criticism without having been created by a proper authority."[10] This argument rests on Munzer's conception of norm "existence," which is tied, but not identical to, norm "efficacy." In elucidating the latter concept, he distinguishes among elements of the following: (a) "action-conformity" (the factual conformity of behavior to the rule); (b) "agent-conformity" (the awareness of this fact); and (c) "agent-following" (the adequate intention).[11] Consequently, a typical duty-imposing norm ("DI-rule")[12] "is efficacious if and only if on most occasions the actions of XS conform to the rule, and if on some occasions of action-conformity Xs conform to the rule, and if on some occasions of agent-conformity XS

[6] *Ibid*, 7–8.

[7] Hans Kelsen, *General Theory of Law and State* (Cambridge, Mass.: Harvard University Press, 1949), 30.

[8] For a comprehensive jurisprudential discussion of this problem from a positivist standpoint, *see, e.g.*, Andrzej Grabowski, *Juristic Concept of the Validity of Statutory Law – A Critique of Contemporary Legal Nonpositivism* (Heidelberg: Springer, 2013).

[9] Stephen Munzer, *Legal Validity* (The Hague: Martinus Nijhoff, 1972), 42.

[10] *Ibid*, 42–43.

[11] "(a) The actions of Xs conform to the rule that all Xs must Φ in C if and only if Xs Φ in C. (b) XS conform to this rule if and only if the actions of Xs conform to the rule and XS know that their actions do so. (c) XS follow this rule if and only if XS conform to the rule and intend that their actions should so conform." *Ibid*, 33.

[12] There are also power-conferring norms ("PC-rules"), but their efficacy "is closely tied to the efficacy of DI-rules." (*Ibid*, 33) Hence, "efficacy is centrally a mark of DI-rules and is affirmed of PC-rules primarily in virtue of their relation to efficacious DI-rules." *Ibid*, 34.

follow the rule."[13] When turning to a relation between concepts of "efficacy" and "existence," Munzer says that "we shall not always wish to withhold the predicates 'exist(s)' and 'is (are) in existence' in the case of non-efficacious elements."[14] For instance, a DI-rule will be inefficacious if action-conformity (and hence agent-conformity and agent-following) are lacking. However, "if its violators were invariably or almost invariably punished, there would be no ground for denying the existence of that rule."[15]

This last remark, however, implies a further distinction between agents' rule-efficacy and officials' rule-efficacy perspective. Officials are empowered with competence to impose sanctions on disobedient actors.[16] If the rule is inefficient from both agents' and officials' efficiency perspective, then, according to Munzer, it ceases to exist as well. Officials' rule-efficacy, thus, becomes the necessary element of the rule's existence. This, however, seems to bring Munzer's approach closer to Kelsen's position. First, both of them understand "validity" in terms of certain criteria of membership in the given normative order.[17] The major criterion concerns the creation/annulment of a norm according to the accepted standard (Hart's rule of recognition) of what is to count as a formal source of law in the given legal order.[18] Whether this criterion of validity is satisfied is normally ascertained by law-applying institutions, most prominently courts.[19] This affirms the centrality of these institutions for law as a distinctive social practice that was discussed earlier. Having this in mind,

[13] *Ibid*, 33.

[14] *Ibid*, 35.

[15] *Ibid*.

[16] Rules conferring competences may be treated as a special type of power-conferring rule, insofar as they contain elements of both rights and duties. Hence, whereas officeholders (e.g., judges) have the exclusive right to determine that the requested actor's behavior was non-conformant and that the sanction shall be imposed on him, they, at the same time, have the duty to duly perform their office.

[17] Munzer, *Legal Validity*, 38.

[18] According to Kelsen, a norm is first and foremost "a valid legal norm if a) it has been created in a way provided for by the legal order to which it belongs, and b) it has not been annulled . . . in a way provided for by that legal order." Two additional ways of annulling the validity of a norm have to do with its inefficacy: *desuetudo* and inefficacy of the legal order as a whole. Kelsen, *General Theory of Law and State*, 120.

[19] Hart attaches the emergence of the "rule of recognition" to a mature legal order possessing systemic quality. This rule abolishes uncertainty among both norm-actors and officials as to what shall count as a valid legal rule. However, even in simpler legal orders, where no such certainty existed, it was upon law-applying institutions to determine whether some rule passed the threshold criteria of the given order to count as a valid, i.e., applicable legal rule. To say this is not necessarily to imply that the decision of a law-applying institution in such simpler societies is constitutive of something being a valid legal norm (although some such legal orders may have existed). It is merely to acknowledge that in conditions of uncertainty as to what

Munzer's insistence on the distinction between "existence" and "validity" in the case of a properly enacted norm that is, nonetheless, not applied by officials is hardly sustainable.[20] This is what Kelsen qualifies as "*desuetudo*" – the situation in which "an enduring lack of efficacy … ends the validity" of the given legal norm.[21] Although conceivable within Munzer's approach, even less tenable would be a proposition that the vast majority of properly created norms of paramount importance that are neither obeyed nor applied can be said to be "valid," and yet "non-existent." In fact, the described situation amounts to "the phenomenon of revolution," in which inefficacy of the legal order as a whole cancels the validity of each legal norm belonging to that order.[22]

A different sort of attempt to challenge Kelsen's claim proceeds from the distinction between formal and substantive aspects of validity. According to this view, "the establishment of entrenched constitutions … has led to the split, within positive law, between the validity and the existence," where the latter "is a weaker form of validity." That is, "[s]omething can be considered a law not only because it is produced according to some formal standards recognized in a legal order, but also because its content is consistent with the substantive constraints provided by the constitution and higher norms."[23]

counted as a valid/applicable legal norm, it was ultimately upon these institutions to settle this problem. For this reason, Hart acknowledges that even a simpler society "which has rules of adjudication is necessarily also committed to a rule of recognition of an elementary and imperfect sort. This is so because, if courts are empowered to make authoritative determinations of the fact that a rule has been broken, these cannot avoid being taken as authoritative determinations of what the rules are. So the rule which confers jurisdiction will also be a rule of recognition, identifying the primary rules through the judgments of the courts and these judgments will become a 'source' of law." Hart, *The Concept of Law*, 97.

20 Equally problematic is Munzer's claim that an improperly created norm that is nonetheless sanctioned by law-applying institutions shall be treated as an "invalid," but "existent" legal norm. This claim can hardly be vindicated by any known legal practice, which normally treats norms that are applied by the courts and implemented by law- enforcing institutions as "valid legal norms."

21 Kelsen does speak of a norm's inefficacy in both senses – that it is "not obeyed and not applied" (Kelsen, *General Theory of Law and State*, 119), but having in mind his thesis that "the primary norm" of a typical legal rule is the one addressing state actors who ought to execute, apply, or implement the law, it is clear that "enduring lack of efficacy" is ultimately to be tested from the officials' rule-efficacy perspective. *See*, Drury D. Stevenson, "Kelsen's View of the Addressee of the Law: Primary and Secondary Norms," in D. A. Jeremy Telman (ed.), *Hans Kelsen in America – Selective Affinities and the Mysteries of Academic Influence* (Berlin: Springer, 2016), 297–318.

22 "The efficacy of the entire legal order is a necessary condition for the validity of every single norm of the order. A *conditio sine qua non*, but not a *conditio per quam*." Kelsen, *General Theory of Law and State*, 119.

23 This is, for instance, how Luigi Ferrajoli distinguishes between formal and substantive validity – "the former being sufficient for the existence of a norm, i.e. for its recognition within a certain legal order; the latter being necessary for its (full) validity." Paolo Sandro, "An Axiomatic Theory of Law" (2011) 17 *Res Publica* 4: 348.

In cases where a norm satisfies conditions of formal validity, but its content is manifestly unconstitutional, so the argument goes, it remains valid, but non-existent, until it is revoked in the process of constitutional review or substituted by the competent authority with the constitutionally coherent norm stemming from the same source of law.[24]

Although appealing, this argument rests on a dubious idea that material criteria of validity of the given legal norm – its coherence with the higher, constitutional norm – can be authoritatively assessed somehow independently of the institutions (be they regular or constitutional courts) in charge of performing this task.[25] While it is clear that legal scholars, practitioners, and even officials may hold the view that some norm is in blatant violation of constitutional law or that the judicial review resulted in the wrong decision of the court, this norm will remain valid as long as it is treated as such by those very officials.[26] Put differently, the relevant practice of officials – and particularly of courts of last instance, acting in the capacity of the final authority – places a stamp of validity on any practiced norm, irrespective of whether in someone's opinion this norm was incorrectly created (formal validity), or is in conflict with the constitution (material validity). Consequently, "the conventional criteria of legality recognize even the court's mistaken holdings as establishing content of the law."[27]

## 2 EPISTEMOLOGICAL PERSPECTIVE AT THE INTERNATIONAL LEVEL – ON FORMAL SOURCES OF INTERNATIONAL LAW

All the aforementioned seems to justify Kelsen's treatment of "validity" as the specific form of "existence" of all norms, including legal ones. This existence

[24] *Ibid.*

[25] In discussing whether a norm's "validity" amounts to its "membership in the legal system" Grabowski fosters a similar claim, by distinguishing between "the institutional validity of rulings and their correctness." Grabowski, *Juristic Concept of the Validity of Statutory Law*, 291.

[26] Himma takes the example of the controversial *Roe* v. *Wade* decision of the US Supreme Court. He says: "Many people believe that the Roe decision is *incorrect* as a matter of constitutional law and interpretation." Moreover, "such critics of Roe include congressional representatives, the attorney general, and a number of Supreme Court Justices – the very officials whose practices, in Hart's view, ultimately determine the content of the legality criteria." And yet, "[e]ven those officials who believe the Roe decision is mistaken as a matter of constitutional law nonetheless regard the decision as establishing the content of the law." All this, however, "is not surprising since lawyers are trained to regard the holdings of the court with final authority as establishing the content of the law." Kenneth Einar Himma, "Final Authority to Bind with Moral Mistakes: On the Explanatory Potential of Inclusive Legal Positivism" (2005) 24 *Law and Philosophy* 1: 9.

[27] Hence, "what officials collectively treat as the law under some recognition norm *is* the law in that legal system." *Ibid*, 11.

(the so-called legal reality[28]) is verifiable due to some observable facts, such as the facts of legal norm-creation (e.g., a legislative, judicial, or administrative act) and legal norm-observance by both citizens and law-applying institutions (efficacy). For this reason, ascertaining valid norms of the municipal legal order, i.e., "oughts" as the objective meaning of norm-creating acts of will, is significantly easier than in the case of other normative orders.[29] Things are, however, much more complex at the international level. As noted by Shaw, the lack of a centralized legislative body and a hierarchized system of courts with comprehensive and compulsory jurisdiction opens "the problem of discovering where the law is to be found and how one can tell whether a particular proposition amounts to a legal rule. This perplexity is reinforced because of the anarchic nature of world affairs and the clash of competing sovereignties."[30] According to certain views, all this has gradually led international legal scholars to become "much less sensitive to the necessity of rigorously distinguishing law from non-law."[31]

Although one of the arguments advanced so far was that, under the preferable prototypical approach, the concept of law as a genre is at times hardly distinguishable from other normative orders, it should by no means be read as a call for abandoning this distinction upon which the entire specialization of the legal profession is built. Despite the obvious distinctiveness of its institutional design, norms of international order are after all "ascertainable." Namely, "[t]here are 'sources' available from which the rules may be extracted and analysed."[32] This, in particular, means that "law is ascertained by its pedigree defined in formal terms and that, as a result, identifying the law boils down to a formal pedigree test."[33] Moreover, "speaking like an

[28] "The difference between natural reality and legal reality is that legal reality as described by legal science consists of facts which have – under the condition that the validity of the basic, non-positive, norm is presupposed – specific meaning: the meaning of positive norms." Hans Kelsen, "Science and Politics" (1951) 45 *The American Political Science Review* 3: 651.

[29] Take the example of a moral order. Since it is not guaranteed by coercive enforcement mechanisms, and there are no separate institutions for its application and administration, it is far less clear what would constitute a by and large effective positive moral order. The same sort of uncertainty applies to the moral-creating acts, because the vast majority of moral norms stem from an unwritten source, such as custom. Without the conclusive existence of these two sorts of facts, there exists no "moral reality" comparable to that of "legal reality."

[30] Shaw, *International Law*, 70.

[31] Jean D'Aspremont, *Formalism and the Sources of International Law – A Theory of the Ascertainment of Legal Rules* (Oxford: Oxford University Press, 2011), 1.

[32] Shaw, *International Law*, 70.

[33] d'Aspremont, *Formalism and the Sources of International Law*, 13.

international lawyer entails, first and foremost, the ability to deploy the categories put in place by the sources of international law."[34]

And yet, there are a number of potential difficulties in pursuing this project at the international level. When speaking about sources of international law, Besson reminds us that one can, firstly, "refer to *processes* by which international legal norms are created, modified, and annulled." In addition, one can speak of "the *places* where their normative outcomes, i.e., valid international legal norms, may be found."[35] The latter usage is in accordance with the original meaning of "source" as a geological concept, and it literally denotes "places where law 'comes to light.'"[36] This, however, does not necessarily enable the smooth ascertainment of valid legal norms. D'Aspremont, thus, argues in favor of the formal conception of law-ascertainment.[37] This conception requires "formal standardization [that] will materialize itself in predefined formal indicators. These predefined indicators can be linguistic or material." Whereas linguistic indicators refer to both written text and oral language, material ones concern "the use of a more or less deliberate given procedure."[38] In contrast, non-formal conceptions operate with "non-formal

[34] Samantha Besson and Jean d'Aspremont, "The Sources of International Law – Introduction," in Samantha Besson and Jean D'Aspremont (eds.), *The Oxford Handbook on the Sources of International Law* (Oxford: Oxford University Press, 2017), 1.

[35] Samantha Besson, "Theorizing the Sources of International Law," in Besson and Tasioulas (eds.), *The Philosophy of International Law*, 170. Thirlway, for his part, differentiates between "the place, normally a written document, where the terms of the rule can be found conveniently stated: this is the *material* source; and the legal element that gives to the rule its quality as law: this is the *formal* source." Hugh Thirlway, *The Sources of International Law* (Oxford: Oxford University Press, 2014), 3–4. This distinction, however, has the potential of further obfuscating the debate, insofar as the term "material sources of law" has a completely different meaning in the continental legal tradition. According to it, "[m]aterial sources influence the content of the new rule of law without being law themselves." Robert Heinsch, *Die Weiterentwicklung des humanitären Völkerrechts durch die Strafgerichtshöfe für das ehemalige Jugoslawien und Ruanda (Zur Bedeutung von internationalen Gerichtsentscheidungen als Rechtsquelle des Völkerstrafrechts)* (Berlin: Berliner Wissenschafts-Verlag, 2007), 342. The same view is expressed by some prominent Anglo-Saxon international scholars. Hence, Fitzmaurice uses "material source" to denote "the stuff out of which the law is made." Sir Gerald G. Fitzmaurice, "Some Problems Regarding the Formal Sources of International Law," in Frederick Mari van Asbek (ed.), *Symbolae Verzijl* (The Hague: Martinus Nijhoff, 1958), 153.

[36] Maarten Bos, "The Recognized Manifestations of International Law" (1977) 20 *German Year Book of International Law*: 10.

[37] Nonetheless, d'Aspremont explains that while "formalism" is preferred "for its virtues in terms of distinguishing law from non-law and ascertaining international legal rules," it is "not ... construed as a tool to delineate the whole phenomenon of law." d'Aspremont, *Formalism and the Sources of International Law*, 5. For instance, formalism in law ascertainment is "fundamentally different" from "the formalism accompanying formal interpretation of international legal rules." *Ibid*, 160.

[38] *Ibid*, 12.

or hybrid law-ascertaining criteria" as well.[39] A final preliminary distinction to be introduced is borrowed from Bos, who asks what "is the purpose of the quest for 'sources.'" Whereas the initial purpose "must be to know *where the law may be found*," so that one can pursue "legal" reasoning, at the next stage the purpose of inquiry "is to find out *what the law is*" in the given case.[40]

In order to enhance analytical clarity in this somewhat cacophonic talk about "formal sources of law,"[41] I will proceed from a conceptual ramification that is fairly rooted in continental legal education. In an introductory law course it is common to speak of the three constitutive elements of the *form* of each legal instrument (act) through which norms are created. These are: a) the actor authorized to create the norm (*competence*); b) the formalized steps in the process of norm-creation (*procedure*); and c) various means (e.g., written or oral language, conclusive behavior, or signs) to provide external existence of the norm-content (*materialization*). Hence, when the actor (e.g., parliament) and materialization (e.g., a single, written text) happen to be the same in the case of both constitution and statute, the distinction between them can be made according to the element of procedure. The fact that the procedure for the creation of a constitution is much more complex than in the case of a statute (e.g., a qualified versus simple majority vote) explains not only how they are, in formal terms, different legal instruments (acts), but also why the former is a hierarchically higher legal act.

Now, the term "formal source of law" is used to designate an adequate form – "container"[42] – in which the external existence of the norm-content is contained. In that respect, both civil and common law legal systems recognize as formal sources of law only those "containers" that "for law-appliers generate binding legal norms" to be applied on a class of alike cases.[43] These may be general legal acts (constitution, statute), individual legal acts (judicial precedent), patterns of behavior accompanied with the requisite belief that such behavior is mandatory (custom), or commentaries (primarily written) of the relevant doctrinal authorities (legal science). Typically, not all "containers"

39 *Ibid.*

40 Bos, "The Recognized Manifestations of International Law," 11.

41 This talk reflects the fact that "there hardly is another subject to be found on which such radically divergent opinions are being held." *Ibid*, 10. Without denying the need for philosophical debates about the formal sources of international law, Judge Higgins notes that "we should not ignore that the need for them is a damaging acknowledgement of inadequacies in a legal system." Rosalyn Higgins, *Problems and Process: International Law and How We Use It* (Oxford: Oxford University Press, 1994), 17.

42 D'Aspremont uses this label exclusively for written instruments. d'Aspremont, *Formalism and the Sources of International Law*, 174.

43 Bernd Rüthers, *Rechtstheorie (3. Auflage)* (München: Verlag. C.H. Beck, 2007), 144.

are treated as having the same relevance – some are recognized as primary (direct), while some others as secondary (indirect) "sources of law." Moreover, they are normally classified in a hierarchical order.

As rightly pointed out by Bos, for both law-applying institutions and law-obeying actors the ultimate purpose of inquiry of what is within a legal order recognized as a "place where law 'comes to light'" is to determine "*what the law is*" in the case at hand. Thus, Kelsen, who is very critical of this concept,[44] seems to have a point when saying that "any superior legal norm is the source of the inferior legal norm." In this sense, "the constitution of a state is the source of the statutes created on the basis of the constitution, a statute is the source of the judicial decisions based thereon, a judicial decision is the source of the duty it imposes upon the party, and so on."[45] This way of putting things, however, is in apparent contradiction with the conventional doctrinal usage at the municipal level, where, for instance, the term "source of law" is never employed to designate a contract, which is otherwise considered a valid "source" of rights and obligations for contracting parties. Only the statute upon which the contract is based can be properly labeled as the "formal source of law."

Therein rests the first big distinctiveness of the doctrinal usage of the term at the international level. A bilateral treaty, for instance, is considered a "source of international law" despite the fact that it normally creates rights and obligations only for the contracting states.[46] The same holds for unilateral declarations of states which, according to the well-known dictum of the International Court of Justice in the *Nuclear Test Case*, "may have the effect of creating legal obligations."[47] Despite not being explicitly mentioned in Article 38 of the Statute of the International Court of Justice,[48] which is commonly taken as

44 He considers "source of law" to be "a figurative and highly ambiguous expression." Kelsen, *Principles of International Law*, 303.

45 *Ibid.*

46 *Ibid*, 318.

47 "When it is the intention of the State making the declaration that it should become bound according to its terms, that intention confers on the declaration the character of a legal undertaking, the State being thenceforth legally required to follow a course of conduct consistent with the declaration." *Nuclear Tests (Australia* v. *France)*, Judgment, I.C.J. Reports 1974, Rep 253, par. 43.

48 It states as follows: "1. The Court, whose function is to decide in accordance with international law such disputes as are submitted to it, shall apply: a. international conventions, whether general or particular, establishing rules expressly recognized by the contesting states; b. international custom, as evidence of a general practice accepted as law; c. the general principles of law recognized by civilized nations; d. subject to the provisions of Article 59, judicial decisions and the teachings of the most highly qualified publicists of the various nations, as subsidiary means for the determination of rules of law. 2. This provision shall not prejudice the power of the Court to decide a case *ex aequo et bono*, if the parties agree thereto."

enumerating formal sources of international law,[49] unilateral acts of states[50] are regularly regarded as unlisted sources of international law,[51] alongside some other instruments (e.g., decisions of international organizations).[52] The practice of the ICJ also gives rise to the claim that some such instruments (e.g., recommendations of international organizations or the so-called gentlemen's agreements) may be qualified as "quasi-sources" of international law.[53]

All this, in turn, brings the inquiry of what shall *abstractly* count as a valid international legal norm closer to the determination of what shall be the applicable international law in the *concrete* case.[54] The possibility that both a general and an individual norm serve as equally good "sources of international law" stems from the fact that the classical international law knows of no hierarchy between the two main sources of law – custom and treaty. Despite the fact that "the custom-creating process was general in nature and brought about rules binding on the whole international community, such rules could not override a contrary treaty entered into by two or more States in derogation from the customary rule."[55] Put differently, the personal sphere of validity of international legal norms, which may generate the division between "general" and "particular" international law,[56] does not, in principle, affect their hierarchical status within the international legal order.

*Statute of the International Court of Justice*, June 26, 1945, T.S. 993. For a comprehensive legal analysis of this article, *see*, Alain Pellet, "Article 38," in Andreas Zimmerman, Christian Tomuschat, and Karin Oellers-Frahm (eds.), *The Statute of the International Court of Justice – A Commentary (2nd ed.)* (Oxford: Oxford University Press, 2012), 677–792.

49 According to a contrary view, "article 38 has never been more than a provision that modestly aims to define the law applicable by the International Court of Justice (ICJ)." d'Aspremont, *Formalism and the Sources of International Law*, 149.

50 On their legal nature, *see, e.g.*, Camille Goodman, "Acta Sunt Servanda? A Regime for Regulating the Unilateral Acts of States at International Law" (2006) 25 *Australian Year Book of International Law*: 43–74.

51 Rüdiger Wolfrum, "Sources of International Law," in *Max Planck Encyclopedia of Public International Law* (Oxford: Oxford University Press, 2013), par. 10. Thirlway, however, expresses reservation with respect to this view. He proposes "to see a unilateral act on the international plane as a sort of inchoate treaty, completed by subsequent events." Thirlway, *The Sources of International Law*, 20–21.

52 Wolfrum, "Sources of International Law," par. 10. Thirlway is, again, cautious in crediting these decisions with the label of "sources." Thirlway, *The Sources of International Law*, 22–23.

53 Although they are "not binding," Pellet notes that "it appears from a careful study of the caselaw of the Court that they are not 'non-legal.'" Pellet, "Article 38," 714, par. 108.

54 *Cf.* d'Aspremont, *Formalism and the Sources of International Law*, 13.

55 The reason for this was that "States did not intend to place limitations on their sovereign powers they had not expressly or implicitly accepted." Antonio Cassese, *International Law* (2nd ed.) (Oxford: Oxford University Press, 2005), 198.

56 Kelsen employs this division. Whereas "general" international legal norms "are valid for all the states of the world," "particular" international legal norms are "valid only for certain states." Kelsen, *Principles of International Law*, 188.

Attempts at the strict hierarchization of international legal rules are, in that respect, a rather recent phenomenon.[57] While no hierarchy has been introduced among different sources of international law, a special class of general rues "has been endowed with a special legal force: they are peremptory in nature and make up the so-called *jus cogens*."[58] What the concept of *jus cogens* "encapsulates is a rule of hierarchy *senso strictu*,"[59] because these "peremptory norms have a rank and status superior to those of all the other rules of the international community."[60] Yet again, these norms themselves are not sources of international law, and although they are placed at the top of the legal hierarchy, they may, in principle, be found in various sources of international law.[61]

From everything said so far, a number of intricate issues arise: a) how to ascertain and distinguish valid norms of the international legal order, i.e., "oughts" as the objective meaning of norm-creating acts of will, from the mere, unilateral acts of will; b) how to ascertain a valid customary legal rule; c) how to ascertain what is a *jus cogens* rule; d) how to ascertain what is an *erga omnes* obligation; and e) how to ascertain invalidity of an international rule based on its inefficacy (*desuetudo*). I will briefly tackle each one of these questions, which are extensively dealt with in the international scholarship.

57 Yet, it is commonly stated that Article 20 of the League of Nations Covenant introduced a rudimentary hierarchy between international legal obligations. Paragraph 1 of this Article read as follows: "(1) The Members of the League severally agree that this Covenant is accepted as abrogating all obligations or understandings inter se which are inconsistent with the terms thereof, and solemnly undertake that they will not hereafter enter into any engagements inconsistent with the terms thereof." This has led Lauterpacht to treat the Covenant as "the higher law." (*See*, Hersch Lauterpacht, "The Covenant as the Higher Law" (1936) 17 *British Year Book of International Law*: 54–65.) The UN Charter follows this model, by stipulating in Article 103: "In the event of a conflict between the obligations of the Members of the United Nations under the present Charter and their obligations under any other international agreement, their obligations under the present Charter shall prevail." While "[t]he precise scope of Article 103 is a subject of debates in doctrine and practice . . . it is indisputable that it establishes the case of normative hierarchy by giving precedence to certain norms over others." Alexander Orakhelashvili, *Peremptory Norms in International Law* (Oxford: Oxford University Press, 2006), 7.

58 Cassese, *International Law*, 199.

59 International Law Commission, *Fragmentation of International Law: Difficulties arising from the Diversification and Expansion of International Law (Report of the Study Group of the International Law Commission, finalized by Martti Koskenniemi)* A/CN.4/L.682 of 13 April 2006, (2006), par. 365.

60 Cassese, *International Law*, 199.

61 Besson, "Theorizing the Sources of International Law," 171.

### a) How to Ascertain a Valid International Legal Norm

Probably the most sensitive area of discussing the difference between valid international legal rules and mere acts of will concerns the domain of threat or the actual use of force by states. Regulating the employment of force between states in the international sphere was from the beginning perceived as the main subject of the law of nations.[62] Hence, Grotius begins his treatise *De Iure Belli ac Pacis* by saying that "all Affairs that regard the Rights of War and Peace" belong properly to the realm of the law of nations.[63] Kelsen goes even further by arguing that this problem is the test case for determining whether international law is "law in the true sense of the term." According to him, international law will pass this test if it determines "a certain conduct of states as the condition of certain enforcement actions, and thus make[s] this conduct an international delict, the enforcement actions having the character of sanctions."[64]

Not only does the UN Charter enshrine the prohibition on the threat or the actual use of force in international relations,[65] but it also "expressly confers upon the Security Council the competence to exercise the force monopoly of the Organization."[66] It does so by conferring "on the Security Council primary responsibility for the maintenance of international peace and security" (Art. 24[1]) and by stipulating that it is upon this body to "determine the existence of any threat to the peace, breach of the peace, or act of aggression," as well as to "make recommendations, or decide what measures shall be taken" (Art. 39). Enforcement measures involving the use of armed force are, in that respect, envisaged as last resort measures that are supposed to be taken only in case the peaceful measures[67] "would be inadequate or have proved to be inadequate" (Art. 42).

Therefore, despite the fact that the UN Charter operates with the more neutral term "measures," Kelsen is justified in holding that that there is such a thing as international legal "sanction."[68] As rightly pointed out by Reisman,

[62] *Cf.* Verdross, *Völkerrecht*, 10.

[63] Thus, he praises Cicero, "who rightly commended the Excellence of this Science." Grotius, *The Rights of War and Peace (Book I)*, 75.

[64] Kelsen, *Principles of International Law*, 22.

[65] *Cf.* Art. 2(4) of the UN Charter.

[66] Kelsen, *Principles of International Law*, 45.

[67] "These may include complete or partial interruption of economic relations and of rail, sea, air, postal, telegraphic, radio, and other means of communication, and the severance of diplomatic relations." (Art. 41)

[68] The problem of international legal "delicts" of states and "sanctions" for their wrongful actions or omissions is further developed in International Law Commission, *Draft Articles on Responsibility of States for Internationally Wrongful Acts*, November 2001, Supplement No. 10 (A/56/10), chp.IV.E.1. I will return to this issue in Chapter 6.

the very term "sanctions" is, thus, meaningfully employed *only* with reference to the measures that "are used by or with the authority of the international community." In contrast, "[w]hen they are used by individual states without the authorization of an international organization, the states using them try to appropriate the word 'sanctions,' but in fact these are forms of intense unilateral violence."[69] No wonder, thus, that "[u]nilateralism undeniably has a strong pejorative connotation" in the contemporary world. The state regarded as guilty of unilateralism is "the one that puts the triumph of its interests before that of the collective interest, without even speaking of the 'common good.'"[70]

But, what if a unilateral action is undertaken with a view to fostering some international "common good"? Can this attempt at "unilateral enforcement of collective will"[71] blur the line between a valid international legal rule (sanction) and a mere act of will?[72] There were several recent enforcement actions of that sort – most notably those of Iraq[73] and Kosovo – which raised the aforementioned doubt. While I will here tackle only the latter case, an important preliminary reminder was given in the context of the legality assessment of the 2003 use of force against Iraq, namely, that "nowhere is the interrelationship between law and policy more evident than in the *jus ad bellum*."[74] This dictum is equally applicable to the Kosovo case, which has triggered profound legal, political, and ethical debates regarding the use of force against states in which sovereign powers of government were presumably

69 Reisman adds that this does not necessarily turn these acts into unlawful ones, because it is a separate issue. W. Michael Reisman, "Sanctions and International Law" (2009) 4 *Intercultural Human Rights Law Review* 1: 11.

70 Pierre-Marie Dupuy, "The Place and Role of Unilateralism in Contemporary International Law" (2000) 11 *European Journal of International Law* 1: 20.

71 Nico Krisch, "Unilateral Enforcement of Collective Will: Kosovo, Iraq, and the Security Council" (1999) 3 *Max Planck Year Book of International Law*: 59–103.

72 This would amount to Munzer's earlier mentioned case of the "existent" yet "invalid" rule.

73 For a legal assessment of the United States's and the United Kingdom's 1998 use of force against Iraq, *see, e.g.*, Krisch, *ibid*, 64–79. For a legal assessment of the 2003 invasion of Iraq, *see, e.g.*, Sean D. Murphy, "Assessing the Legality of Invading Iraq" (2004) 92 *Georgetown Journal of International Law* 2: 173–257.

74 Andru E. Wall, "Was the 2003 Invasion of Iraq Legal?" (2003) 86 *International Law Studies*: 69–70. This point is best illustrated by a brief poll, conducted by *The Guardian*, in which some of the leading international legal experts were asked about the legality of the 2003 use of force in Iraq. While Shaw said that "there was a credible and reasonable argument in favor of the legality of the war," Chinkin responded negatively, because there was no Security Council decision on the enforcement action. Sir Roberts, for his part, said that "[t]here was in principle a possible case for the lawfulness of resort to war by the US and its small coalition," while Crawford simply concluded that the assessment of legality boiled down "to a political judgment." Owen Bowcott, "Was the war legal? Leading lawyers give their verdict," https://www.theguardian.com/politics/2004/mar/02/uk.internationaleducationnews

used in a manner inconsistent with international legal obligations on human rights protection.

Without going into detail, I will first clarify what we are trying to ascertain in the Kosovo case. Put in Kelsenian terms, a complete duty-imposing legal norm "is split into two separate norms, two 'ought' statements" – one directed at some subject who "'ought' to observe certain conduct," and the other directed at a law-applying actor who "ought to execute a sanction in case the first norm is violated."[75] The aforesaid analysis of the UN Charter shows that there is a general duty of states to abstain from threatening or breaching the peace. The Security Council determined in two of its Resolutions, pursuant to Art. 39, that this general duty was violated in the case of Kosovo and that the "Federal Republic of Yugoslavia constitutes a threat to peace and security in the region."[76] In both of the resolutions, thus, the Security Council provided for more specific duties of all the involved actors, but primarily of the FRY government.[77] In the course of January 1999 events in the village of Račak,[78] the Security Council's President issued a press statement, in which it was stated that "all of these events" were considered "violations of its resolutions and of relevant agreements and commitments calling for restraint."[79] After the

75 Kelsen believed in the conceptual primacy of the latter norm ("primary norm"), by holding that "[i]f at all existent, the first norm is contained in the second, which is the only genuine legal norm." Kelsen, *General Theory of Law and State*, 60–61. He tried to explain all legal norms in terms of this structure, but was often criticized for using duty-imposing rules, typical of criminal law, as representative of all legal norms.

76 SC Resolution 1199 speaks of "the deterioration of the situation in Kosovo" (S/RES/1199 [1998]), while SC Resolution 1203 refers to "the unresolved situation in Kosovo" S/RES/1203 (1998).

77 SC Resolution 1199 demands, inter alia, the FRY to "implement immediately the following concrete measures towards achieving a political solution to the situation in Kosovo" (par. 4). SC Resolution 1203 demands, inter alia, that the FRY "comply fully and swiftly with resolutions 1160 (1998) and 1199 (1998) and cooperate fully with the OSCE Verification Mission in Kosovo and the NATO Air Verification Mission over Kosovo," which were agreed upon. (par. 2)

78 Despite the fact that the EU-commissioned forensic expert report did not contain any evidence of torture, deliberate mutilation, or a "massacre" (J. Rainioa, K. Lalu, and A. Penttila, "Independent Forensic Autopsies in an Armed Conflict: Investigation of the Victims from Racak, Kosovo" (2001) 116 *Forensic Science International* 2: 171–185), events were dubbed by the Security Council as "the massacre of Kosovo Albanians" (S/PRST/1999/2). In a separate investigation, a Byelorussian forensic team came to the conclusion that there were no traces of the execution performed from close vicinity. Heinz Loquai, *Der Kosovo-Konflikt – Wege in einen vermeidbaren Krieg (Die Zeit von Ende November 1997 bis März 1999)* (Baden-Baden: Nomos, 2000), 50, fn. 60. Controversies surrounding legal qualifications of this event are an apt reminder of one of the weaker points of international legal order, its lack of credible fact-finding institutions. *See, infra* 189.

79 S/PRST/1999/2

failure of negotiations in Rambouillet[80] and withdrawal of the OSCE Kosovo Verification Mission,[81] NATO began airstrikes against the FRY. Therefore, the key question to be asked is whether this use of force can be deemed a valid sanctioning "measure" within the confines of Art. 42 of the UN Charter.

A caveat. The term "sanction" is often used to denote both the "ought" statement addressing the law-applying institution *and* the material act of punishment, despite the fact that the latter is only an act of execution of the sanctioning rule. Hence, "sanction" is *stricto sensu* only a rule prescribing a certain penalty (e.g., imprisonment) for the given delict, while the forcible act of putting a convictee into jail is, for instance, a material act of enforcement of the court sentence. By way of analogy, an international legal "sanction" is only a rule prescribing a certain "measure" as a consequence for the violation of the established duties, whereas the action by the authorized actor is merely a material act of execution of the stated sanctioning measure. One of the specificities of the sanctioning mechanisms enshrined in Chapter VII of the UN Charter is that they are not concretized in advance for the enumerated delicts, but it is upon the Security Council to specify them in each particular case after determining that the delict has occurred.[82] The other specificity is "decentralization" of international law, which means that there are no special organs of the international community to take such enforcement actions.[83]

80 *See, e.g.*, Marc Weller, "The Rambouillet Conference on Kosovo" (1999) 75 *International Affairs* 2: 211–251.

81 According to NATO, "the OSCE Kosovo Verification Mission was withdrawn from the region, having faced obstruction from Serbian forces to the extent that they could no longer continue to fulfill their task." ("NATO's role in relation to the conflict in Kosovo," available at http://www.nato.int/kosovo/history.htm) In contrast, the retired general of the German *Bundeswehr*, Heinz Loquai, who was a member of the OSCE mission in the province, argues that "[t]he actual situation in Kosovo does not support this rationale." In fact, the OSCE report on March 18th, just six days before the NATO airstrikes began, was as follows: "[T]he situation in the region remains generally tense, but calm. On this day the OSCE carries out 120 patrols with no difficulty." Heinz Loquai, "Kosovo – A Missed Opportunity for a Peaceful Solution to the Conflict?" (1999) *OSCE Yearbook*: 89.

82 As noted by Tomuschat, "there is a need to ascertain, in each and every instance, whether the gravity of the breach justifies imposing a particularly harsh regime of sanctions." Christian Tomuschat, "Reconceptualizing the Debate on Jus Cogens and Obligations Erga Omnes – Concluding Observations," in Christian Tomuschat and Jean-Marc Thouvenin (eds.), *The Fundamental rules of the International Legal Order – Jus Cogens and Obligations Erga Omnes* (Leiden: Martinus Nijhoff, 2006), 429.

83 Kelsen, *Principles of International Law*, 22. Thus, in the absence of some standing international law-enforcement body, the question is whether NATO could be considered an authorized law-enforcing actor in the Kosovo case. There are several general legal grounds for this claim (e.g., Art. 48, 51, and 53 of the UN Charter). However, addressing this question is dependent on the Security Council determining the relevant sanctioning measure in the first place. Without such a decision, it makes no sense to ask whether NATO (or any other actor for

None of the authorities in the field seems to be ready to argue that the use of force against the FRY can be deemed a valid sanctioning norm of international law. As the above-mentioned analysis of the UN Charter demonstrates, it is upon the Security Council not only to ascertain the existence of such grave delicts of international law as threats or breaches of peace, which it did in two resolutions, but also to determine explicitly what sort of specific sanctioning "measure" – the one not involving the use of armed force (Art. 41) or the one involving the use of armed force (Art. 42) – is to be employed as the consequence of the violation of established legal duties. In the absence of such a determination by the Security Council any enforcement measure taken against the violating state cannot be considered a valid international legal norm (sanction), but a mere act of will, expressed in the form of "intense unilateral violence" (Reisman).

No such determination existed in the case of Kosovo. Cassese, thus, concludes that "a group of states has deliberately resorted to armed action against sovereign state without authorization to do so by the Security Council."[84] In that respect, labeling the NATO use of force as a "humanitarian intervention" by no means turns this unilateral action into a valid international legal sanction, because, as noted by Dinstein, "forcible intervention on humanitarian grounds is still forcible intervention" and "only the Security Council can unleash the use of force against a sovereign State under any circumstances exceeding the bounds of self-defense in response to an armed attack."[85] Simma argues in a similar fashion: "[I]f the Security Council determines that massive violations of human rights occurring within a country constitute a threat to the peace (*delict*, M. J.), and then calls for or authorizes an enforcement action to put an end to these violations (*sanctioning rule*, M. J.), a "humanitarian intervention" by military means (*execution of sanction*, M. J.) is permissible." Short of such an explicit authorization, "military coercion employed to have the target state return to a respect for human rights

that matter) was authorized to materialize the determined sanction – the use of force against the FRY.

84 Antonio Cassese, "*Ex iniuria ius oritur*: Are We Moving towards International Legitimation of Forcible Humanitarian Countermeasures in the World Community?" (1999) 10 *European Journal of International Law* 1: 24.

85 Yoram Dinstein, "The Thirteenth Waldemar A. Solf Lecture in International Law" (2000)166 *Military Law Review*: 95. As pointed out by the ICJ in the Nicaragua case, "under international law in force today – whether customary international law or that of the United Nations system – States do not have a right of 'collective' armed response to acts which do not constitute an 'armed attack.'" *Military and Paramilitary Activities in and against Nicaragua, Merits*, ICJ Reports (1986), p. 110, par. 211.

constitutes a breach of Article 2(4) of the Charter."[86] Finally, the lack of subsequent condemnation of NATO airstrikes by the Security Council cannot be construed to mean an implicit authorization of the use of force.[87] As pointed out by Krisch, "apart from the fact that the rejection was not motivated by a wish to approve the strikes, the Charter requires the positive decision by the Council, not the absence of a negative one – otherwise the veto power of the permanent members would be pointless."[88]

Without the legal ground to ascertain the use of force against the FRY as the valid sanctioning rule within the purview of the UN Charter, what one is mostly left with is the discussion about *moral legitimacy* of this unilateral act of force. It transpires that even authors who are ready to defend the "legality" of the NATO action are actually framing their argumentation primarily in terms of moral values that were allegedly served by the use of force.[89] Similarly, those very scholars who admit that the use of force in the Kosovo case cannot be deemed a valid international legal sanction are prone to move from the *de lege lata* analysis to the ethical perspective. Hence, after exhausting all possible venues for legal justification, Simma concludes that "only a thin red light separates NATO's action on Kosovo from international legality"[90] and that "we would be well advised" to treat this use of force "as a singular case in which NATO decided to act without Security Council authorization out of overwhelming humanitarian necessity."[91] Cassese goes a step further and asks legal

86 Bruno Simma, "NATO, the UN and the Use of Force: Legal Aspects" (1999) 10 *European Journal of International Law* 1: 5.

87 Henkin hints at this direction, when contending that "Council ratification after the fact in Resolution 1244 – formal ratification by an affirmative vote of the Council effectively ratified what earlier might have constituted unilateral action questionable as a matter of law." Louis Henkin, "Kosovo and the Law of 'Humanitarian Intervention'" (1999) 93 *American Journal of International Law* 4: 827.

88 Krisch, "Unilateral Enforcement of Collective Will: Kosovo, Iraq, and the Security Council," 86.

89 Take, for example, Klinton's "legal case" for the NATO intervention. Although he explicitly states that "NATO's decision to intervene in Kosovo was a clear breach of the U.N. Charter," as well as "a breach of NATO's own founding document" (447), he nonetheless refers to "the moral imperative" of the action (442), which stems from humanitarian reasons (440–442) and massive refugee flows (445–448). There is an additional, geopolitical reason for preventing the Balkans's "powder keg" from exploding further (442–445). Klinton does at times employ legal grounds for action, such as "an emerging body of international law that permits armed intervention for humanitarian purposes" (441), or "customary international law" concerning human rights protection (448), but he offers no evidence in support of these claims. Alexander W. Klinton, "NATO's Intervention in Kosovo: The Legal Case for Violating Yugoslavia's National Sovereignty in the Absence of Security Council Approval" (2000) 22 *Houston Journal of International Law* 3: 403–449.

90 Simma, "NATO, the UN and the Use of Force: Legal Aspects," 22.

91 He adds that "no general conclusion ought to be drawn" from this case. *Ibid*, 14. Franck subscribes to this position, by claiming that "[e]very nation has an interest in NATO's actions

scholars to "stretch [their] minds further" and ask themselves whether the "NATO armed intervention [was] at least rooted and partly justified by contemporary trends of the international community."[92] He argues that such a conclusion is warranted[93] and that "this particular instance of breach of international law may gradually lead to the crystallization of a general rule" on humanitarian intervention.[94]

The Kosovo case has obviously led many international legal scholars to take this "ambivalent" position that the employed use of force "was both formally illegal and morally necessary."[95] This "turn to ethics" of the international legal scholarship[96] is probably best exemplified in two rhetorical questions raised by Henkin: "Is it better to leave the law alone, while turning a blind eye (and a deaf ear) to violations that had compelling moral justification? Or should Kosovo move us to push the law along, to bring it closer to what the law ought to be?"[97] Dworkin takes this approach to be "dangerous," particularly if fostered by "an eminent international lawyer."[98] According to him, "'[i]nternational law is fragile, still nascent and in critical condition. The proposition that a sense of moral duty can justify violations of international law threatens to strangle the child."[99] Put in less dramatic terms, Henkin's proposal to blur the distinction between *lex lata* and *lex ferenda* leaves us without precise criteria for ascertaining what shall count as a valid legal norm. To appeal, for instance, to "moral standards" of "human conscience," as suggested by Pellet,[100] rather than to a recognized formal source law, as the ultimate criterion for

being classified as the exception, not the rule." Thomas M. Franck, "Lessons of Kosovo" (1999) 93 *American Journal of International Law* 4: 859.

92 Cassese, "*Ex iniuria ius oritur*: Are We Moving towards International Legitimation of Forcible Humanitarian Countermeasures in the World Community?," 25.

93 After tracing those "nascent trends in the world community," Cassese lists conditions under which even an unauthorized use of force for the purposes of humanitarian necessity may be justified. *Ibid*, 27.

94 *Ibid*, 29. Contrary to his own treatment of sanctions in international law, Reisman argues in a similar vein that it is "incumbent upon international scholars" to envisage "the *exceptio* for that very small group of events that warrant or even require unilateral action when the legally designated institution or procedure proves unable to operate." W. Michael Reisman, "Kosovo Antinomies" (1999) 93 *American Journal of International Law* 4: 860.

95 This is how Koskenniemi characterizes his own position. Martti Koskenniemi, "'The Lady Doth Protest Too Much': Kosovo, and the Turn to Ethics in International Law," in *The Politics of International Law* (Oxford: Hart Publishing, 2011), 115.

96 *Ibid*, 116.

97 Henkin, "Kosovo and the Law of 'Humanitarian Intervention,'" 827.

98 He had in mind Franck's similar approach to the subject matter. Dworkin, "A New Philosophy for International Law," 23.

99 *Ibid*.

100 Alain Pellet, "Brief Remarks on the Unilateral Use of Force" (2000) 11 *European Journal of International Law* 2: 386.

ascertaining validity of a rule, opens up the space for the discretion and arbitrariness of those who are in the position to act – and these are the most powerful states.[101] Therefore, sticking to "formalism" in ascertaining what shall count as a valid legal norm is "precisely about setting limits to the impulses – 'moral' or not – of those in decisionmaking positions in order to fulfil general, instead of particular, interests."[102] Judge Cançado Trindade aptly summarizes what would the world look like if we were to do otherwise. He says,

> to allow unilateral acts to be performed (in the course of international legal proceedings), irrespectively of their discretionary – if not arbitrary – character, and to accept subsequent assurances or "undertakings" ensuing therefrom, is to pave the way to uncertainties and unpredictability, to the possibility of creation of *faits accomplis* to one's own advantage and to the other party's disadvantage. The certainty of the application of the law would be reduced to a mere probability.[103]

Leaving aside here potential legal and political consequences of NATO's unlawful intervention,[104] the subsequent emergence of the "responsibility to

[101] Koskenniemi reminds one of the realities of the world, by noting that "it is never Algeria that will intervene in France, or Finland in Chechnya." Koskenniemi, "'The Lady Doth Protest Too Much': Kosovo, and the Turn to Ethics in International Law," 127.

[102] *Ibid*, 128. Some political philosophers have tested whether the alleged morality of the NATO military intervention can be put in this *de lege ferenda* perspective. Buchanan's analysis leads him to conclude that NATO's action "was not credible as an act directed towards reform of the international law of humanitarian intervention." Allen Buchanan, "Reforming the International Law of Humanitarian Intervention," in J. L. Holzgrefe and Robert E. Jeohane (eds.), *Humanitarian Intervention – Ethical, Legal and Political Dilemmas* (Cambridge: Cambridge University Press, 2003), 170.

[103] Judge Antônio A. Cançado Trindade, *The Construction of a Humanized International Law: A Collection of Individual Opinions (1991–2013)*, Vol. 3 (Leiden: Brill, 2017), 713.

[104] As is well known, the most important political and legal implication of the NATO action is the self-proclaimed independence of Kosovo. In its Advisory Opinion on Kosovo, the ICJ was asked to address the following question: "Is the unilateral declaration of independence by the Provisional Institutions of Self-Government of Kosovo in accordance with international law?" (UNGA A/63/L. 2) While finding that the Kosovo unilateral declaration of independence did not violate international law, the Court stated that the submitted question "does not ask about the legal consequences of that declaration. In particular, it does not ask whether or not Kosovo has achieved statehood. Nor does it ask about the validity or legal effects of the recognition of Kosovo by those States which have recognized it as an independent State." (International Court of Justice, *Accordance with international law of the unilateral declaration of independence in respect of Kosovo*, Advisory Opinion, No. 2010/25, 22 July 2010, par. 51) In a separate opinion, Judge Cançado Trindade addressed the problem of legal consequences of unlawful acts, by stressing that "[t]he principle *ex injuria jus non oritur* applies to all those grave breaches ... U.N. Security Council resolution 1244 (1999) cannot thus be read as endorsing wrongful acts of any origin or kind, nor as taking advantage of them." (Separate Opinion of

protect (R2P)" doctrine[105] testifies to the poor, if at all existent, moral transformative potential of the Kosovo-style unilateralism in international relations.[106]

### b) How to Ascertain a Valid Customary Rule of International Law

Even sticking to what are widely perceived as formal sources of international law does not always yield a reliable ascertainment of valid rule. This is particularly true of customary international law (CIL), which is often viewed as "the most anarchic source of international law."[107] The major problem stems from the fact that the term CIL applies both to "the process through which certain rules of international law are formed" and to "the rules formed

Judge A. A. Cançado Trindade, par. 134. [emphasis in the original]) On April 29, 1999, the FRY instituted proceedings before the ICJ against ten NATO countries "for violation of the obligation not to use force," submitting a request for the indication of provisional measures, but the ICJ noted that it was unable to decide on those measures without first establishing *prima facie* jurisdiction in a case. (*Case Concerning Legality of Use of Force [Yugoslavia v. Belgium]* [Provisional Measures], Order of 2 June 1999) In 2004, the ICJ dismissed separate complaints filed in 1999 by Serbia and Montenegro against eight NATO member states. According to the Court's unanimous Judgments, Serbia and Montenegro at that moment lacked standing to sue before the ICJ. (*Legality of Use of Force [Serbia and Montenegro v. Belgium]*, Judgment of December 15, 2004) Finally, there were attempts to investigate and prosecute NATO leaders and personnel at the ICTY, but they were dismissed by the chief prosecutor. For a legal analysis, *see, e.g.*, Andreas Laursen, "NATO, the War over Kosovo, and the ICTY Investigation" (2002) 17 *American University International Law Review* 4: 765–814. *Cf.* Anne-Sophie Massa, "NATO's Intervention in Kosovo and the Decision of the Prosecutor of the International Criminal Tribunal for the Former Yugoslavia Not to Investigate: An Abusive Exercise of Prosecutorial Discretion?" (2006) 24 *Berkley Journal of International Law* 2: 610–649.

105 It was endorsed for the first time in a report by the International Commission on Intervention and State Sovereignty (ICISS): *The Responsibility to Protect* (Ottawa: International Development Research Centre, 2001). Even though the report as such was never adopted by some UN body, the R2P doctrine was eventually incorporated into the 2005 UN World Summit Outcome Document, T 134, U.N. Doc. A/RES/60/1 (September 16, 2005). One of the most important features of the UN-based model of R2P is that it reaffirms the position of the Security Council in determining the use of force as a sanctioning measure. *See*, Miodrag Jovanović, "Responsibility to Protect and the International Rule of Law" (2015) 14 *Chinese Journal of International Law* 4: 757–776.

106 In the UN GA 2009 debate on the R2P concept, Special Adviser to the Secretary General explicitly stated: "This is not 1999. Ten years ago the Assembly addressed the concept of humanitarian intervention and found it wanting. Unilateral armed intervention under the guise of humanitarian principles was – and is – seen as morally, politically, and constitutionally unacceptable. That is not the UN way." Edward C. Luck, "Remarks to the General Assembly on the Responsibility to Protect (R2P)" (New York, 23 July 2009), at 2, http://www.ipacademy.org/images/pdfs/luck_ga_statement23july2009.pdf

107 Birgit Schlütter, *Developments in Customary International Law (Theory and the Practice of the International Court of Justice and the International ad hoc Criminal Tribunals for Rwanda and Yugoslavia)* (Leiden: Martinus Nijhoff Publishers, 2010), 13.

through such a process."[108] Put succinctly, "[c]ustomary law is law created by custom."[109] When phrased in the aforementioned terminology of elements of legal *form*, we are dealing with "an unwritten process whereby normativity is behaviorally generated short of any written instrument."[110] This implies that the "container" of valid customary rule is hardly distinguishable from the very process of the coming into existence of the rule,[111] and according to the traditional wisdom it consists of two elements: a habitual course of action, i.e., "a long-established practice of states" (*corpus*), which is "accompanied by the opinion that this conduct is obligatory or right" (*animus*).[112]

Art. 38 is, in that respect, a potential source of confusion, because it speaks of "international custom, *being evidence* (M. J.) of a general practice accepted as law." Kelsen, for instance, takes the first part of the provision to denote the habitual course of action (fact), and the second part to depict the customary rule of law (norm); hence, he concludes that this wording erroneously implies that "this norm is created by another fact than custom, that the true creator of law stands – so to speak – behind custom."[113] Hillier interprets these linguistic phrases in quite the opposite way. Thus, he contends that it would have been more correct if Art. 38 "had said 'international custom *as evidenced* (M. J.) by a general practice accepted as law,' for it is not the custom or customary rule of international law which is evidence of the general practice, but rather the general practice accepted as law that provides evidence of the customary rule."[114] On the other hand, it does not seem incorrect to contend that "the existence of the customary rule attests that, 'upstream,' a practice has developed which then became accepted as law."[115] In any case, all this puts us in

108 Tulio Treves, "Customary International Law," in Wolfrum (ed.), *The Max Planck Encyclopedia of Public International Law*, par. 1.

109 Kelsen, *Principles of International Law*, 307.

110 Jean d'Aspremont, "The Decay of Modern Customary International Law in Spite of Scholarly Heroism" (2015) *The Global Community Yearbook of International Law and Jurisprudence*: 11.

111 "The essential characteristic which customary international law rules have in common is the way they have come into existence and the way their existence may be determined." Treves, "Customary International Law," par. 3.

112 Kelsen, *Principles of International Law*, 307.

113 *Ibid*, 309. This view is, for instance, attributable to the natural law doctrine. *Ibid*, 311.

114 Tim Hillier, *Sourcebook on Public International Law* (London: Cavendish Publishing Limited, 1998), 78. *Cf.* Higgins, *Problems and Process: International Law and How We Use It*, 18.

115 Pellet, "Article 38," 749, par. 207. Namely, "since the practice in question is followed by states because it is believed by them to be already legally obligatory, the source of the obligation must precede the custom (meaning: customary rule, M. J.) to which the practice gives rise: in this sense the custom (meaning: customary rule, M. J.) may correctly be regarded as the evidence of the practice accepted as law, not its source." Robert Jennings, Arthur Watts (eds.), *Oppenheim's International Law: Volume 1 Peace* (9th ed.) (Oxford: Oxford University Press, 2008), 26, fn. 5.

front of the fundamental "epistemic question of how to determine whether a practice in fact reflects customary law."[116] More precisely, "when is this process – which seems to be cumulative of a practice and an acceptance – achieved?"[117]

Uncertainty surrounding the identification of CIL has led some international scholars to harshly criticize it. It is argued that it is being imbued with some significant limitations;[118] that the application of the traditional two-element doctrine *in concreto* "has proved extremely vexatious for practitioners";[119] and finally, that it "has evolved into a meaningless concept," which as such must be abandoned in the development of international law.[120] Is this gloomy, even demonizing portrayal of CIL warranted? Without a doubt, there are some obvious deficiencies of this formal source of international law. Virtually all of them belong to "the meta-law of customary international law."[121] To begin with, how is the practice of a juristic person to be ascertained – in particular, acts of which physical persons are attributable to state? Even more importantly, which acts/omissions constitute the relevant state practice? If one, for example, has to ascertain a prohibitive customary international rule, does this really turn attempts at identification of relevant inaction of state into "a speculative venture into nothingness"?[122] One of the best illustrations that this may indeed be so is the ICJ's reasoning in the *Nuclear Weapons* Advisory Opinion, in which the Court had to ascertain whether

116 Samuel Estreichner, "Rethinking the Binding Effect of Customary International Law" (2003) 44 *Virginia Journal of International Law* 1: 7.

117 Pellet, "Article 38," 749, par. 207.

118 "CIL has several important limitations: (i) it cannot be made in a coordinated manner in advance of events; (ii) it cannot be made with sufficient detail; (iii) it cannot be made with sufficiently heterogeneous reciprocity between states; (iv) it cannot be made with specifically designed organizational support; (v) it is generally not subject to national parliamentary control; (vi) it purports to bind states that did not consent but failed to object to its formation; and (vii) it provides excessive space for auto-interpretation by states, or for sometimes insufficiently disciplined interpretation by judges." Joel P. Trachtman, "The Growing Obsolescence of Customary International Law," in Curtis A. Bradley (ed.), *Custom's Future – International Law in a Changing World* (Cambridge: Cambridge University Press, 2016), 173.

119 d'Aspremont, "The Decay of Modern Customary International Law in Spite of Scholarly Heroism," 18.

120 As such, it "furnishes neither a coherent nor objective means of determining the norms of international law, how and when they come into existence, and which nations are bound." J. Patrick Kelly, "The Twilight of Customary International Law" (2000) 40 *Virginia Journal of International Law* 2: 452–453.

121 Jörg Kammerhofer, *Uncertainty in International Law – A Kelsenian Perspective* (London: Routledge, 2011), 59.

122 d'Aspremont, "The Decay of Modern Customary International Law in Spite of Scholarly Heroism," 26.

there existed a customary rule prohibiting the threat or use of nuclear weapons. The Court contrasted the widespread inaction of the large majority of states (albeit, primarily of those outside of the circle of nuclear powers) with the "'policy of deterrence,' to which an appreciable section of the international community adhered for many years."[123] It ultimately concluded "that it cannot reach a definitive conclusion as to the legality or illegality of the use of nuclear weapons by a State in an extreme circumstance of self-defence, in which its very survival would be at stake."[124] However, as noted by Judge Shi in a separate Declaration, the examined policy

> is within the realm of international politics, not that of law. It has no legal significance from the standpoint of the formation of a customary rule prohibiting the use of nuclear weapons as such. Rather, the policy of nuclear deterrence should be an object of regulation by law, not vice versa. The Court, when exercising its judicial function of determining a rule of existing law governing the use of nuclear weapons, simply cannot have regard to this policy practice of certain States as, if it were to do so, it would be making the law accord with the needs of the policy of deterrence.[125]

Equally if not more troublesome is ascertainment of *opinio juris*. While Article 38 speaks of "a general practice *accepted* (M. J.) as law," thereby leaving the impression that states have to consent, i.e., to acquiesce to the right/obligation generated by the relevant practice, some of the ICJ's decisions pull in the opposite direction. Most famously, in the *North Sea Continental Shelf* case, the Court referred to the state's "belief":

> Not only must the acts concerned amount to a settled practice, but they must also be such, or be carried out in such a way, as to be evidence of a *belief* (M. J.) that this practice is rendered obligatory by the existence of a rule of law requiring it . . . The States concerned must therefore *feel* (M. J.) that they are conforming to what amounts to a legal obligation. The frequency, or even habitual character of the acts is not in itself enough. There are many international acts, e.g., in the field of ceremonial and protocol, which are performed almost invariably, but which are motivated only by considerations of courtesy, convenience or tradition, and not by any *sense* (M. J.) of legal duty.[126]

123 *Legality of the Threat or Use of Nuclear Weapons*, ICJ Reports (1996), p. 263, par. 96.

124 *Ibid*, par. 97.

125 Declaration of Judge Shi, p. 277.

126 *North Sea Continental Shelf*, ICJ Reports (1969), p. 45, par. 77. This stance is reiterated in the Nicaragua case. *Military and Paramilitary Activities in and against Nicaragua*, pp. 108–109, par. 207.

Acceptance and belief are, however, two quite distinctive things. "It is one thing to take notice of a practice, and a completely different thing to agree to that practice."[127] Neither of them is easily discernable though. The belief-theory is criticized for being heavily anthropomorphic when imputing "beliefs," "feelings," and "senses" to a juristic person.[128] The acceptance-theory is charged with lacking proper methodology for determining whether states have indeed accepted some practiced behavior as a rule of law.[129]

A separate problem for the traditional doctrine concerns the relation between the two constitutive elements. None of them can be discharged or favored "without this engendering immediately the objection that custom is either apologist (because it makes no distinction between might and right) or utopian (because we cannot demonstrate its norms in a tangible fashion)."[130] And yet, international legal theory has been for quite some time operating with two distinctive approaches to customary law. Simma and Alston, for instance, argue that the old-style approach emphasizes the "material," i.e., "objective" element – state practice. The ascertainment of a valid customary rule is to be undertaken through *inductive* reasoning, which boils down to the procedure of "look[ing] into the past to identify customary patterns of State practice and then to turn this empirical result into a normative projection for the future."[131] In contrast, the "modern," new-style approach is far less concerned with state practice, and, instead, relies heavily on the "subjective" element.[132] According to it, "the only task practice ever had to perform ... was to bring consent or *opinio juris* to the fore." This new approach might be dubbed as "radical," insofar as it relies on *deductive*

[127] Christian Dahlman, "The Function of Opinio Juris in Customary International Law" (2012) 81 *Nordic Journal of International Law* 3: 331.

[128] Jean d'Aspremont, "The Doctrine of Fundamental Rights of States and the Functions of Anthropomorphic Thinking in International Law" (2015) 4 *Cambridge Journal of International and Comparative Law* 3: 504.

[129] "Without a defined process whereby states can express their consent or acceptance, the conclusion that a norm is accepted as obligatory is fictitious." Kelly, "The Twilight of Customary International Law," 475.

[130] Martti Koskenniemi, *From Apology to Utopia – The Structure of International Legal Argument (Reissue with a new Epilogue)* (Cambridge: Cambridge University Press, 2005), 410.

[131] Bruno Simma and Philip Alston, "The Sources of Human Rights Law: Custom, Jus Cogens and General Principles" (1988–1989) 12 *Australian Yearbook of International Law*: 89.

[132] Probably the most radical proposal, in that respect, comes from Bin Cheng, who argues in favor of "instant" customary rule of international law. Bin Cheng, "United Nations Resolutions on Outer Space: 'Instant' International Customary Law?," in *Studies in International Space Law* (Oxford: Clarendon Press, 1993), 138.

approach, which turns the process of customary law-making "into a self-contained exercise in rhetoric."[133]

One might have expected some clarificatory job to be done by the ICJ, but it transpires that "the Court has hardly ever stated its methodology for determining the existence, content and scope of the rules of customary international law that it applies."[134] Talmon's meticulous analysis demonstrates that the ICJ oscillates between methods of "induction"[135] and "deduction,"[136] thereby ascribing different weight to each of the two elements. In apparently prioritizing the former method, neither does the Court make a sharp distinction between the so-called "traditional" and "modern custom,"[137] nor does it manage to avoid criticism – regularly reserved for the employment of deductive method – for being subjective, unpredictable, and performing quasi-legislative function. This is so because examining the practice and *opinio juris* of states, upon which a valid customary rule is to be ascertained, "is not a mathematical exercise of simply counting state behaviour but, rather, a process prone to subjectivity and selectivity." The ICJ is faced with the practical impossibility of observing and investigating the practice and *opinio juris* of merely two hundred states. Consequently, "any customary rule will, by necessity, be based on a selection of state practice – a selection made by the Court."[138]

Talmon's analysis led him to eventually conclude that the ICJ's primary method is in fact "assertion." Not only does the Court assert what may be

133 Simma and Alston, "The Sources of Human Rights Law: Custom, *Jus Cogens* and General Principles," 89. According to one such approach, "[a] customary international norm arises when states generally believe that it is desirable now or in the near future to have an authoritative legal principle or rule prescribing, permitting, or prohibiting certain state conduct. This belief constitutes *opinio juris*, and it is sufficient to create a customary law norm." Brian D. Lepard, *Customary International Law: A New Theory with Practical Applications* (Cambridge: Cambridge University Press, 2010), 8.

134 Stefan Talmon, "Determining Customary International Law: The ICJ's Methodology between Induction, Deduction and Assertion" (2015) 26 *The European Journal of International Law* 2: 418.

135 This method "may be defined as inference of a general rule from a pattern of empirically observable individual instances of State practice and *opinio juris*." *Ibid*, 420.

136 "The deductive method, on the other hand, may be defined as inference, by way of legal reasoning, of a specific rule from an existing and generally accepted (but not necessarily hierarchically superior) rule or principle." *Ibid*. Moreover, the Court does employ at least three different methods: normative, functional, and analogical deduction. *Ibid*, 423ff.

137 "The use of the terms 'traditional' and 'modern' suggests a chronological sequence and implies a change of methodology in determining custom over time ... But the deductive method is not a recent or modern phenomenon; it was used by the Court's predecessor, the Permanent Court of International Justice (PCIJ)." *Ibid*, 431.

138 *Ibid*, 432.

regarded as an existent, i.e., valid customary rule, but "it has also denied the existence of (alleged) rules of customary international law simply by stating that there is no 'uniform and widespread State practice' without providing any support for this assertion."[139] That this is so becomes obvious from several ICJ decisions in which the Court uses laconic phrases, such as "the Court would observe,"[140] "the Court observes,"[141] and "in the Court's opinion,"[142] thereby ascertaining the existence of a customary rule without grounding it in any evidentiary practice of states and the relevant *opinio juris*.[143] Hence, some international scholars are prone to conclude in dismay that "after decades of jurisprudence ... almost anything goes in the ascertainment of custom."[144]

All this raises profound questions as to why the Court is not more attentive to devising a clear methodology and why states are not more concerned about this.[145] At this point, it is crucial to be aware of a potential "methodological trap," which pertains to the fact that unlike in municipal law, where the court's jurisdiction is compulsory, and "it is at least feasible (if not wholly correct) to think of law in terms of what a judge will do," in the international legal order "adjudication is the exception, not the rule." A more frequent actor who identifies and applies law "is the government official, engaged either in advising his or her own government, or in negotiating with others."[146] There is an obvious difference in their "observational standpoint(s)" – whereas the international judge or arbitrator is called upon "to decide whether the processes for the creation of custom had been completed by the critical date," the state official

139 *Ibid*, 434.

140 *Arrest Warrant of 11 April 2000 (Democratic Republic of the Congo* v. *Belgium)*, ICJ Reports (2002), p. 20, par. 51.

141 *Armed Activities on the Territory of the Congo (Democratic Republic of the Congo* v. *Uganda)*, ICJ Reports (2005), p. 229, par. 172.

142 *Reparation for Injuries Suffered in the Service of the United Nations*, ICJ Reports (1949), p. 185.

143 Talmon notes that the Court has developed several techniques of assertion, such as referring to the work of the International Law Commission (ILC), *ex cathedra* observation that a certain treaty provision is reflective of customary international law, as well as referring to certain provisions of UN GA resolutions or even entire resolutions as being reflective of customary international law. *Ibid*, 437ff. Sender and Wood reject Talmon's analysis and qualifications and argue that the ICJ is resorting to "the pragmatic approach." Omri Sender and Michael Wood, "The International Court of Justice and Customary International Law: A Reply to Stefan Talmon," *EJIL: Talk!*, November 30, 2015, at www.ejiltalk.org/the-international-court-of-justice-and-customary-international-law-a-reply-to-stefan-talmon/

144 Christian J. Tams, "Meta-Custom and the Court: A Study in Judicial Law-Making" (2015) 14 *The Law and Practice of International Courts and Tribunals* 1: 79.

145 Harlan G. Cohen, "Methodology and Misdirection: Custom and the ICJ," *EJIL: Talk!*, December 1, 2015, at www.ejiltalk.org/methodology-and-misdirection-a-response-to-stefan-talmon-on-custom-and-the-icj/

146 Hillier, *Sourcebook on Public International Law*, 78.

"need not be so objective."[147] However, the international court's putative objectivity should not be equated with its ability to "step into the state's shoes," because it can hardly do so. This is due to the fact that any international court – including the ICJ – "is engaged in a fundamentally different activity than a state discerning a rule to guide its actions or jockeying for its favoured interpretation in relations with other states."[148] Hence, in ascertaining the existence, i.e., validity of a customary international rule, the court is not bound by the arguments advanced by the parties to the dispute – "[r]ather, courts have a theory as to what customary international law is and how it is formed, which is brought to the bench regardless of what the parties say."[149]

Due to all this, even the staunch defenders of CIL are prone to admit that this formal source of international law is facing serious challenges. Probably the main one is "to at once retain its dynamism and its legitimacy."[150] Proponents of the "modern" version of customary rulemaking see it as an apt vehicle for the dynamic transformation of international law in accordance with some values and goals that hardly any actor on the international plane dares to confront. Take, again, the Kosovo case. Despite acknowledging that the NATO use of force was contrary to the UN Charter, and even to its own founding document, the 1949 North Atlantic Treaty, one of the authors who tries to legally justify this action simply states that "the legal case for intervening in Yugoslavia without Security Council approval *can be made* (M. J.) under customary international law." In doing so, he offers no evidence of state practice and *opinio juris*.[151] Asserting that something is customary rule merely in virtue of serving some universally endorsed values, such as humanitarian need and human rights protection, becomes, thus, "a convenient argumentative instrument," which serves as "an expedient tool to vindicate the progressive development of international law and its expansion in areas which are perceived insufficiently regulated by law."[152] Humanitarian intervention was

147 *Ibid*, 79.

148 Cohen, "Methodology and Misdirection: Custom and the ICJ," at www.ejiltalk.org/methodology-and-misdirection-a-response-to-stefan-talmon-on-custom-and-the-icj/

149 Sir Michael Wood, "Formation and Evidence of Customary International Law, Address to the International Law Commission, Geneva, 30. July 2012" (2013) 12 *The Law and Practice of International Courts and Tribunals* 2: 275.

150 David J. Bederman, *Custom as a Source of Law* (Cambridge: Cambridge University Press, 2010), 166.

151 He merely utters that the NATO use of force was "consistent with previous interventions in Somalia, Haiti, and Bosnia" without offering further arguments why this was so. Klinton, "NATO's Intervention in Kosovo: The Legal Case for Violating Yugoslavia's National Sovereignty in the Absence of Security Council Approval," 448.

152 d'Aspremont, "The Decay of Modern Customary International Law in Spite of Scholarly Heroism," 22.

largely perceived as one such area.[153] Customary rulemaking is, thus, often endorsed as an "alternative pedigree,"[154] whereas in many situations it is nothing but a "fake" argumentative construct. As pointed out by Teson,

> [T]he practitioner of fake custom tries to convince an audience who believes in custom as a source of international law that a rule is custom when in reality it is not. He really wants the rule to be law (he is a norm entrepreneur), and one of the ways to achieve that is to convince others that the rule is law. But fake customary rules are rules that are not law under any plausible theory of legitimate lawmaking. They are pieces of advocacy disguised as law. The speaker asserts them as law, but they are putative rules of law. That is, the speaker who asserts fake custom utters a false proposition of law.[155]

Let us keep in mind that due to its institutional specificities (lack of a centralized legislation, hierarchy of courts, and compulsory jurisdiction), international law, more than its municipal counterpart, can be adequately depicted as "an argumentative practice." That is, international law "is about persuading target audiences such as courts, colleagues, politicians and readers of legal texts about the legal correctness – lawfulness . . . of the position one defends." And the "[k]ey to persuasiveness is that the argument is recognizable as a good legal argument."[156] Having this in mind, Bederman rightly warns against dispensing with, or relaxing, either of the two constitutive elements of custom. To do so would be "a misguided attempt to increase CIL's dynamism and relevance (especially to pursue favored objectives, such as the promotion of human rights)," which would, in turn, "fatally undermine its legitimacy." Similarly, "to abandon customary international law's strong positivist intellectual roots in favor of a new naturalism (whether expressed in the idiom of the 'rationality' or 'humanity' of favored norms) would also be folly."[157]

153 As concluded in one of the studies in the once burgeoning literature on humanitarian intervention: "There are many aspects of international law that require reform, but humanitarian intervention is presented as uniquely important." Aidan Hehir, *Humanitarian Intervention – An Introduction* (New York: Palgrave Macmillan, 2010), 261.

154 "If a rule cannot be found in a treaty or ascertained by virtue of conventional law-identification mechanisms, customary international law will offer the best alternative pedigree – and thus foundation – for such rule." d'Aspremont, "The Decay of Modern Customary International Law in Spite of Scholarly Heroism," 22.

155 "Fake custom is hard to unmask. The speaker hopes that if enough people repeat the proposition 'X is custom,' X will become custom in the eyes of most people, even if it is not." Fernando R. Tesón, "Fake Custom," in Brian D. Lepard (ed.), *Reexamining Customary International Law* (Cambridge: Cambridge University Press, 2017), 87.

156 Martti Koskenniemi, "Methodology of International Law," in Wolfrum (ed.), *The Max Planck Encyclopedia of Public International Law*, par. 1.

157 David J. Bederman, *Custom as a Source of Law* (Cambridge: Cambridge University Press, 2010), 166.

In light of these findings, can the ILC's continuous work bring more clarity in this area? The ILC Drafting Committee's 2016 Draft conclusions on the identification of customary international law[158] seem to strengthen the traditional view of custom as a formal source of international law. First, the document reaffirms the two-element doctrine.[159] Second, it specifies that "it is primarily the practice of States that contributes to the formation, or expression, of rules of customary international law." (DC 4[1])[160] Third, it clarifies whose acts are attributable to the state. It states that the relevant practice "consists of conduct of the State, whether in the exercise of its executive, legislative, judicial or other functions." (DC 5) Furthermore, it specifies that forms of practice include "both physical and verbal acts," and that "[i]t may, under certain circumstances, include inaction." (DC 6[1])[161] Finally, it states that the state practice shall be "assessed as a whole" (DC 7[1]), and that the determinant criterion is not some "particular duration" (DC 8[2]), but the quality of practice – that it is "general," meaning "sufficiently widespread and representative, as well as consistent." (par. 1) Fourth, the ILC Draft conclusions specify *animus*, by stating that the practice must be "undertaken with a sense of legal right or obligation" (DC 9[1]), and that this is what differentiates custom from "mere usage or habit." (par. 2) As in the case of practice, evidence of *opinio juris* may take different forms. In case the state practice is evidenced in state's inaction, the requested *opinio juris* shall be determined on the basis of the fact that "States were in a position to react and the circumstances called for some reaction." (DC 10[3]) Finally, the ILC Draft conclusions aspire to clarify the significance of certain materials – treaties,[162] resolutions,[163] decisions of courts and tribunals,[164] and

158 International Law Commission, *Identification of customary international law*, A/CN.4/L.872

159 DC 3(2) specifies that "[e]ach of the two constituent elements is to be separately ascertained. This requires an assessment of evidence for each element."

160 DC 4 also states that, whereas in certain cases, the practice of international organizations may be taken into account (par. 2), conduct of other actors is not practice that contributes to the formation, or expression, of rules of CIL (par. 3).

161 Forms of State practice may vary (par. 2), but "no predetermined hierarchy" exists among them (par. 3).

162 A treaty rule may a) codify the pre-existing customary rule; b) contribute to the crystallization of an emerging customary rule; or c) give rise to a new rule of customary law. (DC 11[1])

163 A resolution adopted by an international organization or at an intergovernmental conference "cannot, of itself, create a rule of customary international law." (DC 12[1]) It may "provide evidence" of the existence of a customary rule of law, or it may "contribute to its development" (par. 2).

164 Decisions of courts and tribunals, and particularly of the ICJ, concerning the existence and content of CIL "are a subsidiary means for the determination of such rules." (DC 13[1]) Where "appropriate," decisions of national courts may serve as "a subsidiary means" for the

teachings[165] – for the identification of customary international law and they reaffirm the "persistent objector" doctrine[166] as well as the differentiation between general and "particular" CIL.[167]

Those who were already critical of the CIL's state of affairs will hardly be dissuaded by the ILC's work.[168] The Draft conclusions by no means settle all the intricate issues belonging to the "meta-law" on customary international law-making.[169] Nevertheless, the ILC's attempt to reinvigorate, after over sixty-five years, "ways and means for making the evidence of customary international law more readily available,"[170] in the form of a questionnaire, "may indeed prove useful" for a more reliable ascertainment of valid customary rules of international law.[171] It remains to be seen whether this will fully prevent international law-applying actors, most particularly courts, from resorting to the argumentative strategy of the ascertainment of customary rules despite the lack of evidence of the existence of either (or both) of the elements of custom.[172] Notwithstanding the fact that their decisions remain "subsidiary means for the determination" of

determination of CIL. (par. 2) For the analysis of the latter issue, *see*, International Law Commission, "The role of decisions of national courts in the case law of international courts and tribunals of a universal character for the purpose of the determination of customary international law" (2016) A/CN.4/691.

165 Teachings of the "most highly qualified" international scholars "may serve as a subsidiary means" for the determination of CIL. (DC 14)

166 "Where a State has objected to a rule of customary international law while that rule was in the process of formation, the rule is not opposable to the State concerned for so long as it maintains its objection." (DC 15[1]) The objection must be "clearly expressed, made known to other States, and maintained persistently." (par. 2)

167 A rule of particular CIL may be "regional, local, or other," and "it applies only among a limited number of States" (DC 16[1]).

168 Talmon, for instance, charges the ILC with creating "the idyllic world," which leaves "the impression that the determination of the existence and content of rules of customary international law is an exact science." Stefan Talmon, "Determining Customary International Law: The ICJ's Methodology and the Idyllic World of the ILC," *EJIL: Talk!*, December 3, 2015, at www.ejiltalk.org/determining-customary-international-law-the-icjs-methodology-and-the-idyllic-world-of-the-ilc/

169 Murphy, in particular, underlines problems regarding inaction as practice and/or evidence of acceptance as law, practice of international organizations, and the concept of "particular" custom. Sean D. Murphy, "Identification of Customary International Law and other Topics: The Sixty-Seventh Session of the International Law Commission" (2015) 109 *American Journal of International Law* 4: 826ff.

170 *See*, International Law Commission, "Ways and means for making the evidence of customary international law more readily available, Report of the International Law Commission" (1950) *Yearbook of the International Law Commission*, Vol. II: 366–374.

171 International Law Commission, *Fourth report on identification of customary international law by Michael Wood, Special Rapporteur* (2016) A/CN.4/695, par. 48.

172 Taking the ICJ's *Gabcikovo-Nagymaros* case (1999) as a paradigmatic illustration, Benvenisti argues that, since the "face-value application of the doctrine often fails to yield customary norms . . . in such circumstances the ICJ or other tribunals 'cheat' by inventing what they refer

CIL, especially the ICJ's ascertainment of something as a customary rule will undoubtedly put on it a more authoritative stamp of validity than in the case of assertions of other international actors.[173]

### c) *How to Ascertain a* Jus Cogens *Rule*

So far it has been shown that while sources of international law generally serve to delineate between valid norms and putative power-utterances, it is not always easy to ascertain instances of "behaviorally generated normativity,"[174] that is, the empirical existence of certain facts (practice + acceptance) that have the status of "law-creating facts,"[175] i.e., valid customary rules of international law. It is now to be examined whether the ascertainment of valid international legal norms additionally depends on the distinction between formal and substantive aspects of validity, which was in municipal law largely a corollary of the establishment of entrenched constitutional rules with the higher legal force.

Although the core of the traditional scholarship, by basing international law on the state's sovereign will, essentially draws its inspiration from private law,[176] there were always scholars, primarily within the jusnaturalist camp, who emphasized that this body of law cannot be composed solely of *jus dispositivum*.[177] Just as the natural law doctrine at the municipal level paved the way for the subsequent emergence of peremptory constitutional norms that put limits on the legislative power,[178] so the same doctrine at the

to as custom." He furthermore argues "why they are fully authorized and expected to do so." Eyal Benvenisti, "Customary International Law as a Judicial Tool for Promoting Efficiency," in Eyal Benvenisti and Moshe Hirsh (eds.), *The Impact of International Law on International Cooperation – Theoretical Perspectives* (Cambridge: Cambridge University Press, 2004), 87.

173 And this is so in spite of the fact that "[t]he decision of the Court has no binding force except between the parties and in respect of that particular case" (Art. 59 of the ICJ Statute).

174 d'Aspremont, "The Decay of Modern Customary International Law in Spite of Scholarly Heroism," 11.

175 Kelsen, *Principles of International Law*, 308.

176 *See*, Hersch Lauterpacht, *Private Law Sources and Analogies of International Law: With Special Reference to International Arbitration* (Hamden: Archon Books, 1927), 5. For a rather skeptical view, *see, e.g.*, Evangelos Raftopoulos, *The Inadequacy of the Contractual Analogy in the Law of Treaties* (Athens: Publications of the Hellenic Institute of International and Foreign Law, 1990).

177 Simply put, even private law "is still law," and as such it "carries an inescapable public element with it." Claudio Michelon, "The Public Nature of Private Law?," in Claudio Michelon et al. (eds.), *The Public in Law Representations of the Political in Legal Discourse* (Farnham: Ashgate, 2012), 195. The stamp of "publicness" of international rules is further given by the very name of "public international law."

178 It is, however, to be borne in mind that "peremptoriness" has a far broader scope at the municipal level, which stretches beyond constitution and strict hierarchy of norms. *See* in more detail in Robert Kolb, *Peremptory International Law – Jus Cogens: A General Inventory*

international level has professed for a long time the existence of peremptory norms that would limit the state's putative absolute power of the international treaty making.[179] The arguments of that sort may be found in the writings of the early international scholars,[180] but balder statements in that respect can be traced to the nineteenth-century literature. A notable example is Bluntschli's claim that, since the legal validity of the treaty law "is based on the legal consciousness of humanity ... [t]reaties whose contents violate the generally accepted human rights or the binding laws of international law are ... invalid."[181] According to him, "the recognized human rights" would be violated by treaties that introduce, spread, and protect slavery; strip foreigners of any rights; prevent free navigation on the open sea; and order persecution of persons on the basis of their faith.[182]

As already noted, the introduction of Article 20 in the League of Nations Covenant has prompted the argument that this constituted "the higher law" in the body of international legal rules.[183] More generally, Verdross claimed in the mid-1930s that there were two sorts of "*jus cogens* rules": the first consisted of different compulsory norms of CIL, whereas the second concerned the general prohibition of states from concluding treaties *contra bonos mores*.[184] Although this question was never considered settled among international

(London: Hart Publishing, 2015), 3ff. Whether international jus cogens is of the same type as its municipal counterpart "is essentially a matter of degree and depends also on the evolution of the concept of international *jus cogens*, which, compared with its municipal counterpart, is still in its infancy." *Ibid*, 5, fn. 13.

179 "Given that individual States appear in international law as law-makers, the concept of *jus cogens* resembles conceptually ... the constitutional limitations in terms of on what the law-makers can freely enact." Orakhelashvili, *Peremptory Norms in International Law*, 10. *Cf.* Antonio Cassese, "For an Enhanced Role of Jus Cogens," in Antonio Cassese (ed.), *Realizing Utopia – The Future of International Law* (Oxford: Oxford University Press, 2012), 159.

180 Frowein notes that "[a] great deal of the discussion between the early Spanish scholars centred around the question as to what kind of limits had to be respected by States under all circumstances." Similarly, one can find in the index of *De jure belli ac pacis* fifteen entries under *jus strictum*. Jochen Abraham Frowein, "Jus Cogens," in *Encyclopedia of Public International Law*, Vol. 7 (Amsterdam: Elsevier, 1984), 328.

181 Johann Caspar Bluntschli, *Das moderne Volkerrecht der civilisirten Staaten als Rechtsbuch dargestellt* (Nordlingen: Druck und Verlag der C.H. Beck'schen Buckhandlung, 1872), par. 410.

182 *Ibid*, par. 411.

183 "[W]hile the Covenant of the League is no more 'law-making' than any other treaty, the substance of its law differs so radically from other international conventions in its scope and significance as a purposeful instrument in the process of political integration of mankind as to deserve the designation of a 'higher law.'" Lauterpacht, "The Covenant as the Higher Law," 64–65.

184 Alfred von Verdross, "Forbidden Treaties in International Law" (1937) 31 *American Journal of International Law* 4: 572.

scholars,[185] the introduction of Article 103 in the UN Charter was deemed as further evidence that international law established the basic hierarchy of norms. And yet, international scholars only recently have started more courageously to employ constitutionalist rhetoric when referring to international law.[186] The emphasis is on "[t]he normative, as opposed to the institutional, dimension of international constitutionalism."[187] This dimension was fully highlighted with the stipulation of Articles 53 and 64 of the VCLT. Article 53 defines a *jus cogens* norm as "a norm accepted and recognized by the international community of States as a whole as a norm from which no derogation is permitted and which can be modified only by a subsequent norm of general international law having the same character." Article 64, on the other hand, specifies that "[i]f a new peremptory norm of general international law emerges, any existing treaty which is in conflict with that norm becomes void and terminates."

To the extent that the introduction of these provisions attracts an immediate comparison with the history of municipal law, in which the emergence of constitutional norms signified the entrenchment of a robust norm-hierarchy, one cannot escape the following analogy: The wording of Art. 53 reminds one of a norm introduced into a municipal law statute that says that there exists something called a "constitutional norm" from which no statutory norm can derogate. Surely, no lawyer would nowadays fail to notice the oddness of such a *contentless* "constitutional norm." No wonder, thus, that despite the general hype with which the hierarchization of international law was met, there are international lawyers who persist in emphasizing the same oddness of the jus cogens norm.[188]

D'Amato is one of them. He argues that any adequate theory of jus cogens has to answer the following three questions: (1) "What is the utility of a norm of *jus cogens*?" (call it "the utility question"); (2) "How does a purported norm of *jus cogens* arise?" (call it "the emergence question"); and (3) "Once one arises, how can international law change it or get rid of it?" (call it "the revision

185 Kelsen, *Principles of International Law*, 344. *Cf.* Alfred Verdross, "Jus Dispositivum and Jus Cogens in International Law" (1966) 60 *American Journal of International Law* 1: 55.

186 *See, e.g.*, Bardo Fassbender, *The United Nations Charter as the Constitution of the International Community* (Leiden: Martinus Nijhoff, 2009). For a general assessment, *see, e.g.*, Jan Klabbers, Anne Peters, and Geir Ulfstein, *The Constitutionalization of International Law* (Oxford: Oxford University Press, 2011).

187 That is, "hierarchically ordered norms, even without the backing of adequate institutional mechanisms, could fulfil constitutional functions." Andrea Bianchi, "Human Rights and the Magic of Jus Cogens" (2008) 19 *European Journal of International Law* 3: 494.

188 For a summary of various criticisms of jus cogens, *see*, Kolb, *Peremptory International Law – Jus Cogens: A General Inventory*, ch. 2.

question").[189] It appears that all three questions revolve around the problem of identification of a putative jus cogens norm. This is one of the common points of departure of many criticisms in the literature. Addressing the problem of identification of a peremptory norm, Shelton notes that "this is akin to watching the many differing visual representations of literary creations or simply reading a classic novel; each person brings a particular vision to the characters."[190] D'Amato argues that elusiveness surrounding this concept enables "any writer to christen any ordinary norm of his or her choice as a new *jus cogens* norm, thereby in one stroke investing it with magical power."[191] Bianchi, similarly, contends that international lawyers could be said to assume the role of "magicians," by "administering the rites of *jus cogens* and invoking its magical power." While "[a]cting under the different guise of scholars, counsel, international judges, and legal advisers," they "have succeeded in making *jus cogens* part and parcel of the fabric of the international law discourse."[192]

These criticisms seem to prioritize "the emergence question," by asking whether there exists some objectively verifiable way for a jus cogens norm to arise. If no such way exists, as D'Amato obviously believes, then "the utility question" is solved as well – jus cogens is merely an "exclamation point" that has no value other than "rhetorical."[193] Finally, if no solution to "the emergence question" is available, "the revision question" also cannot be addressed properly. Without knowing the way for the emergence of one such norm, we are hopeless in detecting a matching procedure of its modification.

Let us start from "the emergence question." Part of it has to do with the valid source of international law from which one such norm of "general international law" may arise. International scholars are not in unison in addressing this problem. While Besson rather broadly states that a jus cogens norm "may be found in various sources of international law,"[194] Cassese is specific in saying that such a general rule may be created only by custom.[195] However, it seems possible that such a norm emerges either through "customary international law or through adherence to treaties containing them

189 Anthony D'Amato, "It's a Bird, It's a Plane, It's a Jus Cogens!" (1990) 6 *Connecticut Journal of International Law* 1: 6.
190 Dinah Shelton, "Sherlock Holmes and the Mystery of Jus Cogens" (2015) 46 *Netherlands Yearbook of International Law*: 24.
191 D'Amato, "It's a Bird, It's a Plane, It's a Jus Cogens!," 2.
192 Bianchi, "Human Rights and the Magic of *Jus Cogens*," 494.
193 D'Amato, "It's a Bird, It's a Plane, It's a Jus Cogens!," 6.
194 Besson, "Theorizing the Sources of International Law," 171.
195 Cassese, *International Law*, 199.

by all states,"[196] despite the fact that the latter form of emergence is less feasible.[197]

If custom is the most common way for a jus cogens norm of international law to emerge,[198] then all the problems connected to the identification of CIL apply here as well. Except that these problems are here also coupled with the additional implication stemming from the process of identification – that of ascribing to one such norm the status of a hierarchically highest international legal norm. Now, one may note that the wording of Art. 53 implies a somewhat different process for the emergence of a jus cogens norm than the one required by the traditional two-element process of CIL. Namely, Art. 53 speaks of a norm being "accepted and recognized by the international community of States as a whole." This still need not be an insurmountable obstacle if the earlier-created norm of CIL is subsequently vested with the legal quality of peremptoriness.[199] Nevertheless, the question then arises as to what is "the international community of States as a whole" and what it means for such a community to "accept" and "recognize" one norm as a jus cogens norm. Cassese offers a ready-made solution:

> As for the method by which to ascertain the birth of a peremptory norm, it may suffice for the majority of members of the world community to evince

196 Shelton, "Sherlock Holmes and the Mystery of Jus Cogens," 24. *Cf.* Kolb, *Peremptory International Law – Jus Cogens: A General Inventory*, 9.

197 And yet, there are multilateral treaties that are ratified by all states. Tomuschat refers, in that respect, to Article 6 (1), second clause, of Geneva Convention III on the Treatment of Prisoners of War, by which "the contracting States themselves have committed themselves to never proceeding to lower the level of protection," as an example of a jus cogens norm whose source is an international treaty. (Tomuschat, "Reconceptualizing the Debate on *Jus Cogens* and Obligations *Erga Omnes* – Concluding Observations," 427) For Shelton, however, the example of humanitarian law conventions, as well as of some other major treaties, such as the UN Charter, or some environmental treaties, testifies to the fact that the real problem is "one of ensuring compliance by states with obligations they have freely accepted, and not one of imposing obligations on dissenting states." Shelton, "Sherlock Holmes and the Mystery of Jus Cogens," 47.

198 Orakhelashvili, *Peremptory Norms in International Law*, 113.

199 In the *Questions relating to the Obligation to Prosecute or Extradite*, the ICJ seems to indicate this chronological order, by stating that "the prohibition of torture is part of customary international law and *it has become* a peremptory norm (*jus cogens*)." (emphasis mine) The Court, then, notices that the said "prohibition is grounded in a widespread international practice and on the *opinio juris* of States." (*Questions relating to the Obligation to Prosecute or Extradite [Belgium* v *Senegal]*, ICJ, Judgment of 20 July 2012, par. 99) This last ICJ formulation leaves us, however, with doubt as to whether it merely reiterates the two-element basis of all customary rules, including the one on the prohibition of torture, or, as argued by Shelton, grounds the emergence of this particular jus cogens norm in the same two customary elements – state practice and *opinio juris*. Shelton, "Sherlock Holmes and the Mystery of Jus Cogens," 34.

> their "acceptance" of a customary rule as having the rank of a peremptory norm. Such "acceptance" does not necessarily involve actual conduct, or a positive assertion; it may involve an express or tacit manifestation of will, which can take various forms. No consistent practice of states and other international legal subjects *(usus)* is necessary.[200]

It is surely tempting to circumvent the literal meaning of the phrase "the international community of States *as a whole*" by seeking the support of "the majority of members of the world community." Similarly, it seems pragmatic to ask for a "tacit manifestation of will," not necessarily grounded in a consistent state practice, as a sign of "acceptance and recognition." After all, sticking to the literal meaning of Art. 53 may lead to a somewhat paradoxical implication – the emergence of a jus cogens norm, whose purported function is to put limits on the state's sovereign will as the source of international law-making, would eventually depend on the robustly expressed will of those very states, and all of them. The question is, nonetheless, whether Cassese's interpretation of the key formulations of Art. 53 is justified.[201]

"The emergence question" becomes even more complicated to address if the newly *emerging*[202] customary rule is one that is conceived to be of a peremptory nature. Notwithstanding the plausibility of this scenario in practice,[203] Art. 53 principally allows for one such development.[204] This, then, opens a series of intricate issues. First, such an emerging peremptory norm would obviously have to pass the two-element test envisaged for

200 Cassese, "For an Enhanced Role of *Jus Cogens*," 158.

201 Cassese argues that "[i]t can be inferred from authoritative statements of some of the protagonists of the Vienna Conference that what is required is the acceptance by the majority of states provided that such majority includes states which are representative of the various political and geographic areas of the world." *Ibid*, 165.

202 I will return to the question of "emerging" norms in the section on relative normativity.

203 In the *Nicaragua* case, the ICJ does not employ this temporal dimension but, interestingly enough, it refers to the peremptoriness of the prohibition on the use of force as additional evidence that the rule belongs to CIL. "A further confirmation of the validity as customary international law of the principle of the prohibition of the use of force . . . may be found in the fact that it is frequently referred to in statements by State representatives as being not only a principle of customary international law but also a fundamental or cardinal principle of such law," i.e., jus cogens. (*Military and Paramilitary Activities in and against Nicaragua, Merits*, p. 100, par. 190). *Cf.* Orakhelashvili, *Peremptory Norms in International Law*, 42, fn. 38.

204 Cassese seems to reject this possibility when noting that "[t]he task of the body charged with inquiring into *jus cogens* would only consist of establishing whether, *in addition* (M. J.) to being a customary rule or principle, the norm at issue has also been endowed with the higher rank of a peremptory norm." He nonetheless adds that "in practice the two logically distinct phases of investigation may tend to merge." Cassese, "For an Enhanced Role of *Jus Cogens*," 164.

CIL. Second, provided that Cassese's aforementioned reading is warranted,[205] this would imply that there are two separate tracks for the emergence of a jus cogens norm, depending on whether its customary character and peremptoriness are acquired simultaneously or successively. Not only does the VCLT not envisage such a distinction, but it would be highly detrimental to the much needed unity of the international legal order, one of whose most potent facilitators is exactly the concept of peremptory norms.[206] Finally, if in the process of emergence such a rule is challenged by a persistent objector,[207] then this objection would seem to have the additional legal effect of vetoing the putative peremptoriness of the given rule.[208] Such an implication would, however, be at odds with the very *raison d'être* of jus cogens norms[209] – "the very idea of non-derogability of peremptory norms implies a superior limit of

205 This is, however, far from certain. Take the French rebuttal in the "white paper," issued in the course of the *Nuclear Tests* case, regarding an alleged jus cogens prohibition of atmospheric testing (interestingly enough, neither New Zealand, nor Australia had raised that point before the ICJ). Referring to the qualification from Art. 53, the French government noted that "at least two countries have already expressed an opposite view: France . . . and China. Now, these two countries, which represent many more than 800 million people, i.e. a substantial proportion of the world population, are two of the five permanent members of the Security Council." According to Ragazzi, this "is further evidence of the variety and controversial nature of any attempts to define the requirement of recognition and acceptance of a norm of *jus cogens* by the international community of States as a whole." Maurizio Ragazzi, *The Concept of International Obligations Erga Omnes* (Oxford: Clarendon Press, 1997), 208.

206 "*Jus cogens* is a legal technique which protects against fragmentation of the law into a plurality of separately applicable legal regimes under the guise of private autonomy." Kolb, *Peremptory International Law – Jus Cogens: A General Inventory*, 3. By centering upon "non-derogability," this author departs from the idea that jus cogens is "a sort of new constitutional legal order of the international community." *Ibid*, 8.

207 As noted by Green, there is broad agreement, strengthened now by the ILC Draft conclusions on CIL, that for the persistent objector rule "to take effect the objector must *object, persistently* and *consistently*, to an *emerging* norm of custom *before that norm crystallizes* into binding customary international law." James A. Green, *The Persistent Objector Rule in International Law* (Oxford: Oxford University Press, 2016), 276.

208 Although most commentators reject the effect of the persistent objector rule in the case of jus cogens norms, Linderfalk shows that there are no principle reasons for such a stance if "the emergence question" is to be solved on the positivistic grounds, by relying on formal aspects of the norm creation. Ulf Linderfalk, "Understanding the Jus Cogens Debate: The Pervasive Influence of Legal Positivism and Legal Idealism" (2015) 46 *Netherlands Yearbook of International Law*: 63.

209 This is pointed out by Roberto Ago, who presided over the Vienna Conference on the Law of Treaties. He asks what is meant by the phrase "international community as a whole": "Did we mean all members of the international community? Obviously not, or we would end up giving a right of veto to a single State." Roberto Ago, "The Concept of 'International Community as a Whole': A Guarantee to the Notion of State Crimes," in Joseph H. H. Weiler, Antonio Cassese, and Marina Spinedi (eds.), *International Crimes of State – A Critical Analysis of the ILC's Draft Article 19 on State Responsibility* (Berlin: Walter de Gruyter, 1989), 252–253.

permissibility of the exercise of State will in disposing the interests protected by peremptory norms."[210]

Formal aspects, thus, seem to be unable to furnish reliable grounds for addressing "the emergence question." After all, while drafting what became Art. 53, the ILC clearly stated that "[i]t is not the form of a general rule of international law but the particular nature of the subject-matter with which it deals that may . . . give it the character of *jus cogens*."[211] While this reprimand leads us toward substantive aspects, Orakhelashvili rightly points out that "[t]he two aspects are interdependent and mutually supportive." That is, "[f]ormal characteristics depend on material elements, for there must be a clear reason why that norm is non-derogable."[212] This takes the discussion back to "the utility question" and to the putative constitutionalist function of jus cogens rules. Just as certain rules, by virtue of their content – those concerning fundamental rights and governmental structure[213] – were at some point in history given specific constitutional form, which made them hierarchically the highest norms in municipal law, so, according to this line of reasoning, some rules of international law deserve to be endowed with the quality of peremptoriness. Constitutional content, in that respect, preceded its form. In comparison to statutory norms, the revision of constitutional norms – as an element of their formal aspect – was made more difficult precisely because the content of the aforementioned norms was deemed as being of special relevance for the given political community. This may sound conspicuously like natural-law reasoning. But the truth is that legal positivism has nothing to say about *materiae constitutionis*. The substantive aspect of the concept of constitution was historically shaped by political forces that were heavily infused with the natural-law ideas about social contract, limited government, and inalienable rights of individuals.[214] The core of

210 Orakhelashvili, *Peremptory Norms in International Law*, 44.

211 (1966) *Yearbook of the International Law Commission*, Vol. II (UN Doc A/CN.4/SER.A/1966/Add. 1), at 248, par. 2.

212 Orakhelashvili, *Peremptory Norms in International Law*, 44.

213 According to Squires, the concept of constitutionalism comprises two elements: rights provisions (safeguarding various rights and liberties) and structural provisions (installing the representative system, separation of powers, federal or unitary form of state, etc.). Judith Squires, "Liberal Constitutionalism, Identity and Difference" (1996) 44 *Political Studies* 3: 621.

214 As noticeable from the drafting of the very first modern written constitution, that of Massachusetts, "[t]he notion that unalienable natural rights are somehow basic to human nature, as well as being very desirable, is reflected in the first article of the Declaration of Rights of the Constitution of 1780." This article states as follows: "All men are born free and equal, and have certain natural, essential, and unalienable rights; among which may be reckoned the right of enjoying and defending their lives and liberties; that of acquiring,

constitutional substance has stabilized throughout the subsequent rise of constitutionalism in virtually all parts of the world.[215]

Now, the question is whether something akin is traceable at the international level. Specificity of that issue at the international level stems from the fact that the actors, whose seemingly absolute power of law creation has to be limited, are at the same time the ones who must "accept and recognize" some norms as non-derogable. This apparent paradox is captured in Orakhelashvili's remark that the subject matter of jus cogens "must be something independent of the will of States."[216] This creates a principal problem for the employment of the contractualist argument in the international sphere, despite the fact that "social contract theory [is] particularly suitable for structuring an analysis of *jus cogens* in international law."[217] No wonder then that the critical push came not from states, but from international scholars working in the natural-law tradition who have been continuously advocating for the introduction of a constitutionalist element in international law. The urge for such a development also has been voiced in international legal practice.[218] For

possessing, and protecting property; in fine, that of seeking and obtaining their safety and happiness." (Ronald M. Peters, *The Massachusetts Constitution of 1780: A Social Compact* [Amherst: University of Massachusetts Press, 1978], 77–78) In contrast, one of the founding fathers of modern legal positivism, Bentham, considered the concept of "natural rights" as "nonsense upon stilts." (Bentham, "Anarchical Fallacie," 501) Similarly, one of the leading legal positivists of the present, Raz, questions the "special status" of constitutional rights, that is, "their constitutional entrenchment which makes them superior to ordinary legislation." What makes them special, according to him, is that they are put under the court's, instead of the legislature's, authority. (Joseph Raz, "Rights and Politics" (1995) 71 *Indiana Law Journal* 1: 41, 42) Raz also rejects "foundationalist" doctrines of human rights, and instead fosters "a political conception of human rights." *See*, Joseph Raz, "Human Rights Without Foundations," in Besson and Tasioulas (eds.), *The Philosophy of International Law*, 321–337. Joseph Raz, "Human Rights in the Emerging World Order" (2010) 1 *Transnational Legal Theory* 1: 31–47.

215 *See*, Bruce Ackerman, "The Rise of World Constitutionalism" (1997) 83 *Virginia Law Review* 4: 771–797.

216 Orakhelashvili, *Peremptory Norms in International Law*, 44.

217 Thomas Weatherall, *Jus Cogens – International Law and Social Contract* (Cambridge: Cambridge University Press, 2015), 14. "A contractarian understanding of the international community begins with its organization in terms of the higher interests common to its members … The higher interests of a community articulated through the social contract reflect those particular values and interests deemed necessary for a community to establish peaceful, social coexistence. The doctrine of *jus cogens* invites just such a conceptualization as a category of norms necessary to the social coexistence of the international community." (*Ibid*, 100) Somewhat similar is a public order approach, in which "public order" is understood "as a restriction upon acts which are thought to be harmful to the community." Orakhelashvili, *Peremptory Norms in International Law*, 46.

218 "Irrespective of the difficulty of finding a general vocabulary that would express the role of the sense of importance of particular norms, the practice of international law has always recognized the presence of some norms that are superior to other norms and must therefore be

example, just before the adoption of the VCLT, Judge Tanaka, in his dissenting opinion in the *South Africa* case, stated: "If we can introduce in the international field a category of law, namely *jus cogens* . . . a kind of imperative law which constitutes the contrast to *jus dispositivum* ... surely the law concerning the protection of human rights may be considered to belong to the *jus cogens*."[219] If such "higher law" was to be introduced, not only would it outlaw those practices that were once considered a legitimate part of international law-making,[220] but, analogously to constitutional provisions, it would be alterable only by rules of the same legal quality.

Having all this in mind, René-Jean Dupuy, the Holy See representative at the Vienna conference, noted that the eventual entrenchment of norms of hierarchy in the VCLT enabled "progressive integration of natural into positive law."[221] However, unlike the drafters of initial political declarations of human rights who operated with seemingly exhaustive lists of fundamental rights that were meant to limit the use of governmental power, the ILC drafters did not dare to include some such list of jus cogens norms in the VCLT.[222] Its

given effect." International Law Commission, *Fragmentation of International Law: Difficulties arising from the Diversification and Expansion of International Law*, par. 326.

219 Judge Tanaka, Dissenting Opinion (*Ethiopia* v. *South Africa; Liberia* v. *South Africa*), Second Phase, Judgment [1966] ICJ Rep, 298.

220 Taking the prohibition of slavery as one such undisputable example of plausible jus cogens norm, one has to bear in mind that "[s]lavery took a particularly pernicious form in the Atlantic world between the sixteenth and nineteenth centuries ... International law was surprisingly central to this enterprise. At the beginning of this period, international law was used to justify the slave trade." (Jenny S. Martinez, *The Slave Trade and the Origins of International Human Rights Law* [Oxford: Oxford University Press, 2012], 16) D'Amato mocks the utility of jus cogens, by explaining how it supposedly functions: "[W]hen a putative treaty provision becomes so senseless that it is unimaginable that states would actually include it in a treaty . . . [e.g.] an agreement to exchange slaves . . . then *jus cogens* theory snaps into action to make sure that such senselessness, should it occur, would have no legal effect." (D'Amato, "It's a Bird, It's a Plane, It's a Jus Cogens!," 4) However, as the practice of the slave trade aptly demonstrates, what is "unimaginable" in the eyes of the contemporary "international community of States as a whole" not only once was, but still nowadays in someone's head might be considered morally acceptable.

221 This was his remark at the meeting of the Committee of the Whole on April 30, 1968. UN Conference on the Law of Treaties, First Session Vienna, 26 Mar. – 24 May 1968, Official Records, Summary records of the plenary meetings of the Committee of the Whole, at 258, par. 74.

222 The ILC declined to do so for two reasons: "First, the mention of some cases of treaties void for conflict with a rule of *jus cogens* might, even with the most careful drafting, lead to misunderstanding as to the position concerning other cases not mentioned in the article. Secondly, if the Commission were to attempt to draw up, even on a selective basis, a list of the rules of international law which are to be regarded as having the character of *jus cogens*, it might find itself engaged in a prolonged study of matters which fall outside the scope of the present articles." (1966) *Yearbook of the International Law Commission*, Vol. II, at 248, par. 3.

absence, nonetheless, does not mean either that a norm's peremptory character cannot be clarified on an individual basis,[223] or that there exist no prima facie examples of such norms in international law. In the drafting process, for instance, the ILC referred to the following examples of jus cogens norms: prohibitions of unlawful use of force, genocide, piracy, slavery, and crimes against humanity; and the right of self-determination.[224] Despite the fact that the major criticism of the jus cogens concept underlines the lack of a wide consensus when it comes to the identification of all plausible candidates for the quality of non-derogability,[225] this is not its biggest deficit. After almost fifty years of existence in the world community, none of the aspects of its peremptoriness[226] has been so far triggered, "namely: (i) to bring about the nullity of a treaty contrary to a peremptory norm, or at a minimum (ii) to be relied upon in legal disagreements between states as one of the major issues in dispute, or (iii) to be used by an international judicial body as the *ratio decidendi* of one of its judgments."[227] This means that, notwithstanding the fact that legal practice "has breathed new life" into the concept,[228] "the utility question" – understood as the constitutionalist function of jus cogens – has yet to be fully realized.[229]

### d) *How to Ascertain an* Erga Omnes *Obligation*

The preceding analysis largely applies to the concept of *erga omnes* obligations as well. As is well known, its life in international law is owed to *obiter dicta* of

223 Orakhelashvili, *Peremptory Norms in International Law*, 43.

224 (1966) *Yearbook of the International Law Commission*, Vol. II, 248, par. 3. The ILC's Fragmentation report also includes the prohibition of racial discrimination and apartheid and the prohibition of the violation of the basic rules of international humanitarian law. (International Law Commission, *Fragmentation of International Law: Difficulties arising from the Diversification and Expansion of International Law*, par. 374) In the Draft Articles on State Responsibility, the ILC introduces in addition the prohibition against torture. International Law Commission, *Draft Articles on Responsibility of States for Internationally Wrongful Acts*, p. 113, par. 5.

225 As pointed out by Linderfalk, "[w]hen international lawyers move beyond exemplification and try to make the list of *ius cogens* complete, their various compilations of norms come out as widely disparate ... in the end, very little agreement exists" with respect to the content of the substantive, "first order rules of *ius cogens.*" Ulf Linderfalk, "Normative Conflict and the Fuzziness of the International ius cogens Regime" (2009) 69 *Zeitschrift für ausländisches öffentliches Recht und Völkerrecht*: 963–964.

226 This is what Linderfalk labels as "the second order rules of *jus cogens*" regime and they pertain to situations of "normative conflicts." *Ibid*, 964–965.

227 Cassese, "For an Enhanced Role of *Jus Cogens*," 159.

228 *Ibid*, 160–162.

229 *Ibid*, 170–171.

the ICJ's *Barcelona Traction* case, in which the Court made the distinction between "absolute" and "unqualified" state obligations "towards the international community as a whole, and those arising vis-à-vis another State in the field of diplomatic protection." Since "the former are the concern of all States ... all States can be held to have a legal interest in their protection; they are obligations *erga omnes*."[230] By way of exemplification, the Court referred to some such already existing international legal obligations, stemming "from the outlawing of acts of aggression, and of genocide, as also from the principles and rules concerning the basic rights of the human person, including protection from slavery and racial discrimination."[231]

It is notable that all the mentioned obligations derive from norms of jus cogens,[232] which inevitably calls for the analysis of the relationship between the two concepts. In doing so, it is advisable to follow Tomuschat in breaking down this analysis into two phases. Whereas in the initial phase, "the task is to identify the relevant rules of conduct to which some higher legal rank – whatever that may be – is ascribed," in the subsequent phase, it is necessary "to spell out which special legal consequences ensue from any breach of such 'superior' principles and rules."[233] International scholars largely acknowledge the difference stemming from the second stage of investigation. Hence, Kadelbach contends that while the effect of jus cogens norms "is to make conflicting treaties void," *erga omnes* obligations "have been considered so far, by and large, as a concept of State responsibility." That is, the latter "impose special duties on the offending State which may go beyond the bilateral reparation scheme which applies in reciprocal legal relationships."[234] However, no agreement exists with respect to the hierarchical status of *erga*

230 *Barcelona Traction*, ICJ Reports 1970, p. 32, par. 33. In its subsequent jurisprudence the Court has affirmed the concept of *erga omnes* obligations, although it has been cautious in applying it. *Cf. e.g.*, *East Timor*, ICJ Reports 1995, p. 102, par. 29; *Crimes of Genocide*, ICJ Reports 1996, p. 616, par. 31.

231 *Barcelona Traction*, p. 32, par. 34.

232 This applies equally to the right to self-determination, which, according to the ICJ's finding in the *East Timor* case, also creates *erga omnes* obligations. *East Timor (Portugal* v. *Australia)*, Judgment, I.C.J. Reports 1995, p. 102, par. 29.

233 Tomuschat, "Reconceptualizing the Debate on *Jus Cogens* and Obligations *Erga Omnes* – Concluding Observations," 428–429.

234 One of the elements of *erga omnes* obligations "is the right of States not directly affected by an internationally wrongful act to invoke the responsibility of the violator, be it on their own behalf, on behalf of subjects of international law who are not in a position to bring a claim themselves, or simply as members of the international community of States." Stefan Kadelbach, "Jus Cogens, Obligations Erga Omnes and other Rules – The Identification of Fundamental Norms," in Tomuschat and Thouvenin (eds.), *The Fundamental rules of the International Legal Order – Jus Cogens and Obligations Erga Omnes*, 26. *See* Art. 48(1) *Draft Articles on Responsibility of States for Internationally Wrongful Acts.*

*omnes* obligations. While Tomuschat and Kadelbach put them in the same basket with jus cogens rules and treat them respectively as "superior"[235] and "fundamental"[236] rules of international law, the ILC's *Fragmentation* report explicitly states that "[t]he *erga omnes* nature of an obligation . . . indicates no clear superiority of that obligation over other obligations."[237]

When it comes to the central task of the first phase, ascertaining valid international obligations endowed with the special quality of being *erga omnes* is the task that once again brings to the fore the distinction between formal and substantive elements. Unlike the category of jus cogens norms, whose legal status was determined in the VCLT,[238] the emergence of *erga omnes* obligations was linked to neither of the two main sources of international law. It was introduced by the ICJ, but not even in the *ratio decidendi* part of the decision, which caused immediate concerns of some international scholars. One of the ILC's prominent members, McCaffrey, belongs to the camp of skeptics. Addressing possible formal grounds for the existence of distinctive *erga omnes* international obligations, he says that the *Barcelona Traction* case "can hardly be taken as authority" for that purposes. True, the Court did introduce this concept, "but it uttered [it] in what you might call a quintessential dictum in the context of a case whose facts and legal issues hardly required such a pronouncement." And, yet, "this gratuitous statement has opened a door which has since proved impossible to close." McCaffrey, thus, concludes reluctantly that the category of *erga omnes* obligations "is something with which we must deal."[239]

Ragazzi's analysis of the four examples of *erga omnes* obligations mentioned by the ICJ reveals that they share five common elements: 1) they refer to "narrowly defined obligations"; 2) they are all negative obligations, i.e., prohibitions; 3) put in Hohfeldian terms,[240] they are all strict obligations, i.e.,

[235] Tomuschat, "Reconceptualizing the Debate on *Jus Cogens* and Obligations *Erga Omnes* – Concluding Observations," 429.

[236] Kadelbach, "*Jus Cogens*, Obligations *Erga Omnes* and other Rules – The Identification of Fundamental Norms," 26.

[237] This is so because unlike the norms of jus cogens, which "are distinguished by their normative power – their ability to override a conflicting norm – obligations *erga omnes* designate the scope of application of the relevant law, and the procedural consequences that follow from this." International Law Commission, *Fragmentation of International Law: Difficulties arising from the Diversification and Expansion of International Law*, par. 380.

[238] Some international scholars argue that ever since, it has become customary international law. *See, e.g.*, Cassese, "For an Enhanced Role of *Jus Cogens*," 169.

[239] Stephen McCaffrey, "Lex Lata or the Continuum of State Responsibility," in Weiler, Cassese, and Spinedi (eds.), *International Crimes of State – A Critical Analysis of the ILC's Draft Article 19 on State Responsibility*, 242.

[240] Wesley Newcomb Hohfeld, *Fundamental Legal Conceptions as Applied in Judicial Reasoning and Other Legal Essays* (New Haven: Yale University Press, 1919).

duties; 4) they all stem from jus cogens norms; and 5) they are all "instrumental to the main political objectives of the present time, namely the preservation of peace and the promotion of fundamental human rights."[241] These five common features are, however, "merely descriptive." That is, they cannot "be regarded as prescriptive criteria that an international obligation must satisfy to be an obligation *erga omnes*," although they may provide "a useful framework" for the analysis of some prospective candidates for such international legal status.[242]

All of this pushes the process of the ascertainment of *erga omnes* obligations toward the fifth element, which is substantive in nature.[243] Hence, Ragazzi himself acknowledges that the starting point for the first phase of analysis is to find "the rationale for the universal opposability of obligations *erga omnes*." It is ultimately to be found "in the recognition of the universal validity of the basic moral values that these obligations are meant to protect."[244] More specifically, the identification should be taken along the lines of the ICJ's qualifications of *erga omnes* obligations as "absolute," "unqualified," and the "the concern of all States." Yet again, no compiled inventory of existing or emerging *erga omnes* obligations is available,[245] which leave us, just as in the case of jus cogens rules, with a general reprimand that, since those obligations "reflect basic moral values," they have to be "identified rigorously."[246]

If international legal practice has endorsed and recognized the existence of a class of international legal norms endowed with the quality of

241 Ragazzi, *The Concept of International Obligations Erga Omnes*, 132–134.

242 *Ibid*, 134.

243 The ILC's *Fragmentation* report concludes in a similar vein that "the source of a norm cannot be said to be decisive on whether that norm does give rise to obligations *erga omnes* or not. It is rather the character of primary [substantive, M. J.] norms which determines the nature of secondary rules [legal effects, M. J.]." International Law Commission, *Fragmentation of International Law: Difficulties arising from the Diversification and Expansion of International Law*, par. 402.

244 Ragazzi, *The Concept of International Obligations Erga Omnes*, 183.

245 In the comment to Art. 48(1b) of *Draft Articles on Responsibility of States for Internationally Wrongful Acts*, which concerns invocation of responsibility by a State other than an injured State in the case of *erga omnes* obligations, the ILC states that it is not "the function of the articles to provide a list of those obligations which under existing international law are owed to the international community as a whole. This would go well beyond the task of codifying the secondary rules of State responsibility, and in any event, such a list would be only of limited value, as the scope of the concept will necessarily evolve over time." International Law Commission, *Draft Articles on Responsibility of States for Internationally Wrongful Acts*, p. 127, par. 9.

246 Ragazzi, *The Concept of International Obligations Erga Omnes*, 188. Bederman also warns that "any attempts to expand the scope of the *jus cogens* and *erga omnes* doctrines must be restrained." Bederman, *Custom as a Source of Law*, 166.

peremptoriness, as well as of international legal obligations that are *erga omnes* in nature, and yet remained somewhat undecided with respect to the precise content of such norms/obligations, the crucial issue is who shall have the ultimate authority to ascertain this content.[247] Cassese is, in that respect, without any doubts. In the discussion of the "who" question with respect to jus cogens norms, which *mutatis mutandis* applies to *erga omnes* obligations, he says:

> I submit that the task of authoritatively determining whether a peremptory norm exists cannot be entrusted to either the UN General Assembly or to any other political body. Nor can pronouncements of individual states or by other members of the international society be tantamount to more than expressions of legal views by such international subjects, expressions which of course may have powerful weight for any international organ pronouncing on the issue. To make such an authoritative determination requires being endowed with judicial powers. It is therefore chiefly for international judicial courts and tribunals to make such a finding. Both inter-state and international criminal courts are empowered to undertake this task.[248]

Whether the court's ascertainment of the specific content of jus cogens rules and *erga omnes* obligations will be authoritative enough for other international legal actors "depends on how persuasively they make their findings." In this case, "as in any other matter, the cogency of the court's reasoning has a decisive bearing on its likelihood to be taken up by other courts and tribunals."[249] Notwithstanding the fact that in the absence of international institutional hierarchy the proposed solution may potentially be harmful for the unity of international legal order,[250] it reaffirms the previously made general point that it is ultimately upon law-applying institutions to determine whether some content-specific rule passes the threshold criteria of the given order so as to count as a valid, i.e., applicable legal rule.

247 This problem also occurred during *travaux préparatoires* of Article 20 of the League of Nations Covenant. Lauterpacht points out that the major question "which weighed on the minds of the draftsmen" when they introduced the hierarchy of international legal norms "seems to have been who will decide as to the alleged inconsistency" between lower and higher norms. Lauterpacht, "The Covenant as the Higher Law," 55.

248 Cassese, "For an Enhanced Role of *Jus Cogens*," 164.

249 *Ibid.*

250 Maarten den Heijer and Harmen van der Wilt, "Jus Cogens and the Humanization and Fragmentation of International Law" (2015) 46 *Netherlands Yearbook of International Law*: 18.

### e) *How to Ascertain Invalidity of an International Legal Norm Based on Its Inefficacy* (Desuetudo)

As already pointed out in the general discussion regarding "validity" and "efficacy," the former quality of a single legal norm may be lost due to the absence of the latter. More precisely, "[i]f the norm remains permanently inefficacious, the norm is deprived of its validity by '*desuetudo*.'" In that respect, "[*d*]*esuetudo* is the negative legal effect of custom."[251] Having in mind Kelsen's insistence on the sanctioning rule as the "primary" element of the norm-structure, it was concluded that officials' rule-efficacy perspective is decisive for ascertaining *desuetudo*. This is so despite the fact that inefficacy from the officials' rule-efficacy perspective normally comes up as a corollary of the preceding inefficacy from the agents' rule-efficacy perspective.

Despite generally being recognized by theorists, "the scholarly literature of international law presents no comprehensive theory of desuetude."[252] Still, the concept is commonly defined "as the rejection of a rule through subsequent non-enforcement *or* (M. J.) non-compliance."[253] The definition's employment of alternative forms of *desuetudo* seems to suggest that the required level of a rule's inefficacy may be assessed either from the officials' (non-enforcement) or from the agents' (non-compliance) perspective. That this is indeed so becomes obvious when one takes into account that these two perspectives in international law are intricately connected, because the state is not just the subject of international law, but it is also its *agency*, its *official*, "so far as the administration and enforcement of IL is concerned."[254] The other important distinctiveness of international law is that the major source of legal rights and duties is treaty, whereby actors, instead of being subjected to the imposed will of a legislator, autonomously and consensually regulate their mutual relations. For this very reason, *desuetudo* in international law is often assessed from the actors' rule-efficacy perspective.

Since *desuetudo* may be a principal ground for the invalidity of norms stemming from different sources of international law,[255] the question emerges

[251] Kelsen, *General Theory of Law and State*, 119.

[252] Michael J. Glennon, "How International Rules Die" (2005) 93 *Georgetown Law Journal* 3: 939.

[253] Jan Wouters and Sten Verhoeven, "Desuetudo," in Wolfrum (ed.), *The Max Planck Encyclopedia of Public International Law*, par. 1.

[254] Jeremy Waldron, "Are Sovereigns Entitled to the Benefit of the International Rule of Law?" (2011) 22 *European Journal of International Law* 2: 330.

[255] Wouters and Verhoeven, "Desuetudo," par. 1. Nevertheless, these authors emphasize that "[i]t is doubtful whether desuetudo will ever constitute the legal ground for terminating a unilateral act." *Ibid*, par. 16.

as to what it means for a norm to be inefficacious. When it comes to the international law of treaties,[256] it is, first, important to bear in mind that the VCLT does not recognize *desuetudo* as a valid legal ground for the termination of treaties.[257] While it was in the drafting process envisaged as one such possible ground,[258] the Special Rapporteur, Gerald Fitzmaurice, eventually took the position that there was no "objective principle of law terminative of treaties on the mere ground of age, obsolescence, or desuetude as such." Insofar as the treaty is based on the consent of contracting parties, the Rapporteur noted that "by failing to apply or invoke it, or by other conduct evincing lack of interest in or reliance on it," states actually express "a tacit agreement . . . by conduct, to disregard the treaty and to consider it as being at an end."[259] Some international scholars are, thus, explicit in stating that "treaties cannot be terminated by *desuetudo*."[260] Rather, "repeated incompatible practices of all parties" can be taken as sufficient factual evidence for triggering the valid legal ground – "tacit agreement" – for the termination and modification of a treaty.[261]

256 Although the two concepts are commonly discussed together, one should not confuse *desuetudo* with *rebus sic stantibus*; the latter concerns the termination or revision of a treaty through fundamental and unforeseen conditions after the conclusion of the treaty. For a thorough discussion of the two concepts, *see*, Athanassios Vamvoukos, *Termination of Treaties in International Law: The Doctrine of Rebus Sic Stantibus and Desuetude* (Oxford: Clarendon Oxford, 1985).

257 *See* section 3 of the VCLT.

258 *See* Art. 15, which speaks of "mutual desuetude." Gerald G. Fitzmaurice, Special Rapporteur, "Second Report on the Law of Treaties" (1957) Yearbook of the International Law Commission, Vol. II: 28.

259 *Ibid*, 48, par. 86.

260 Maarten Bos, "The Identification of Custom in International Law" (1982) 25 *German Yearbook of International Law*: 39. For a contrary view, *see* Vamvoukos, *Termination of Treaties in International Law: The Doctrine of Rebus Sic Stantibus and Desuetude*, 303.

261 *See* Art. 54(b) of the VCLT. Wouters and Verhoeven, "Desuetudo," par. 10. Blurring of the actors' and officials' rule-efficacy perspectives at the international level may contribute to the controversy as to whether we are dealing with *desuetudo* or the case of "subsequent practice in the application of the treaty which establishes the agreement of the parties regarding its interpretation" (Art. 31.3[b] of the VCLT). Hence, while Wouters and Verhoeven speak of Art. 27(3) of the UN Charter as "[t]he most famous instance of desuetudo" (Wouters and Verhoeven, "Desuetudo," par. 5), Crawford and Nicholson, using the same example, contend that "it is much more likely that the provisions of the Charter – a living instrument – will be interpreted with sufficient flexibility to reflect any new consensus and to respond to emerging needs." (James Crawford and Rowan Nicholson, "The Continued Relevance of Established Rules and Institutions Relating to the Use of Force," in Marc Weller, Alexia Solomou, and Jake William Rylatt [eds.], *The Oxford Handbook of the Use of Force in International Law* [Oxford: Oxford University Press, 2015], 111) In the case at hand, Art. 27(3) states that a UN Security Council resolution requires nine affirmative votes to pass, including the concurring votes of the SC permanent members. However, the subsequent state practice emerged that

Things are far more complex when it comes to CIL. What would constitute requested inefficacy in the case of a two-element rule? Bos remarks that just "[a]s much as practice may be proof of *opinio iuris*, desuetude, i.e., inactivity of all, or a number of, the parties concerned, may be evidence of an *opinio iuris* which faded away." He then stresses that the word "inactivity" in this context implies that "participants for some time fail to apply an existing rule of customary international law in circumstances which, on the face of them, call for its application."[262] Glennon similarly talks of "the excessive violation of a rule."[263] The "excessiveness" can be explained in the following way: "Where a rule of international law has been repeatedly disregarded by a significant number of states over a long period of time there is no longer reason to believe that states feel obliged to comply with that rule." Put differently, there is a tipping point at which "state practice that is inconsistent with a norm is simply too thick to justify the conclusion that states really accept the norm as obligatory."[264]

Both of these views focus only on the actors' rule-efficacy perspective, but while Bos speaks of a "slow dying process" that "increase[s] difficulties in the matter of evidence" as to when a valid international rule eventually dies out,[265] Glennon tries to formulate *desuetudo* in far more simple terms: "If a rule is breached by a significant number of states a significant number of times over a significant period of time, I would not call it international law."[266] Furthermore, whereas for Bos "one is entitled to believe that the rule has lapsed, especially because of the disappearance of the *opinio iuris* sustaining it,"[267] Glennon's rational choice approach pushes him toward states' practice – "one has to know how often a rule has been breached to know whether the rule is law."[268]

This eventually led Glennon to baldly conclude that one of the foundational international rules – that of the prohibition of the threat or use of force –

abstention by a permanent member does not bar the adoption of a SC resolution if it receives nine affirmative votes. The ICJ verified this practice in *Legal Consequences for States of the Continued Presence of South Africa in Namibia (South West Africa) notwithstanding Security Council Resolution 276 (1970)*, Advisory Opinion, ICJ Reports 1971, p. 22.

262 Bos, "The Identification of Custom in International Law," 39.

263 He holds that *desuetudo* applies both to treaty and customary rules of international law. Glennon, "How International Rules Die," 940.

264 *Ibid*, 960.

265 Bos, "The Identification of Custom in International Law," 40.

266 Glennon, "How International Rules Die," 960.

267 Bos, "The Identification of Custom in International Law," 39.

268 He adds that counting violations does not provide concrete guidance as to when and where the tipping point occurs: "precisely where desuetude sets in – where the line between binding legal rules and nonbinding norms is to be drawn – will always be a matter of opinion." Glennon, "How International Rules Die," 964.

enshrined in Art. 2(4) of the UN Charter, is no longer a valid legal rule.[269] This claim, however, reveals weaknesses of Glennon's somewhat simplistic approach. If the prohibition in question is treated as a treaty rule, it was shown that its demise may come as a result of either explicit or tacit agreement of all the contracting parties as to that effect. No evidence of some such agreement exists here. Neither do all UN member states agree that this prohibition was at some "tipping point" supplanted by what Glennon calls "the freedom principle,"[270] which is functionally equivalent to no rule,[271] nor can it be said that they all agreed to amend the Charter by way of their subsequent practice.[272] At this point, one should also take into account the officials' rule-efficacy perspective, which Glennon disregards completely. Despite manifest and numerous breaches of Art. 2(4) since the adoption of the UN Charter, the ICJ, in its 1996 *Nuclear Weapons* Advisory Opinion, nonetheless referred to it as a valid rule of international law.[273] Finally, even if it could somehow be shown that the treaty rule on the prohibition of the threat or use of force was modified or ceased to be valid, "[i]t would ... *also* have to be shown that the parallel customary prohibition on the use of force no longer operated." Having in mind that this is presumably a jus cogens norm, it could have been modified only by a norm of the same quality of peremptoriness. However, "[t]here is not the slightest evidence of this."[274]

One can conclude from the above that ascertaining the invalidity of an international legal norm by virtue of its inefficacy is burdened with all the problems of "the fundamental methodology of customary international law formation."[275] Consequently, just as in the case of the emergence of a new valid customary rule, the cure for the uncertainty surrounding the ascertainment of *desuetudo* should be searched for in authoritative decisions of law-applying institutions, primarily international courts and tribunals.[276]

269 *Ibid*, 958ff.

270 This is a well-known Lotus principle: [S]ince "[t]he rules of law binding upon States ... emanate from their own free will ... [r]estrictions upon the independence of States cannot therefore be presumed." The Case of the S.S. "Lotus," 1927 PCIJ (ser. A) No. 10, p. 18.

271 Glennon, "How International Rules Die," 940.

272 Crawford and Nicholson, "The Continued Relevance of Established Rules and Institutions Relating to the Use of Force," 112.

273 *Legality of the Threat or Use of Nuclear Weapons*, par. 38.

274 Crawford and Nicholson, "The Continued Relevance of Established Rules and Institutions Relating to the Use of Force," 113.

275 Glennon, "How International Rules Die," 970.

276 In that respect, one should bear in mind that the ICJ, for instance, "has never explicitly recognized desuetudo." Wouters and Verhoeven, "Desuetudo," par. 7.

## 3 PERSPECTIVE OF PRACTICAL RATIONALITY – HOW NORMS PROVIDE REASONS FOR ACTION

Raz essentially follows Kelsen in holding that validity is a specific form of the norm's existence, but what is for him even more important is that "[o]nly valid norms are valid or good reasons"[277] and "the main difficulty in explaining rules is to understand their relations to reasons for action."[278] This is the *perspective of practical rationality*, which is concerned with the "general human capacity for resolving, through reflection, the question of what one is to do."[279] Since rules are normative in the sense that they purport to guide and regulate our behavior, by employing this perspective, one is interested in elucidating the second *how* question of normativity – namely, *how norms provide us with reasons for action*. This *how* question reveals another set of puzzling issues. For the purposes of this treatise, I will confine myself to the most important points of this vast philosophical debate.[280]

Insofar as agents, when engaging in practical reasoning, "attempt to assess and weigh their reasons for action, [that is] the considerations that speak for and against alternative courses of action that are open to them,"[281] reasons in question must be such that they "count in favour of that for which they are reasons." That is, they have to have potential to "justify and require that which they favour."[282] Thus, Raz calls them "normative reasons."[283] Insofar as an agent is acting rationally, her deliberation about action presumably generates

277 Raz, *Practical Reason and Norms*, 84.

278 *Ibid*, 9.

279 Jay R. Wallace, "Practical Reason," in Edward N. Zalta (ed.), *The Stanford Encyclopedia of Philosophy* (Spring 2018 ed.), at https://plato.stanford.edu/archives/spr2018/entries/practical-reason

280 For a basic overview of the relevant philosophical standpoints, *see, e.g.*, Timothy O'Connor and Constantine Sandis (eds.), *A Companion to the Philosophy of Action* (Oxford: Wiley-Blackwell, 2010). For a more nuanced discussion on general philosophical matters, *see, e.g.*, Sergio Tenenbaum (ed.), *Desire, Practical Reason and the Good* (Oxford: Oxford University Press, 2010); Constantine Sandis (ed.), *New Essays on the Explanation of Action* (Basingstoke: Palgrave Macmillan, 2009) For a discussion related to law, *see, e.g.*, George Pavlakos and Veronica Rodriguez-Blanco (eds.), *Reasons and Intentions in Law and Practical Agency* (Cambridge: Cambridge University Press, 2015).

281 Wallace, "Practical Reason," at https://plato.stanford.edu/archives/spr2018/entries/practical-reason

282 Joseph Raz, "Reasons: Explanatory and Normative," in Sandis (ed.), *New Essays on the Explanation of Action*, 187.

283 Raz considers them "facts," which, apart from being normative, are also "explanatory in that when there is a normative reason for which an agent acted then that reason explains (i.e. it features in an explanation of) that action." *Ibid*, 184.

appropriate intentions,[284] which in turn calls for a practical account of normative agency that would have to show how normative reasons/intentions "*feature in agency qua agency-guiding items*."[285]

Irrespective of the fact that there are many normative orders, normativity is one and the same across all of them.[286] This means that the reason-giving nature of norms has the same logical form. As pointed out by Raz, "statements of the form 'x ought to $\phi$' are logically equivalent to statements of the form 'There is reason for x to $\phi$.'"[287] A universal mechanism of various normative orders through which they give us reasons to behave in a certain way is by installing obligations. Hence, rules of etiquette install the obligation to be the first to greet the older ones; moral rules install the obligation not to lie and cheat; religious rules install the obligation of worshipping; customary rules install the obligation of morning for deceased loved ones; fashion rules install the obligation to follow latest trends when picking our clothes, etc. Consequently, it is in the very nature of an obligation *of any kind* that it provides reasons for action.[288]

In the classical phase of his teaching, Kelsen fostered the claim that the concept of "ought" was a general and "umbrella concept" (*Sammelbegriff*), "which simply embraces all deontic modalities."[289] However, in the last stage of his work, he retreated from this position by noting: "Although ... the word 'ought' can have different meanings, it does seem too far removed from ordinary usage to say, of behaviour that is empowered or is permitted, that one 'ought' so to behave."[290] Raz develops an argument along similar lines. He says that "[i]t

284 Conversely, practical irrationality (*akrasia*) "involves a failure to form the attitudes that one acknowledges to be called for by the considerations one has reflected on." Wallace, "Practical Reason," at https://plato.stanford.edu/archives/spr2018/entries/practical-reason

285 George Pavlakos and Veronica Rodriguez-Blanco, "Introduction," in Pavlakos and Rodriguez-Blanco (eds.), *Reasons and Intentions in Law and Practical Agency*, 1.

286 As pointed out by Spaak, "[T]here is only one sense of normativity, only one sense of 'ought,' so that although we may with good sense speak of the normativity of law or the normativity of morality, etc., there is no specifically moral or legal or prudential *type* of normativity, but only normativity plain and simple." Torben Spaak, "Legal Positivism, Conventionalism, and the Normativity of Law" (2018) 9 *Jurisprudence* 2: 323.

287 Raz, *Practical Reason and Norms* (2nd ed.), 29.

288 This is by no means an orthodox view in jurisprudence. Hart, for instance, notes that rules of etiquette "use characteristic normative vocabulary," such as "You ought to take your hat off," but then he immediately adds that "to use in connection with rules of this kind the words 'obligation' or 'duty' would be misleading and not merely stylistically odd. It would misdescribe a social situation." Hart, *The Concept of Law*, 86. The problem with this observation is that Hart seems to assume that the rule *installing obligation* in the form "x ought to $\phi$" is *necessarily obligatory* for a norm-subject, which is not the case.

289 Robert Alexy, "Hans Kelsens Begriff des Relativen Apriori," in Robert Alexy et al. (eds.), *Neukantianismus und Rechtsphilosophie* (Baden-Baden: Nomos, 2002), 186.

290 Hans Kelsen, "Validity and Efficacy of the Law" (1967), in Carlos Bernal et al. (eds.), *Essays in Legal Philosophy – Eugenio Bulygin* (Oxford: Oxford University Press, 2015), 58, fn. 6.

would be correct but highly misleading to state, in normal circumstances, that an act which in fact one ought to perform is permitted."[291] Neither "permissive" nor "power-conferring" norms can be classified as "mandatory," insofar as "[w]hat one ought to do depends on whether one desires or has other reasons for or against bringing about the relevant normative change." Yet, they are "normative and can be said to guide behaviour because of their contribution to practical inferences, to the solution of practical problems."[292]

Consequently, the normative function of guiding human behavior can be achieved through the use of two related, yet distinctive mechanisms – that of ordering and prohibiting (through *obligations*) and that of entitling (through *rights*). This is particularly true of law as a normative order.[293] However, while the latter mechanism does not lead to a moral squabble because it is up to an addressee's will to trigger the normative function of a rule, the former mechanism seems to open up a far more intricate moral problem of accounting for the fact that an installed obligation by its nature *purports to bind* subjects whose behavior it regulates irrespective of their will. Now, we normally use words "binding" and "obligatory" as synonyms. Does this imply that *all* rules installing obligations are "binding"? Such conclusion would not be in line with a common way of thinking, according to which "binding" rules are "mandatory," in the sense that they are *non-optional* for norm-subjects. Yet, a cursory inspection of the aforementioned examples reveals that not every obligation-installing rule manages to meet this standard, insofar as a putative norm-addressee may simply opt out from being subjected to it. Hence, a nonbeliever may opt out from being subjected to any religious rule; someone not having means for or interest in following fashion rules may completely disregard how he/she ought to dress, etc. At the same time, we are all aware of social contexts in which those norms are taken by some of their addressees as fully "binding" – the very same religious rules will be "binding" for devoted believers, just as some fashion rules may be regarded as "mandatory" for those who want to be trendy.

Among various normative orders, law is typically conceived as the one whose obligations are "binding," i.e., "non-optional" for all its addressees. In the mainstream legal philosophy this stance is often grounded in a direct link made between the concepts of "normativity," "validity," and "bindingness." Kelsen holds that when we state that a norm is valid "we assume that it has 'binding force' for those whose behavior it regulates."[294] Raz comes to the

[291] Raz, *Practical Reason and Norms*, 89–90.
[292] *Ibid*, 106. Moreover, these norms have the same structure as "mandatory" ones. *Ibid*, 96.
[293] Raz, *The Concept of a Legal System*, 169.
[294] Kelsen, *General Theory of Law and State*, 30.

same conclusion when distinguishing between "requests" and "orders." The former "cannot be said to be binding." To utter "'I am asking you to do A and this is binding' is to say that I am not making a request but giving an order." Thus, it makes sense to speak of "a (normative) power to command," but it is senseless to speak of "a (normative) power to request." Raz concludes that "an order can be binding because if valid it requires that its addressee shall act on it disregarding other considerations."[295] Finally, Hart states: "[W]here there is law, there human conduct is made in some sense non-optional or obligatory."[296]

### *a) Are Legal Norms "Non-optional"?*

How are we to understand this claim about legal normativity? One way to interpret it would be to say that the addressee cannot but comply with the required behavior. This reading would equate "non-optionality" of a legal rule with some sort of physical incapacity of the norm-subject to resist the course of action prescribed by the rule. But this is surely not the sense of "non-optionality" we have in mind when referring to the alleged "binding" nature of legal rules. If we were to employ this meaning of "non-optionality," a tax law requiring the paying of taxes would have the same "binding" force for its norm-subjects as the law of gravitation has for all the objects. However, as Kelsen aptly demonstrates, one should differentiate between laws of nature and human laws. According to him, legal theory uses the principle of "imputation" to describe positive law as the object of its study. In doing so, the employed principle has "a function analogous to that which the principle of causality has in the natural laws by which natural science describes nature."[297] The crucial difference lies in the fact that in a "rule of law" (*Rechtsaatz*)[298] both A and B depend on human's will. Whereas A stands for a norm created by an act of will of a legal authority,[299] the requested behavior – B – does not come out of necessity as in the case of laws of nature, because it is upon the norm-subject's will to decide whether to follow the norm or not. As put by Kelsen: "The rule of

[295] Raz, *Practical Reason and Norms*, 101.

[296] Hart, *The Concept of Law*, 82.

[297] Hans Kelsen, "Causality and Imputation" 60 *Ethics* 1: 1–2.

[298] In describing its object, legal science uses a particular statement, which Kelsen originally labeled as *Rechtsaatz*. In his works in English, this word was translated as "rule of law" or "rule of law in descriptive sense," which was one of the matters of contestation during Kelsen and Hart's meeting at the Berkeley Law School in November 1961. *See*, Herbert Hart, "Kelsen Visited" (1963) 10 *UCLA Law Review* 4: 709–728.

[299] Kelsen, *Pure Theory of Law*, 77.

law does not say, as the law of nature does: when A is, 'is' *B*; but when *A* is, *B* 'ought' to be, *even though B perhaps actually is not* (M. J.)."[300]

Another way of interpreting the "non-optionality" of legal rules – far more promising and often endorsed by contemporary legal philosophers – is to ascribe to them some special normative force that necessarily guides a norm-subject's practical reasoning in the direction of the requested behavior. This is how Raz approaches the subject matter. According to him, normativity cannot be adequately exposed by investigating what people do, practice, or believe. The normative force of law can be elucidated only by explaining the "mandatory" nature of its rules. Since all rules are reasons for action, it is necessary to demonstrate how rules, and particularly "mandatory" ones, are any different from other reasons for action. This is a proper order of steps.[301] So, what is for Raz the distinguishing feature of "mandatory" norms? While they are first-order reasons, that is, reasons for performing or refraining from a certain act, they are *additionally* "exclusionary reasons," that is, negative second-order reasons, i.e., reasons to refrain from acting for some conflicting reasons.[302] A special type of "mandatory" rules is the one issued by an "authority."[303] Such a rule is the "content-independent" reason for action.[304] The reason in question is "in the apparently 'extraneous' fact that someone in authority has said so, and within certain limits his saying so would be reason for any number of actions."[305] Since "the law's claim to authority" is part of its nature of being law,[306] elucidating the normativity of law ultimately requires unpacking the concept of "authority."

Raz argues that the "normal" way to think of authority is to think of an actor (individual or institutional) claiming "the right to rule," which triggers the correlative "obligation to obey."[307] This in turn makes the solution to the puzzle of legal normativity dependent on the prior clarification of the

300 *Ibid.*

301 Raz, *Practical Reason and Norms*, 58.

302 *Ibid*, 39.

303 *Ibid*, 58–59.

304 "A reason is content-independent if there is no direct connection between the reason and the action for which it is a reason." Joseph Raz, *The Morality of Freedom* (Oxford: Clarendon Press, 1986), 35.

305 *Ibid.*

306 "The law's claim to authority is manifested by the fact that legal institutions are officially designated as 'authorities,' by the fact that they regard themselves as having the right to impose obligations on their subjects, by their claims that their subjects owe them allegiance, and that their subjects ought to obey the law as it requires to be obeyed." Joseph Raz, "Authority, Law, and Morality" (1985) 68 *The Monist* 3: 300.

307 Raz, *The Morality of Freedom*, 23.

problem of legitimate authority.[308] Authorities are legitimate, according to Raz's "normal justification thesis" (NJT),[309] if they provide us "service" by freeing us from the task of balancing a complex set of reasons for which we may lack sufficient expertise or information.[310] More precisely, "an authority is legitimate when one complies better with one's duty overall by submission to authority than by trying to act on the basis of one's own assessments of what is right and wrong in each instance."[311] In order to do that, authoritative directives should be based only on "dependent reasons," that is, "reasons which already independently apply to the subjects of the directives and are relevant to their action in the circumstances covered by the directive."[312] Once an actor claiming authority satisfies the legitimacy standards,[313] its directives "pre-empt" all other reasons for action that might be taken into account.[314] Hence, under the pre-emptive thesis, "a subject should treat a legitimately authoritative directive as an action-guiding rule."[315] Finally, since the key legitimacy test is whether following the authority's instructions improve "one's conformity with reason,"[316] the NJT "invites a piece-meal approach to the question of the authority of governments, which yields the

308 For this reason, Raz's is an "externalist" theory of legal normativity, which "do[es] not explain the normativity of law from resources within the law itself." Roger A. Shiner, "Law and Normativity," in Dennis Patterson (ed.), *A Companion to Philosophy of Law and Legal Theory* (2nd ed.) (Oxford: Wiley-Blackwell, 2010), 418.

309 Raz says: "[T]he normal way to establish that a person has authority over another person involves showing that the alleged subject is likely better to comply with reasons which apply to him (other than the alleged authoritative directives) if he accepts the directives of the alleged authority as authoritatively binding and tries to follow them, rather than by trying to follow the reasons which apply to him directly." Raz, *The Morality of Freedom*, 53.

310 Raz lists several typical situations in which individuals are likely to benefit from authoritative directives. *Ibid*, 75.

311 Tom Christiano, "Authority," in Edward N. Zalta (ed.), *The Stanford Encyclopedia of Philosophy* (Spring 2013 ed.), at http://plato.stanford.edu/archives/spr2013/entries/authority/.

312 Raz, *The Morality of Freedom*, 47. "[T]he restriction imposed upon a putative authority by this thesis is that its directives ought to be issued in the service of the subjects in that the directives are tracking reasons that already apply to them." Kenneth Ehrenberg, "Joseph Raz's Theory of Authority" (2011) 6 *Philosophy Compass* 12: 886.

313 Raz emphasizes that the NJT is the "normal," but not the only, way to legitimize the authority. (*Ibid*, 53) Moreover, meeting the NJT and dependence thesis is necessary but not sufficient for an authoritative directive to become legitimate. Approaching sufficiency requires also meeting the "independence" ("autonomy") condition, according to which the matter directed "is not the one on which it is more important that people should decide for themselves than that they should decide correctly." Joseph Raz, "Facing Up: A Reply" (1989) 62 *Southern California Law Review* 3–4: 1180.

314 This is the essence of "the pre-emption thesis." Raz, *The Morality of Freedom*, 46.

315 Ehrenberg, "Joseph Raz's Theory of Authority," 887.

316 Raz, *The Morality of Freedom*, 74.

conclusion that the extent of governmental authority varies from individual to individual."[317]

What is the implication of the alleged "pre-emptive" and "exclusionary" nature of legal norms for the practical agency of those who follow them? According to Rodriguz-Blanco, Raz fosters a model of legitimate legal authority that connects legal rules and reasons for action, while simultaneously arguing that "there is no need to evaluate the grounding reasons of legal rules to determine how they bind us."[318] However, practical agency requires acting for reason, and to act for reason is to act *intentionally*.[319] Raz seems to contradict this, when claiming that it suffices that the agent *conforms to* reasons for action, without necessarily *acting for* reasons. In Raz's words, "we cannot reliably conform to reason unless much of the time we do so automatically and unthinkingly."[320] On the other hand, he stresses that "no blind obedience to authority is ... implied" by his account.[321] Rodriguez-Blanco responds to this apparent tension within Raz's account by noting that "[t]o merely follow the authority's order *unintentionally*, though conforming to reason, is not to exercise our practical reasoning."[322] Therefore, to follow legal rules "intentionally and not blindly" is "to 'tap into' the grounding reasons of legal rules."[323] This eventually raises *the paradox of intentionality*: "[I]f we follow legal rules intentionally, then legal rules cannot be exclusionary reasons." And vice versa, "[i]f we do not follow legal rules intentionally, then legal rules do not have a reason-giving character." Consequently, "either

317 *Ibid*, 80.

318 Veronica Rodriguez-Blanco, *Law and Authority under the Guise of the Good* (Oxford: Hart Publishing, 2014), 139.

319 Rodriguez-Blanco, *Law and Authority under the Guise of the Good*, 153. In conceiving intentionality, we need to abandon "the standard view," according to which intentions are "mental states." This view cannot provide an adequate explanation of the fact that, when acting intentionally, "we know the reasons why we are doing this or that, and this knowledge enables us to achieve the end of our action in a controlled manner." (Veronica Rodriguez-Blanco, "Legal Authority and the Paradox of Intention in Action," in Pavlakos and Rodriguez-Blanco (eds.), *Reasons and Intentions in Law and Practical Agency*, 121) The primary explanation of an intentional act requires employing "the guise of the good" model, which, by using the why-question methodology, helps one to explicate her performed action (including the rule-following) in terms of the grounding reasons for action as good-making characteristics. For the full exposition of "the guise of the good model" *see*, Rodriguez-Blanco, *Law and Authority under the Guise of the Good*, ch. 3. Raz defends "the guise of the good model," but he considers it inapplicable in the explication of legal normativity. *See*, Joseph Raz, "On the Guise of the Good," in Tenenbaum (ed.), *Desire, Practical Reason and the Good*, 111–137.

320 Joseph Raz, *Engaging Reason – On the Theory of Value and Action* (Oxford: Oxford University Press, 1999), 94.

321 Raz, "Authority, Morality and Law," 215.

322 Rodriguez-Blanco, *Law and Authority under the Guise of the Good*, 159.

323 Rodriguez-Blanco, "Legal Authority and the Paradox of Intention in Action," 122.

legal rules cannot be exclusionary reasons or legal rules do not have a reason-giving character."[324]

Hurd highlights another, related paradox arising from Raz's account – "the paradox of practical authority." On the one hand, there is "a canon of practical rationality" that dictates that we act on the balance of reasons that are available to us. On the other hand, Raz's conception of authority implies that a government has practical authority "if it can command us to act in ways that may not comport with the balance of reasons as we see it."[325] According to Hurd, this leads to the paradoxical consequence that "obedience to law of the sort required by the exercise of practical authority violates a central principle of rationality." In pursuing this principle, one may justifiably wonder "[h]ow could it ever be rational to act contrary to the balance of reasons as one sees it solely because one has been told to do so?"[326]

On both of these readings, the key problem of Raz's approach is that he initially formulates the moral puzzle of legal authority from the deliberative, first-person perspective of practical reasoning,[327] but then provides the solution from the theoretical, third-person perspective.[328] Take the following example. Suppose that for business reasons, I move to Tel Aviv. I live in a part of the city that is far away from my office and due to a less efficient and reliable public transportation system, I am forced to drive both directions each day. Since I am one of the executives in the firm, I tend to go to the office almost every day during the week, irrespective of the official working hours. The nature of my work is such that I cannot do it from home. At some point, I realize that I spend too much time in my car and that it would be good for my health if I could walk more. Moreover, if I decide not to drive, I could spend more time with my family because I would not be able to go to the office by foot, and using other means of transportation would conflict with my goal of investing more time in walking. Finally, I have serious concerns about the high level of pollution in my new city of residence, and this is additional reason for me to consider not driving my car for at least one day of the week. On the other side, I am aware that if I decide to pursue my plan, the productivity of my firm, which operates in international markets, may suffer

324 Rodriguez-Blanco, *Law and Authority under the Guise of the Good*, 157.

325 Heide M. Hurd, *Moral Combat* (Cambridge: Cambridge University Press, 1999), 69.

326 *Ibid.*

327 As pointed out by Wallace, when engaged in practical reasoning, agents "do this from a distinctively first-personal point of view, one that is defined in terms of a practical predicament in which they find themselves." Wallace, "Practical Reason," at https://plato.stanford.edu/archives/spr2018/entries/practical-reason

328 Rodriguez-Blanco, *Law and Authority under the Guise of the Good*, 160.

considerably. In addition, even if I pick as a non-driving day Saturday – which is the official nonworking day in Israel – my bosses at the central office would surely not be happy with this decision and this might prevent me from being further promoted in the firm. On the balance of reasons, I am inclined to quit driving for one day, preferably Saturday, but have not yet decided what to do.

Imagine the state drafts the *Law on the Transport Rationing Mechanism*, with the purpose of "controlling pollution levels by restricting the number of on-road vehicles per day" and "improving overall health condition of citizens in urban areas" (the official preamble of the drafted legislation). The legislator intends to achieve this goal by introducing the method of odd–even rationing, i.e., banning vehicles with odd license plates from driving on Sundays and Tuesdays, and those with even license plates from driving on Mondays and Wednesdays. Now, is the NJT satisfied? Let us recall that this thesis states that "a directive that is not actually getting subjects to comply better with the balance of reason will not generally be legitimately authoritative."[329] How is one to determine what "the *correct* balance of reasons" requires, or what is "*better*" for me as the subject of the given directive, and whether the directive enables me to comply better with a "*right*" reason? It is surely possible to argue that the legislation does me "service" by tracking some of the reasons that already apply to me ("the dependence thesis") and that I will be better off by following the directive, because it managed to strike the "correct" balance between the conflicting reasons for action. On the other hand, the directive bars me from driving my car for two days and I was deliberating on quitting driving for not more than a day in the week; furthermore, it prevents me from driving the car on two weekdays, whereas my preferable choice was Saturday, which is the official nonworking day. In both of these aspects, thus, the drafted legislation increases the costs of the choice of quitting driving, which would have made it in the first place the less attractive option in my deliberation.

There are two principle options. I can treat the directive as the first-order content-dependent reason for action, which, when weighted with conflicting reasons, may turn out to be the "right" reason for my action. But, then, the directive would not be authoritative in the Razian sense, since the outcome of the balancing process may very well be the entirely different one. In order to be authoritative, the directive would also have to function as the "exclusionary," i.e., negative, second-order reason – a reason that excludes all the reasons for acting contrary to what is required by the directive. However, the legitimacy conditions of the directive would then have to be assessed from some third-person perspective. That is, one would need some external, theoretical

329 Ehrenberg, "Raz's Service Conception of Authority," 886.

perspective from which to say that I would do better at complying with the correct balance of reasons by obeying the directive than by determining on my own what the balance of reasons requires. How is this to be squared with Raz's fundamental premise that "[a] reason for an action is a consideration that renders its choice intelligible"?[330] In what sense is the choice favored by the directive "intelligible" if "in balancing the various requirements that apply to her, the 'reflective individual' found that abiding by the law actually takes her away from the path of 'right reason'?"[331] In this central aspect, Raz's "answer seems unsatisfactory from the deliberative viewpoint" of practical rationality.[332] Consequently, in order for legal rules to guide our behavior and provide us with reason for action they have to be *deliberatable*, which essentially makes them *non*-non-optional for norm-subjects.[333] Were it any different, legal rules would have been transformed "into mere habits devoid of any normative meaning."[334]

Having said all this, the only remaining venue for the treatment of "non-optionality" of legal rules for norm-subjects[335] is that of taking into account the

330 Raz, "The Problem of Authority: Revisiting the Service Conception," in *Between Authority and Interpretation – On the Theory of Law and Practical Reason*, 128–129.

331 Sylvie Delacroix, *Legal Norms and Normativity – An Essay in Genealogy* (Oxford: Hart Publishing, 2006), 149.

332 Rodriguez-Blanco, "Legal Authority and the Paradox of Intention in Action," 139.

333 Himma notes that, in Raz's view, exclusionary reasons do not preclude an agent "from deliberating to determine what the balance of excluded reasons would require by way of acting; they *simply preclude* (M. J.) her acting on the basis of those reasons or her assessment of those reasons." ( Kenneth Einar Himma, "Authority," in Giorgio Bongiovanni et al. (eds.), *Handbook of Legal Reasoning and Argumentation* [Dordrecht: Springer, 2018], 203) First, as pointed out by Hurd, Raz himself is not quite clear on this point (Hurd, *Moral Combat*, 76–77). Second, even if Himma's interpretation of Raz's view is correct, it would be pointless from the first-person perspective of practical agency to argue that one reason is "deliberatable" with other reasons, while at the same time necessarily "precluding" an agent from acting on other conflicting reasons. Such a nature of one reason makes it essentially non-deliberatable for a practicing agent. This, then, pushes Raz's stance toward Hart's position, according to which norms of practical rationality would be violated if in the case of "peremptory" reasons an agent would deliberate on the class of conflicting reasons. Hart says: "[T]he commander characteristically intends his hearer to take the commander's will instead of his own as a guide to action and so to take it in place of any deliberation or reasoning of his own: the expression of a commander's will that an act be done is intended to preclude or cut off any independent deliberation by the hearer of the merits pro and con of doing the act . . . This, I think, is what is meant by speaking of a command as 'requiring' action and calling a command a 'peremptory' form of address." Herbert L. A. Hart, "Commands and Authoritative Reasons," in *Essays on Bentham* (Oxford: Oxford University Press, 1982), 253. Himma considers Hart's stance "problematic" for a number of reasons. Himma, "Authority," 204ff.

334 Delacroix, *Legal Norms and Normativity – An Essay in Genealogy*, 154.

335 From everything said so far, it is clear that normativity of rules is discussed primarily from the perspective of those actors whose behavior is supposed to be guided by the given norms.

law-applying institutions that are in charge of their enforcement. A legal rule is, then, considered "non-optional" in the sense that its breach triggers the enforcement of sanction against the will of a disobeying norm-subject. In this view, the "bindingness" of a legal rule can be explicated by recourse to the "idea of a legitimate response to deviation in the form of demands and pressure for conformity."[336] However, to hold this view is not to claim that coerciveness is the ground of legal bindingness, because it is obviously not. As eloquently put by Radbruch, "while power may indeed serve as a basis for the 'must' of compulsion, it never serves as a basis for the 'ought' of obligation."[337] Even under the hardly attainable condition of the full efficacy of the sanctioning regime, it would still be the case that "[i]nternalization – determining whether, the extent to which, and the way in which a rule provides a reason for action – is located initially and primarily within individual decision-makers."[338] Bix formulates this idea in the following way:

> We certainly say that the law of a country "applies" to its citizens (and often non-citizens resident in the country) whether those individuals "accept" the law or not. By this, we mean in part that if those individuals act contrary to law's prescriptions, they may be subjected to sanctions. However, while law's *coercion* may be inescapable, its *normativity* is not.[339]

Coercive guarantees are, thus, only "auxiliary reasons" for the actions of norm-subjects.[340] Nevertheless, they normally help law as a complex institutionalized normative order to function with a higher level of efficiency than other normative orders. Or, as famously put by Hart, "'sanctions' are ...

[336] In his 1988 interview, Hart takes this to be "the central component of obligation," which he failed to highlight adequately in the *Concept of Law*. Herbert Hart, "Answers to Eight Questions," in d'Almeida, Edwards, and Dolcetti (eds.), *Reading HLA Hart's The Concept of Law*, 283.

[337] Gustav Radbruch, "Statutory Lawlessness and Supra-Statutory Law (1946)" (2006) 26 *Oxford Journal of Legal Studies* 1: 6.

[338] Frederick Schauer, *Playing By the Rules – A Philosophical Examination of Rule-Based Decision-Making in Law and in Life* (Oxford: Clarendon Press, 1991), 128.

[339] Brian Bix, "The Nature of Legal Obligation," in Kenneth Einar Himma, Miodrag Jovanović, and Bojan Spaić (eds.), *Unpacking Normativity: Conceptual, Normative, and Descriptive Issues* (Oxford: Hart Publishing, 2018)

[340] Rodriguez-Blanco, *Law and Authority under the Guise of the Good*, 199. It is important to recall that, in his discussion about "necessary and natural" elements that constitute the minimum morality that makes a legal system possible, Hart sends essentially the same message. He says that if no one "would have any reason to obey except fear" – and this would happen were the legal rules to deny even minimal "essential benefits and protection" stemming from "natural necessity" – than the legal system would "sink to the status of a set of meaningless taboos." Herbert Hart, "Positivism and the Separation of Law and Morals," in *Essays in Jurisprudence and Philosophy*, 81–82.

required not as the normal motive for obedience, but as a *guarantee* that those who would voluntarily obey shall not be sacrificed to those who would not." Therefore, "what reason demands is *voluntary* co-operation in a *coercive* system."[341]

### b) Law as "The Signaler of Last Resort"

All this leads to a rather surprising and unconventional conclusion – since law is only one among many normative systems that we use as signalers that something ought to be done, its normative force competes with the normative force of other normative orders. Consequently, "[l]aw's power to bind us and impose upon us some non-optional mode of conduct is a property that needs rebuilding on a constant basis. This 'rebuilding' occurs every time a person enters a practical deliberation aimed at balancing law's requirements with other types of demands." This, in turn, implies that "the reasons provided by law may sometimes, on balance, fail to give rise to an obligation."[342]

Can legal rules under those conditions be perceived as authoritative? Rodriguez-Blanco believes that a "weaker reading" of Raz's "service conception" is good enough to resolve the seemingly inherent tension between the authoritativeness of legal rules and the practical agency of norm-subjects.[343] She holds that "we *can* act according to a presumption of the goodness of the rules and therefore a *presumption* of the authoritative force of legal rules."[344] Perry uses a somewhat different strategy for showing that a directive need not function as a second-order exclusionary reason in order to be authoritative. He introduces the concept of "*reweighting* reason" as "a subjective second-order reason," which can be defined as "a reason to treat a reason as having a greater or lesser weight than the agent would otherwise judge it to possess in his or her subjective determination of what the objective balance of reasons requires."[345]

341 Hart, *The Concept of Law*, 198. (emphasis in the original)

342 "Far from being detrimental to law's normative dimension, these opportunities to challenge law's legitimacy are vital to maintaining legal normativity 'alive' so to speak." Delacroix, *Legal Norms and Normativity – An Essay in Genealogy*, 154.

343 This reading proceeds from the idea that "authorities create legal rules or authoritative directives based on grounding reasons as good-making characteristics that are *transparent* to the addressee of the legal rule or authoritative directive so that their will is engaged with it." Rodriguez-Blanco, *Law and Authority under the Guise of the Good*, 169.

344 *Ibid*, 142. Acting according to a presumption implies acting "as if something were correct or as if we have a justified belief." *Ibid*, 160.

345 Stephen Perry, "Second Order Reasons, Uncertainty, and Legal Theory" (1989) 62 *Southern California Law Review*: 932.

He explains the nature of a "reweighting reason" in the context of authority in the following way:

> I might take the judgment of the authority into account only to the extent of introducing an element of systematic bias into my practical reasoning; I would treat the case for the conclusion which is favored by the authority as being stronger to some specified degree than it actually appears to me to be. I would thus be deferring to the judgment of the authority only partially, in the sense that I would never permit my own judgment to be preempted completely by that of the authority.[346]

The proposed alternatives suggest, then, that in order for law to be treated as "the signaler of last resort . . . people must adopt in advance a certain attitude to it." The attitude in question "is respect for the law as a source of salience."[347] Interestingly enough, Raz fully shares this idea.[348] He speaks of "respect for law" as "an aspect of identification with society (the reverse of alienation)."[349] More specifically, "the attitude of respect is a manifestation of loyalty," which "gives rise to . . . an obligation to obey, to . . . an acknowledgment of authority."[350] Raz introduces this "attitude" in the overall picture about the authoritativeness of law, because he holds that there is no "obligation to obey the law," understood as "a general obligation applying to all the law's subjects and to all the laws on all the occasions to which they apply."[351] To establish the existence of one such general obligation, one has to search for adequate "grounds," which "need not be the same for everyone or for every occasion, but they should be of sufficient generality so that a few general sets of considerations will apply to all on all

346 *Ibid*, 932. Alexander fosters a similar claim, that "law cannot itself constitute a second-order, exclusionary reason to disregard all or any non-legal first-order reasons; what it can (and should) do is *demand* that it be responded to as if it had, and *perhaps claim* that it be regarded as having, *overriding normative weight.*" Larry Alexander, "Law and Exclusionary Reasons" (1990) 18 *Philosophical Topics* 1: 5.

347 Jeremy Waldron, "Authority for Officials," in Lukas H. Meyer, Stanley L. Paulson and Thomas W. Pogge (eds.), *Rights, Culture and the Law – Themes from the Legal and Political Philosophy of Joseph Raz* (Oxford: Oxford University Press, 2003), 54.

348 Marmor also emphasizes that if there is an obligation to follow the law, it "must come from moral and political considerations. The reasons for obeying the law cannot be derived from the norms that determine what the law is." (Andrei Marmor, "The Conventional Foundations of Law," in Stefano Bertea and George Pavlakos [eds.], *New Essays of the Normativity of Law* [Oxford: Hart Publishing, 2011], 152) Schauer similarly stresses that "the decision of any agent . . . to internalize a rule is . . . a function of something outside the rule itself." Schauer, *Playing By the Rules*, 126.

349 Joseph Raz, "Respect for Law," in *The Authority of Law – Essays on Law and Morality* (2nd ed.) (Oxford: Oxford University Press, 2009), 259.

350 *Ibid*, 261.

351 Joseph Raz, "The Obligation to Obey the Law," in *The Authority of Law*, 234.

occasions."[352] Raz, however, believes that neither morality nor prudence can serve as such generalized grounds,[353] not even in the case of "a good society whose legal system is just."[354] In this way, Raz fosters the view that the question of legitimate authority is a moral problem related to, but distinct from, the problem of the grounds of a general obligation to obey the law.[355] Moreover, in advancing a "patchwork" conception of authority, he believes that "government is authoritative over different citizens with regard to different ranges of issues."[356] And yet within the given, individually tailored range of issues limited by "the independence thesis," a directive of an authority satisfying the legitimacy conditions stated in the NJT "is binding" on norm-subjects and "they are duty-bound to obey it."[357]

But, again, what does Raz actually *mean* by the statement that a legitimate directive "is binding" for its norm-subjects? At some point he offers a "rough" clarification of his stance when saying that where such directive intervenes to require certain behavior, we are "not allowed to question its force," even though we are allowed to deliberate upon it, that is, "to question its wisdom and advocate its reform."[358] Whatever is assumed under the term "force" – be it "validity" or purported "bindingness" of the directive – the implication of

352 *Ibid.*

353 Prominent political philosophers dealing with this issue also acknowledge that "there can be numerous reasons to obey particular laws." (George Klosko, *Political Obligations* [Oxford: Oxford University Press, 2005], 100) Moreover, they are aware of the fact that "[n]ot every 'member' of a polity will stand in the same relation to its laws ... which means that it is a mistake to think that everyone must have the same general obligation to obey." However, the common response in recent years has consisted not in rejecting the idea that there can be a general obligation to obey the law, but in offering "hybrid," i.e., multiple principal theories of political obligation. Richard Dagger and David Lefkowitz, "Political Obligation," in Edward N. Zalta (ed.), *The Stanford Encyclopedia of Philosophy* (Fall 2014 ed.), at https://plato.stanford.edu/archives/fall2014/entries/political-obligation.

354 Raz, "The Obligation to Obey the Law," 233.

355 "Obligations to obey the law need not depend on the legitimacy of its authorities." (Raz, "The Problem of Authority: Revisiting the Service Conception," 127) He is by no means alone in holding this view. Schauer speaks of "the asymmetry of authority," which is reflected in the fact that "the lack of a (good moral) reason for obeying authority does not entail the lack of a (good moral) reason for imposing it." And vice versa. Schauer, *Playing By the Rules*, 129. *Cf.* Liam Murphy, *What Makes Law? An Introduction to the Philosophy of Law* (Cambridge: Cambridge University Press, 2014), 116.

356 Donald H. Regan, "Reasons, Authority, and the Meaning of 'Obey': Further Thoughts on Raz and Obedience to Law" (1990) 3 *Canadian Journal of Law and Jurisprudence* 1: 21.

357 Raz, "The Problem of Authority: Revisiting the Service Conception," 134. Ehrenberg, thus, concludes that "Raz's notion of an obligation is an exclusionary reason that applies categorically." Kenneth Ehrenberg, "Critical Reception of Raz's Theory of Authority" (2011)6 *Philosophy Compass* 11: 780.

358 "This is, roughly, what I mean when I say that legitimate laws, and the directives of legitimate authorities generally, preempt the background reasons that might militate against the

the norm-subject's disregarding the directive would be that law-applying institutions, most notably courts, would normally refer to the issued directive (reason) "as justification for not excusing someone who acts on [conflicting reasons] and breaks the law."[359] However, in order to show that this is what is implicated by "bindingness," i.e., "non-optionality," of legitimate legal rules (directives), one need not rely on a dubious "pre-emption thesis," which seems to be in an irresolvable tension with the requests of practical rationality.[360]

The treatment of law as "the signaler of last resort" can be well explained with reference to the aforementioned "respect" for law. This respect can be manifested differently and generated for various reasons. True, the overall belief in the legitimacy of political authorities has proven to be the strongest ground for treating legal rules as binding.[361] However, legal rules might be at times treated by norm-subjects as "binding" for prudential reasons associated with legal sanctions,[362] just as "*some* legal norms might *sometimes* trigger ... general moral reasons" for action,[363] even when they are issued by plainly illegitimate authorities.[364] Finally, norm-subjects might find themselves with other members of the polity in different interconnected legal statuses (e.g., students, employees, companies) in which treating obligation-installing

authoritative directives and replace them with their own requirements." Raz, "The Problem of Authority: Revisiting the Service Conception," 141.

359 Joseph Raz, "The Claims of Law," in *The Authority of Law*, 32.

360 Whenever openly trying to reconcile them, Raz seems to be closer to the view that, just like other norms, even legitimate legal directives are *non*-non-optional for norm subjects – "in following authority, just as in following advice, or being guided by any of the technical devices, one's ultimate self-reliance is preserved, for *it is one's own judgment which directs one to recognize the authority of another* (M. J.), just as it directs one to keep one's promises, follow advice, use technical devices and the like." Raz, "The Problem of Authority: Revisiting the Service Conception," 140.

361 For Buchanan, "the crucial idea [is] that the rules of a legitimate institution *have a privileged status vis 'a vis our reasons for acting and that their having this privileged status is not dependent on their content.*" (Allen Buchanan, "The Legitimacy of International Law," in Besson and Tasioulas (eds.), *The Philosophy of International Law*, 83) Rodriguez-Blanco argues that there are reasons that enable us to create a presumption of the goodness, i.e., legitimacy, of legal authority. There are two of them. First, authorities make claims about their legitimacy and moral correctness. And second, authorities make claims on complying with Fuller's eight desiderata of the Rule of Law. Rodriguez-Blanco, *Law and Authority under the Guise of the Good*, 160–161.

362 Schauer, *Playing By the Rules*, 123.

363 Brian Bix, "Kelsen and Normativity Revisited," at ssrn.com/abstract=2287870, 18. (Published in Spanish, Brian H. Bix, "De Nuevo sobre Kelsen y la normatividad," in Carlos Bernal and Marcelo Porciuncula (eds.), *Kelsen para erizos. Ensayos en honor a Stanley L. Paulson* (Bogota: Universidad Externado de Colombia, 2017), 273–296)

364 This would, for instance, be the case with various criminal law prohibitions (e.g., on murder, theft) issued by a totalitarian state.

norms as binding is connected to reciprocal benefits stemming from the concomitant right-conferring norms.[365]

In any event, "even if a significant number of people believe that law *qua* law gives them reasons for action, this may be a matter calling more for a psychological or sociological explanation rather than a philosophical one."[366] It seems, thus, that the most that jurisprudence can convey in the form of a concluding message is that the overall authority (and the concomitant higher level of efficiency) of law as a normative order is a result of a complex and combined effect of the interrelated typical features of law – normativity, institutional nature, (coercive) guaranteeing, and justice-aptness – and should not be erroneously translated into the alleged "exclusionary" nature of legal norms as reasons for action.

## 4 PERSPECTIVE OF PRACTICAL RATIONALITY AT THE INTERNATIONAL LEVEL

If we now try to bring the perspective of practical rationality into the discussion about the nature of international law, we are initially faced with the question whether its main subjects – states – do possess the requisite capacity for rational deliberation that can generate appropriate intentions. It seems that the most elaborate affirmative answer, if there is one, can be expected from the scholarship that tries to elucidate international law by employing the rational choice theory. In a well-known attempt of that sort, Goldsmith and Posner note that the initial premise "that states act rationally to further their interest is not self-evident," insofar as all of its components "are open to question."[367] Yet, they believe that each of them is defensible. To begin with, states are realities of the legal world in the same way as corporations are and, hence, "they arrange themselves to act like agents." Their "corporate identity" is recognized by both municipal and international law.[368] Although more difficult for ascertainment than in the case of corporations, interests of the state can be defined as "state's preferences about outcomes" and they are to be

365 This is basically what Hart has in mind when speaking of "mutuality of restrictions," which exists "in many spheres of life." He explains it in the following way: "[W]hen a number of persons conduct any joint enterprise according to rules and thus restrict their liberty, those who have submitted to these restrictions when required have a right to a similar submission from those who have benefited by their submission." Herbert L. A. Hart, "Are There Any Natural Rights?" (1955) 64 *The Philosophical Review* 2: 185.

366 Bix, "Kelsen and Normativity Revisited," 18.

367 Jack L. Goldsmith and Eric A. Posner, *The Limits of International Law* (Oxford: Oxford University Press, 2005), 4.

368 *Ibid*, 5.

identified in the preferences of the "political leadership,"[369] which is legally organized through institutions and internationally recognized as state's representatives.[370] All this, according to Goldsmith and Posner, warrants the adoption of the rational choice lens through which a state's behavior in the international realm can be perceived as a rational maximization of its interests.[371]

One by no means needs to follow Goldsmith and Posner's approach in order to find the aforementioned basic assumptions justifiable. They all lead to the conclusion that states, acting through their representatives, are capable of practical reasoning that gives rise to their intentional actions. After all, the idea that states do have "intentions" when "freely" expressing "consent" is in the very basis of international treaty law,[372] just as the ascription of a "psychological" element to states is crucial for the creation of customary international law.[373] This, then, clears the way for investigating how international law provides its subjects with reasons for action. Now, one source of skepticism with respect to the "true legality" of international law might stem from the idea, discussed earlier, that legal normativity implies "bindingness," i.e., "non-optionality," of its rules. Since international law is largely consent based, and states can opt out of being subject to entire legal regimes (e.g., international criminal law)[374] or a specific treaty (through reservations)[375] and customary rules (through the persistent objector rule),[376] its normativity is, according to skeptics, somehow deficient in comparison to that of the "true law." Accordingly, in order to meet this challenge, international legal scholars

369 *Ibid*, 6.

370 As the Permanent Court of International Justice remarked in its 1923 advisory opinion: "States can act only by and through their agents and representatives." *Certain questions relating to settlers of German origin in the territory ceded by Germany to Poland*, Advisory Opinion, [1923] Publ. PCIJ, Series B, no. 6, at 22.

371 Goldsmith and Posner, *The Limits of International Law*, 7.

372 *See*, Art. 12 of the VCLT.

373 *See*, DC 9 of the ILC Draft conclusions on the identification of customary international law.

374 For instance, two of the four states that conducted the Nuremberg prosecutions – United States and Russia – are not parties to the Rome Statute. For the US position toward international criminal law, *see, e.g.*, Leila N. Sadat and Mark A. Drumbl, "*The United States and the International Criminal Court: A Complicated, Uneasy, Yet at Times Engaging Relationship*" (2016) Washington University in St. Louis Legal Studies Research Paper Series, at https://scholarlycommons.law.wlu.edu/cgi/viewcontent.cgi?article=1504&context=wlufac; for the Russian stance, *see, e.g.*, Gennady Esakov, "International Criminal Law and Russia: From 'Nuremberg' Passion to 'The Hague' Prejudice" (2017) 69 *Europe-Asia Studies* 8: 1184–1200.

375 *See*, Section 2 of the VCLT.

376 *See*, DC 15 of the ILC Draft conclusions on the identification of customary international law.

would need to show that international legal rules are placed on the same axis that connects concepts of "normativity," "validity," and "bindingness."

Besson, for instance, defends the full-fledged "legality" of international law exactly by elucidating its normativity via the concept of "bindingness." In contending that Raz's approach is applicable beyond the state level,[377] she argues that just as legal normativity at the municipal level "corresponds to the law's claim to authority," i.e., to "its claim to create obligations to obey the law that in principle preclude some countervailing reasons for action," so at the international level it corresponds to the law's claim to give its subjects "exclusionary albeit *prima facie* reasons for action."[378] Although Besson underlines that these reasons "differ depending on the subjects" (e.g., individuals versus collectives), as well as on "the lawmakers" (e.g., treaty versus customary rules), she feels it necessary to add that international law's "normativity has increased and diversified over the years."[379] This, in particular, means that

> some international legal norms bind subjects who have not agreed to them (e.g. third-party effect of treaties) or who have expressly objected to them (e.g. limitations on persistent objections to customary law), be they states or individuals; they bind them even if they have made reservations when agreeing to them; and, finally, they sometimes bind them in an imperative fashion.[380]

Put differently, the maturity of international legal normativity has been confirmed by the fact that the "bindingness" of some of its rules is no longer grounded in the consent of its norm-subjects.

D'Aspremont, for his part, offers a somewhat different defense of international legal "bindingness," which "has long constituted the very DNA of the discipline of international law."[381] Namely, he treats it as "the expression of the validity of a rule and its membership to the international legal order," which enables international lawyers to preserve their binary world of "legal" and "nonlegal" phenomena.[382] However, bindingness is not to be confused with

377 She nonetheless urges "a revised" and "re-interpreted" version of Raz's theory for international law. Samantha Besson, "The Authority of International Law – Lifting the State Veil" (2009) 31 *Sydney Law Review* 3: 343–380.

378 Besson, "Theorizing the Sources of International Law," 173–174.

379 *Ibid*, 174.

380 *Ibid.*

381 Jean d'Aspremont, "Bindingness" (2015) ACIL Research Paper 2015–19, at https://ssrn.com/abstract=2690155, 1. (forthcoming in Jean d'Aspremont and Sahib Singh (eds.), *Concepts for International Law – Contributions to Disciplinary Thought* (London: Edward Elgar, 2019)

382 *Ibid*, 4.

"authority," that is, "sense of obligation." Although related, they are not completely the same concepts. Consequently, bindingness is only "one of the reasons for action which may or not be sufficient to convince addressees of international legal rules to comply with the latter."[383] In that respect, the fact that a rule is valid, i.e., legally binding, "has never been a guarantee for compliance" and this can easily be verified empirically.[384]

The previous analysis, which debunks the direct link between the concepts of "normativity," "validity," and "bindingness," sheds a completely new light on common worries of international legal scholars that the subject of their interest is somehow defective in comparison to municipal law. It transpires that these worries are largely misplaced since the nature of law cannot be elucidated by trying to show that there is something special about the normativity of legal rules. Take, for starters, Raz's empirical observations upon which he built the central case of legitimate authority, without which one is unable to comprehend legal rules as "exclusionary reasons" for action. First, authorities of a country normally claim that the inhabitants are bound to obey them. He says that we can imagine a situation in which they do not do so, "but in which the population does acquiesce in their rule."[385] Not only is it highly unlikely that such a society ever existed, but even if it were to exist, "we would not regard it as being governed by authority," because such institutions would be too far from what "we normally regard as authorities."[386] Second, the normal view of authorities involves the contention that we as subjects are faced with directives that are deliberately imposed on us by another. This leads Raz to conclude that consent-based explanations of authority "fly in the face of reality."[387] Finally, we normally proceed from the idea that those receiving directives are in the position of subordination. That is, "the normal understanding is that authority involves a hierarchical relationship, that it involves imposition on the subjects."[388]

383 *Ibid*, 6. Çali similarly argues that "[a] piece of international law may well be legally binding, but it may not enjoy authority in the sense that it does not have the capacity to impose a specific pre-emptive duty or the duty it imposes could be rebuttable by other considerations. The binding nature of international law, therefore, is a necessary, but insufficient condition for the authority of international law over domestic orders." Başak Çali, *The Authority of International Law – Obedience, Respect, and Rebuttal* (Oxford: Oxford University Press, 2015), 11.

384 d'Aspremont, "Bindingness," 13.

385 Raz, *The Morality of Freedom*, 27.

386 *Ibid*.

387 Raz, "The Problem of Authority: Revisiting the Service Conception," 162.

388 *Ibid*, 165.

Now, what happens with the concept of authority, and concomitantly with the concept of legal rules as "exclusionary reasons" for action, in a case in which the underlying empirical premises are different than those envisaged by Raz? What if we paradigmatically do not have specially designed institutions for imposing rules; what if actors who create, execute, and are subject to rules are, normally, one and the same; what if hierarchy and subordination are not regular states of affairs; what if conflict-resolution institutions normally operate upon prior consent, even the consent of an actor being charged of breaking a rule, etc.? An easy way out would be to state that we are no longer able to speak of "authorities" and a normative order called "law."[389] And yet, in the presence of the aforementioned empirical conditions at the international level, all relevant actors refer to some rules of conduct as rules of international law;[390] most of them obey those rules most of the time, making the international law an overall effective normative order;[391] some institutions are by and large perceived as international authorities; decisions of conflict-resolution institutions are commonly treated as binding and are executed accordingly, etc. Simply put, we have a landscape with all the patterns typically associated with law as we know it at the municipal level.

### a) *Relative Normativity of International Law*

If the preceding general analysis, with attention primarily on the rules of municipal law, demonstrated that legal normativity does not exhaust in its "bindingness," i.e., "non-optionality," then elucidation of international law in terms of practical rationality can proceed without unsubstantiated "conceptual baggage of domestic law."[392] The most important implication of this move is that it opens up room for *gradation*. But, what exactly is the object of gradation? Weil's famous cautiousness, in that respect, is certainly warranted. He remarks that, unlike sociologists, who "note down and allow for the infinite gradations of social phenomena," lawyers are trained in treating "a simplifying

389 In spite of all this, Raz states that his theory of authority applies to international bodies as well, without further elaborating this claim. Raz, "Why the State?," 22.

390 Even Morgenthau, as a prominent realist scholar, conceded that to deny the existence of international law "flies in the face of all the evidence." Hans J. Morgenthau, *Politics among Nations: The Struggle for Power and Peace* (2nd ed.) (New York: Alfred A. Knopf, 1954), 251.

391 As famously put by Henkin: "Almost all nations observe almost all principles of international law and almost all of their obligations almost all the time." Louis Henkin, *How Nations Behave* (New York: Columbia University Press, 1979), 47.

392 Çali speaks of different negative pieces of such baggage, Raz's theory of authority being the most problematic one. Çali, *The Authority of International Law*, 54ff.

rigor" as "essential" for their professional vocation.[393] The implication of the mainstream jurisprudence's thesis that there is an overlap between "validity," "normativity," and "bindingness"[394] is that if it is possible to gradate one concept, then it is necessarily possible to gradate others as well. But just as the initial assumption is unsubstantiated, so is the resulting conclusion.

Let us start with validity. While providing the case for "soft law," Peters and Pagotto emphatically announced recently that no "compelling justification of the binarist assertion that 'legality' is like virginity" has been offered. Consequently, they argue that "[j]ust as a norm can be more or less 'just' or 'efficient,' it can also be more or less 'legal.'"[395] Validity, however, cannot to be gradated. It is a specific existence of norms, and sources of law are there to help us distinguish between the realms of "legal" and "non-legal."[396] Credibility of the entire legal profession crucially depends on the principle possibility of differentiating between these two realms; law-applying institutions both perceive themselves and are perceived by norm-subjects as called upon to resolve conflicts by justifying their decisions on legal grounds; and finally, the argument that the rule of law is preferable to the rule of power, insofar as it implies "the supremacy of law over the supremacy of individual will,"[397] which is of even greater importance in the international realm, is meaningful only under the presupposition that law is distinguishable from politics. Hence, when it comes to the validity of both municipal and international law, the traditional binary view is a warranted sign of the "simplifying rigor" of the legal mind.

Admittedly, the sources test in international law is not as reliable as it is at the municipal level due to the lack of hierarchy of both sources of law and judiciary. This is, as we saw, particularly true of the ascertainment of the validity of customary rules of international law. Having this in mind, Besson argues that international law-making processes can result in "complete legal norms," but also in "intermediary legal products." Although the latter "are not yet valid legal norms, [they] may be vested with a certain evidentiary value in the next stages of the law-making process."[398] For instance, UN General

393 Prosper Weil, "Towards Relative Normativity in International Law?'" (1983) 77 *American Journal of International Law* 3: 441.

394 According to this view, "*the essence of law is its normativity (or: legal bindingness, or legal validity as synonyms)*." (emphasis in the original) Peters and Pagotto, "Soft Law as a New Mode of Governance: A Legal Perspective," 6.

395 *Ibid*, 9.

396 The additional criteria concern rules governing the temporal scope of validity and conflict of laws.

397 Denise Meyerson, "The Rule of Law and the Separation of Powers" (2004) 4 *Macquarie Law Journal* 1: 1.

398 Besson, "Theorizing the Sources of International Law," 170.

Assembly resolutions were long ago recognized as some such products with "nascent legal force."[399] They "may provide evidence of both state practice and *opinio juris* which might then support the final development of a customary norm."[400]

In no other area of law can one find more references to "emerging legal norms" than are found in the area of international law. Nevertheless, a norm that is emerging is not yet existent, i.e., valid, but it may have some legal bearing insofar as it becomes a legitimate point of reference in an ongoing argumentative international legal practice. One may come across different examples of these "emerging" norms of international law. Take the controversy regarding the R2P doctrine. Even a cursory overview of the burgeoning literature on the subject will reveal a dubious status of its "legality."[401] It is argued that "the doctrine has the potential to develop from an emerging norm into a rule of customary international law";[402] that part of the doctrine can already be qualified as international customary law;[403] that it is "an important new political commitment, perhaps akin to soft law";[404] that the R2P "is construed primarily as a nonlegal concept,"[405] etc.

Despite not always being easily ascertainable, validity is the key quality of a legal norm. No norm can qualify for the status of "legality" unless it satisfies recognized criteria of its validity specified in some source of law. Bindingness, however, is no such quality. For any norm – including a legal one – to be binding, it has to generate a "sense of obligation," i.e., authoritativeness among norm-subjects. It is plainly clear that not every valid legal rule can be said to be

399 Castaneda wrote that resolutions were "embryonic norms" or "quasilegal rules." Jorge Castaneda, *Legal Effects of United Nations Resolutions* (New York: Columbia University Press, 1969), 176.

400 Besson, "Theorizing the Sources of International Law," 171. This is confirmed in the DC 12(2) of the ILC Draft conclusions on the identification of customary international law: "A resolution adopted by an international organization or at an intergovernmental conference may provide evidence for establishing the existence and content of a rule of customary international law, or contribute to its development."

401 For a comprehensive overview of the doctrine and its applicability in various parts of the world, *see, e.g.*, Vasilka Sancin (ed.), *Responsibility to Protect: Where Do We Stand Ten Years After?* (Ljubljana: University of Ljubljana Press, 2015).

402 Alison McCormick, "From Sovereignty to Responsibility: An Emerging International Norm and Its Call to Action in Burma" (2011) 18 *Indiana Journal of Global Legal Studies* 1: 576.

403 Rachel E. VanLandingham, "Politics or Law? The Dual Nature of the Responsibility to Protect" (2012) 41 *Denver Journal of International Law & Policy* 1: 101.

404 Jonah Eaton, "An Emerging Norm – Determining the Meaning and Legal Status of the Responsibility to Protect" (2011) 32 *Michigan Journal of International Law* 4: 803.

405 Mehrdad Payandeh, "With Great Power Comes Great Responsibility? The Concept of the Responsibility To Protect Within the Process of International Lawmaking" (2010) 35 *Yale Journal of International Law* 2: 515.

binding in the aforementioned sense. D'Aspremont is certainly correct when noting that lawyers routinely refer to all valid legal norms as "legally binding."[406] However, this is merely *façon de parler* – a figurative and conventional expression of the legal profession. More precisely, it is a phrase that denotes that, in the case of conflict, a valid legal norm will be treated by law-applying institutions, most notably courts, as potentially applicable. Accordingly, there is no need to substitute "validity" for "bindingness," when the latter term more aptly corresponds to the aforementioned "sense of obligation" (authoritativeness). Only with this conceptual clarification in mind does it make sense to treat them as the two "distinct notions which can be apprehended and discussed separately."[407]

Bindingness can be gradated, because normativity can be gradated. When primarily understood as the capacity to give rise to obligations,[408] legal normativity can clearly be endowed with relative weight. If all norms, including legal ones, are taken as reasons for action, then norm-subjects are the ones who ultimately bestow upon different norms different normative weight. At times – actually, in most legal orders, most of the time – norm-subjects "internalize" legal norms and treat them as conclusive reasons for action, just as sometimes they disregard them altogether or give preference to the rules of other normative orders.[409] Gradation of international legal normativity, thus, has nothing to do either with the source of law from which the installed obligation is derived or with the hierarchical status of the given legal norm. Let me explain this.

Although being on diametrically opposite doctrinal poles, Besson and Weil essentially hold the identical, erroneous view that the normative power of an international legal rule crucially depends on it being grounded in state consent. While for Besson the spread of non-consensually based rules of international law is a welcome sign of "increased" normativity,[410] for Weil, as a proponent of the "voluntarist" basis of international law, it is a marker of

406 He says that "bindingness continues to perform an ontological and identifying function in the discipline today." d'Aspremont, "Bindingness," 2.

407 *Ibid*, 6.

408 As stated previously, this is a morally more problematic aspect of law's normativity than the one that refers to the law's capacity to entitle norm-subjects by granting them rights. Furthermore, as pointed out by both Kelsen and Raz, right-conferring norms can hardly be elucidated with the reference to the concept of "bindingness."

409 "Patterns of internalization across numerous decision-makers may of course develop, or be inculcated by education, or be enforced by sanctions. But the way in which and the extent to which, if at all, rules become a part of a decisional process is ultimately determined by the decision-maker alone." Schauer, *Playing By the Rules*, 128.

410 Besson, "Theorizing the Sources of International Law," 174.

the negative trend toward "relativization" of international legal normativity.[411] It is, however, principally irrelevant whether the installed obligation stems from a treaty or customary rule or from a unilateral act of state. True, it is to be presumed that the norm of a treaty or unilateral declaration that requires certain behavior by installing obligation will more easily generate the "sense of obligation," insofar as it was created with the consent of the norm-subject, i.e., the state. Nevertheless, for various reasons this need not be the case. Take, for example, the doctrine of the "efficient breach" of contract law, which concerns a voluntary breach of contract by a party who concludes that paying damages would be less costly than performing under the contract.[412] Economically driven international legal scholarship has been arguing for quite some time that the doctrine is applicable to the elucidation of the functioning of international treaty law,[413] particularly in the area of international trade law.[414]

On the other hand, the normative power of a customary rule may be highest, thereby creating the requisite "sense of obligation," even for the state upon which the installed obligation was imposed without its consent (for instance, in the case of a newly emerging state). Consequently, irrespective of the source of law, "[i]nternational laws encompass variable forms of authority relationships with domestic orders depending on the capacity of the specific international laws to impose duties themselves."[415] However, just like in the case of municipal legal norms, inquiries into the sources of authoritativeness, that is, into the reasons why states would consider as binding norms to which they have not consented, belong more to the province of sociology or international relations than to legal philosophy.[416]

411 Weil, "Towards Relative Normativity in International Law?," 441.

412 For a general account in contract law, *see, e.g.*, Gregory Klass, "Efficient Breach," in Gregory Klass, George Letsas, and Prince Saprai (eds.), *The Philosophical Foundations of Contract Law* (Oxford: Oxford University Press, 2014), 362–387.

413 *See, e.g.*, Eric Posner and Alan O. Sykes, "Efficient Breach of International Law: Optimal Remedies, Legalized Noncompliance, and Related Issues" (2011) 110 *Michigan Law Review* 2: 243–294.

414 But *see*, Krzysztof J. Pelc, "Eluding Efficiency: Why Do We Not See More Efficient Breach at the WTO?" (2010) 9 *World Trade Review* 4: 629–642.

415 According to Çali, "these authoritative relationships range from overriding authority to qualified authority and rebuttable authority." They are grounded in "minimal deference to international law," which as a "general duty to take international law into account at the very least includes a deliberation about what kind of an authority structure a specific international law imposes on state officials." Çali, *The Authority of International Law*, 11.

416 For example, working at the intersection of international relations theory and international law, Guzman has offered a "reputational" theory of states' compliance. Andrew T. Guzman, *How International Law Works: A Rational Choice Theory* (Oxford: Oxford University Press, 2008)

What jurisprudence can offer is yet another conceptual clarification that concerns the relation between "relative normativity" and the hierarchization of the international legal order. Weil's erroneous assumption is that the former is merely a corollary of the latter.[417] He says that unwelcome gradation of international legal normativity leads to "graduated," i.e., "enhanced" normativity, which is manifested in the belief that "some norms are now held to be of greater specific gravity than others, to be more binding than others."[418] The norms in question are jus cogens rules and international crimes. Weil argues that their proponents endow these rules with some form of unjustifiable "supernormativity."[419]

The hierarchical status of a legal norm, however, by no means affects its capacity to give rise to obligation. The highest legal norms of municipal legal order, enshrined in a constitution, are not somehow more binding than the rules of by-laws. In fact, every historical instance of revolution aptly demonstrates that the change of legal regime begins with norm-subjects' disrespect for the most fundamental constitutional rules and not for, say, traffic rules.[420] Therefore, it is the nature of normativity as such, and, thus, (international) legal normativity as well, that invites the talk of gradation and relativity. International scholars may rightly pinpoint some problems regarding the ascertainment of the content of peremptory norms and *erga omnes* obligations or the presumed legal consequences stemming from their existence in international legal order,[421] but this fact alone cannot be taken as an indication – either positive or negative – of the "relative normativity" of international law.

### *b) Soft Law*

A subject far more adequately discussed under the rubric of "relative normativity" of international law is the concept of "soft law." Just like many other concepts already mentioned, soft law is also a matter of great controversy in the international legal scholarship. The debate is often framed as consisting of two

417 Shelton replicates this mistake when explicitly claiming that "'[r]elative normativity' is a question of hierarchy of norms." Dinah Shelton, "International Law and 'Relative Normativity,'" in Malcolm D. Evans (ed.), *International Law* (1st ed.) (Oxford: Oxford University Press, 2003), 145.

418 Weil, "Towards Relative Normativity in International Law?," 421.

419 *Ibid*, 429.

420 For a critical account of the theory of legal discontinuity of the Kelsenian sort, *see*, John Finnis, "Revolutions and Continuity of Law," in *Philosophy of Law – Collected Essays: Volume IV* (Oxford: Oxford University Press, 2011), 407–435.

421 Most of Weil's criticisms are in fact phrased in such a way. Weil, "Towards Relative Normativity in International Law?," 429ff.

camps with opposing views as to the binary nature of (international) law. According to this division, while anti-binarists take "soft law" as the expression of "the complexity of the international exercise of public authority in a pluralized world," binarists take "the notion as redundant because it turns into either hard law or not law at all."[422] While the former believe that the binary image "is increasingly being challenged, paving the way for the growing acceptance of a mid-way concept of 'soft law' that would occupy some space in between,"[423] the latter hold strongly to the view that "law itself, for all its binariness, is capable of reflecting a whole spectre of subtleties and nuances ... that law itself can accommodate various shades of grey without losing its binary character."[424]

This division is, however, potentially simplifying and misleading. Again, everything hinges upon the prior question of what is there to gradate. Since validity cannot be the subject of gradation, then it is clear that "soft law" has to pass the recognized threshold in order to qualify for the status of "law." Hence, phrases such as "non-legal soft law," which Chinkin uses to denote "non-binding or voluntary resolutions and codes of conduct formulated and accepted by international and regional organisations,"[425] can be akin to Besson's "intermediary legal products," accepted as a heuristic tool for analyzing certain instruments which, despite being able to trigger some legal effects,[426] are not "legal" after all.[427] On the other hand, once the alleged necessary "bindingness" of legal norms is exposed as unsubstantiated, it becomes possible to elucidate the capacity of some non-legal normative

422 Jean d'Aspremont and Taanja Aalberts, "Which Future for the Scholarly Concept of Soft International Law? Editors' Introductory Remarks" (2012) 25 *Leiden Journal of International Law* 2: 309, 310.

423 Melaku Geboye Desta, "Soft Law in International Law: An Overview," in Andrea K. Bjorklund and August Reinisch (eds.), *International Investment Law and Soft Law* (Cheltenham: Edward Elgar, 2012), 40.

424 Jan Klabbers, "The Redundancy of Soft Law" (1996) 65 *Nordic Journal of International Law* 2: 180.

425 Christine M. Chinkin, "The Challenge of Soft Law: Development and Change in International Law" (1989) 38 *International and Comparative Law Quarterly* 4: 851.

426 "[T]hey can play a role in the *internationalization of the subject-matter*, provide guidelines for the interpretation of other legal acts, or pave the way for further subsequent practice which may one day be taken into account for the emergence of customary international norm." Jean d'Aspremont, "Softness in International Law: A Self-Serving Quest for New Legal Materials" (2008) 19 *European Journal of International Law* 5: 1082. *Cf.* Tadeusz Gruchalla-Wesierski, "A Framework for Understanding 'Soft Law'" (1984) 30 *McGill Law Journal* 1: 37–88, especially part II.

427 Weil is here warranted in claiming that "sublegal obligations are neither 'soft law' nor 'hard law': they are simply not law at all." Weil, "Towards Relative Normativity in International Law?," 415, fn. 7.

instruments to give rise to obligations of their addressees,[428] as well as to fully comprehend reasons why states and other international actors often opt for their adoption.[429] Whatever those reasons are, one thing is clear – by regulating their behavior by non-legal instruments, international actors choose not to rely on the judicial enforcement of the undertaken obligations.[430]

If "soft law" instruments cannot be explained by reference to their relative legality, then we should turn to the exposition of their "softness." Despite being critical of the idea of the relative normativity of international law, Weil notes, in a footnoted remark, that it seems "better to reserve the term 'soft law' for rules that are imprecise and not really compelling."[431] These are fully fledged valid legal instruments/rules whose normative function of guiding human behavior is generally low.[432] This may be so because fulfilling this function is not a condition of their international legal validity.[433] Therefore, international actors are free to adopt a legal instrument "which fails to provide any precise directive as to which behaviour its authors are committed to." Put differently, they may "soften its content by ensuring that it does not lay down any specific obligation and design it in such a way that the addressee retains a right to opt out or to define its scope of application."[434] Again, this is possible because the formulation of clear obligations is not the prerequisite of the legal character of an international act.[435]

[428] Although she mistakenly uses the adjective "binding" to denote all valid legal norms, Shelton accurately observes that "[i]n some instances, compliance with non-binding (i.e., non-legal, M. J.) norms and instruments is extremely good and probably would not have been better if the norms were contained in a binding (i.e., legal, M. J.) text." She concludes that "[t]hey are not law and they do not need to be in order to influence conduct in the desired manner." Shelton, "International Law and 'Relative Normativity,'" 170. *Cf.* Michael Bothe, "Legal and Non-Legal Norms – A Meaningful Distinction in International Relations?" (1980) 11 *Netherlands Yearbook of International Law*: 65–95. Jovanović, "Theorizing 'Unidentified Normative Objects' of Global Regulatory Regimes", 227–250.

[429] Shelton believes that "[t]he considerable recourse to and compliance with non-binding norms may represent a maturing of the international system." Shelton, "'International Law' and 'Relative Normativity,'" 170.

[430] *Cf.* Weil, "Towards Relative Normativity in International Law?," 417–418.

[431] Weil, "Towards Relative Normativity in International Law?," 415, fn. 7. In that respect, he follows in the footsteps of Bexter, who was among the first to acknowledge that "there are norms of various degrees of cogency, persuasiveness, and consensus which … may be described as 'soft' law." Richard R. Baxter, "International Law in 'Her Infinite Variety'" (1980) 29 *International and Comparative Law Quarterly* 4: 549.

[432] Besson argues that "in terms of degree of normativity," international law "now ranges from low-intensity or soft law to imperative law." Besson, "Theorizing the Sources of International Law," in Besson and Tasioulas (eds.), *The Philosophy of International Law*, 165.

[433] *Cf.* d'Aspremont, "Softness in International Law," 1085.

[434] Hence, d'Aspremont labels such an instrument as "soft negotium." *Ibid*, 1084.

[435] *Ibid*, 1084–1085.

D'Aspremont speaks of several types of such international instruments with "soft *negotium*." First, there are instruments with "potestative" provisions, which "have no normative character, as they fail to provide any directive as to which behaviour the parties should adopt irrespective of their own will."[436] Second, provisions may be "purely indicative or suggestive," thereby not formulating any obligations whatsoever. Finally, there are "agreements which are not self-sufficient in the sense that they require complementary instruments for their scope to be fully defined."[437] Although the adopted language of instruments may suggest their "softness" in one of the aforementioned senses, d'Aspremont judiciously warns against hasty conclusions, because it may transpire that some such allegedly potestative provisions actually enable third parties, including tribunals, to determine the content of the required behavior.[438]

436 d'Aspremont, "Softness in International Law," 1085.
437 *Ibid*, 1086.
438 *Ibid*, 1087.

# 5

# International Law as an Institutionalized and (Coercively) Guaranteed Order

The discussion so far demonstrates that the nature of law as a normative order cannot be reduced to its normativity. That is, the fact that law is typically taken by its norm-subjects as the signaler of last resort cannot be elucidated with recourse to some alleged specificity of the reasons for action that it provides. As rightly pointed out by Delacroix, the mainstream legal theory has a "propensity to consider the normative dimension of law as a *given*." From this standpoint, "explaining legal normativity involves considering its impact on individuals, its potential conflicts with other forms of normativity, but never what conditions its possibility."[1] This latter task can be accomplished with the employment of the *genealogical* method, whose point "is to bring out the artificial character of a certain kind of institution. It typically aims at those institutions that seem to be able to construct their legitimacy only by 'forgetting' that they were brought into existence by a historical process."[2]

The analysis undertaken in the previous chapters has partly relied on this approach by trying to shed light on law as a complex social artifact, whose nature and authoritativeness cannot be fully analyzed without taking into account its social interaction with other normative orders, as well as its other typical features. One such feature, which law shares with some other normative orders (e.g., religious), is that it is an "institutionalized abstract artifact."[3] According to MacCormick, institutionalization of a normative order implies primarily institutionalization of judgment, because "normative order involves judgment." That is, "to think normatively is to think judgmentally."[4] It is not uncommon that within a given societal setting one behavior is subjected to

[1] Delacroix, *Legal Norms and Normativity – An Essay in Genealogy*, 102.
[2] *Ibid*, 100.
[3] Ehrenberg, *The Functions of Law*, 12.
[4] MacCormick, "Institutional Normative Order: A Conception of Law," 1057.

plurality of judgments. In a case where each of the judgments, some of which may be conflicting, is "conclusive within a particular order," one is faced with the question: "[W]hich ought to prevail?"[5] From the perspective of each of the normative orders involved, "such a question is of course self-answering," whereas from the perspective of the agent whose behavior is the subject of a plurality of judgments, the answer to the question has "both prudential and moral aspects." Addressing the question in a prudential manner will be, among other things, affected by "power relations," and insofar as this is the case, the problem we are facing is "one of politics."[6] MacCormick concludes that "political power" rests with a normative order that can guarantee that its judgment will "prevail in the last resort," and "[i]n the world as it has been, and still to a very large extent is . . . [t]he coercively predominant normative orders have been those of states."[7] This turns (coercive) guaranteeing into yet another important and typical feature of law as a normative order.

Our exposition of international legal normativity required an extensive detour into the debate about general problems of legal normativity, which was in the mainstream jurisprudence taken almost exclusively with municipal law in mind. When it comes to the typical features of institutionality and (coercive) guaranteeing, this will not necessarily be the case. This is due to the aforementioned fact that empirical circumstances at the international level are entirely different from those at the state level. Simply put, the said "power relations" are distinctively shaped in the international arena, and this profoundly affects theoretical ramification of the discussed issues. Finally, unlike in the case of municipal law, international legal theorists are not prone to presume authoritativeness of the international legal order by "forgetting" how it was brought into life through a specific historical process. Hence, the following analysis will to a certain extent rely even more robustly on the genealogical approach, whose ambition is "to trace the social and cultural factors that have contributed to bringing about the phenomenon in question"[8] – in this case, international law as an institutionalized and (coercively) guaranteed order.

## 1 INSTITUTIONALIZATION OF THE INTERNATIONAL ORDER

At the beginning of the opening chapter it was acknowledged that the international law talk is sensible under an assumption of the existence of a world of

5 *Ibid*, 1059.
6 *Ibid*.
7 *Ibid*, 1060.
8 Delacroix, *Legal Norms and Normativity – An Essay in Genealogy*, 96.

multiple political communities, conscious of the idea that it is preferable to be ruled from the inside than from the outside, as well as of the choice between rule-based or rule-less relations among them. From the very emergence of distinctive political communities, i.e., "state-level societies,"[9] they had a principal choice between the two general foreign policy courses. They could either follow something akin to the ancient ideal of *autarkeia*, i.e., self-sufficiency (αὐτάρκεια),[10] or they could try to position themselves better politically in the "outer world." Throughout history, the former has never been an ideal cherished by more than a handful of political communities.[11] As for the latter foreign policy option, for a long period of time it was primarily to be achieved through the use of armed force and the mastery of the art of war,[12] which at times could be fully accomplished only in larger military associations or polities.[13] This by no means implies that other means for the promotion of this foreign policy objective, such as diplomacy or trade, were nonexistent. On the contrary, even ancient political communities were also committed to developing friendly relations with their close or more distant neighbors. As rightly pointed out by Bederman, without this ability to commit themselves to such acts of friendship, "[n]ot only would it have been

9 This is the notion Fukuyama uses to denote a political organization of society that is in several respects different from the preceding "tribal society." *See*, Francis Fukuyama, *The Origins of Political Order – From Prehuman Times to the French Revolution* (New York: Farrar, Straus and Giroux, 2011), ch. 5.

10 *See*, Aristotle, *Politics* (translated, with introduction and notes, by C.D.C. Reeve) (Indianapolis: Hackett Publishing Company, 1998), 1326b, 1372a. For an overview of the concept of *autarkeia* from a political rather than ethical point of view, *see, e.g.*, Neil Morpeth, "Autarkeia: Notes on its Cultural and Historical Context" (1993) 25 *Prudentia (Supplementary Number: Multarum Artium Scientia)*: 126–130.

11 A notable historical example was the isolationist foreign policy of the Japanese Tokugawa shogunate, which was called "sakoku" (closed country) and lasted for more than two centuries. *See, e.g.*, Tashiro Kazui, "Foreign Relations during the Edo Period: Sakoku Reexamined" (1982) 8 *Journal of Japanese Studies* 2: 283–306. One can take as a contemporary example the North Korean *Juche* ideology (commonly translated as "self-reliance"), developed by Kim Il Sung. *See, e.g.*, Bruce Cumings, *Korea's Place in the Sun: A Modern History* (New York: W.W. Norton, 2005), ch. 8.

12 As famously put by the founder of modern political science, Machiavelli: "A prince, therefore, must not have any other object nor any other thought, nor must he adopt anything as his art but war, its institutions, and its discipline; because that is the only art befitting one who commands." Niccolò Machiavelli, *The Prince* (Translated and edited by Peter Bondanella) (Oxford: Oxford University Press, 2005), 50.

13 In Ancient Greece, the alliances could be defensive (*epimachia*) or offensive (*symmachia*). "The latter typically featured a stipulation that partners to the alliance were to have the same friends and enemies, a stipulation found also in earlier treaties of the Near East." Sheila L. Ager, "Treaties, Archaic and Classical Greece," in Roger S. Bagnall et al. (eds.), *The Encyclopedia of Ancient History* (1st ed.) (Hoboken: Blackwell Publishing, 2013), 6837.

impossible for ancient States to pledge their faith with one another in a positive law-making act ... but no other rule of State conduct could have had any force and effect."[14] And although there were not many doctrinal norms of international antiquity, they "were broad in importance and capable of eliciting certainty and security of expectation."[15] For that reason, it is possible to claim that "a common *idea* or *tradition* that international relations were to be based on the rule of law"[16] was born already in ancient times.

To say this, however, is not necessarily to foster the idea "of historic continuity between the ancient and modern worlds" of international law.[17] The birth of the latter is commonly attributed to the Peace of Westphalia in 1648, which ended the thirty-year religious conflict in Europe, and is considered the "first major instance of organized international co-operation."[18] It "marks the end of an epoch and the opening of another. It represents the majestic portal which leads from the old into the new world."[19] The Westphalian Peace was a novel political project that abandoned "the idea of hierarchical structure of society" and replaced it with a new system, whose main features were: a) peaceful coexistence of a multiplicity of states, b) each sovereign within its territory, c) equal to one another, and d) free from any external earthly authority.[20] This newly introduced system rested on the idea of *horizontality* of international law and the balance of power – "a law operating between rather than above states and a power operating between rather than above states."[21] As such, it gave predominant shape to the modern international legal order and was a strong impetus for all its subsequent developments.[22]

14 Bederman, *International Law in Antiquity*, 135.

15 According to Bederman, they included rules regulating "(1) the conduct of embassies, immunities granted to envoys, and protections afforded to foreigners; (2) the sanctity given to treaties and alliances; and (3) the constraints of a nation declaring war and the limits on the actual conduct of hostilities." *Ibid*, 7.

16 *Ibid*, 6.

17 *Ibid*, 4.

18 Shaw, *International Law*, 1282.

19 Leo Gross, "The Peace of Westphalia, 1648–1948" (1948) 42 *American Journal of International Law* 1: 28.

20 *Ibid*, 28–29.

21 *Ibid*, 29.

22 It is to be borne in mind that fixing the birth of modern international law to this particular event is to a certain extent "a historical simplification." As pointed out by Besson, "[m]odern sovereignty was in fact largely established well before 1648, on the one hand, and sovereignty was still questioned later on and until the end of the Austro-Hungarian Empire, on the other." Samantha Besson, "Sovereignty," in *Max Planck Encyclopedia of Public International Law*, par. 14. *Cf.* Stéphane Beaulac, *The Power of Language in the Making of International Law – The Word Sovereignty in Bodin and Vattel and the Myth of Westpahila* (Leiden: Martinus Nijhoff, 2004).

In the formative period, this order was almost exclusively concerned with the regulation of potential conflicts. This led Friedmann to famously label this phase of development as the international "law of coexistence," insofar as it aimed primarily to maintain the existence of a small number of states. Nevertheless, alongside this continuing aspect, an international "law of cooperation" was also developing.[23] The two aspects were from the very beginning – and to a large extent still are – in constant tension,[24] insofar as they reflect the principles of formal independence (sovereignty) of states and their actual interdependence. At the same time, this tension "has produced the paradox that, in order to exercise their functions and to remain as independent as possible, states [were] forced to cooperate due to the unavoidable reality of interdependence." One may even claim that it was international cooperation that enabled states "to control external influences."[25] Hence, in pre-World War I Europe, whenever a problem arose in relations between the states, international congresses and conferences were summoned. According to the earlier proposed broad definition of institutions, these congresses did possess some proto-institutional aspects of "an interlocking double-structure of persons-as-role-holders . . . and of social practices involving both expressive and practical aims and outcomes."[26] In that respect, they "constituted an important prelude to the establishment of international institutions." Nonetheless, at some point it became clear that they were "inadequate to fulfil the job they had been intended to do."[27] Namely, they were set up on an ad hoc basis upon the initiative of one or more of the states involved in the international crisis; only invited states could participate and decisions were to be made unanimously. All this "severely restricted the utility of the system."[28]

[23] Wolfgang Friedmann, *The Changing Structure of International Law* (New York: Columbia University Press, 1964)

[24] Dupuy's remarks, stated two decades ago, still seem to be valid. Pierre-Marie Dupuy, "International Law: Torn between Coexistence, Cooperation and Globalization. General Conclusions" (1998) 9 *European Journal of International Law* 2: 278–286.

[25] Henry G. Schermers and Niels M. Blokker, *International Institutional Law – Unity within Diversity* (5th revised ed.) (Leiden: Martinus Nijhoff, 2011), 2.

[26] Harré, *Social Being*, 98.

[27] Shaw, *International Law*, 1283.

[28] *Ibid.* There were some notable exceptions, which "had given the small states a taste for international activism." The 1907 Hague peace conference, for instance, "approached universal participation, with forty-four states being represented." Furthermore, "due in part to its near-universal participation, organizational experiments took place, one of them being that recommendations (so-called voeux) of the conference were passed by a majority vote, instead of unanimity." Jan Klabbers, *An Introduction to International Institutional Law* (Cambridge: Cambridge University Press, 2002), 17.

Once the hierarchical nature of the old world was dismantled, states were keen to preserve these new horizontally structured legal and power relations as far as possible. In such a situation, the question of the authoritativeness of a putative international order was shaped along profoundly different lines than those envisaged by Raz when discussing the case of municipal law. Raz says: "The aspect of the moral problem we are confronting is not the limits to one's freedom that the law or other authoritative directives pose. It is that the limits are imposed deliberately, and that they are imposed by another. They are not limits set by me."[29] As already pointed out by Kant, no such "external constraints" existed in the case of sovereign states. Hence, what he hoped for as a realistic second-best solution to the ideal of a *civitas gentium* (an international state) was a *foedus pacificum*, which would emerge as a result of states' willingness to "renounce their savage and lawless freedom."[30]

The historical record shows that this willingness is reflective of "a consciousness of common interests between states," which "comes into being when there is tangible evidence that action has to be taken."[31] In particular, it was the horror of two world wars that forced states to set limits on their sovereign freedom by establishing a global institutional structure – the League of Nations after World War I, and the United Nations (UN) following World War II. The Great War was the first instance of "an all-out war," which has crystallized the conviction that peace was "a common interest for all states." Similarly, the Great Depression of the 1930s has shown that "national wealth and economic growth had become a matter of international concern." In both of these cases, the newly detected common interests of states were given their international institutional forms.[32] And the awareness of this "commonness" was clearly expressed in President Wilson's address at the Paris Peace Conference in which he presented the Draft of the Covenant of the League of Nations, when he said that the resulting document symbolized "the union of wills in a common purpose, a union of wills which cannot be resisted and which I dare say no nation will run the risk of attempting

[29] Raz, "The Problem of Authority: Revisiting the Service Conception," 162.

[30] Kant, "Perpetual Peace: A Philosophical Sketch," 105.

[31] Elisabeth Zoller, "Institutional Aspects of International Governance" (1995) 3 *Indiana Journal of Global Legal Studies* 1: 124.

[32] In the case of the global economic institutions, they refer to the post-World War II Bretton Woods System (International Monetary Fund and World Bank) and General Agreement on Tariffs and Trade (GATT), which was transformed into the World Trade Organization (WTO). *Ibid.*

to resist."[33] Despite the fact that its success, or lack thereof, is commonly judged upon the subsequent events, most notably World War II,[34] some more nuanced expositions persuasively show that "[w]ith the League of Nations as the first international organization whose secretariat had extra-territorial prerogatives, a new, more formal and global era in the history of international organizations started."[35] Moreover, irrespective of some noticeable differences in the institutional structure between the League and its successor,[36] it would also be fair to conclude that "the United Nations is in large measure the result of a continuous evolutionary development extending well into the past."[37]

## 2 INSTITUTIONS OF INTERNATIONAL LAW

Despite sharing all typical features of an international organization (IO) – that it is created by states, on the basis of a treaty, and that it has a will distinctive from its members[38] – the UN is the most important global institutional structure.[39] It is not only a universal membership

[33] "Address of President Wilson on Presenting the Draft of the Covenant of the League of Nations to the Third Plenary Session of Peace Conference at Paris, February 14, 1918" (1919) 13 *American Journal of International Law* 3: 571–572.

[34] One may also judge it upon the fact that Wilson had not managed to persuade the Congress that the United States should become a member of the League of Nations.

[35] Madeleine Herren, "International Organizations, 1865–1945," in Jacob Katz Cogan, Ian Hurd, and Ian Johnstone (eds.), *Oxford Handbook of International Organizations* (Oxford: Oxford University Press, 2016), 108. For a contrary view, that "[t]he League of Nations was never intended to be, nor is it, a revolutionary organization," *see, e.g.*, Alfred Zimmern, *The League of Nations and the Rule of Law* (London: MacMillan and Co., 1936).

[36] In one such analysis, provided immediately after the formation of the UN, it is noted that the "[t]he over-all rule of unanimity is abandoned; no tests of aggression are stated, and the Council is left a wide discretion in determining what constitutes an act of aggression; the specialized agencies have room for more functional operation; there are more bodies of the United Nations which can ask the Court for an advisory opinion or which can call to the attention of the Security Council matters dangerous to peace." Clyde Eagleton, "Covenant of the League of Nations and Charter of the United Nations: Points of Difference" (1945) 13 *The Department of State Bulletin* 321: 263–269.

[37] Leland M. Goodrich, "From League of Nations to United Nations" (1947) 1 *International Organization* 1: 4.

[38] These features are not present in the same form in each instance of an international organization. This is particularly true of the last mentioned feature. Klabbers, *An Introduction to International Institutional Law*, 9ff.

[39] As early as 1949, the ICJ took the position in the *Reparations* case that the UN has a distinct international legal personality. It concluded that the UN is an "international person," that is, "a subject of international law," which is "capable of possessing international rights and duties," and, thus, with the "capacity to maintain its rights by bringing international claims." *Reparation for Injuries Suffered in the Service of the United Nations (Advisory Opinion)* (1949) ICJ Rep. 174, p. 179.

organization,[40] but the one based on the foundational treaty with a number of constitutional elements,[41] which enables[42] it to assume all three traditional governing roles – legislative, judicial, and executive – at the global level. Although "it is a long way from being a world government,"[43] the UN clearly provides a blueprint for global "governance without a government."[44] As enshrined in its charter, the UN's function[45] is both to facilitate coordination of international relations in a number of areas in a cooperative manner and toward the achievement of "common ends," as well as to provide means for the "adjustment or settlement of international disputes" (Art. 1). Since it has already been emphasized that the main function of law is coordination and dispute settlement,[46] it is clear that the UN institutional framework is in the service of the international law's function of the same sort. And yet, the UN does not provide for an institutional structure comparable to the municipal law – that of a single global legislative body, a global executive branch, and a global court of the last instance. Consequently, the discussion about international law-making and law-applying institutions cannot boil down to a detailed exposition of the composition, prerogatives, and practices of the UN organs.[47]

40 There are other international organizations with this aspiration, although membership conditions may affect the scope of their "universality." A notable example is the WTO. *See, e.g.*, Lisa Toohey, "Barriers to Universal Membership of the World Trade Organization" (2012) 19 *Australian International Law Journal*: 97–115.

41 It is argued that the UN Charter has the following constitutional elements: tendency toward perpetuity; indelibleness; primacy; and allocation of functions to governing bodies. Simon Chesterman, Ian Johnstone, and David M. Malone, *Law and Practice of the United Nations – Documents and Commentary* (2nd ed.) (Oxford: Oxford University Press, 2016), xxxiii.

42 As noted by Peters, "international law constitutes, enables, and constrains international organizations." The first two functions are related primarily to the "effectiveness" of IOs, and Peters labels them "constitutionalism 1.0." Anne Peters, "International Organizations and International Law," in Cogan, Hurd, and Johnstone (eds.), *Oxford Handbook of International Organizations*, 33.

43 Chesterman, Johnstone, and Malone, *Law and Practice of the United Nations*, xxxii.

44 "Governance means setting priorities and using power to attain them. It can take many forms, such as setting rules and regulations, providing incentives and support, promising rewards, or threatening punishments." (Zoller, "Institutional Aspects of International Governance," 122) For a more elaborated account of global governance, *see, e.g.*, Robert O. Keohane, *Power and Governance in a Partially Globalized World* (London: Routledge, 2002).

45 As pointed out by Kelsen, the stated purposes of the UN constitute "functions" of the organization to be carried out by its organs. Hans Kelsen, *The Law of the United Nations – A Critical Analysis of Its Fundamental Problems (With Supplement)* (London: Stevens & Sons Ltd., 1951), 15.

46 *See, supra* p. 110.

47 For one such analysis, *see, e.g.*, Benedetto Conforti, *The Law and Practice of the United Nations* (3rd revised ed.) (Leiden: Martinus Nijhoff, 2005).

More precisely, despite a dense web of mutually interconnected IOs and other international actors, with the UN as the focal institution, the regime of horizontality is still very much in place, insofar as most of the international legal life still begins and ends with the actions of states. As already pointed out, states are primary actors who create, execute, and are subjected to rules of international law. Hence, this is a necessary point of departure for the discussion of institutionalism as a typical feature of international law. It basically narrows it down to the elucidation of two central themes: 1) the role of other, non-state institutional actors in the process of international law-making; and 2) judicialization of international law through the formation of international adjudicative and dispute-settlement institutions.

### *a) Non-state Institutional Actors of International Law-Making*

Notwithstanding the fact that preliminary findings regarding typical features of law as a genre of normative orders revealed the conceptual primacy of law-applying institutions, insofar as without them legal order would be inconceivable,[48] the function of law-making both logically and chronologically precedes the function of law-application. Accordingly, in those instances of legal orders in which separate institutions are vested with the power of law-making, an analysis of the institutionalist feature of law dictates that they are first exposed. The question is, nonetheless, whether international law is one such order. According to Buchanan, it is possible to differentiate between the three main types of "international law-making institutions (ILIs)" – the institution of treaty making, the institution of customary international law, as well as "global governance institutions," which range from the UN organs, such as the Security Council, to various global regulatory regimes, such as the WTO or Kyoto Protocol institutional environmental framework.[49] The first two types of "institutions" refer primarily to the most important "processes" of international law-making,[50] in which states usually assume two roles – they are lawmakers *and* norm-subjects. Since those processes were largely dealt with in Chapter 4.2 on the sources of international law,[51] the focus here will be on the role of non-state international institutional actors.[52]

48 *See, supra* p. 72.
49 Buchanan, "The Legitimacy of International Law," 80.
50 This is how Besson speaks of them and equates them with the "sources of international law." Besson, "Theorizing the Sources of International Law," 170.
51 *See, supra* pp. 83–128.
52 I prefer this label, insofar as Buchanan's proposed term may be potentially confusing, so as to include some global regulatory regimes of dubious legal nature. On the nature of these global

It is often claimed that, although created and sustained through state-made treaties, these institutions "are increasingly taking on law-making functions."[53] This argument, however, crucially depends on what counts as an act of "law-making" in international law. This, on the other hand, necessarily takes us back to the complex story of the formal sources of international law. We should be reminded, first, of the fact that the international legal doctrine is almost united in holding that Art 38(1) of the ICJ Statute provides a nonexhaustive list of formal sources of law. Secondly, the concept of a "formal source of law" in the international realm is taken in terms that are broader than those at the municipal level, insofar as it refers to all "containers" of the norm-content from which rights and obligations of norm-subjects can be derived. For instance, regardless of whether the treaty is multilateral, thereby creating general norms, or bilateral, thereby creating individual norms,[54] both are international law-making acts and, as such, formal sources of international law.[55] Accordingly, if it can be shown that there are certain *acts* of non-state international institutional actors that determine legal rights and/or obligations of norm-subjects, one can, then, justifiably speak of those institutions as international law-making ones.[56]

The preceding remarks take us eventually to the problem of the nature of various acts, i.e., instruments of IOs. The way that they are created, and their nature, are in principle determined by what the founding treaty stipulates.

regulatory regimes, *see, e.g.*, Jovanović, "Theorizing 'Unidentified Normative Objects' of Global Regulatory Regimes." For a possible defense of the distinctive sources of global/transnational law, *see, e.g.*, Miodrag Jovanović, "'Global/Transnational Law' Challenges to Theorizing About Law," in Jorge Luis Fabra-Zamora (ed.), *Jurisprudence in a Globalized World* (Cheltenham: Edward Elgar Publishing, forthcoming 2019). Finally, the concept of "non-state international institutional actors" is much narrower than the concept of "non-state actors," which is now widely used in the discussions about international legal subjectivity. *Cf.* Thirlway, *The Sources of International Law*, 17.

53 Buchanan, "The Legitimacy of International Law," 80.

54 One should bear in mind what the Rapporteur Fitzmaurice remarked in the process of drafting the VCLT. He said that "the purely numerical element is not always conclusive in determining the character of the treaty. Thus, a treaty with three or four parties only may be nearer to a bilateral than to a multilateral treaty in its real character." Fitzmaurice, Special Rapporteur, "Second Report on the Law of Treaties," 20.

55 Kelsen, *Principles of International Law*, 320.

56 I give here two caveats. First, even if there are some such acts of law-making (e.g., certain decisions of IOs or their bodies), this will not necessarily solve the dispute among international scholars whether such acts should have the status of an independent source of international law. Second, I am leaving aside here the contribution of IOs in the form of initiators and facilitators of treaty-making conferences, which is nowadays a "usual way in which organizations contribute to the development of international law." They can do so in different ways. Klabbers, *An Introduction to International Institutional Law*, 217ff. *Cf.* Wolfrum, "Sources of International Law," par. 40. For a comprehensive treatment of this problem, *see*, José E. Alvarez, *International Organizations as Law-makers* (Oxford: Oxford University Press, 2005), chapters 5 and 6.

The situation is, however, not so simple. First, the constituent documents "are not always clear on the types of acts (and their nature) to be adopted." Second, even where this is the case, "practice tends to come up with examples that do not fit the mould of the constituent document."[57] One way to proceed would be to follow Klabbers in classifying all the potential acts of law-making in three categories. According to him, there are, first, those instruments that "aspire to be of a law-making nature, laying down more or less general abstract rules of general application, binding upon all subjects of a given legal system." Then, there are acts "in the nature of applying the law to certain configurations of facts," which are "more or less the equivalent of administrative acts" in municipal law.[58] Finally, there are the so-called acts of a household nature, which relate "to the (largely internal) functioning of the organization," such as making the budget or selection of the IO's officials.[59]

Although appealing, this classification has its potential drawbacks. First, while invoking a clear-cut distinction between general and individual legal acts of non-state international institutional actors, it reserves the label of "law-making" only for the former instruments. This is, however, already problematic from the perspective of Art. 38(1) of the ICJ Statute, which recognizes "judicial decisions," i.e., individual legal acts, as subsidiary formal sources of international law. The endorsed distinction is even more dubious if one takes into account the oft employed argument in the contemporary international legal scholarship that "the inevitable generation of legal normativity in the course of international adjudication should be understood as judicial lawmaking."[60] Second, Kelsen's remark that "[c]reation and application of law are only relatively, not absolutely, opposed to each other" may be of specific relevance for international law.[61] In particular, this may be the case

57 Klabbers, *An Introduction to International Institutional Law*, 197.

58 *Ibid*, 200.

59 *Ibid*, 201. Klabbers mentions as the fourth category acts "which aim to influence behaviour, but without creating law." *Ibid*.

60 Armin von Bogdandy and Ingo Venzke, "International Courts as Lawmakers," in Rüdiger Wolfrum and Ina Gätzschmann (eds.), *International Dispute Settlement: Room for Innovations?* (Heidelberg: Springer, 2013), 162.

61 Thus, he says that "[b]y 'source' of law not only the methods of creating law but also the methods of applying law may be understood." (Kelsen, *Principles of International Law*, 304) Venzke argues that "[t]he making of international law is in significant parts a result of processes that cannot be convincingly captured in doctrines of sources." According to him, "[s]ources picture lawmaking as a one-time act," while his "theoretical perspective sets out to elucidate legal change in the dynamics of continuous norm-application," that is, in the process of "communicative practice" in which the crucial question is who possesses the "semantic authority" to determine the normative meaning of legal provisions. (Ingo Venzke, *How Interpretation Makes International Law – On Semantic Change and Normative Twists*

when bodies of IOs are vested by founding treaties with powers that are supposed to be exercised in accordance with broadly defined goals and purposes of the given organization. Finally, the aforementioned "household" acts normally pose neither theoretical, nor practical challenges, because they are expressly provided for in the founding treaties. Put differently, they are acts taken under the doctrine of "attributed powers," which was already confirmed by the Permanent Court of Justice in the 1926 *European Commission for the Danube* case. The Court stated: "As the European Commission is not a State, but an international institution with a special purpose, it only has the functions bestowed upon it by the Definitive Statute with a view to the fulfilment of that purpose, but it has power to exercise these functions to their full extent, in so far as the Statute does not impose restrictions upon it."[62] This doctrine goes hand in hand with the conventional *Lotus* principle, according to which states are bound only by the international legal obligations to which they consented.

However, as noted by Klabbers, the doctrine of attributed powers is faced with at least two problems. Firstly, "[i]f an organization's powers are limited to those powers explicitly granted, then the organization remains, in effect, merely a vehicle for its members rather than an entity with a distinct will of its own."[63] One can, then, sensibly question the *raison d'être* of their existence. Even more importantly, organizations are "dynamic and living creatures, in constant development, and it is accepted that their founding fathers can never completely envisage the future." This has led to the question of whether IOs can exercise "implied powers" that are not expressly granted by a founding treaty.[64] In many ways, this problem is "at the heart" of the discussions regarding powers of IOs.[65]

[Oxford: Oxford University Press, 2012], 30) Sources are, however, understood here as "all the facts or events that provide the ways for the creation, modification, and annulment of valid legal norms" (Besson, "Theorizing the Sources of International Law," 169) For the discussion of the institutional aspect of law, it makes sense to distinguish between separate acts of norm-creation and norm-application, even under the assumption that the normative meaning of each created legal provision can be discerned only in the process of norm-application.

62 *Jurisdiction of the European Commission of the Danube between Galatz and Braila (Advisory Opinion)* [1926] Publ. PCIJ, Series B, no. 14, par. 179.

63 Klabbers, *An Introduction to International Institutional Law*, 65–66.

64 They "follow from the original purposes, functions or powers which remain firmly anchored in the organization's constitution." In that respect, "[i]mplied powers are subsidiary to the express powers." (Krzysztof Skubiszewski, "Implied Powers of International Organizations," in Yoram Dinstein (ed.), *International Law at a Time of Perplexity – Essays in Honour of Shabatai Rosenne* (Dordrecht: Martinus Nijhoff, 1989), 858). In the *Reparations* case, the ICJ stated with respect to the powers of the UN: "Under international law, the Organization must be deemed to have those powers which, though not expressly provided in the Charter, are conferred upon it by necessary implication, as being essential to the performance of its duties." *Reparation for Injuries Suffered in the Service of the United Nations (Advisory Opinion)*, par. 182.

65 Klabbers, *An Introduction to International Institutional Law*, 66.

Having all this in mind, the most intriguing issues related to the law-making capacity of non-state international institutions concern the following questions: whether some of their acts presumably adopted outside of the scope of "expressed powers" do create rights and obligations of norm-subjects; whether some of their acts, which are not intended by founding treaties to be of a legal nature, do produce legal effects and whether those effects amount to law-making; and, whether some of their acts, applying "at certain configurations of facts" can count as instances of "judicial lawmaking."

### 1) UN Security Council as an International Law-Making Institution

The most obvious candidate for the status of non-state international institution of law-making is the UN Security Council (SC). First, it is clearly vested with expressly conferred powers of making "decisions" within the confined "responsibility for the maintenance of international peace and security."[66] Of particular importance are responsibilities under Chapter VII. Normally, SC resolutions clearly indicate when the SC is taking actions within this chapter. For example, in the aforementioned SC Resolution 1199 concerning the Kosovo case, the Council explicitly states that it is "[a]cting under Chapter VII of the Charter of the United Nations," and it then proceeds to "demand" and "request" certain behavior from the involved parties, to "insist" upon their action or inaction, and to "decide" on certain matters. However, what is the nature of a SC resolution that is not taken within the purview of Chapter VII? Take the SC Resolution 2334 (2016). The Council does not specify under which of the chapters it is taking action, and yet it "*[r]eaffirms* that the establishment by Israel of settlements in the Palestinian territory occupied since 1967, including East Jerusalem, has no legal validity and constitutes a flagrant violation under international law" (par. 1) and it "*[r]eiterates* its demand that Israel immediately and completely cease all settlement activities in the occupied Palestinian territory" (par. 2).[67] There is a line of argumentation according to which any resolution not taken within Chapter VII "is not legally binding."[68]

66 Art. 24 and 25 of the UN Charter

67 S/RES/2334 (2016)

68 According to one such analysis, the Resolution "was adopted under the sixth chapter of the UN Charter (Pacific Settlement of Disputes) and as such is not mandatory. It contains a series of political determinations and recommendations to the international community." Alan Baker, "The Dangers of UN Security Council Resolution 2334 (2016)" (2016), available at www.europarl.europa.eu/meetdocs/2014_2019/documents/d-il/dv/thedangersofunscresolution2334_/thedangersofunscresolution2334_en.pdf

The problem with this reasoning is that the ICJ stated long ago that the purported legal bindingness of the SC resolution was not premised upon it being taken under the Chapter VII prerogatives. In the Advisory Opinion in the *Namibia* case, the ICJ ventured into the normative meaning of the text of SC Resolution 276, which did not employ words such as "demands" or "decides," but instead used the much toned-down phrase of "calls upon." The ICJ asked itself whether this is an instance of "exhortatory rather than mandatory language," and came to the conclusion that

> [i]n view of the nature of the powers under Article 25, the question whether they have been in fact exercised is to be determined in each case, having regard to the terms of the resolution to be interpreted, the discussions leading to it, the Charter provisions invoked and, in general, all circumstances that might assist in determining the legal consequences of the resolution of the Security Council.[69]

This has led some scholars to argue that "[a]ny *decision* of the Security Council is legally binding upon all U.N. member states, whether or not the text of the resolution explicitly references Chapter VII."[70] Even if this reading of the Charter is warranted, everything hinges upon the interpretation of the nature of the given resolution – whether it is to be treated as a decision or a recommendation. As the aforementioned ruling of the ICJ "was not necessarily making a general statement about the interpretation of SCRs, but was dealing with the question whether particular SCRs had binding effect,"[71] there is a pressing need for a more developed doctrine of the interpretation of the SC resolutions.[72] While the ICJ has provided further general guidelines for

69 *Legal Consequences for States of the Continued Presence of South Africa in Namibia (South West Africa) notwithstanding Security Council Resolution 276 (1970) (Advisory Opinion)* (1971) ICJ Rep 16, par. 114.

70 Dan Joyner, "Legal Bindingness of Security Council Resolutions Generally, and Resolution 2334 on the Israeli Settlements in Particular" (2017) *EJIL: Talk!*, available at www.ejiltalk.org/legal-bindingness-of-security-council-resolutions-generally-and-resolution-2334-on-the-israeli-settlements-in-particular/

71 Wood, nonetheless, states that "its remarks in this case may offer some guidance to the more general issues" and in the remainder of the paper he tries to develop some tentative guidelines for the interpretations of SC resolutions. Michael C. Wood, "The Interpretation of Security Council Resolutions" (1998) 2 *Max Planck Yearbook of United Nations Law*: 75.

72 For an updated version of Wood's approach to this question, *see*, Michael C. Wood, "The Interpretation of Security Council Resolutions, Revisited" (2017) 20 *Max Planck Yearbook of United Nations Law*: 1–35. *Cf.* Alexander Orakhelashvili, "The Acts of the Security Council: Meaning and Standards of Review" (2007) 11 *Max Planck Yearbook of United Nations Law*: 143–195.

addressing this problem,[73] the crux of the matter revolves around the legal and institutional limitations of the SC actions. It enjoys a wide discretion in characterizing certain events and situations as threats to international peace and security[74] and, thus, there is a tangible worry that "the scope of the SC's binding powers, if combined with an overriding binding force, would make the SC a dauntingly powerful organ."[75] This problem was additionally reinvigorated with novel actions of a law-making kind, such as issuing the so-called thematic resolutions (e.g., regarding women, children, civilians, and international terrorism),[76] as well as resolutions "not related to a particular incident or limited in time," but instead purporting to impose "general obligations on all states in a broad issue area for an indefinite period."[77] Particularly with respect to the latter resolutions, the SC has taken an unprecedented move, thereby assuming the power of a "world legislator" (*Weltgesetzgeber*).[78] And while it is true that the Council has an interest in enhancing the acceptance of its acts, because it "has no way of enforcing legislation unpopular with the wider membership of the United Nations,"[79] the possibility of the judicial review[80]

73 In the Advisory Opinion on the *Kosovo* case, the ICJ stressed the difference between interpretation of treaties and SC resolutions: "While the rules on treaty interpretation embodied in Articles 31 to 33 of the Vienna Convention on the Law of Treaties may provide guidance, differences between Security Council resolutions and treaties mean that the interpretation of Security Council resolutions also require that other factors be taken into account. Security Council resolutions are issued by a single, collective body and are drafted through a process that is very different from that used for the conclusion of a treaty." *Accordance with International Law of the Unilateral Declaration of Independence in Respect of Kosovo (Advisory Opinion)*, par. 94.

74 A notable example is SC Resolution 2177 (2014), in which the Council determined "that the unprecedented extent of the Ebola outbreak in Africa constitutes a threat to international peace and security."

75 Marko Divac Öberg, "The Legal Effects of Resolutions of the UN Security Council and General Assembly in the Jurisprudence of the ICJ" (2005) 16 *European Journal of International Law* 5: 885.

76 *See*, Rosanna Deplano, *The Strategic Use of International Law by the United Nations Security Council – An Empirical Study* (Cham: Springer, 2015), 33.

77 These were the post 9/11 resolutions on terrorism, such as SC Resolution 1373 (2000), SC Resolution 1540 (2004), and SC Resolution 2178 (2014). Chesterman, Johnstone, and Malone, *Law and Practice of the United Nations*, 145ff.

78 Klaus Dicke, "Weltgesetzgeber Sicherheitsrat" (2001) 49 *Vereinte Nationen* 5: 163–168.

79 Stefan Talmon, "The Security Council as World Legislature" (2005) 99 *American Journal of International Law* 1: 187. On various instances of states' resistance to the SC resolutions, including the justifiable form of civil disobedience that might foster the development of the UN law, *see*, Sufyan Droubi, *Resisting United Nations Security Council Resolutions* (London: Routledge, 2014).

80 Somewhat surprisingly, the EC Court of First Instance undertook in the famous *Kadi* case the judicial review of the SC resolutions on targeted sanctions on individuals suspected of terrorism. The Court concluded that it had jurisdiction to review "indirectly, the lawfulness

of the Security Council's acts and measures[81] seems to be of vital importance if constitutionalist aspects[82] of the UN legal-institutional structure are to be strengthened.[83]

## 2) UN General Assembly as an International Law-Making Institution

The second candidate for the status of non-state international institution of law-making is the UN General Assembly (GA). This is so despite the fact that, apart from the competence in the "household" matters of budget and membership, the UN Charter explicitly vests this body only with the power of issuing "recommendations," which are traditionally classified as "acts without

of the resolutions of the Security Council at issue, in the light of the higher rules of international law falling within the ambit of *jus cogens*, in particular the mandatory prescriptions concerning the universal protection of the rights of the human person." (par. 282) (*Yassin Abdullah Kadi* v. *Council of the European Union and Commission of the European Communities*, Case T-315/01 [2005]) The ruling expectedly sparked a vigorous debate, especially regarding the relationship between the EU and UN law. *See, e.g.*, Peter Hilpold, "The EU Law and the UN Law in Conflict: The Kadi Case" (2009) 13 *Max Planck Yearbook of United Nations Law*: 141–182. With respect to the role of the ICJ, Orakhelashvili argues that it "has never ruled out the possibility of judicial review of decisions of other principal organs of the United Nations." Orakhelashvili, "The Acts of the Security Council: Meaning and Standards of Review," 192. Drawing from the Lockerbie cases, Martenczuk argues that "this review is implicit in the exercise of the judicial function of the Court; it does not constitute an independent 'power of judicial review.'" Bernd Martenczuk, "The Security Council, the International Court and Judicial Review: What Lessons from Lockerbie?" (1999) 10 *European Journal of International Law* 3: 527.

81 For instance, one of the "unexpected" exercises of its powers concerned the creation of international tribunals to bring to trial persons accused of war crimes and crimes against humanity in the former Yugoslavia and Rwanda. Chesterman, Johnstone, and Malone, *Law and Practice of the United Nations*, xxxix. Although it was raised among international scholars, "[a] challenge to the competence of the Security Council to establish the ICTY was," according to Shahabuddeen, "repelled." Mohamed Shahabuddeen, *International Criminal Justice at the Yugoslav Tribunal: A Judge's Recollection* (Oxford: Oxford University Press, 2012), 24.

82 These aspects are emphasized by the ICTY in the *Tadić* case. The Court stated: "The Security Council is an organ of an international organization, established by a treaty which serves as a constitutional framework for that organization. The Security Council is thus subjected to certain constitutional limitations, however broad its powers under the constitution may be. Those powers cannot, in any case, go beyond the limits of the jurisdiction of the Organization at large, not to mention other specific limitations or those which may derive from the internal division of power within the Organization. In any case, neither the text nor the spirit of the Charter conceives of the Security Council as *legibus solutus* (unbound by law)." ICTY, *The Prosecutor* v. *Dusko Tadić*, IT-94-1-AR72, Appeals Chamber, Decision (1995), par. 28.

83 While the question of the desirability of constitutionalization of international law has obvious normative dimensions that fall outside the scope of this book, some aspects of this issue have important implications for the discussion about the (lack of) systemic features of the international legal order, which will be tackled in Chapter 7.

binding force."[84] As pointed out by Klabbers, the primary reason for paying so much attention to the GA acts is the fact that this is a body of the only universal organization that has a broad competence in a whole range of topics. Therefore, "[i]t is somewhat curious and unsatisfactory to consider the possibility that all this work may be legally inconsequential, or at best have indirect consequences."[85] During the Cold War era this view was fostered by the Third World states, which claimed "that *some* types of General Assembly resolutions ... are, in some way, sources of legal obligations." According to a strong version of the argument, they are binding per se, while a weak version stipulates that they "are binding by virtue of some special relationship they have to some of the traditional sources of international law."[86]

Proponents of the strong thesis may single out a class of the GA acts enacted under the name of "declarations." As put by Asamoah in one of the earliest comprehensive treatises on the legal nature of these GA acts, "there is the feeling that these declarations are of greater significance than ordinary resolutions."[87] While these acts "are not intended to become treaties," they nonetheless "purport to declare principles of international law."[88] The most notable examples include the Universal Declaration of Human Rights,[89] the Declaration on the Granting of Independence to Colonial Peoples,[90] the Declaration on the Prohibition of the Use of Nuclear and Thermonuclear Weapons,[91] the Declaration on the Inadmissibility of Intervention in the Domestic Affairs of States and the Protection of Their Independence and Sovereignty,[92] and the Declaration on Principles of International Law concerning Friendly Relations and Cooperation among States.[93]

84 Conforti, *The Law and Practice of the United Nations*, 217. The ICJ endorses this classical view in the *South West Africa* case, when noting that "[t]he persuasive force of Assembly resolutions can indeed be very considerable, but this is a different thing. It operates on the political not the legal level: it does not make these resolutions binding in law." *South West Africa Cases (Ethiopia* v. *South Africa; Liberia* v. *South Africa)*, second phase, [1966] ICJ Reports 6, par. 98.

85 Klabbers, *An Introduction to International Institutional Law*, 211.

86 Oscar M. Garibaldi, "The Legal Status of General Assembly Resolutions: Some Conceptual Observations" (1979) 73 *Proceedings of the Annual Meeting (American Society of International Law)*: 325.

87 Obed Y. Asamoah, *The Legal Significance of the Declarations of the General Assembly of the United Nations* (The Hague: Martinus Nijhoff, 1966), 19.

88 Chesterman, Johnstone, and Malone, *Law and Practice of the United Nations*, 152.

89 A/RES/3/217 A (1948)

90 A/RES/15/1514 (1960)

91 A/RES/1653(XVI) (1961)

92 A/RES/20/2131 (1965)

93 A/RES/25/2625 (1970)

The legal nature of a GA act, however, can hardly be discerned from mere reference to its name. On one occasion this has been clarified by the Office of Legal Affairs of the UN Secretariat, which stated as follows:

> In the practice of the United Nations a Declaration is a formal and solemn instrument suitable for those occasions when principles considered to be of special importance are being enunciated. Apart from the solemnity and formality associated with a declaration there is legally no distinction between a declaration and a recommendation which is less formal. In the practice of the United Nations all declarations of major importance have been adopted by resolution of the General Assembly or by special United Nations conferences.[94]

Hence, in order to determine potential legal effects of a GA act, including its capacity to create obligations,[95] one should employ a far more complex methodology. As noted by Chesterman, Johnstone, and Malone, the legal weight that these declarations shall be given "depends in part on the clarity of intention by participating states: Is the declaration meant to reflect a refinement or codification of international law?" Furthermore, it depends "on how much support the declaration receives: Is the vote unanimous? Did key states vote against it?" The ultimate question to be addressed is "whether the declaration itself is ever enough to create new law. Must there also be evidence of state practice outside the General Assembly supporting the proposition that the declaration is regarded as the law?"[96]

Both the practice and the doctrine, in that respect, point in the direction of the weaker thesis, which assigns legal effects to the GA acts due to some relationship with the main sources of international law. The most commonly stated relations are that the GA act is declaratory of an already existing international legal norm, or that it provides "evidence of a not-yet-existing but future norm."[97] The ICJ has confirmed the first type of connection in the *Nicaragua* case, when discussing the legal effects of the Declaration on Friendly Relations. It stated that "the effect of consent to the text of such

94 *United Nations Juridical Yearbook* (1981), p. 149.

95 "Legal effects themselves are not limited to force or obligation but cover a wide area including matters of status and operation." Blaine Sloan, "General Assembly Resolutions Revisited (Forty Years Later)" (1988) 58 *British Yearbook of International Law*: 105.

96 Chesterman, Johnstone, and Malone, *Law and Practice of the United Nations*, 152.

97 Garibaldi discharges the possibility that GA resolutions are either "interpretation" or "evidence" of some "preexisting norm" of international law, because this necessarily takes us back to the stronger thesis, which he deems both in its empirical and normative versions unwarranted. Garibaldi, "The Legal Status of General Assembly Resolutions: Some Conceptual Observations," 327.

resolutions cannot be understood as merely that of a 'reiteration or elucidation' of the treaty commitment undertaken in the Charter. On the contrary, it may be understood as an acceptance of the validity of the rule or set of rules declared by the resolution by themselves."[98] The connection of the second type is confirmed in the ICJ's *Nuclear Weapons* ruling. The Court stated "that General Assembly resolutions, even if they are not binding, may sometimes have normative value. They can, in certain circumstances, provide evidence important for establishing the existence of a rule or the emergence of an *opinio juris*." The Court further on emphasized that "[t]o establish whether this is true of a given General Assembly resolution, it is necessary to look at its content and the conditions of its adoption; it is also necessary to see whether an *opinio juris* exists as to its normative character." Similarly, "a series of resolutions may show the gradual evolution of the *opinio juris* required for the establishment of a new rule."[99]

All this seems to justify the scholarly characterization of the GA acts as "intermediary legal products,"[100] insofar as they "are in the process of becoming something more."[101] Although not acts of genuine law-making, the GA acts are, nonetheless, "an important link in the development of either a conventional or customary norm, and may by themselves or combined with other factors have important legal effects on the growth of law."[102] This conclusion can be *mutatis mutandis* extended to some of the acts of other territorially or functionally specialized international organizations, whose potential legal effects are usually not of the universal scope.

This leaves us with the question whether individual acts of the international dispute-settlement institutions may in some sense qualify for the status of law-making acts. The answer to this question largely depends on the understanding of the process of interpretation and law-application, as well as on the precedential nature of the given adjudicative regime. Since these issues highlight the aforementioned relativity of the distinction between law-making and

98 *Military and Paramilitary Activities in and against Nicaragua*, par. 188.

99 In the case at hand, the Court noted that "several of the resolutions under consideration in the present case have been adopted with substantial numbers of negative votes and abstentions; thus, although those resolutions are a clear sign of deep concern regarding the problem of nuclear weapons, they still fall short of establishing the existence of an *opinio juris* on the illegality of the use of such weapons." *Legality of the Threat or Use of Nuclear Weapons*, par. 70–71. According to the ILC's DC 12(2), a resolution adopted by an international organization may "provide evidence" of the existence of a customary rule of law, or it may "contribute to its development."

100 Besson, "Theorizing the Sources of International Law," 170.

101 Sloan, "General Assembly Resolutions Revisited (Forty Years Later)," 108.

102 *Ibid*, 124.

law-applying institutions at the international level, they will be addressed in the following section on the judicialization of the international legal order.

### *b) Judicialization of the International Legal Order*

As pointed out at the beginning of this chapter, normative orders imply judgment, insofar as in the process of norm-application it is possible to "judge" whether the undertaken behavior is in accordance with the prescribed rule. There are normative orders (e.g., morality) that rely on some such "judgments" of the very norm-subjects whose behavior is regulated by the given norm. Other normative orders, however, turn to institutionalization, which primarily means that the function of judgment is assigned to a specially devised institution. Law is one such order, which typically empowers an adjudicative body of some sort to make a "judgment" in case there are doubts whether the undertaken behavior of a norm-subject was in conformity with the stipulated rule. Institutionalization of judgment at the municipal level is strengthened by the fact that jurisdiction of the established judicial bodies is compulsory for norm-subjects, which means that they may be forcibly brought before the court. It was emphasized already that one of the specificities of the international legal order concerns the fact that its main norm-subjects, states, still largely serve as its *agencies*, i.e., *officials*, when it comes to the administration and enforcement of international law.[103] Furthermore, the international legal order knows of no general system of compulsory jurisdiction and hence, "adjudication is the exception, not the rule."[104] All this has profound implications for the discussion about non-state international actors of law-application.

Judicialization can be defined as "the process through which judicial authority over the institutional evolution of a society is constructed."[105] In the formative period of the modern, Westphalian international legal order,[106] whose central features were horizontality and the law of coexistence, diplomatic mediation and arbitration were the main forms of settling disputes between norm-subjects who disagreed whether the undertaken behavior was in contravention with the given rule of international law. In fact, these forms of

103 Waldron, "Are Sovereigns Entitled to the Benefit of the International Rule of Law?," 330.

104 Hillier, *Sourcebook on Public International Law*, 78.

105 Alec Sweet Stone, *The Judicial Construction of Europe* (Oxford: Oxford University Press, 2004), 2.

106 For an overview of the historical instances of international arbitration in antiquity, *see, e.g.*, Jackson Harvey Ralston, *International Arbitration from Athens to Locarno* (Stanford: Stanford University Press, 1929), especially Ch. XV.

dispute settlement dominated interstate relations until the aforementioned turning events of the twentieth century,[107] which generated the consciousness of international "commonness" and the gradual formation of a more integrated international community. Thus, one may argue that the process of the court-like form of judicialization of the international legal order accelerated with the establishment of the two post-war global institutional structures, each with its own "world court"[108] – the Permanent Court of International Justice (PCIJ) after World War I and the International Court of Justice (ICJ) following World War II.[109] Already the first of them "was a historic 'melting-pot' of ideals about international justice and . . . international community as well as notions of international law. It was the culmination so far of a persistent movement towards, in prosaic terms, more effective settlement of international disputes."[110]

The existing "world court" is only a part of the advanced international dispute resolution order.[111] This order is principally grounded in Art. 33 of the UN Charter, which stipulates that the parties to a dispute that may endanger international peace and security shall "seek a solution by negotiation, enquiry, mediation,

107 Early attempts at establishing some international court-like institutions were met with the determinate resistance of states, thereby revealing their "strong preference for maintaining arbitration as a flexible, autonomous procedure which, while adjudicative in character, remains pliable to their will throughout its course." Georges Abi-Saab, "Fragmentation or Unification: Some Concluding Remarks" (1999) 31 *New York University Journal of International Law and Politics* 4: 923.

108 This label is traditionally reserved for "the principal judicial organ" of the world organization (Art. 92 of the UN Charter). There are other judicial bodies operating at the global level: the WTO Dispute Settlement System; the International Tribunal for the Law of the Sea (ITLOS); and the International Criminal Court (ICC). There are also some global international arbitral bodies, the most important of which are the Permanent Court of Arbitration (PCA) and the International Center for the Settlement of Investment Disputes. Cesare P. R. Romano, "Litigating International Law Disputes: Where To?," in Natalie Klein (ed.), *Litigating International Law Disputes – Weighing the Balance* (Cambridge: Cambridge University Press, 2014), 461.

109 The PCIJ was preceded by the PCA, established under the 1899 and 1907 Conventions for the Pacific Settlement of International Disputes. Its name, however, "was a misnomer," insofar as it was not composed of permanent judges, but had to be summoned on an ad hoc basis for each case of dispute settlement. Ole Spierman, *International Legal Argument in the Permanent Court of International Justice – The Rise of the International Judiciary* (Cambridge: Cambridge University Press, 2005), 4.

110 *Ibid*, 3.

111 Some scholars in the field speak of the "international dispute resolution system." *See, e.g.*, Anna Spain, "Integration Matters: Rethinking the Architecture of International Dispute Resolution" (2010) 32 *University of Pennsylvania Journal of International Law* 1: 1–55. I am for the moment deliberately avoiding the word "system" because it implies that there are structural relations between various international dispute settlement actors that possess the systemic quality. This is, however, debatable. I will return to this problem in Chapter 7.

conciliation, arbitration, judicial settlement, resort to regional agencies or arrangements, or other peaceful means of their own choice."[112] A more rapid multiplication of new or significantly reformed international dispute settlement institutions,[113] however, started only in the 1990s, and it was further marked with qualitative changes in terms of the nature and competencies of these bodies.[114]

What is an upshot of the judicialization of the international legal order? One way of approaching this issue is by linking it to the debate about the alleged fragmentation of international law. Simply put, even if one were to believe that nothing is wrong with the multiplication of international adjudicative institutions, "one will still have to address questions relating to their interaction and how to delimit their respective roles."[115] I will return to this problem in Chapter 7. The alternative way of addressing this issue requires elucidation of the possible influence of these institutions on the development of international law. International adjudicative institutions were all formed with the primary purpose of settling disputes on the basis of the applicable law. However, as famously noted by Lauterpacht, "[i]nstitutions set up for the achievement of definite purposes grow to fulfil tasks not wholly identical with those which were in the minds of their authors at the time of their creation."[116] Hence, some commentators argue that "it is no longer convincing" to think of these institutions solely in "their role of settling disputes."[117]

112 Art. 37 states that should the disputing parties "fail to settle it by the means indicated in that Article, they shall refer it to the Security Council."

113 Romano provides a detailed taxonomy of the "international rule of law institutions." They are first divided into classes of "adjudicative" and "non-adjudicative" means, where the former ones issue binding decisions and are composed of independent members. The class of "international adjudicative means" can be further divided in at least three distinct "orders": (a) international courts and tribunals; (b) arbitral tribunals; and (c) international claims and compensations bodies. Cesare P. R. Romano, "A Taxonomy of International Rule of Law Institutions" (2011) 2 *Journal of International Dispute Settlement* 1: 241–277. Since the purpose of this section is not to provide a clear-cut classification of all the international dispute settlement bodies, which is any way hardly possible, but to address the problem of law-application at the international level, I will focus on the class of "adjudicative" institutions understood in this broader sense. *Cf.* John G. Merrills, *International Dispute Settlement* (5th ed.) (Cambridge: Cambridge University Press, 2011).

114 Cesare P. R. Romano, "The Proliferation of International Judicial Bodies: The Pieces of the Puzzle" (1999) 31 *New York University Journal of International Law and Politics* 4: 710.

115 Thomas Buerganthal, "Proliferation of International Courts and Tribunals: Is It Good or Bad?" (2001) 14 *Leiden Journal of International Law* 2: 267–268.

116 Sir Hersch Lauterpacht, *The Development of International Law by the International Court* (Cambridge: Cambridge University Press, 1982), 5.

117 von Bogdandy and Venzke, "International Courts as Lawmakers," 162. For a recent proposal that international adjudicative institutions should not only function as dispute settlers, but also as "peacemakers," *see*, Anna Spain, "Examining the International Judicial Function: International Courts as Dispute Resolvers" (2011) 34 *Loyola of Los Angeles International and Comparative Law Review* 1: 5–31.

Despite the fact that parties to a dispute normally do not resort to the means of international litigation with the idea "to swell international jurisprudence, the decisions of courts and tribunals often have just that effect."[118] The question is, then, whether international adjudicating institutions are merely contributing to the development of international law or are also assuming the function of genuine law-making. The response hinges upon the characterization of the process of judicial decision-making mentioned earlier, as well as on the potential precedential nature of the adjudicative decisions.

Traditional wisdom says that there is no formal system of precedent in international law and, since they have binding force only for the parties to a dispute, judicial decisions are only subsidiary sources of international law. However, such categorization of these decisions "only partly captures, and may even understate their impact on the development of international law."[119] Even the skeptics with respect to the law-making power of international adjudicative institutions are not ready to deny that at least part of the ICJ's jurisprudence does have the effect of "*fertilizing* [traditional] modes of law-formation."[120] On the other hand, von Bogdandy and Venzke believe that there is enough empirical evidence to support the stronger claim that international courts act like lawmakers. Their belief is grounded in the assumption that the nature of adjudicative interpretation is not that of cognition.[121] This is a well-known stance of "interpretive realism,"[122] according to which "ascribing meaning to normative texts is a noncognitive activity – not a matter of cognition, but rather a matter of decision."[123] Proponents of this view hold that the search for applicable law in the given factual circumstances most commonly

118 John Merrills, "The Place of International Litigation in International Law," in Klein (ed.), *Litigating International Law Disputes – Weighing the Balance*, 15.

119 Shane Darcy, *Judges, Law and War: The Judicial Development of International Humanitarian Law* (Cambridge: Cambridge University Press, 2014), 37.

120 Berman offers a handful of landmark ICJ cases that affected the subsequent treaty and/or customary international law. Sir Franklin Berman, "The International Court of Justice as an 'Agent' of Legal Development," in Christian J. Tams and James Sloan (eds.), *The Development of International Law by the International Court of Justice* (Oxford: Oxford University Press, 2013), 20.

121 von Bogdandy and Venzke, "International Courts as Lawmakers," 166.

122 Interpretive legal realism is commonly opposed to "legal formalism," which proceeds from the idea that "the law is 'rationally' determinate" and that "judicial decision-making involves nothing more than mechanical deduction on the model of the syllogism." (Brian Leiter, "Legal Realism and Legal Formalism: What Is the Issue?" (2010) 16 *Legal Theory* 2: 111) Only under the premise of some form of legal formalism can one speak of court's substantive and procedural "errors." *See*, A. Mark Weisburd, *Failings of the International Court of Justice* (Oxford: Oxford University Press, 2016)

123 Riccardo Guastini, "A Realistic View on Law and Legal Cognition" (2015) 27 *Revus – Journal for Constitutional Theory and Philosophy of Law*: 46.

does not yield one determinate result,[124] but instead prompts judges to get into "the process of *finding* decisions."[125] In doing so, they often reason by providing abstract and categorical legal statements that go beyond the actual case at hand[126] and, as such, may serve "as authoritative reference points for later legal practice."[127] These statements refer to legal matters that are not only substantive, but also procedural, such as, for instance, evidentiary issues.[128]

Even if one subscribes to this view of the nature of judicial interpretation,[129] it is far from clear what legal weight is attributed to some such decisions of international adjudicative institutions,[130] that is, whether they are treated as binding in subsequent cases.[131] For example, detailed studies of the practice of the ICJ, the WTO adjudicative bodies, or investment treaty arbitration

124 Otherwise, the practice of international adjudication would not be that much packed – criticists would say overloaded – with separate and dissenting opinions and declarations. The only ICJ case, for example, which was decided with no appended individual or joint opinion to a judgment/advisory opinion, was *Maritime Delimitation in the Black Sea (Romania* v. *Ukraine)*, Judgment, I.C.J. Reports 2009, p. 61.

125 This view, however, does not necessarily "detract from the deductive model of legal reasoning." This reasoning is "an instrument for controlling and legitimizing judicial power. It regards the modus of *justifying* decisions and not the process of *finding* decisions." von Bogdandy and Venzke, "International Courts as Lawmakers," 167, 168.

126 This is particularly true of advisory opinions, because they, "by their very nature, may address legal norms of consequence for all States." Darcy, *Judges, Law and War*, 26. In her thorough study of the advisory function of the ICJ, Aljaghoub comes to the conclusion that "the primary motive for most advisory opinions rendered so far has been for clarification of the law and guidance for future action, rather than judicial legitimisation of decisions already taken." Mahasen M. Aljaghoub, *The Advisory Function of the International Court of Justice: 1946 –2005* (Heidelberg: Springer, 2006), 223. However, "the clarification or identification of legal rules is situated at the boundary between simply stating the existing law, law-development, and law-making, which are not separated by a precise definition." Karin Oellers-Frahm "Lawmaking through Advisory Opinions?" (2011) 12 *German Law Journal* 5: 1046.

127 von Bogdandy and Venzke, "International Courts as Lawmakers," 171.

128 It is, for instance, argued that the ways in which the ICJ "chose to resolve" procedural issues of evidence and fact finding in *Nicaragua* v. *United States* were "precedent-setting and have continued to guide the Court in its treatment and evaluation of evidence ever since." Paul S. Reichler and Yuri B. Parkhomenko, "Nicaragua v. United States and Matters of Evidence Before the International Court of Justice," in Edgardo Sobenes Obregon and Benjamin Samson (eds.), *Nicaragua Before the International Court of Justice – Impacts on International Law* (Cham: Springer, 2018), 44.

129 Needless to say, this view is heavily contested in contemporary legal philosophy. For a recent overview of the problematics, but mostly from the Anglo-American perspective, *see*, Brian G. Slocum (ed.), *The Nature of Legal Interpretation: What Jurists Can Learn about Legal Interpretation from Linguistics and Philosophy* (Chicago: University of Chicago Press, 2017).

130 As put by Darcy, "they do carry legal weight, although a precise value cannot be easily determined." Darcy, *Judges, Law and War*, 26.

131 A special aspect of this problem concerns the treatment of judicial decisions by adjudicative institutions belonging to different specialized international legal regimes. I will address this problem in Chapter 7.

tribunals, demonstrate that *some form of precedential weight* is assigned to the decisions of the respective adjudicative institutions. At the same time, commentators commonly emphasize that the ICJ "does not regard its previous decisions as laying down the law with binding effect";[132] that the adopted WTA panel reports "are not binding precedent and do not control subsequent panels";[133] and, that normative expectations generated by a coherent jurisprudence "cannot encompass the expectation that investment treaty tribunals will always decide consistently or may not deviate from earlier jurisprudence – an expectation that would result in arbitral precedent being binding."[134]

In that respect, most of the international adjudicative institutions seem to function on the premises of the highest common law courts, which "even where they aver that they are treating their former decisions as 'normally binding,' their power to depart 'when it appears right to do so' means that they are not strictly bound."[135] Therefore, the requisite "sense of obligation" to follow earlier decisions, i.e., their authoritativeness, seems to be generated primarily by the quality of their reasoning.[136] It is, thus, noted that in the absence of the formal doctrine of *stare decisis*, the precedential weight of the ICJ's jurisprudence depends on whether it is "highly persuasive."[137] Similarly, it is argued that adopted reports of the WTO panels "have strong persuasive power and may be viewed as a form of nonbinding precedent."[138] In the same vain, it is stressed that "investment treaty tribunals create a system of persuasive

[132] Mohamed Shahabuddeen, *Precedent in the World Court* (Cambridge: Cambridge University Press, 1996), 12.

[133] David Palmeter and Petros C. Mavroidis, "The WTO Legal System: Sources of Law" (1998) 92 *American Journal of International Law* 3: 401.

[134] Stephan W. Schill, "System-Building in Investment Treaty Arbitration and Lawmaking" (2011) 12 *German Law Journal* 5: 1108.

[135] Shahabuddeen, *Precedent in the World Court*, 10. Unlike the highest common law courts, lower common law courts are bound by the established precedents, whereas continental courts are, normally, only authorized "to consider previous decisions as part of the general legal material from which the law may be ascertained." *Ibid*, 9.

[136] In the words of von Bogdandy and Venzke, "[t]he lawmaking effect of judicial decisions ... does not only depend on the *voluntas*, but also on its *ratio*." von Bogdandy and Venzke, "International Courts as Lawmakers," 174. Darcy also speaks of the "persuasive authority" of international adjudicative institutions. Darcy, *Judges, Law and War*, 30. This stance is shared even by those who are otherwise skeptical of the law-making function of international adjudicative institutions. Focusing on the ICJ's role, Berman says that its decisions "will be tested in the rumbustious market-place of ideas, and so they should be; those that convince by the quality of their reasoning (and, I add, by the convincingness of their fact-finding) will have profound effects ... while those that don't (on either score) will fade." Berman, "The International Court of Justice as an 'Agent' of Legal Development," 21.

[137] Shahabuddeen, *Precedent in the World Court*, 128.

[138] Palmeter and Mavroidis, "The WTO Legal System: Sources of Law," 401.

and non-binding precedent that States and investors generally focus on in developing normative expectations."[139]

The additional source of the ascribed precedential weight and authoritativeness may be found in the belief that *consistency* and *coherence* are somehow inherent in the adjudicative function.[140] Legal reasoning is about "supporting judicial decisions by arguments or reasons which cumulate, form chains, or form cumulation-nets."[141] Coherence in adjudication, thus, amounts to forming "coherent cumulations, chains, or nets of reasons."[142] Consistency, on the other hand, is implicit in the belief that like cases should be decided in a like manner.[143] That is, "[c]onsistency may provide a rationale for a limited exercise of analogy. Where an earlier case has settled some indeterminacy in the application of the law, and where the rationale for the earlier decision is equally applicable to the later facts, then it would be inconsistent to decide the later case differently."[144] Hence, although perfectly permissible, departure from the established jurisprudence is considered justifiable only if there are not sufficient grounds for some form of analogical reasoning.[145] Where some such grounds

139 Schill, "System-Building in Investment Treaty Arbitration and Lawmaking," 1109.

140 Needless to say, it is a matter of jurisprudential contestation whether "somehow" boils down to the claim that coherence is "necessary, sufficient or desirable" in legal reasoning. *See*, Julie Dickson, "Interpretation and Coherence in Legal Reasoning," in Zalta (ed.), *The Stanford Encyclopedia of Philosophy* (Winter 2016 ed.), at https://plato.stanford.edu/archives/win2016/entries/legal-reas-interpret/.

141 Arguments are cumulated in the following way: "The reasons which justify *ORx* are $r_1$ and $r_2$ and $r_3$ and $r_n$." They form chains when "[t]he reasons which justify *ORx* are $r_1$ because of $p_1$." Finally, they form cumulation nets in the following way: "The reasons which justify *ORx* are $r_1$ because $p_1$ and $r_2$ because $p_1$ and $p_2$" Leonor Moral Soiano, "A Modest Notion of Coherence in Legal Reasoning. A Model for the European Court of Justice" (2003) 16 *Ratio Juris* 3:297, fn. 3–5.

142 *Ibid*, 297.

143 See in more detail in Neil MacCormick, *Legal Reasoning and Legal Theory* (with a revised foreword) (Oxford: Clarendon Press, 1994), chapters VII and VIII. For a skeptic's view of the value of coherence in adjudication, *see*, Joseph Raz, "The Relevance of Coherence," in *Ethics in Public Domain – Essays in Morality of Law and Politics* (revised ed.) (Oxford: Clarendon Press, 1995), 301ff.

144 Grant Lamond, "Precedent and Analogy in Legal Reasoning," in Zalta (ed.), *The Stanford Encyclopedia of Philosophy* (Spring 2016 ed.), at https://plato.stanford.edu/archives/spr2016/entries/legal-reas-prec/

145 In general, "[a]n *analogy* is a comparison between two objects, or systems of objects, that highlights respects in which they are thought to be similar." Paul Bartha, "Analogy and Analogical Reasoning," in Zalta (ed.), *The Stanford Encyclopedia of Philosophy* (Winter 2016 ed.), at https://plato.stanford.edu/archives/win2016/entries/reasoning-analogy/ Again, it is disputable what sort of analogical reasoning can be justified by resorting to the values of consistency and coherence. For instance, while dispelling "strong analogy," which "amounts to the application of basically the same reasons to novel cases," Marmor argues in favor of "weak analogy," whereby treating like cases alike amounts to the application of "*a similar*

exist,[146] treating like cases alike is additionally considered as realizing justice in "its simplest form,"[147] as well as enhancing legitimacy of the given adjudicator.[148]

As already emphasized, the general belief in legitimacy of political authorities has proven to be the strongest ground for treating legal rules as binding reasons for action. Raz highlight this intricate link when noting that "international institutions cannot be legitimate without their directives being accepted and respected by people generally."[149] This is of particular relevance for international adjudicative institutions, which in contrast to their municipal counterparts "lack a monopoly of enforcement power, and have only the power to persuade the addressees of their decisions that those decisions are correct."[150]

## 3 (COERCIVE) GUARANTEES IN INTERNATIONAL LAW

One of the most commonly raised objections against the full-fledged "legality" of international law concerns its lack of coercive enforcement mechanisms. As Austin famously noted, by "being rules set and enforced by *mere opinion*" rules of "international law" belong to a class of "objects frequently but *improperly* termed *laws*."[151] Simply put, horizontality of international relations is irreconcilable with Austin's command theory of law.[152] This means two things: neither international law knows of "a sanction properly so called," which "is an evil annexed to a command," nor the party who will enforce rules set by general opinion against any future violator is ever "determinate and assignable."[153]

*principle*" and "is justified by a direct appeal to the value of coherence in adjudication." Andrei Marmor, *Law in the Age of Pluralism* (Oxford: Oxford University Press, 2007), 194.

146 It is important to bear in mind that consistency requires an adequate caseload. Discussing the case of the "world court," Berman notes that "the occasional and adventitious nature of the ICJ's caseload has the almost automatic consequence that the Court is unlikely to be given the opportunity to revisit successively particular areas of substantive international law." Berman, "The International Court of Justice as an 'Agent' of Legal Development," 20.

147 This is, in Hart's opinion, "justice in the application of the law." Hart, "Postscript," 206. I will return to this issue in Chapter 6.

148 Palmeter and Mavroidis, "The WTO Legal System: Sources of Law," 402.

149 Raz, "Why the State," 23.

150 Palmeter and Mavroidis, "The WTO Legal System: Sources of Law," 402.

151 Austin, *The Province of Jurisprudence Determined*, 20.

152 Lars Vinx, "Austin, Kelsen, and the Model of Sovereignty: Notes on the History of Modern Legal Positivism," in Michael Freeman and Patricia Mindus (eds.), *The Legacy of John Austin's Jurisprudence* (Dordrecht: Springer, 2013), 66.

153 Austin, *The Province of Jurisprudence Determined*, 125.

For Weber, the former point is less relevant, insofar as law's guarantees may come in the form of either "physical or psychological coercion."[154] In that respect, he explicitly states that "the means of coercion are irrelevant." For example, "[e]ven a 'brotherly admonition,' such as has been used in various religious sects as the first degree of mild coercion of the sinner, is 'law' provided it is regulated by some order and applied by a staff."[155] Hence, Weber takes the latter point on institutionalization as crucial for the emergence of law as a distinctive normative order. That is, for a set of rules to be classified as "law" there has to be "a staff engaged in enforcement."[156] His reluctance to straightforwardly label international law as "true" law comes exactly from this source:

> As is well known, it has often been denied that international law could be called law, precisely because there is no legal authority above the state capable of enforcing it. In terms of the present terminology this would be correct, for we could not call "law" a system the sanctions of which consisted wholly in expectations of disapproval and of the reprisals of injured parties, which is thus guaranteed entirely by convention and self-interest without the help of a specialized enforcement agency.[157]

Kelsen also distinguishes law from other normative orders by stressing its coercive nature. Law coercively sanctions its violators "in the sense that certain possessions are taken from ... [them] against their will, if necessary by the employment of physical force."[158] For Kelsen, however, it is not the special, centralized "staff" that is crucial for the existence of law as a normative order, but the fact that the undertaken coercive measures are authorized. Hence, he says that "[i]nternational law is true law if the coercive acts of states ... are, in principle, *permitted* (M. J.) only as a reaction against a delict," that is, if such coercive acts "can be interpreted as a reaction of the international legal community."[159] Put differently, international law is true law provided that acts of force can, in the form of coercive sanctioning measures, be attributed to the international legal order as such.[160] In that respect, whether a centralized

154 Weber, *Economy and Society*, 34.
155 *Ibid*, 35.
156 *Ibid*, 34.
157 Despite all this, Weber somewhat laconically concludes that "for purposes of legal terminology exactly the opposite [to treat international law as law] might well be acceptable." *Ibid*, 35.
158 Kelsen, *General Theory of Law and State*, 19.
159 Kelsen, *Principles of International Law*, 18.
160 One is, then, able to differentiate between acts of "retorsion" and "reprisals," insofar as only in the latter case the employment of physical force is permitted, i.e., authorized, and thus can be qualified as a sanctioning measure in international law. *Ibid*, 25.

("collective security"), or decentralized ("self-help") force monopoly prevails is a contingent matter[161] that normally has bearing on the efficiency of the regime,[162] but it does not affect its legal nature.

Although Kelsen was the sole important legal philosopher of the twentieth century to deal extensively with international law, he is still nowadays criticized for grounding international law's "legality" in coercion. In dismissing theories of international law that put force to the forefront, Shaw, for instance, argues that to treat, as Kelsen does, the states' rights of self-defense and reprisals as the sanctions of international law "is to misunderstand the role of sanctions within a system because they are at the disposal of the states, not the system itself."[163] Moreover, one should not overlook the fact that the present trend in international law is "to restrict the use of force as far as possible, thus leading to the absurd result that the more force is controlled in international society, the less legal international law becomes."[164] Criticism of this sort, however, misses the point about Kelsen's argument. It is not so much about the quantity of force used in interstate relations, as it is about the quality. As already pointed out, what Kelsen wants to underscore is that the truly legal nature of international rules decisively depends on the fact that coercion is allowed only as an authorized act of sanctioning. It is of secondary importance who is authorized to undertake the act of sanctioning.[165]

Shaw is, nonetheless, on the right track when claiming that "one cannot discover the nature of international law" by grounding it in a force-centered account.[166] Yet, he may be right for differing reasons. To begin with, coercion may be irrelevant for the conceptualization of international law simply because it is not a necessary feature of the concept of law. As indicated earlier, some prominent contemporary legal philosophers belonging to the camp of metaphysically driven conceptual analysts (e.g., Raz, Green), hold this view with respect to the nature of law. However, as Chapter 2 shows, the metaphysically driven conceptual analysis is problematic for a number of reasons. When it comes to this particular argument, the alleged counterexample of "society of angels," employed within the possible-worlds methodology, is so

161 Already at the time of publication of his *Principles of International Law*, in 1952, Kelsen believed that the "process of centralization [of international law] is steadily increasing" by the multiplication of international tribunals and executive agencies. *Ibid*, 403.

162 "It stands to reason that collective security is more effective if the force monopoly of the community is centralized than if it is decentralized." *Ibid*, 15.

163 Shaw, *International Law*, 5.

164 *Ibid*.

165 "Even if the principle of self-help prevails, legal and illegal employment of force are to be distinguished." Kelsen, *Principles of International Law*, 14.

166 Shaw, *International Law*, 5.

remote from the actual world in which we live[167] that it simply fails to tell us anything interesting about law as a human social practice.[168] Hence, it is safe to argue within the proposed alternative of the prototype theory that one of the typical features of law is that it is institutionally guaranteed by *some means* of coercion.[169]

If this is so, in what sense, then, is Shaw heading in the right direction with his dismissal of force-centered accounts of international law? First, the claim about coercive guarantees as the typical feature of law is not to be understood in an Austinian sense, as the claim that law necessarily threatens with the infliction of "evil and pain." If this was so, international law, or at least large parts of it, would hardly qualify for the status of law. However, such a reading is inconceivable even at the municipal level, because sanctioning measures may come in a variety of forms and need not necessarily take the shape of sheer physical force. Even Austin in one place – probably unintentionally – speaks of inflicting "evil or *inconvenience*" (M. J.) as forms of sanctioning measures.[170] And indeed, legal norms might be backed up by all sorts of "inconveniences" for norm violators – from subjecting them to acts of physical violence to merely depriving them of some earlier acquired entitlements and benefits. What is far more important is that, regardless of the form, norm violators shall be exposed to some such "inconveniences" against their will. As explicated, this is the only sense in which one may speak of law as being "non-optional" for its norm-subjects.[171]

167 As pointed out by Jackson, "[t]he key point is that the right way to describe a counterfactual world sometimes depends in part on how the actual world is, not solely on how the counterfactual world is in itself. The point is not one about the space of possible worlds in some newly recognized sense of 'possible,' but instead one about the role of the actual world in determining the correct way to describe certain counterfactual possible worlds." Jackson, *From Metaphysics to Ethics – A Defence of Conceptual Analysis*, 77–78.

168 Himma rightly notes that "[i]t seems counterintuitive to think that law applies to beings that are so very different from us when *our* concept of law, as Raz keenly observes, is constructed by *our* social practices; and those practices are intended to regulate the behaviour of self-interested beings like us in conditions of material scarcity." Himma, "The Authorization of Coercive Enforcement Mechanisms as a Conceptually Necessary Feature of Law," 603.

169 Although Himma insists on the metaphysically driven conceptual analysis as an adequate methodological approach, his conclusion about "the centrality of coercive enforcement mechanisms in every paradigm instance of law we have ever known" (*ibid*, 593) is far more easily defendable within the prototype theory, because it implies that not all instances covered by the concept-term "law" are equal (i.e., some are non-paradigm or nontypical). *Cf.* Schauer, *The Force of Law*, 43.

170 Austin, *The Province of Jurisprudence Determined*, 126. The reason to believe that the choice of the word "inconvenience" is careless stems from the fact that throughout the book Austin persistently uses the phrase "evil or pain." *Ibid*, 21, 30, 139, 148.

171 *See, supra* pp. 137–139.

This leaves us with the alternative claim that law necessarily relies on forcible enforcement mechanisms, which yet again casts doubt on the "legality" of international law. Once more, unjustifiably. Even municipal law relies on two tiers of enforcement mechanisms – "primary" and "secondary." As stressed by Hathaway and Shapiro, primary enforcement is "addressed to the conduct rule violators."[172] That is, in many instances a norm violator will be called upon to execute the ordered sanctioning measure by herself (e.g., to demolish an illegally built residential unit, to report to jail, to leave the country, etc.). Only if she fails to do so, will the secondary enforcement mechanism be put into effect and the respective enforcement agency will be employed to do that, if necessary by the use of force.

With these distinctions in mind, Hathaway and Shapiro offer the most elaborate account of enforcement in international law. They proceed by arguing that all versions of skepticism toward international law boil down to what they label as "the Modern State Conception," which "requires legal systems to (1) possess *internal* enforcement mechanisms (2) that use the threat and exercise of *physical force*."[173] However, as already indicated, this conception is defunct even at the municipal level due to "its parochial definition of law enforcement."[174] Namely, legal orders, even municipal ones, may rely on the method of "*external outcasting*." It is qualified as "outcasting," insofar as "the coercion used to enforce the law need not involve the threat and exercise of violence [but] it may involve the threat of exclusion."[175] It is "external" because it is "frequently carried out by those outside the regime."[176] Consequently, "allowing the Modern State Conception to set the terms of the debate over international law leads us to ask and answer the wrong questions."[177]

The fact that international law typically relies on "external outcasting" does not imply that internalization and the use of physical force are completely absent at the international level. Hence, when all the instruments of international law enforcement are presented along the axes internal/external and physical/non-physical, it is possible to operate with the following categories: (1) internal and physical; (2) external and physical; (3) internal and nonphysical; and (4) external and nonphysical. It is noticeable that the Modern State Conception knows only of the first category, while the remaining three fall

172 Hathaway and Shapiro, "Outcasting: Enforcement in Domestic and International Law," 271.
173 *Ibid*, 269.
174 *Ibid*, 300.
175 *Ibid*, 256.
176 *Ibid*, 258.
177 *Ibid*, 302.

outside of the scope of that account.[178] To begin with, nearly all use of physical force in international law is externalized. Despite the UN Charter drafters' intentions to encourage the establishment of the UN standing troops (Art. 43), in practice all forcible sanctioning actions are taken by states with the approval of the UN Security Council.[179] On the other hand, an internal form of outcasting is employed any time an international legal regime itself sanctions lawbreaking behavior of a state by excluding it from participating in the treaty bodies. For instance, if the state party fails to provide the mandatory contribution to the World Health Organization (WHO), the World Health Assembly shall sanction the violating state by denying it the benefits of participation in this governing body.[180] A final enforcement mechanism is external outcasting, which "is so pervasive that it is fair to say that it is the primary mode of law enforcement utilized by international legal regimes."[181] One of the notable examples is the WTO compulsory dispute resolution system. The WTO's Dispute Settlement Body's sanctioning measures are not enforced by the WTO regime, but by the aggrieved state party. And instead of the use of force, "enforcement is limited to specific, approved, retaliatory trade measures."[182] There are numerous instances of external outcasting in international law, which can be further classified and systematized.[183] Differences between the enforcement regimes are not accidental, but "are predictable responses to the underlying characteristics of the legal systems in which they operate."[184]

Despite all its apparent strengths, the enforcement model of external outcasting has its obvious limitations. Hathaway and Shapiro single out four of them. First, external outcasting is dependent upon a higher degree of cooperation between the participating norm-subjects in the given legal regime. When there is a low level of cooperation, the enforcement regime of outcasting becomes powerless.[185] Second, the factual inequality of states as primary subjects of international law comes here especially to the fore. Simply put, "[l]arger, more powerful states will find outcasting less threatening –

[178] *Ibid*, 303.
[179] *Ibid*, 304.
[180] *Ibid*, 306.
[181] *Ibid*, 308.
[182] *Ibid*, 307.
[183] Hathaway and Shapiro classify various externalized outcasting regimes according to the following criteria – whether they are (1) permissive or mandatory; (2) adjudicated or non-adjudicated; (3) in-kind or non-in-kind; (4) proportional or non-proportional; and (5) first parties only or third parties as well. *Ibid*, 310ff.
[184] *Ibid*, 310.
[185] *Ibid*, 340.

particularly if the state threatening to put in place an outcasting sanction is smaller, weaker, or more dependent on the outcast state."[186] This affects both the legitimacy and the long-term effectiveness of the given international legal regime. Third, since external outcasting is a form of "nonviolent exclusion," there is a credible danger "that the outcast will not heed a toothless attempt at exclusion unless physically forced to do so."[187] Finally, this enforcement guarantee relies on detection of violations: "Where violations of the law are difficult to detect, an outcasting regime will likely be ineffective in generating compliance."[188]

There is not much to be added to this meticulous analysis of the role of coercive guarantees in international law. Its major contribution is in highlighting the model of outcasting as a predominant enforcement regime in the international legal order. Hence, only a couple of remarks should be made. In her brief response to Hathaway and Shapiro's account, Besson rightly observes that the internal versus external divide in outcasting crucially depends on the criteria for treating one set of international legal rules as a self-contained legal regime.[189] Without entering here into the discussion about this issue, which will be the subject matter of Chapter 7, it suffices to say that the aforementioned divide is indeed rather blurry insofar as it does not pay enough attention to the role of states as officials, i.e., agents, of the general or a particular international legal order. To qualify "external" actors as those "outside of the regime" is potentially misleading, because it may leave the impression that their actions are taken without the authorization of the regime. Since this obviously is not what Hathaway and Shapiro have in mind, it indeed may be well to treat such actors as part of the internal institutional structure of the regime. Hence, Besson does have a point when noting that the aforementioned WTO example may also be read as a case of internal outcasting, insofar as "state institutions acting for the WTO" may be regarded "as agents of internal enforcement of the organization."[190] For that reason, it seems far more adequate to keep Kelsen's traditional divide between centralized and decentralized forms of outcasting, where the yardstick for centralization would concern the creation of specially designed enforcement agencies of the given international legal regime. Unlike with Kelsen, however, the employed distinction would not

186 *Ibid*, 342.

187 *Ibid*.

188 *Ibid*, 340, fn. 270.

189 Samantha Besson, "International Legality – A Response to Hathaway & Shapiro" (2011), at http://opiniojuris.org/2011/11/15/international-legality—a-response-to-hathaway-shapiro/

190 *Ibid*.

necessarily treat centralization in normative terms, as a sign of advancement of the regime in question,[191] insofar as the history of international organizations has amply demonstrated that flexible, decentralized models of enforcement can also produce a high level of regime effectiveness.[192]

Finally, a caveat regarding Hathaway and Shapiro's warning about apparent limitations of the external outcasting for the effectiveness of the given regime. In addressing their warnings in reverse order, one can, first, only agree with their observation that "any enforcement regime relies on detection of violations."[193] Yet, it is important to stress a particular vulnerability of various international legal regimes to the problem of credible fact-finding. Even if special fact-finding institutions are set up, such as in the case of the Fact Finding Mission of the Organization for the Prohibition of Chemical Weapons (OPCW),[194] their capacity of detecting potential violations of international law may prove to be questionable due to the lack of political will. Hence, in response to recent allegations of a chemical weapons attack in the Syrian town of Douma, the Security Council, voting on three separate draft resolutions, failed to rally the votes needed to launch an "independent mechanism of investigation" into the incident.[195]

In that respect, the authors rightly stress that an enforcement mechanism such as external outcasting crucially depends on cooperative benefits. International law of cooperation, on the other hand, is dependent upon there being a sufficient level of "commonness" in the given area of international relations. This "commonness," as the earlier mentioned historical examples taught us, need not be the upshot of states' conscious and self-interested willingness to limit their sovereignty. It may also be the result of some great necessities or unavoidable consequences of the processes of rapid globalization.[196] Irrespective of the

191 The reason why centralization of enforcement has normative flavor in Kelsen's account is that he does proceed from something akin to the Modern State Conception, treating it as an ideal toward which international law should aspire.

192 The history of the European project of integration is in that respect particularly remarkable.

193 Hathaway and Shapiro, "Outcasting: Enforcement in Domestic and International Law," 340, fn. 270.

194 In response to persistent allegations of chemical weapons attacks in Syria, the OPCW Fact Finding Mission (FFM) was set up in 2014 "to establish facts surrounding allegations of the use of toxic chemicals, reportedly chlorine, for hostile purposes in the Syrian Arab Republic." www.opcw.org/special-sections/syria/the-fact-finding-mission/

195 SC/13288, at www.un.org/press/en/2018/sc13288.doc.htm

196 At the most general level, globalization "can be described as the name that has been given to a multi-facetted process of expansion of human activities to the entire globe and assorted cognitive frames of reference … globalization, as the very archetype of an overarching, all-inclusive phenomenon cannot be expected to leave international law untouched." Frédéric Mégret, "Globalization," in *Max Planck Encyclopedia of Public International Law*, par. 1.

causes,[197] whenever there is a higher level of "commonness" and cooperation, the given legal regime tends to function as a more contained one. When opting out of a developed international legal regime of cooperation is too costly, outcasting measures of depriving cooperative benefits have far better chances to be effective despite being pacifist and nonviolent.[198] Take the general international legal order with the UN as its institutional architecture. Raz says that "[o]pting out of it would be very isolating. Remaining in it is as free as remaining in your home country. You can emigrate (sometimes) but it is a life-changing decision. And in the case of the UN there is no alternative to go to. The alternative is more like going to a desert island."[199] Or, take another legal regime with universalist aspirations – WTO. Its "importance and dominance in various aspects of international trade makes membership highly prized, and exit is very costly."[200] Self-containedness of such regimes may to a certain extent even help to buffer the existing factual inequalities between different norm-subjects.[201] Finally, in such regimes, it is neither the physical force, nor the threat of force, but the "*seriousness* of social pressure behind the rules [that] is the primary factor determining whether they are thought of as giving rise to obligations."[202] This is what eventually enables them to function as reasonably efficient legal orders.

197 This is a proper object of study of legal sociologists, although Twinning is warranted in holding that globalization, understood in a broad sense, as "all modern tendencies to transnationalisation," calls for a redefinition of the "theoretical or more abstract part" of the discipline of law known under the name of jurisprudence. William Twining, *Globalisation and Legal Scholarship* (Oisterwijk: Wolf Legal Publishers, 2011), 2–3.

198 Potentially, they may be seen by the norm violators as more coercive than traditional forcible sanctions. As put by Payandeh, "[I]n the age of globalization the exclusion of a state from international cooperation may be a much harsher sanction for violations of international law than a 'classical' coercive sanction." Payandeh, "The Concept of International Law in the Jurisprudence of H.L.A. Hart."

199 Raz, "Why the State," 14.

200 *Ibid*, 16.

201 See an interesting exchange of arguments on this issue, spawned by Anthony D'Amato's comment "Does International Law Bind Superpowers?," at http://opiniojuris.org/2005/08/14/does-international-law-bind-superpowers/.

202 Hart, *The Concept of Law*, 86.

# 6

# Justice-Aptness of International Law

As preliminary remarks regarding the central case of law as a genre demonstrate, law generates belief among its norm-subjects that in successfully performing its general function of coordination and dispute settlement it can bring about the value of justice. The same is true of international law.[1] Both the Preamble and opening articles of the UN Charter demonstrates the cardinal importance of justice as an international legal value. The Preamble states as one of the UN "ends" the establishment of "conditions under which justice and respect for the obligations arising from treaties and other sources of international law can be maintained." In Article 1(1), the observance of justice and international law is explicitly limited to a special function of the UN: to bringing about adjustments or settlements of disputes and situations that might lead to a breach of the peace. Whereas this general obligation from Article 1 is directed at the UN itself, Article 2(3) addresses member states, by stipulating that they "shall settle their international disputes by peaceful means in such a manner that international peace and security, and justice, are not endangered."[2]

Justice is by no means the only value that international law is supposed to deliver in its functioning. As the opening article of the Charter clearly indicates,

[1] As pointed out by Focarelli, "[a] good number of people expect international law to provide global responses to current global challenges and to bring about more justice in the world." Carlo Focarelli, *International Law as Social Construct – The Struggle for Global Justice* (Oxford: Oxford University Press, 2012), 1.

[2] In providing a first detailed interpretative account of the UN law, as enshrined in the Charter, Kelsen makes a comment with respect to inconsistences in these two introductory articles: "It is hardly understandable why the Organisation shall bring about adjustment or settlement of international disputes or situations which might lead to a breach of the peace in conformity with the principles of justice and international law, whereas the Members in pursuit of this Purpose shall settle all their international disputes, but not 'situations,' in conformity with 'justice' but not with 'international law.'" Kelsen, *The Law of the United Nations*, 18.

peace and security are also regarded as the paramount values of the international legal order. The primary purpose of this chapter is not to investigate the relation between these values,[3] although they may obviously come in conflict,[4] but to elucidate the most important aspects of justice-aptness of international law in light of its specificities. As already noted, this feature implies that, unlike with other, more particular values, "it necessarily makes sense to ask whether law is just and, where it is found deficient, to demand reform."[5] Moreover, justice-aptness of law is pervasive, insofar as it "applies as much to the substance of law as it does to its administration and procedures."[6] However, before focusing on the specificities of justice-aptness of international law, it is necessary to say something about different forms of justice.

According to Aristotle's traditional distinction, *distributive* justice requires that things should be distributed so that all involved parties get their share based on some relevant merit.[7] The other type is *rectificatory*, i.e., corrective justice and it governs relations between parties, both voluntary (stemming from transactions) and involuntary (stemming from delicts).[8] The former form of justice operates according to what mathematicians call "geometrical" proportion,[9] whereas the latter involves "arithmetical" proportion.[10] Whatever its form, justice is always about *allocation* of goods and ills, of benefits and burdens.[11] This allocation is necessarily taken within the following well-known formula: Treat equals equally and unequals unequally. As noted by Radbruch, this is a contentless formula,[12] for neither does it reveal what is to be taken as the standpoint (*Gleichspunkt*) from which to distinguish

[3] For instance, it is noticeable that justice is not mentioned in the first part of Article 1(1) as one of the values that is supposed to be delivered in the UN's "taking of effective collective measures for the prevention and removal of threats to the peace, and for the suppression of acts of aggression or other breaches of the peace." Motions to include justice in the first part have not received the required majority, but according to the report of the President of the Commission, "all those who took the floor to oppose the two motions were agreed that the concept of justice is a norm of fundamental importance; and all affirmed that peace, real and endurable, cannot be based on anything other than on justice." Quoted from Kelsen, *ibid*, 17, fn. 3.

[4] "The values inspiring the rules of international law not only partially overlap, they are also often in competition with one another." Focarelli, *International Law as Social Construct*, 431. Focarelli offers a few value tensions of current international law concerning order versus humanity, wealth versus humanity, and humanity versus humanity. *Ibid*, 432ff.

[5] Green, "Positivism and the Inseparability of Law and Morals," 1050.

[6] *Ibid*.

[7] Aristotle, *Nicomachean Ethics*, 1130b.

[8] *Ibid*, 1131a

[9] *Ibid*, 1131b

[10] *Ibid*, 1132a

[11] Gardner, *Law as a Leap of Faith*, 242.

[12] Hart also speaks of it as "an empty form." Hart, *The Concept of Law*, 159.

between equal and unequal cases, nor does it direct us toward the precise way of their treatment (*die Art der Behandlung*).[13] Without this formula,[14] however, both forms of justice are inconceivable.[15] Its importance is vital in the allocation of both substantive and procedural rights and obligations of norm-subjects.[16] Moreover, only with keeping this formula in mind is it possible to understand Aristotle's distinction between justice and equity, where the latter by its "very nature" is "a correction of law, where it is deficient on account of its universality."[17]

A final preliminary remark with respect to the relation between the two forms of justice: It is important to bear in mind that rectificatory presupposes distributive justice.[18] For instance, voluntary transactions between two parties can be subjected to the arithmetic proportion only if both sides were previously recognized by the given legal order as having capacity to enter into such contractual relation. Hence, what has the logical and conceptual priority is the act of distribution of the status of a legal subject with the capacity to contract, which is taken according to some criterion for distinguishing

[13] Therefore, it has to be filled with the substance that will depend on lawmakers' understanding of desirable goals (*Zweckmäßigkeit*). Gustav Radbruch, *Rechtsphilosophie* (Heidelberg: C. F. Müller Verlag, 2011), 73.

[14] I deliberately use the word formula, even though it is commonly spoken of as the principle of "formal justice." It is contrasted with its content (e.g., criteria for distinguishing some cases as unequal), which is labeled "substantive justice." Hart triggered the debate by arguing that in order for formal justice to be done, it is not necessary that requirements of substantive justice are met as well. Hart, "Postscript," 206. A number of authors have criticized this stance. *See, e. g.*, David Lyons, "On Formal Justice" (1973) 58 *Cornell Law Review* 5: 833–861; Kenneth I. Winston, "On Treating Like Cases Alike" (1974) 62 *California Law Review* 1: 1–39; Green, "The Germ of Justice"; Gardner, *Law as a Leap of Faith*, 246ff.

[15] Gardner argues that Aristotle "espouses nothing that could conceivably be called a principle of formal justice. He never says, as he is sometimes accused of saying, that people act justly whenever they . . . treat like people alike and unalike people unalike." *Ibid*, 247. This is hardly so, having in mind the following of Aristotle's words: "[I]n fact quarrels and complaints arise either when equals receive unequal shares in an allocation, or unequals receive equal shares." Aristotle, *Nicomachean Ethics*, 1131a. This statement makes sense only under the assumption that the guiding principle is that of treating equals equally and unequals unequally.

[16] When embodied in a set of procedural legal rules (e.g., *audiatur et altera pars*, equality of arms, etc.) it is often called "procedural justice." *See, e.g.*, Lawrence B. Solum, "Procedural Justice" (2004) 78 *Southern California Law Review* 1: 181–321.

[17] Aristotle, *Nicomachean Ethics*, 1137b. A familiar example concerns the exact level of punishment for the same criminal offense in case of a person with no criminal record and a recidivist. While justice apparently requires the equal punishment for equal delicts, the factual circumstances of the cases justify resorting to equity, which may lead to a harsher punishment in the latter case.

[18] For a contrary view, *see*, Stephen R. Perry, "On the Relationship Between Corrective and Distributive Justice," in Jeremy Horder (ed.), *Oxforde Essays in Jurisprudence* (Fourth Series) (Oxford: Oxford University Press, 2002), 237–263.

between equals and unequals.[19] Similarly, before a judge can rectify the injustice stemming from the conducted delict, certain ills in the form of sanctions have to be distributed proportionally according to the presumed weight of the stipulated criminal acts.

## 1 ALLOCATIVE CONFLICTS AND INTERNATIONAL LAW-MAKING

In his Oliver Wendell Holmes Lectures, delivered in March 1941, Kelsen at one point says that

> in the last analysis, international morality is the soil which fosters the growth of international law: it is international morality which determines the general direction of the development of international law. Whatever is considered "just" in the sense of international morality has at least a tendency of becoming international law.[20]

This somewhat unexpected statement from one of the champions of legal positivism[21] may be attributed to the fact that it was conveyed at the moment when World War II was dangerously progressing. It was made within Kelsen's discussion on the *bellum iustum* doctrine, which was at the core of international conflicts. He believed that, much like the development of a primitive law, a post-war international legal order should follow the same direction, by first establishing adjudicative and then legislative institutions. More specifically, he argued for the creation of an international court with compulsory jurisdiction, to which "all disputes among member states without exception" would be submitted.[22]

However, to the extent that law is the most suitable normative vehicle for allocating goods and burdens in the form of rights and obligations, "allocative conflicts," that is, "conflicts about who gets how much of what and why,"[23] are not centered so much around law-applying, but around law-making institutions. At the municipal level, those conflicts are largely framed by the fact that subjects in charge of allocation, that is, law-making institutions (e.g., parliament) and recipients of allocation (e.g., citizens) are, normally, not the same.

19 It is well known from the history of law that such status at the municipal level was denied to minors, women, slaves, and members of some professions.

20 Hans Kelsen, *Law and Peace in International Relations, The Oliver Wendell Holmes Lectures, 1940–41* (Cambridge, Mass.: Harvard University Press, 1942), 36–37.

21 Rigaux, for instance, argues that "Kelsen's thought on the 'growth' of international law is not in accordance with his Pure Theory of Law." Rigaux, "Hans Kelsen on International Law," 337.

22 Kelsen, *Law and Peace in International Relations*, 159.

23 Gardner, *Law as a Leap of Faith*, 244.

In that respect, the situation is much different at the international level, insofar as the two main international law-making institutions are the "institutions" of treaty-making and customary law-making. In both of them, states assume the double role of subjects in charge of allocation *and* recipients of allocation. Hence, one may be inclined to argue that the most intriguing allocative conflicts at the international level would be those related to non-state institutional actors in their capacity of international lawmakers.

This plausible viewpoint, however, has to be put in a larger perspective. In order to assess whether international law is just in its capacity of a distributive institutional order, one needs to address a prior question of what is the basic international good, whose allocation was, and still nowadays is, the major source of allocative conflicts. In that respect, Walzer's approach in his influential treatise on distributive justice is of significant help. He says that this idea "presupposes a bounded world within which distribution takes place." The world in question is the relevant "political community." Walzer notes that "[w]e assume an established group and a fixed population, and so we miss the first and most important distributive question: How is that group constituted?" Putting this question at the forefront reveals that "[t]he primary good that we distribute to one another is membership in some human community." What we do with respect to this good shapes all "other distributive choices: it determines with whom we make those choices, from whom we require obedience and collect taxes, to whom we allocate goods and services."[24]

By way of analogy, one may easily conclude that the primary good to be distributed within the international legal order is membership in the international community,[25] that is, *sovereign statehood*. It is important to add that the statehood presupposes the existence of the accompanying good to be distributed – a chunk of territory over which the state can exercise political control.[26] How modern international law fares in terms of the concern for distributive justice can be assessed to a large extent by tracing the history of legal institutionalization of different allocative principles according to which sovereign statehood, i.e., title to

[24] Michael Walzer, *Spheres of Justice – A Defense of Pluralism and Equality* (New York: Basic Books, 1983), 31.

[25] Whether sufficient level of "commonness" has been generated at the international level so that one can credibly employ the phrase "international community" is a matter of contestation. Sir Hersch Lauterpacht did not hesitate to use this label as early as 1933 in his well-known work *The Function of Law in the International Community* (Oxford: Oxford University Press, 2011). For a contemporary assessment of the concept, *see, e.g.*, Mehrdad Payandeh, *Internationales Gemeinschaftsrecht – Zur Herausbildung gemeinschaftsrechtlicher Strukturen im Völkerrecht der Globalisierung* (Heidelberg: Springer, 2010), 17ff.

[26] Paul Gilbert, *The Philosophy of Nationalism* (Boulder: Westview Press, 1998), 91.

territory, was supposed to be distributed.[27] This history is, at the same time, the history of main allocative conflicts at the international level.[28] Let us start with the Westphalian peace treaties, which are considered the cornerstone of the modern international legal order.[29] One of their most important aspects, in Walzer's terms, concerned the "decisions" of the then-existing states to allocate sovereign statehood to some new members (Switzerland and Netherlands). In general, peace treaties, following some major international conflicts, were for a long time the main "institution" of international law-making that served to extend membership to newly admitted sovereign states.[30] Those treaties, however, did not install any forward-looking allocative principle[31] that could subsequently have been invoked for the distribution of sovereign statehood.

[27] "[Q]uestions such as the nature and demarcation of boundaries, the varieties of title to territory, the issues of when and how both boundaries may be changed and title to territory transferred have all come to be regulated by specific, but interlinked, sets of systemic rules. These rules ... now apply globally, and can be said to represent a core element of the institutional structure of international society." Andrew Hurrell, "International Law and the Making and Unmaking of Boundaries," in Allen Buchanan and Margaret Moore (eds.), *States, Nations, and Borders: The Ethics of Making Boundaries* (Cambridge: Cambridge University Press, 2003), 275.

[28] To be a member of the international legal order is to be an international legal subject. States are major, but not the only subjects of international law. International organizations are also members of the international legal order. However, this particular membership is not a good whose distribution according to a certain allocative principle can be expected to generate allocative conflicts. Finally, the denial of individual membership in particular political communities, primarily on the basis of race, has from the 1950s onward become a matter of international concern, leading to the development of international human rights law. This, in turn, has become the principle ground for claiming that individuals also enjoy the status of subjects of international law. (Shaw, *International Law*, 257–259) For an argument that human beings are becoming the primary international legal subjects, *see*, Anne Peters, *Beyond Human Rights: The Legal Status of the Individual in International Law* (Cambridge: Cambridge University Press, 2016) On the international legal subjectivity of various nonstate actors, *see, e.g.*, Jan Klabbers, "(I Can't Get No) Recognition: Subjects Doctrine and the Emergence of Non-State Actors," in Jarna Petman and Jan Klabbers (eds.), *Nordic Cosmopolitanism – Essays in International Law for Martti Koskenniemi* (Leiden: Martinus Nijhoff, 2003), 351–369.

[29] As already indicated, the Westphalian division between the old and new international legal order is largely a construct. Larkins, for instance, challenges the modern conception of territoriality of state, which is also linked to the Westphalian era, by arguing that it can be traced back to the Renaissance. Jeremy Larkins, *From Hierarchy to Anarchy – Territory and Politics before Westphalia* (New York: Palgrave Macmillan, 2010)

[30] This was, for instance, also the case with the Treaty of Berlin, which followed the Russo-Turkish War of 1877–1878. The treaty marked the end of Ottoman rule in the Balkans by extending *de jure* or de facto sovereign statehood to Romania, Serbia, and Montenegro, as well as the autonomy to Bulgaria. For more detail *see*, M. Hakan Yavuz and Peter Sluglett (eds.), *War and Diplomacy: The Russo-Turkish War of 1877–1878 and the Treaty of Berlin* (Salt Lake City: The University of Utah Press, 2011).

[31] For a distinction between forward-looking and backward-looking accounts of distributive justice at the international level, *see*, Daniel Butt, *Rectifying International Injustice – Principles of Compensation and Restitution Between Nations* (Oxford: Oxford University Press, 2009), 31ff.

Toward the end of World War I, President Wilson famously proposed national self-determination as a new allocative principle that was supposed to replace the practice of arbitrary creation and dismemberment of states through the process of balancing power relations between major European states. In Wilson's opinion, expressed in the *Fourteen Points* speech, the war "had its roots in the disregard of the rights of small nations and of nationalities [that] are not to be handed about from one sovereignty to another by an international conference or an understanding between rivals and antagonists." Instead, "peoples may now be dominated and governed only by their own consent." In that respect, self-determination should be taken not as a mere phrase, but as "an imperative principle of action."[32]

Put in the aforementioned terms of Kelsen, Wilson strongly believed that the espoused principle was emanation of international morality that determined the general direction of the future development of international law.[33] Despite obvious problems it could have triggered in the implementation on the complex situation on the ground,[34] the principle of national self-determination was invoked during the political process leading to the Treaty of Versailles.[35] It transpired, however, that self-determination could not serve as a guiding allocative principle for solving territorial and sovereignty conflicts that would arise under the newly formed League of Nations.[36]

32 Fourteen Points (Wilson's Address to Congress, January 8, 1918), in Henry Steele Commager and Milton Cantor (eds.), *Documents of American History (since 1898)*, Vol. II (Englewood Cliffs: Prentice Hall, 1988), 137.

33 In that respect, one may claim that "the 'national model' of self-determination was a very progressive notion." Bartram S. Brown, "Human Rights, Sovereignty, and the Final Status of Kosovo" (2005) 80 *Chicago-Kent Law Review* 3: 241.

34 Wilson's Secretary of State, Robert Lansing, has famously expressed fears that self-determination of peoples will lead to disastrous consequences. (Robert Lansing, *The Peace Negotiations – A Personal Narrative* [Orlando: Houghton Mifflin Company, 1921], 97–98) Referring to Wilson's Thirteenth Point, which states that "an independent Polish state should be erected which should include the territories inhabited by indisputably Polish populations," Neiberg also notes that there was "no 'indisputably Polish' (or, for that matter, indisputably Ukrainian or Czech or Serbian) part of Europe to which all could agree." Michael S. Neiberg, *The Treaty of Versailles – A Concise History* (Oxford: Oxford University Press, 2017), 41.

35 In submitting the proposal for revision of the Treaty, even the German delegation invoked the principle, by arguing that the envisaged request to give up all overseas colonies, by simply transferring them into another imperial administration (British and Belgian), was contrary to the "Fourteen Points." Norman A. Graebner and Edward M. Bennett, *The Versailles Treaty and Its Legacy – The Failure of the Wilsonian Vision* (Cambridge: Cambridge University Press, 2011), 57.

36 In the well-known advisory opinion regarding the status of the Aaland Islands, the International Committee of Jurists clearly stated that, "[a]lthough the principle of self-determination of peoples plays an important part in modern political thought, especially since the Great War, it must be pointed out that there is no mention of it in the Covenant of the League of Nations. The recognition of this principle in a certain number of international treaties cannot be considered as

In fact, this was not its role even after it was integrated in the post-World War II UN Charter, in which it primarily served as one of the principles upon which friendly relations among nations were to be developed (Art. 1[2]).[37] Nevertheless, with this step, the allocative conflicts regarding membership in the international community of states were from that moment on largely tied to the activities of the UN, as the global non-state institutional actor.

At the moment of its creation, the UN had fifty-two member states, and a number of territories were either in the status of non-self-governing territories (Chapter XI), or they were under the international trusteeship system (Chapter XII).[38] However, everything changed between the early 1950s and the 1960s, when upon the request of socialist countries and with the support of the developing countries that had already become independent, "the principle of self-determination was vociferously invoked within the United Nations to legitimize the termination of colonial rule."[39] After the initial reluctance, "Western countries gradually gave way to grudging acceptance of the new trends," which ultimately paved the way for a broad agreement "both about the idea that non-self-governing territories should have the opportunity freely to choose their international status and about the manner in which their right to self-determination would be implemented."[40] The major legal acts that installed self-determination as the allocative principle for the acquisition of sovereign statehood were the UN GA resolutions 1514(XV)[41] and 1541(XV),[42] which were subsequently supplemented with the UN GA Resolution 2625 (XXV).[43] Eventually, the principle of self-determination came (and continues)

sufficient to put it upon the same footing as a positive rule of the Law of Nations." Official Journal of the League of Nations, Special Supplement No. 3, Oct. 1920.

37 Antonio Cassese, *Self-determination of Peoples: A Legal Reappraisal* (Cambridge: Cambridge University Press, 1995), 42–43.

38 On mandates and trust territories and non-self-governing territories, *see* in general, James R. Crawford, *The Creation of States in International Law* (2nd ed.) (Oxford: Oxford University Press, 2007), chapters 13 and 14. The Security Council in 1994 terminated the United Nations Trusteeship Agreement for the last Territory – the Trust Territory of the Pacific Islands (Palau) – after it opted for self-government in its 1993 plebiscite.

39 Cassese, *Self-determination of Peoples*, 71.

40 *Ibid.*

41 UN Doc A/RES/1514(XV) *Declaration on the Granting of Independence to Colonial Countries and Peoples*, 14 December 1960, particularly Articles 2 and 5.

42 UN Doc A/RES/1541(XV) *United Nations General Assembly Resolution 1541(XV) on principles which should guide Members in determining whether or not an obligation exists to transmit the information called for under Article 73e of the Charter*, 15 December 1960, particularly Principle VI.

43 UN Doc A/RES/25/2625(XXV) *Declaration on Principles of International Law concerning Friendly Relations and Co-operation among States in accordance with the Charter of the United Nations*, 24 October 1970.

to be commonly referred to as both a jus cogens norm and an *erga omnes* obligation of international law.[44]

Despite enabling the enlargement of membership of the international community,[45] this principle has by no means eliminated all the statehood disputes around the world. As put by Weller, "the all-or-nothing game of self-determination has helped to sustain conflicts, rather than resolve them."[46] In the decolonization period, in which self-determination served as the dominant allocative principle, the "self" – understood as the relevant population – was in a large majority of cases considered undisputable, due to the reliance on the *uti possidetis* principle that was to define the relevant territorial unit.[47] That is, the self-determining entity was defined by the boundaries drawn by the former colonial powers. However, this has not eradicated cases in which challenges were raised with respect to "the territorial definition of former colonial entities,"[48] or to "the implementation of colonial self-determination."[49]

Finally, with the shift from inter-state to intra-state conflicts,[50] several cases of sovereignty disputes arose outside the colonial context (for example,

44 *See, supra* pp. 109–124. Elsewhere I argued that self-determination is a plausible candidate for the status of a "universal collective right." Miodrag Jovanović, *Collective Rights – A Legal Theory* (Cambridge: Cambridge University Press, 2012), chapter 4.

45 At this moment, there are 193 members of the UN. Vatican City and Palestine are in the status of observer states, and there are several entities that are not members, but are recognized by at least one UN member.

46 Marc Weller, "Settling Self-determination Conflicts: Recent Developments" (2009) 20 *European Journal of International Law* 1: 114.

47 For specificities of the process of decolonization in Latin America, *see, e.g.*, Paula María Vernet, "Decolonization: Spanish Territories," *Max Planck Encyclopedia of Public International Law*; for an assessment of the African decolonization, *see, e.g.*, Malcolm Shaw, *Title to Territory in Africa – International Legal Issues* (Oxford: Clarendon Press, 1986); the ICJ also stressed the differences between the two contexts in *Frontier Dispute (Burkina Faso* v. *Mali)*, 1986 I.C.J. 554, December 22, 1986, paras. 20–26; for a general analysis of the role of *uti possidetis* in territorial disputes, *see*, Suzanne Lalonde, *Determining Boundaries in a Conflicted World – The Role of Uti Possidetis* (Montreal: McGill-Queen's University Press, 2002)

48 "These are cases where a former colony exercised the right to self-determination, but ethnic movements emerging within the newly independent state seek separation" (e.g., Bougainville, Sri Lanka, Philippines, Burma, and India in relation to tribal peoples). Weller, "Settling Self-determination Conflicts: Recent Developments," 113.

49 "These are cases where it is argued that the doctrine of *uti possidetis* was wrongly applied at the point of decolonization, or that an entity was wrongfully incorporated into the newly independent state at that moment" (e.g., Eritrea, Somaliland, and Kashmir, and perhaps Southern Sudan and the Comoros and Mayotte). *Ibid*, 114.

50 Therese Pettersson and Peter Wallensteen, "Armed Conflicts, 1946–2014" (2015) 52 *Journal of Peace Research* 4: 537. *Cf.* David A. Backer, Ravi Bhavnani, and Paul K. Huth (eds.), *Peace and Conflict 2017* (New York: Routledge, 2018)

Chechnya, Corsica, the Basque Country, Kosovo, etc.),[51] "where the concept of self-determination in the sense of secession does not apply at all, given the lack of a colonial nexus."[52] In such cases, where the membership in the international community of states has to be extended to certain entities, normally at the expense of the already existing states whose territorial integrity is protected by international law,[53] the question is what shall serve as the functioning allocative principle. In addressing this issue, international legal scholarship oscillates between two principles. One is the principle of *effectiveness*, according to which an entity is allocated the status of sovereign statehood if it satisfies the criteria enshrined in the Montevideo convention,[54] which are often considered to be part of CIL.[55] The other is the principle of *collective recognition*, according to which an entity is allocated the status of sovereign statehood if it was recognized by a sufficient number of states.[56] A number of views in the field, nonetheless, stress the importance of both principles,[57] just

[51] A special case concerns the scope of self-determination of indigenous peoples. *See, e.g.*, S. James Anaya, *Indigenous Peoples in International Law* (Oxford: Oxford University Press, 2000), chapters 3 and 4.

[52] Weller, "Settling Self-determination Conflicts: Recent Developments," 113.

[53] In case a parent state constitutionally accommodates such a request for independent statehood of its entity, international legal issues will presumably not arise. On the constitutional regulation of secessionist aspirations, *see, e.g.*, Miodrag Jovanović, *Constitutionalizing Secession in Federalized States: A Procedural Approach* (Utrecht: Eleven Publishing International, 2007).

[54] Under the 1933 *Montevideo Convention on the Rights and Duties of States*, a state comes into being by satisfying following criteria – territory, population, government, and capacity to enter into relations with the other states (Art. 1). The convention also states in Art. 3 that "[t]he political existence of the state is independent of recognition by the other states."

[55] See, for instance, the EJIL: *Talk!* debate on this issue. Dapo Akande, "The Importance of Legal Criteria for Statehood: A Response to Jure Vidmar" (2013) EJIL: *Talk!*, available at www.ejiltalk.org/the-importance-of-legal-criteria-for-statehood-a-response-to-jure-vidmar/ (arguing that the Montevideo rule is a customary rule of international law); Jure Vidmar, "The Importance of Legal Criteria for Statehood: A Rejoinder to Dapo Akande" (2013), available at www.ejiltalk.org/the-importance-of-legal-criteria-for-statehood-a-rejoinder-to-dapo-akande/ (arguing that the Montevideo criteria should not be seen as a rule of customary international law).

[56] One of the obvious ways to determine what counts as a "sufficient" number of states would be to treat the UN admission procedure as a form of collective recognition. This is, for instance, Lauterpacht's proposal. Sir Hersch Lauterpacht, *Recognition in International Law* (Cambridge: Cambridge University Press, [1947] 2013), 403.

[57] In a much-celebrated book on the creation of states, Crawford says that "[t]he conclusion must be that the status of an entity as a State is, in principle, independent of recognition," even though recognition "can resolve uncertainties as to status and allow for new situations to be regularized." Crawford, *The Creation of States in International Law*, 28, 27. *Cf.* Shaw, *International Law*, 261.

as some of them emphasize "emerging" international legal conditions of statehood, such as democratic requirements.[58]

This brief survey demonstrates that the international legal order has come a long way from the time when the primary good of sovereign statehood was allocated to, or withdrawn from, an entity on the basis of discretion and sheer power politics. Nevertheless, the international legal order has not completely crystalized and institutionalized the relevant allocative principle(s) for the distribution of this good, which leaves enough room for new allocative conflicts.[59] This is all the more important if one bears in mind that the acquisition of the status of statehood is the precondition for being allocated other important benefits and burdens that are distributed through different acts of international law-making. Some such international goods are: natural resources (UN GA Resolution 1803(XVII) of 14 December 1962, "Permanent sovereignty over natural resources");[60] in the case of coastal states, maritime

58 Anne Peters, "Statehood after 1989: 'Effectivités' between Legality and Virtuality," in James Crawford and Sarah Nouwen (eds.), *Select Proceedings of the European Society of International Law, Vol III* (Oxford: Hart Publishing, 2012), 179. *Cf.* Jure Vidmar, *Democratic Statehood in International Law: The Emergence of New States in Post-Cold War Practice* (Oxford: Hart Publishing, 2013).

59 This is merely to indicate that in the absence of legally institutionalized clear allocative principle(s), the chances for allocative conflicts are much bigger. This by no means implies that if such clear allocative principle had been legally installed this would have necessarily solved all the allocative conflicts. Simply put, such a scenario would have not ruled out the possibility that some putative claimants consider the installed allocative principle as substantively unjust. For instance, the "continental shelf" is the valid allocative principle for the distribution of maritime resources in international law. By being based on "geographical features and political boundaries," it leads "to a widely uneven distribution of marine resources," which, in turn, "raises fundamental problems of distributive justice and of global equity in contemporary international law." Put differently, many excluded, "land-locked and other geographically disadvantaged states" may argue that the distribution according to the installed allocative principle is substantively unjust. (Thomas Cottier, *Equitable Principles of Maritime Boundary Delimitation: The Quest for Distributive Justice in International Law* [Cambridge: Cambridge University Press, 2015], 2.) In that respect, the task of this chapter is not to provide arguments either in favor or against any substantive "conception" of distributive justice as applied at the international level (for one such recent conception, which is based on the two core "pillars" – the promotion of international peace and respect for the basic individual human rights – *see*, Steven R. Ratner, *The Thin Justice of International Law: A Moral Reckoning of the Law of Nations* [Oxford: Oxford University Press, 2015]). Instead, its aim is to analyze to what extent international law is apt for appraisal in terms of the traditional "concept" of distributive justice. On the distinction between "concept" and "conception" of justice, *see*, John Rawls, *A Theory of Justice* (Cambridge, Mass.: The Belknap Press of Harvard University Press, 1971), 5.

60 As noted by Hobe, "[t]here is a high likelihood that most of the important (armed) conflicts in our twenty-first century will be those concerning resources." (Stephan Hobe, "Evolution of the Principle on Permanent Sovereignty Over Natural Resources: From Soft Law to a Customary Law Principle?," in Marc Bungenberg and Stephan Hobe [eds.], *Permanent*

resources[61] (United Nations Convention on the Law of the Sea);[62] in the case of certain northern states, new territories in the Arctic region (Declaration on the Establishment of the Arctic Council), etc.[63] Finally, membership in the community of states is a precondition for equal treatment under international law[64] and for the capacity to enter into treaty relations,[65] as well as for the assumption of responsibility for wrongful international acts.[66] Hence, membership status is also crucial for all the matters of rectificatory justice that may arise at the international level.

## 2 RECTIFICATORY JUSTICE AND INTERNATIONAL LAW-APPLICATION

Just as law-making is about coordinating the behavior of norm-subjects through the distribution of certain benefits and burdens in the form of rights and obligations, a critical portion of law-application is about settling disputes between parties who disagree about whether the installed rule was violated. This is where adjudicative institutions come to the fore. Parties addressing these institutions approach them with a certain expectation, which Aristotle formulated in a famous saying: "To appeal to a judge is to appeal to what is just."[67] The adjudicative institution is there to "restore equality" that was presumably violated by a wrongful act. Hence, the adjudicative institution's task of applying the law in the given case can be appraised in light of the

*Sovereignty over Natural Resources* [Cham: Springer, 2015], 2) Sovereignty over natural resources is widely acknowledged as a bundle of different rights and duties of states. *See, e.g.*, Nico Schrijver, *Sovereignty over Natural Resources – Balancing Rights and Duties* (Cambridge: Cambridge University Press, 1997).

61 The new territorial allocation was prompted by the emergence of the continental shelf doctrine in the 1950s. For an early assessment of the doctrine, *see*, Hans Kelsen, *On the Issue of the Continental Shelf – Two Legal Opinions* (Wien: Springer, 1986).

62 Art. 76. defines the allocative principle of "continental shelf," combining the criteria of natural prolongation with that of distance. See in more detail in, Cottier, *Equitable Principles of Maritime Boundary Delimitation: The Quest for Distributive Justice in International Law*, 1.

63 The Ottawa Declaration was signed by eight states having territorial claims in the region of Arctic. However, it does not prescribe any allocative principle for solving the problem of contrasting claims. It establishes the Arctic Council, with a limited role to "provide a means for promoting cooperation, coordination and interaction among the Arctic States" (Art. 1[a]).

64 One of the founding principles of the UN Charter is "the principle of the sovereign equality of all its Members." (Art. 2[1])

65 "The present Convention applies to treaties between States." Art. 1 of the VCLT

66 "Every internationally wrongful act of a State entails the international responsibility of that State." Art. 1 of the ILC Draft articles on Responsibility of States for Internationally Wrongful Acts

67 Aristotle, *Nicomachean Ethics*, 1132a

concern for rectificatory justice. This concern is manifested in the application of a sanctioning rule in the case of a legally responsible norm-subject. As put by Aristotle, "when the damage has been assessed ... [t]he judge tries to equalize them with the penalty, decreasing the gain that has been made" with the undertaken wrongful act.[68]

Consequently, the aptness of international law for appraisal in terms of rectificatory justice depends primarily on there being rules specifying delicts and responsibility for them, as well as legal consequences stemming from those delicts – that is, sanctions. As already stressed, Kelsen believes that "legality" of international law can be established provided that there is such a thing as "international sanctions." However, by "a sanction," he means "a coercive act," and thus, he argues that "[e]ven if it is admitted that under general international law the violation of an obligation automatically entails the substitute obligation to make reparation, this substitute obligation cannot be considered as having the character of a sanction."[69] This stems from the fact that there is "no objective authority, especially no court, competent to ascertain the existence of a delict." Therefore, the violating state has to repair damages "only if it admits that it has committed a delict." On the other hand, it is "not obliged to comply with any unilateral demand for reparations made by the injured state."[70] Kelsen eventually says that "it is not excluded to assume" that under general international law, neither the delinquent state has the obligation to repair the damages, nor the injured state has the obligation to try to get reparation "before resorting to reprisals or war," which are considered "true" international sanctions.[71]

Kelsen struggles to account for the fact that the international legal order of the 1950s knows of no developed net of centralized law-applying institutions, be they for administering, adjudicating, or enforcing the rules of international law. Hence, he makes a curious conclusion that in the absence of a compulsory international jurisdiction that would authoritatively ascertain the existence of delict, the nature of reparation for incurred damages changes from sanction – and this is how it is treated in municipal tort and

68 Aristotle says that "the word 'gain' is generally employed in such cases, even if it is not appropriate for some of them, such as assault, and the same goes for the use of the word 'loss' of the victim." *Ibid*, 1132a

69 Kelsen, *Principles of International Law*, 21.

70 *Ibid.*

71 Accordingly, "general international law only provides that by an agreement concerning reparation of the moral and material damage caused by the delict, and by the fulfillment of the obligation established by this agreement the delinquent state can avoid the sanctions provided by general international law." *Ibid.*

contract law[72] – to yet another simple rule of conduct.[73] Sanction and obligation, however, "are two different concepts," where the former is necessarily of coercive nature.[74] This ultimately leads Kelsen to be confused as between sanctioning rules and enforcement mechanisms and to treat only authorized usage of force (reprisals and war) as genuine international legal sanctions.[75]

Surprisingly enough, in dismissing reparation as a form of sanction, Kelsen does quote, without commenting, the well-known passage from the *Chorzow* case,[76] in which the PCIJ states that "it is a principle of international law, and even a general conception of law, that any breach of an engagement involves an obligation to make reparation."[77] The Court further elaborates this point in the following way:

> The essential principle contained in the actual notion of an illegal act – a principle which seems to be established by international practice and in particular by the decisions of arbitral tribunals – is that reparation must, as far as possible, wipe-out all the consequences of the illegal act and re-establish the situation which would, in all probability, have existed if that act had not been committed. Restitution in kind, or, if this is not possible, payment of a sum corresponding to the value which a restitution in kind would bear; the award, if need be, of damages for loss sustained which would not be covered by restitution in kind or payment in place of it – such are the principles which should serve to determine the amount of compensation due for an act contrary to international law.[78]

From the mere usage of the word "obligation," Kelsen seems to invoke an unwarranted conclusion that reparation has no sanctioning nature, despite the Court's lengthy elaboration of its restitutive purpose, which corresponds to the legal dictionaries' definition of "damages" in municipal tort law.[79] The PCIJ's avoidance of the word "sanction" is but an illustration of the still existent

[72] Kelsen admits this by saying that "[u]nder national law, the situation is substantially different ... for there are courts competent to ascertain the existence of the delict and to determine the content of the reparation to be made." *Ibid*, 21.

[73] "*Conduct rules* tell people which actions they are obligated, prohibited, or permitted to perform." Hathaway and Shapiro, "Outcasting: Enforcement in Domestic and International Law," 270.

[74] Kelsen, *Principles of International Law*, 22.

[75] He speaks of "international sanctions as enforcement measures" (*ibid*), despite the fact that it is principally possible to distinguish between sanctioning rules and primary and secondary enforcement mechanisms. *See*, *supra* pp. 281–283.

[76] Kelsen, *Principles of International Law*, 20, fn. 4.

[77] *Factory at Chorzow (Germany* v. *Poland)*, 1928 P.C.I.J. (ser. A) No. 17 (Sept. 13), par. 73.

[78] *Ibid*, par. 125.

[79] The Oxford dictionary of law defines "damages" in the following way: "The purpose of damages in tort is to put the plaintiff in the position he would have been if the tort had not

reluctance of international doctrine and practice to employ this term. In the Commentary to the *Draft articles on Responsibility of States for Internationally Wrongful Acts*, the ILC notes that "[t]he term 'sanctions' has been used for measures taken in accordance with the constituent instrument of some international organization."[80] Furthermore, the term has a penal flavor and, thus, its usage may be controversial under the present-day international law, which recognizes neither the state as "the subject of criminal sanctions,"[81] nor the award of punitive damages, "even in relation to serious breaches of obligations arising under peremptory norms."[82] Hence, indeterminacies regarding the adequate labeling of legal consequences stemming from internationally wrongful acts may be attributed to the fact that international law does not generally distinguish between different types of liability according to the source of the breached obligation. As was uttered in the influential *Rainbow Warrior* case,

> the general principles of International Law concerning State responsibility are equally applicable in the case of breach of treaty obligation, since in the international law field there is no distinction between contractual and tortious responsibility, so that any violation by a State of any obligation, of whatever origin, gives rise to State responsibility and consequently, to the duty of reparation.[83]

All the accrued international legal developments in this area[84] were eventually codified in the ILC *Draft articles*[85] which, in Crawford's words, "represent

been committed." Elizabeth A. Martin (ed.), A *Dictionary of Law* (4th ed.) (Oxford: Oxford University Press, 1997), 124.

80 This particularly applies to "Chapter VII of the Charter of the United Nations – despite the fact that the Charter uses the term 'measures,' not 'sanctions.'" International Law Commission, *Draft Articles on Responsibility of States for Internationally Wrongful Acts*, 75.

81 *Prosecutor* v. *Blaškić*, International Tribunal for the Former Yugoslavia, Case IT-95–14-AR 108 *bis*, (1997) ILR, Vol. 110, par. 25.

82 International Law Commission, *Draft Articles on Responsibility of States for Internationally Wrongful Acts*, 111.

83 *Case concerning the difference between New Zealand and France concerning the interpretation or application of two agreements, concluded on 9 July 1986 between the two States and which related to the problems arising from the Rainbow Warrior Affair*, 30 April 1990, Reports of International Arbitral Awards, Vol. XX, p. 251, par. 75.

84 In summarizing the ICJ's caseload on the matter of state responsibility, Higgins note that "since the early 1970s, the periodic findings on State responsibility that the Court has had occasion to make have been pronouncements handed down against the background of intermittent work by the International Law Commission on State responsibility." Rosalyn Higgins, "The International Court of Justice: Selected Issues of State Responsibility," in Maurizio Ragazzi (ed.), *International Responsibility Today – Essays in Memory of Oscar Schachter* (Leiden: Martinus Nijhoff, 2005), 271.

85 They were eventually incorporated in the UN GA Resolution on the Responsibility of States for Internationally Wrongful Acts (adopted on 12 December 2001) (A/RES/56/83)

the modern framework of state responsibility."[86] The *Draft articles* employ the generic concept of "wrongful act," which covers all forms of the state's illegal behavior,[87] and may "give rise to various types of legal relations, depending on the circumstances."[88] The text does, however, introduce "a serious breach" of an obligation arising under a jus cogens norm (Art. 40[1]),[89] in which one of the stipulated legal consequences is that "[n]o State shall recognize as lawful a situation created by a serious breach ... nor render aid or assistance in maintaining that situation." (Art. 41[2]) The concept of state responsibility is construed in such a way as to eschew "any general preconditions for responsibility in international law, such as 'fault' on the part of the wrongdoing state, or 'damage' suffered by any injured state."[90] Part Two of the *Draft articles* deals with legal consequences of the wrongful act. The responsible state has a duty to cease that act and to provide guarantees of its non-repetition (Art. 30). It also has "to make full reparation for the injury," which "includes any damage, whether material or moral, caused by the internationally wrongful act of a State." (Art. 31) Reparation, which has to restore the situation caused by the internationally wrongful act, can take the form of "restitution" (Art. 35), "compensation" (Art. 36), and "satisfaction" (Art. 37), either singly or in combination.[91] This part of the *Draft articles* also envisages the possibility of "countermeasures,"[92] which are "measures, otherwise unlawful, taken against another state in response to an unlawful act by that state and with a view to obtaining cessation and/or reparation."[93] Finally, the text introduces the part on the invocation of state

86 James Crawford, *State Responsibility: The General Part* (Cambridge: Cambridge University Press, 2013), 45.

87 Art. 1 and Art. 2(b). "An internationally wrongful act of a State may consist in one or more actions or omissions or a combination of both." International Law Commission, *Draft Articles on Responsibility of States for Internationally Wrongful Acts*, 32.

88 *Ibid*, 33.

89 "A breach of such an obligation is serious if it involves a gross or systematic failure by the responsible State to fulfil the obligation." Art. 40(2)

90 Crawford, *State Responsibility: The General Part*, 49. Articles 20–25 deal with circumstances which exclude wrongfulness and, thus, international responsibility of the state.

91 For a detailed analysis of the concept of "injury," *see, e.g.*, Julio Barboza, "Legal Injury: The Tip of the Iceberg in the Law of State Responsibility," in Ragazzi (ed.), *International Responsibility Today*, 7–22.

92 Art. 49–54.

93 "The subject proved a vexed one, with some states questioning the wisdom of including them in the ILC's work at all." (Crawford, *State Responsibility: The General Part*, 48) As to the employed terminology, the ILC notices that "countermeasures" have to be differentiated from "reprisals" and "retorsion." Whereas the former term was traditionally used to denote "unlawful action, including forcible action, taken by way of self-help," more recently it "has been limited to action taken in time of international armed conflict; i.e. it has been taken as equivalent to belligerent reprisals." Accordingly "countermeasures" denote "that part of the

responsibility[94] – "an issue which might be analogized to municipal law concepts of standing or the possession of an actionable claim or cause of action."[95]

With the rapid judicialization of international law, all the necessary elements for the appraisal of international law in terms of rectificatory justice are gradually coming into place. Romano does caution that "far from having reached the high-water mark, on aggregate international litigation has just taken off."[96] At the same time, he stresses that "the real revolution" lies in the shift from a traditional "consensual" to a "compulsory" paradigm. This shift is reflected in the fact "that the overwhelming majority of these fora exercise compulsory jurisdiction and that litigation is triggered often and in certain contexts solely unilaterally."[97] Although the jurisdiction of the "world court" is essentially based on the consent of states,[98] it is important to acknowledge that, at the moment of writing, seventy-three states have unilaterally declared that "they recognize as compulsory *ipso facto* and without special agreement, in relation to any other State accepting the same obligation, the jurisdiction of the Court." (Art. 36[2] of the ICJ Statute)[99] The rise of international litigation not only enables the authoritative assessment of the existence of breaches of international obligations,[100] but it also reveals the capacity of international adjudicative institutions to "restore equality" undermined by the putative international wrongful acts. This in the long run increases the international law's aptness for inspection in terms of rectificatory justice.

subject of reprisals not associated with armed conflict." As for "retorsion," it is an "'unfriendly' conduct which is not inconsistent with any international obligation of the State engaging in it even though it may be a response to an internationally wrongful act." International Law Commission, *Draft Articles on Responsibility of States for Internationally Wrongful Acts*, 128.

94 Art. 42–48.

95 Crawford, *State Responsibility: The General Part*, 47.

96 Romano, "Litigating International Law Disputes: Where To?," 469. After mapping the current state of affairs of international litigation, he concludes that "if the establishment of more adjudicative bodies is unlikely . . . the increase in caseload and judicial output of existing adjudicative bodies is likely to continue." *Ibid*, 463–464.

97 Cesare P. R. Romano, "The Shift From the Consensual to the Compulsory Paradigm in International Adjudication: Elements for a Theory of Consent" (2007) 39 *New York University Journal of International Law and Politics* 4: 794. He adds that "[t]his shift is also visible in quasijudicial and implementation control procedures as well in political processes such as determinations of legality by the UN Security Council." *Ibid*, 795, fn. 10.

98 *See, e.g.*, Stanimir A. Alexandrov, "The Compulsory Jurisdiction of the International Court of Justice: How Compulsory Is It?" (2006) 5 *Chinese Journal of International Law* 1: 29–38.

99 www.icj-cij.org/en/declarations

100 Art. 12 of *Draft articles*

# 7

# Fragmentation – A Special Feature of International Law?

One of the central claims of this book is that, at the most abstract level, international law exhibits all four typical features that can be associated with the central case of law as a genre of normative orders. Within the undertaken prototype approach, which is context sensitive, it is possible to detect that international law does display certain specificities with respect to each of the discussed typical features. They are a corollary of the distinctive empirical setting at the international level in which legal regulation of relations between norm-subjects is taking place. This setting is largely determined by the earlier mentioned relations of horizontality, in which states, as principal actors, assume the role of both lawmakers and norm-subjects. All this has resulted in a peculiar institutional structure of the international legal order, without a centralized legislature, courts with compulsory jurisdiction, and special enforcement agencies.

The analysis so far did not address in more detail the question whether international law belongs to a narrower subcategory of "institutionalized systems," because "systematicity" was not treated as a typical feature of law as a genre, but as an attribute of a particular historical form, that of the contemporary legal order.[1] Hart apparently takes a diametrically opposite position, by treating "the legal systems of modern states" as "the clear standard cases" of law.[2] As a result, the aforementioned formal structure of international law reminds him of "a simple regime" of primary rules.[3] Hart, nonetheless,

[1] As such, "systematicity" is by no means unique for law. As noted, institutionally organized religious orders tend to display important elements of "systematicity." *See, supra* p. 73.

[2] Hart, *The Concept of Law*, 3. It is already indicated that Hart's "fable of law's genesis," which commends elements of "systematicity" as remedies for the ills of "primitive communities" (*ibid*, 91), seriously endangers his ambition to provide a morally neutral and descriptive theory of law. Gardner, "Why Law Might Emerge: Hart's Problematic Fable," 85.

[3] *Ibid*, 232.

remarks that to have an order based on mere primary rules is not to strip it of all the characteristics we normally ascribe to the developed municipal law, such as the purported "bindingness" of those rules.[4] However, what we do not have in the given order, and we do possess in the modern day municipal law, is "a way of demonstrating the validity of individual rules by reference to some ultimate rule of the system."[5] This rule – "rule of recognition" – is "not a necessity, but a luxury, found in advanced social systems whose members not merely come to accept separate rules piecemeal, but are committed to the acceptance in advance of general classes of rule, marked out by general criteria of validity."[6] Since, in Hart's opinion, international law does not have such rule of recognition, its operative rules "constitute not a system but a set of rules."[7] Put differently, in the moment of writing his *Concept of Law*, Hart believed that international law had not progressed to the stage of an "advanced" legal order endowed with the "systemic" feature.[8]

One of the deficiencies of such a simple regime, which is supposed to be mended by the introduction of a "rule of recognition," concerns "*uncertainty*." Namely, there is no authoritative way of settling doubts as to what the applicable rule is, what its precise scope is, and how conflicts between several potentially applicable rules are to be solved.[9] Almost half a century after Hart's depiction of international law as lacking the character of a "system" of rules, the ILC came up with a consolidated report on "difficulties arising from the diversification and expansion of international law." While contemporary international law is most certainly not "a simple regime," the persistent absence of a centralized structure of law-making, coupled with the pervading horizontality of international relations and "the expanding legal scope of international concern,"[10] has become a legal order with new sources of uncertainty. They pertain to "the emergence of specialized and (relatively) autonomous rules or rule-complexes, legal institutions and spheres of legal

4 Hart says that "if rules are in fact accepted as standards of conduct, and supported with appropriate forms of social pressure distinctive of obligatory rules, nothing more is required to show that they are binding rules." *Ibid*, 234.

5 *Ibid*, 234.

6 *Ibid*, 235.

7 *Ibid*.

8 "Perhaps international law is at present in a stage of transition towards acceptance of this and other forms which would bring it nearer in structure to a municipal system. If, and when, this transition is completed the formal analogies, which at present seem thin and even delusive, would acquire substance, and the sceptic's last doubts about the legal 'quality' of international law may then be laid to rest." *Ibid*, 236–237.

9 *Ibid*, 92.

10 Shaw, *International Law*, 45.

practice."[11] Once thought of as the province of "general international law," it has gradually evolved into the field of operation of specialized legal regimes of "international trade law," "international human rights law," "international environmental law," etc. These regimes tend to function "with relative ignorance of legislative and institutional activities in the adjoining fields and of the general principles and practices of international law."[12] In short, the employed perspective, according to the ILC report, inclines one to conclude that international law suffers from "fragmentation."

This somewhat gloomy diagnosis raises several important questions. For instance, one may question the very employment of the framework of "systematicity," which is imported from municipal law. Is the request for a "systemic" feature of international law only part of "the conceptual baggage of domestic law," the one which may obfuscate analytical elucidation of the nature of international law?[13] One may, then, ask whether the depicted reality of international law is accurate. Is international law indeed fatally parceled into separate "self-contained legal regimes"?[14] Finally, one may argue that fragmentation is "very much in the eye of beholder."[15] If one changes the lens, is it not after all possible to speak of international law's unity?

## 1 HART'S LENS OF "SYSTEMATICITY"

In Victor Burgin's well-known photograph from the series US77, an observer is assuming the viewpoint of the front-seat passenger of the moving vehicle ahead of which a straight, flat, and empty road is seemingly unfolding. And yet, the photograph is entitled *False Perspective*, as if the author wants to tell us that no matter how simple is the landscape of physical reality, in order for its particles to be coherently linked into a single scene, a viewer has somehow to connect them, thereby necessarily becoming involved in the process of personal construction. The end result of this process is a viewer's "perspective." But, then again, in what sense can something that is the result of an individual construction ever be said to be "false," or "truthful" for that matter? The only plausible way would be to treat the "correctness" of a perspective as the request

[11] ILC, *Fragmentation of International Law*, par. 8.

[12] *Ibid.*

[13] Çali speaks of such "baggage" in the analytical clarification of the concept of authority in international law. Çali, *The Authority of International Law*, 51ff.

[14] For an early account, *see*, Bruno Simma, "Self-contained Regimes" (1985) 16 *Netherlands Yearbook of International Law*: 117.

[15] Jan Klabbers, "Setting the Scene," in Klabbers, Peters, and Ulfstein, *The Constitutionalization of International Law*, 14.

for "coherence" in one's attempt to make some such connections with the purpose of organizing one's own experience.

This exercise in the interpretation of a piece of art[16] has the sole purpose of serving as a reminder of the important methodological dictum of this book – that legal reality is far more complex and that, in trying to make connections between different particles of specific raw data, a legal philosopher has to engage partly in the business of "stipulative regimentation" (Raz) of the empirical knowledge, thereby necessarily imposing on it his/her own theoretical construction of that reality. On this account, "correctness" of a theory of law has to be translated into the request for its "coherence" in light of some predefined theoretical purposes.[17] Hart obviously engages in such business when proposing to treat law "as the union of primary and secondary rules" under the broader perspective of "systematicity."[18] In doing so, however, he oscillates between the claim that "systematicity" is a necessary condition of "legality" (when speaking of the development of "secondary rules" as a "step from the pre-legal to the legal"[19]) and the claim that "systematicity" is only a feature of "the standard case," which differentiates it from "borderline cases" such as "primitive law" or "international law." Although the latter forms of law do not possess this feature, they are not for that reason stripped of their "legality."[20] Since the second claim is employed in the chapter on international law, I will focus on it.[21]

Hart's bold statement, that "international law not only lacks the secondary rules of change and adjudication which provide for legislature and courts, but also a unifying rule of recognition specifying 'sources' of law and providing general criteria for the identification of its rules," is qualified by Waldron as "simply preposterous."[22] And for a good reason. If law's obtaining the "systemic" feature serves the goal of remedying the ills of uncertainty, static

16 Hence, although it may appear so, I am neither engaging in the dispute with Wittgenstein's elaboration of the claim that "[t]he picture depicts reality" (Ludwig Wittgenstein, *Tractatus Logico-Philosophicus* [London: Kegan Paul, Trench, Trubner & Co., 1922], 2.201ff), nor am I trying to offer an argument in favor of some form of epistemic constructivism or the coherence theory of truth. *See, e.g.*, James O. Young, "The Coherence Theory of Truth," in Zalta (ed.), *The Stanford Encyclopedia of Philosophy* (Fall 2018 ed.), https://plato.stanford.edu/archives/fall2018/entries/truth-coherence/

17 *See, supra* p. 60.

18 Hart, *The Concept of Law*, chapters V and VI.

19 *Ibid*, 42, 94, 117, 170.

20 *Ibid*, 15–16.

21 For the analysis of the first claim and its relevance to the discussion about international law, *see*, Payandeh, "The Concept of International Law in the Jurisprudence of H.L.A. Hart," 993–994.

22 Waldron, "International Law: 'A Relatively Small and Unimportant' Part of Jurisprudence?," 222.

character of the rules, and inefficiency,[23] then it is justifiable to employ the functionalist approach in determining whether international law is devoid of this feature.[24] Under this approach, it would be very difficult to claim that, even then, international law did not know of the secondary rules of adjudication and change.[25] Waldron shows that both the constitution of the International Court of Justice (ICJ) as a court, as well as its operation, which, regardless of the absence of compulsory jurisdiction, is marked by the general acceptance of its decisions, cannot be understood differently but in terms of secondary rules.[26] Similarly, it is hardly deniable that the international order has gradually evolved secondary rules specifying the ways of changing the international law, which were subsequently codified in the 1969 VCLT. True, this change is different than the one in a modern municipal system – "it is plenary rather than representative and it works through a principle of voluntary accession rather than majority-decision" – but the crucial point is that it performs the same function.[27]

This leaves us with Hart's insistence that international law needs to possess a *unifying* rule of recognition in order to become a full-fledged legal system.[28] Taken, once again, from the functionalist standpoint, the role of the rule of recognition is twofold: a) to specify criteria for the validity of primary rules; and b) to provide criteria for regulating the relationship between different sources of law.[29] As for the first role, the preceding analysis showed that Art. 38 of the ICJ Statute provides for a nonexhaustive list of sources of international law, whereas the practice of international adjudicative institutions contributes to the crystallization of the status of other potential sources, such as decisions of international organizations.[30] There are further rules (in the VCLT) and authoritative texts (ILC Draft conclusions on the identification of customary international law), which serve the same role of alleviating uncertainties as to what shall count as a valid rule of international law. True, they are unable to

23 Hart, *The Concept of Law*, 92–93.

24 Payandeh, "The Concept of International Law in the Jurisprudence of H.L.A. Hart," 981.

25 As pointed out by Culver and Giudice, "central legislatures and courts with compulsory jurisdiction are only particular forms of law-creating and law-applying institutions, and so do not exhaust the possibilities of institutions capable of practicing secondary rules of change and adjudication. To suggest otherwise is to make an unwarranted claim from the specific experience of the law-state." Keith Culver and Michael Giudice, *Legality's Borders: An Essay in General Jurisprudence* (Oxford: Oxford University Press, 2010), 28.

26 Waldron, "International Law: 'A Relatively Small and Unimportant Part of Jurisprudence?,'" 216.

27 *Ibid*, 218.

28 Hart, *The Concept of Law*, 236.

29 Payandeh, "The Concept of International Law in the Jurisprudence of H.L.A. Hart," 989.

30 *See, supra* p. 88.

completely eliminate them, but "[t]these uncertainties are no more pressing in international law than they are in municipal legal systems,"[31] particularly in the area of constitutional law.[32] Consequently, Hart is not justified in "making greater demands on international law than he makes on municipal law." In any way, under Hart's perspective of "systematicity," differences between the two could only be "differences of degree, not differences of kind."[33]

As for the second role of the rule of recognition, Hart did not explicitly address it in the context of international law. Nevertheless, from his characterization of this body of law as a mere "set" of rules, one may infer the conclusion that he believed that international law possessed no mechanism for regulating conflicts between different sources.[34] This problem is extensively addressed in the ILC's Report on "fragmentation" of international law.

## 2 THE ILC'S LENS OF "FRAGMENTATION"

The ILC's approach to the "systematicity" of international law is triggered by what this body considers as an indisputably positive development – "the rapid expansion of international legal activity into various new fields and the diversification of its objects and techniques."[35] This process, however, has its negative side, which the ILC depicted by the word "fragmentation." The reason for the treatment of this problem lies in the fact that the emergence of new geographically or functionally limited "self-contained regimes" "creates problems of coherence in international law."[36] Coherence, on the other hand, "is valued positively owing to the connection it has with predictability and legal security. Moreover, only a coherent legal system treats legal subjects equally."[37] Fragmentation creates both "institutional and substantive problems,"[38] but the ILC leaves aside the former

[31] Payandeh, "The Concept of International Law in the Jurisprudence of H.L.A. Hart," 991.

[32] *See*, Jack Goldsmith and Daryl Levinson, "Law for States: International Law, Constitutional Law, Public Law" (2009) 122 *Harvard Law Review* 7: 1791–1868. I will return to this problem in the concluding note.

[33] Waldron, "International Law: 'A Relatively Small and Unimportant' Part of Jurisprudence?," 220.

[34] Payandeh, "The Concept of International Law in the Jurisprudence of H.L.A. Hart," 992.

[35] ILC, *Fragmentation of International Law*, par. 14.

[36] *Ibid*, par. 15.

[37] *Ibid*, par. 491.

[38] Andenas and Bjorge speak also of the third aspect – "methodological fragmentation," which has to do with the way law-application institutions at times treat customary rules and treaties. Mads Andenas and Eirik Bjorge, 'Introduction: From Fragmentation to Convergence in International Law', in Mads Andenas and Eirik Bjorge (eds.), *A Farewell to Fragmentation – Reassertion and Convergence in International Law* (Cambridge: Cambridge University Press, 2015), 7ff.

aspect,[39] arguing that this issue "is best dealt with by the institutions themselves."[40] As a consequence, the Report is focused on the problem of normative conflicts in international law and the traditional legal techniques for dealing with them.[41] In the absence of a strict hierarchy of formal sources of international law,[42] the *lex superior* maxim is of limited applicability,[43] and, thus, the larger part of the Report is dedicated to the function and scope of the *lex specialis* maxim,[44] which assumes greater importance in international law.[45]

While rightly stressing that the lack of a hierarchical relation between sources of international law also affects the problem of grasping the nature of a "normative conflict," the ILC, nonetheless, does not offer a more elaborate account of why this is so. Namely, unlike in municipal law, no principal distinction can be made between different sources *ratione materiae*. The subject matter of general legal acts of municipal law (constitution, statute, decree) is directly linked to the three earlier mentioned elements of their

39 It has "to do with the competence of various institutions applying international legal rules and their hierarchical relations *inter se*." ILC, *Fragmentation of International Law*, par. 13.

40 *Ibid.*

41 *Ibid*, par. 18.

42 Curiously enough, the ILC at one point resorts to "an informal hierarchy" of sources of international law. It says: "Inasmuch as 'general law' does not have the status of *jus cogens*, treaties generally enjoy priority over custom and particular treaties over general treaties. In the same vein, it may be assumed ... that local customs (if proven) have primacy over general customary law and, perhaps, the body of customary law has primacy over the general principles of law under article 38 (1) (c) of the ICJ Statute. This informal hierarchy follows from no legislative enactment but, emerges as a 'forensic' or a 'natural' aspect of legal reasoning." *Ibid*, par. 85. Since the aim of this paragraph of the Report is to discuss "the point of *lex specialis*," the unstated assumption is that, in regulating relations between the rules stemming from different sources of international law, this maxim somehow reflects the aforementioned "informal hierarchy." Orakhelashvili also refers to "the hierarchy of norms" when pointing out that "[o]ne norm could prevail over another because it emerged later in time; or because it applies as between certain States in contrast to general international law." Orakhelashvili, *Peremptory Norms in International Law*, 7. However, in solving normative conflicts, neither *lex posterior*, nor *lex specialis* reflects some hierarchy of legal norms. They rely on criteria that has nothing to do with the hierarchical structure of the legal order. Hence, the ILC is hardly justified in relying on an alleged "informal hierarchy" of international law.

43 As previously discussed, there are only some rules, which may originate from different sources of international law, which enjoy the hierarchically superior status in the international legal order. The Report deals with them in Section E.

44 *Ibid*, C. 2 Section. In the international legal doctrine, "the *lex specialis* principle has been categorized either as a general principle of international law, as a rule of customary international law, or as a principle of legal logic." Bruno Simma and Dirk Pulkowski, "Of Planets and the Universe: Self-Contained Regimes in International Law" (2006) 17 *European Journal of International Law* 3: 486, fn. 10.

45 Michael Akehurst, "The Hierarchy of the Sources of International Law" (1976) 47 *British Yearbook of International Law*: 273.

form – competence, procedure, and materialization.[46] Hence, what used to be the substance of statutory law-making was at some point of political history "upgraded" to the subject matter of constitution and protected with a more complex procedure of enactment and change. In that respect, elements of both substance and form provide the reasons why a constitution is considered hierarchically the highest legal act of municipal law. As a consequence, all potential normative conflicts that involve constitutional norms and norms of other general legal acts are resolved according to the *lex superior* maxim in favor of the former. This means that the scope of application of the *lex specialis* maxim in municipal law is narrowed only to conflicts between the norms, which belong to general legal instruments that are hierarchically equally ranked and possess the same normative force. Most commonly, *lex specialis* is there to solve the conflicts between statutory norms.

No such clear-cut picture exists at the international level.[47] Since the form of an international legal instrument does not play the same role as in the municipal legal order, the question of what constitutes a "normative conflict" will apparently have to be solved according to the criterion of substance, i.e., subject matter. In that respect, the ILC rightly notes that "[i]f conflict were to exist only between rules that deal with the 'same' subject-matter, then the way a treaty is applied would become crucially dependent on how it would classify under some (presumably) pre-existing classification scheme of different subjects." The problem is that "no such classification schemes" are available.[48] Hence, the ILC introduces "a wide notion of conflict as a situation where two rules or principles suggest different ways of dealing with a problem."[49] This definition reveals that the determination of the existence and the nature of "normative conflict" is part of the process of legal reasoning and interpretation.[50]

This finding is of general relevance for all the normative conflicts, both in municipal and international law, which are supposed to be solved by the application of the *lex specialis* maxim. Namely, its application "depends on

46 *See*, *supra* p. 86.

47 "Because of the spontaneous, decentralized and unhierarchical nature of international law-making – law-making by custom and by treaty – lawyers have always had to deal with heterogeneous materials at different levels of generality and with different normative force." ILC, *Fragmentation of International Law*, par. 486.

48 *Ibid*, par. 22. In particular, there are no criteria for classifying some norms as belonging to "international human rights law" or "international environmental law." These are "arbitrary labels on forms of professional specialization. There are no rules on how to qualify particular treaty regimes and most regimes could be qualified from a number of such perspectives." *Ibid*, 254.

49 *Ibid*, par. 25.

50 *Ibid*, par. 27.

the *previous identification of distinct rules*." More precisely, "the correlative rules in hand must be identified and ranked in advance in a certain order of lower/higher generality." Accordingly, *lex specialis* cannot serve as "a device to identify (special and general) rules. It is able to come to play when the works of interpreting and identifying rules has already been done."[51] Simma and Pulkowski, for instance, point to the problem of determining whether "non-compliance," within multilateral environmental agreements (MEA), concerns the same subject matter as the rules on state responsibility. Since the latter deal with "the legal consequences of unlawful conduct," that is, "breach,"[52] the question is whether MEA rules of "non-compliance" could be treated as special rules that would prevail on account of the *lex specialis* maxim.[53]

In order for that to be possible, the two rules have to be interpreted as standing in an adequate relationship. That is, a putative special and a general rule have to be perceived "as entities correlated, as … logical classes or geometric sets."[54] There are two principle ways in which law may take account of this relationship – "A particular rule may be considered an application of a general standard in a given circumstance … Or it may be considered as a modification, overruling or a setting aside of the latter."[55] Irrespective of the exact way these two rules are perceived in the process of interpretation, in order for any relationship to be established, the rules in question have to be seen "as part of some 'system.'"[56] This means that no rule "applies in a vacuum," and, hence, determining a particular form of normative relationship always takes place in some "normative environment."[57] Put differently,

51 Silvia Zorzetto, "The Lex Specialis Principle and its Uses in Legal Argumentation: An Analytical Inquire" (2012–2013) 3 *Eunomía. Revista en Cultura de la Legalidad*: 66.

52 Simma and Pulkowski, "Of Planets and the Universe: Self-contained Regimes in International Law," 488.

53 *Ibid*, 489.

54 Zorzetto, "The *Lex Specialis* Principle and its Uses in Legal Argumentation," 65. As stated by the ILC, "[g]enerality and speciality are thus relational. A rule is never 'general' or 'special' in the abstract but in relation to some other rule. This relationality functions in two registers. A rule may be general or special in regard to its *subject-matter* (fact-description) or in regard to the *number of actors* whose behaviour is regulated by it … The registers may overlap." ILC, *Fragmentation of International Law*, par. 112.

55 *Ibid*, par. 88.

56 *Ibid*, par. 32. Cf. Zorzetto, "The *Lex Specialis* Principle and its Uses in Legal Argumentation," 64.

57 ILC, *Fragmentation of International Law*, par. 120. Thus, "whether a rule is seen as an 'application', 'modification' or 'exception' to another rule, depends on how we view those rules in the environment in which they are applied, including what we see as their object and purpose." *Ibid*, par. 97.

"*[n]o general, context-independent answers can be given*" regarding the application of the *lex specialis* maxim.[58]

This conclusion turns out to be of particular relevance for the discussion about the multiplication of "self-contained regimes," which are initially detected as the main source of international law's fragmentation.[59] The ILC differentiates between the three possible ways of defining those regimes. In the narrowest sense, advanced by Simma, a "self-contained regime" pertains to "a special set of secondary rules that determine the consequences of a breach of certain primary rules (including the procedures of such determination)." In a broader sense, it refers to "any interrelated cluster (set, regime, subsystem) of rules on a limited problem together with the rules for the creation, interpretation, application, modification, or termination – in a word, administration – of those rules."[60] Finally, the broadest understanding emerges "from the informal activity of lawyers, diplomats, pressure groups, more through shifts in legal culture and in response to practical needs of specialization than as conscious acts of regime-creation."[61] In that sense, one may speak of "branches of international law," which "are also assumed to function in the manner of self-contained regimes, claiming to be regulated by their own principles."[62]

Which type of relationship exists between the special regime and the general law "will be predominantly a matter of interpreting the treaties that form the regime."[63] However, since "systemic thinking penetrates all legal reasoning, including the practice of law-application,"[64] one is warranted in holding that no regime in international law is truly "self-contained." Even in the case of a well-developed regime, "general law has at least two types of function. First, it provides the normative background that comes in to fulfil aspects of its operation not specifically provided by it . . . Second, the rules of general law also come to operate if the special regime fails to function properly. Such failure might be substantive or procedural."[65] This leads the ILC to conclude that the very label "self-contained regime" is "a misnomer,"[66] and, thus, it pledges for a more adequate tag – "special treaty-regimes." Their

58 *Ibid*, par. 119. (emphasis in the original)

59 The general rationale of special regimes is that "[t]hey take better account of the particularities of the subject-matter to which they relate; they regulate it more effectively than general law and follow closely the preferences of their members." *Ibid*, par. 191.

60 *Ibid*, par. 152.

61 *Ibid*, par. 158.

62 *Ibid*, par. 152.

63 *Ibid*, par. 159.

64 *Ibid*, par. 35.

65 *Ibid*, par. 192.

66 *Ibid*, par. 193.

emergence, according to the Commission's ultimate finding, has not after all *"seriously undermined legal security, predictability or the equality of legal subjects."*[67]

Therefore, what originally appeared as a devastatingly pessimistic portrait of the state of affairs of the international legal order[68] was eventually depicted in far more enthusiastic tones, with the ILC's assertion that the discussed legal techniques "provide a basic professional tool-box that is able to respond in a flexible way to most substantive fragmentation problems."[69] However, interpretative devices for the solution of normative conflicts are not self-applicable. Their usage crucially depends on the institutional actor vested with the law-applying authority. But, as pointed out, the ILC deliberately decided not to tackle the institutional dimension of fragmentation. This seriously undermines the idea of the whole project, having in mind the ILC's stance that the existence of a relationship between various norms, its qualification as "normative conflict," and its solution according to some of the interpretative maxims is upon the very subject of interpretation. Hence, the institutional aspect is of crucial importance for the elaboration of interaction between different, specialized regimes in international law.[70]

## 3 THE "AS *IF*" LENS OF INTERNATIONAL LAW'S UNITY

The discussion so far has revealed that the international legal order is at the present moment diversified and sectored into a number of highly autonomous regimes with their own adjudicative institutions.[71] With the nascent but

67 *Ibid*, par. 492.

68 This starting premise is far from being universally endorsed among international scholars. Greenwood, for instance, argues that the "fragmentation" diagnosis is grounded in three unjustifiable assumptions: first, "that what we are witnessing is a decline from a past golden age in which international law was a single, entirely coherent system"; second, "that the increased diversity of international law must be seen as a problem"; and third, "that unity and diversity must be in conflict." He is particularly interested in dispelling this last claim. Sir Christopher Greenwood, "Unity and Diversity in International Law," in Andenas and Bjorge (eds.), *A Farewell to Fragmentation – Reassertion and Convergence in International Law*, 38–39.

69 ILC, *Fragmentation of International Law*, par. 492.

70 For this reason, Young adopts the following definition of "regimes": They are "sets of norms, decision-making procedures and *organisations* coalescing around functional issue-areas." Margaret A. Young, "Introduction: The Productive Friction between Regimes," in Margaret A. Young (ed.), *Regime Interaction in International Law – Facing Fragmentation* (Cambridge: Cambridge University Press, 2012), 9.

71 Fischer-Lescano and Teubner argue that "self-contained regimes fortify themselves as auto-constitutional regimes," whose defining feature "is not simply that they create highly specialized primary norms (substantive rules in special fields of law), but they also produce, in

palpable shift toward the earlier mentioned paradigm of compulsory jurisdiction, these institutions engage nowadays more often in the process of law-application, in which they also "shift meanings and can establish their own interpretations as new reference points for legal discourse." In that respect, they become *loci* of "semantic struggles" that enable the further development of international law.[72] At the same time, their authoritative ascertainment of something as a valid and applicable international legal rule has the character of the "practice of recognition," which is in the Hartian sense meant to alleviate the factor of uncertainty. A potential problem is that these "practices of recognition" occur across different sectoral regimes and may not always settle on a single rule of recognition.[73] Similarly, in the absence of an institutional hierarchy or some general appeals mechanism, "the risk that each court or tribunal would interpret and apply the rules of international law in its own way, disregarding or challenging the jurisprudence of other courts and tribunals became a matter of serious concern."[74] Put differently, what from the standpoint of a certain international legal regime may look like a move toward erasing uncertainty, from a conflicting stance may simply be apprehended as bringing even more instability to the international legal order. If no institutional structure is available for a categorical settlement of potential conflicts between different autonomous regimes,[75] are we really destined, as Hart believed, to "the obstinate search for unity and system where these desirable elements are not in fact to be found"?[76]

contrast to the generalized secondary norms of international law, their own procedural norms on law-making, law-recognition and legal sanctions." Andreas Fischer-Lescano and Gunther Teubner, "Regime Collisions: The Vain Search for Legal Unity in the Fragmentation of Global Law" (2004) 25 *Michigan Journal of International Law* 4: 1015.

72 Venzke, *How Interpretation Makes International Law*, 71.

73 "While Hart acknowledged that the idea of a rule of recognition was meant to serve as a kind of notional summary or shorthand for referring to a rather complex array of facts, his repeated use of the idea of 'rule of recognition' has unfortunately often given the misleading impression that the various practices of indeterminately identified officials do always unite in and amount to a singular rule wherever there is a legal system." Michael Giudice, "Sources and the Systematicity of International Law – A Philosophical Perspective," in Besson and d'Aspremont (eds.), *The Oxford Handbook on the Sources of International Law*, 592.

74 Greenwood, "Unity and Diversity in International Law," 46.

75 As pointed out by Venzke, "[t]here is usually no stable or sufficiently thick ground for deciding who should prevail – either in law or political theory. Political theory is faced with multiple and overlapping constituencies that make reasonable claims to public autonomy. And law does not seem to offer any meta-ordering between legal orders but appears to be rather speechless when two orders collide." Venzke, *How Interpretation Makes International Law*, 251. *Cf.* Nico Krisch, *Beyond Constitutionalism – The Pluralist Structure of Postnational Law* (Oxford: Oxford University Press, 2010), 298.

76 This criticism was specifically directed at Kelsen's search for a "basic norm" of international law. Hart, *The Concept of Law*, 235–236.

However, it might be the case that this is from the outset a wrong way of approaching the issue. Highlighting the so-called institutional problem fosters an erroneous "view that international law is somehow 'constitutionally deficient,'" which "arises only because of the rather incoherent and unrealistic expectations that we have of the international legal order."[77] For this reason, Fischer-Lescano and Teubner urge "a radical rethinking of conflicts law," arguing that the lawyer's mainstream perspective is "reductionist," "oversimplifying," and "narrow."[78] The mainstream view identifies "a danger to the unity of international law because the conceptual-doctrinal consistency, the clear hierarchy of norms and the effective judicial hierarchy that was developed within the nation-states, is lacking." Accordingly, proponents of this view are in the search for "a hierarchical solution to the problem, which, whilst not wholly reproducing the ideal of legal hierarchies of the nation-state, at least comes somewhere close to it."[79] Instead, these authors argue in favor of a "social theory" perspective, which is able to reveal that what lawyers depict as mere collisions between norms has in fact "its origin in contradictions between society-wide institutionalized rationalities." These contradictions cannot be entirely solved by law. The most one can hope for is "a weak normative compatibility of the fragments." Nevertheless, even this objective "is dependent upon the ability of conflicts law to establish a specific network logic, which can effect a loose coupling of colliding units."[80]

Even this radical pluralist view[81] through the lens of social theory, which purposefully wants to distance itself from the mainstream legal perspective,[82] cannot resist dealing with the subject matter *as if* it represents a unified whole. Not only do Fischer-Lescano and Teubner not shy away from speaking of a "global legal system," but their alternative heuristic devices, such as "network

77 Richard Collins, *The Institutional Problem in Modern International Law* (Oxford: Hart Publishing, 2016), 4.

78 Fischer-Lescano and Teubner, "Regime Collisions: The Vain Search for Legal Unity in the Fragmentation of Global Law," 1002.

79 *Ibid.*

80 *Ibid*, 1004.

81 For an overview of different versions of the pluralist argument, *see, e.g.*, Brian Z. Tamanaha, "Understanding Legal Pluralism: Past to Present, Local to Global" (2008) 30 *Sidney Law Review* 3: 375–411.

82 The urge for distancing seems to be shared by international legal scholars. In making introductory comments for the 25th Anniversary Symposium of the *Michigan Journal of International Law*, entitled "Diversity or Cacophony? New Sources of Norms in International Law?," within which Fischer-Lescano and Teubner's paper was one of the contributions, Simma remarks that "most international lawyers would not regard these two authors as 'mainstream' members of their profession." Bruno Simma, "Fragmentation in a Positive Light" (2004) 25 *Michigan Journal of International Law* 4: 847.

logic"[83] or "regimes compatibility,"[84] are also premised on some such "systemic" idea of merged totality.[85] In fact, they argue, without providing any further justification, that "one *must* (M. J.) proceed from the assumption that law has ... established itself globally as a unitary social system."[86] In arguing so, they seem to return to the perspective that, according to the ILC, "penetrates all legal reasoning."[87] This is a genuine legal perspective of the world of existing norms as one of a logically coherent, integrated, and unified whole. More precisely, lawyers represent their specific reality *as if* it is imbued with these qualities, despite being conscious that this is at times entirely counterfactual. What is more, they normally organize functioning of a legal order in such a way that the burden of proof is on anyone claiming that this is not so. In that respect, the legal perspective appears to be grounded in what Vaihinger famously coined as "*als ob*" (as if) methodology. He says:

> Our natural tendency is to adjust all our representations, to test them by comparison with reality, and to render them free from contradiction ... But the customary modes and results of thought already contain so many subjective and fictional elements that it is not surprising if thought also strikes out along other lines. It must be remembered that the object of the world of ideas as a whole is not the portrayal of reality – this would be an utterly impossible task – but rather to provide us with an *instrument for finding our way about more easily in this world.*[88]

This instrument is the "as if" methodology, which operates with two types of "ideational constructs," i.e., "fictions." The "real" ones are "not only in contradiction with reality but self-contradictory in themselves," while the "semi-fictions" are "constructs which only contradict reality as given, or deviate from

83 Fischer-Lescano and Teubner, "Regime Collisions: The Vain Search for Legal Unity in the Fragmentation of Global Law," 1004.

84 *Ibid*, 1045.

85 This can be easily confirmed by checking the plain dictionary definitions of the words "network" and "compatible." The former is defined as "a *system* of lines or channels resembling a network"; "an interconnected or interrelated chain, group, or *system*" (emphasis mine) (at www.merriam-webster.com/dictionary/network), whereas the latter is defined as "capable of existing together in *harmony*"; "capable of cross-fertilizing freely or *uniting* vegetatively"; "capable of forming a *homogeneous* mixture that neither separates nor is altered by chemical interaction" (emphasis mine), at www.merriam-webster.com/dictionary/compatibility

86 The unity in question "is no longer structure-based ... but is rather process-based, deriving simply from the modes of connection between legal operations, which transfer binding legality between even highly heterogeneous legal orders." *Ibid*, 1007–1008.

87 ILC, *Fragmentation of International Law*, par. 35.

88 Hans Vaihinger, *The Philosophy of 'As if' – A System of Theoretical, Practical and Religious Fictions of Mankind* (translated by C. K. Ogden) (London: Routledge and Kegan Paul, 1925), 15. (emphasis in the original)

it, but are not in themselves self-contradictory."[89] Although Veihinger was mostly concerned with the usage of this methodology in science, one can certainly find its application in the area of law.[90] In fact, it is commonly assumed that both legal practice and legal theory rely on those ideational constructs.[91] Vaihinger, for instance, refers to well-known "juristic fictions."[92] However, one may object that scientific ideational constructs are instruments for the cognition and representation of reality, whereas the task of law is not to discover facts, but to regulate actual human behavior.[93] Thus, in Vaihinger's own sense of the word, it makes sense only to speak of ideational constructs of legal theory.[94]

In that respect, one needs to bear in mind that highly abstract theoretical ideational constructs are rarely, if ever, used in legal practice (e.g., Kelsen's "basic norm,"[95] or Hart's "union of primary and secondary rules"), whereas

89 *Ibid*, 16.

90 Lon Fuller, *Legal Fictions* (Stanford: Stanford University Press, 1967), 125. Fuller provides a comprehensive list of books and articles in the German legal literature that were inspired by Veihinger's monograph, 95, fn. 4.

91 "Just like maps provide a sense of orientation only by means of manipulated, scaled, and simplified representation of physical space, so can law bring order to the world only by creating and imposing a surreal matrix of legal terms and concepts upon that to which it relates." Valentin Jeutner, *Irresolvable Norm Conflicts in International Law: The Concept of a Legal Dilemma* (Oxford: Oxford University Press, 2017), 151.

92 According to him, the term fiction has been "nowhere better known than in jurisprudence where it forms a favourite subject of discussion." Vaihinger, *The Philosophy of 'As if'*, 33.

93 Hence, Kelsen concludes that "due to the lack of any aim of cognition within the legal order – which as such is the object of cognition, and not itself cognition or an expression of cognition – the words of a legal norm can never contain a 'fiction' in Vaihinger's sense." Hans Kelsen, "On the Theory of Juridic Fictions. With Special Consideration of Vaihinger's Philosophy of the As-If," in Maksymilian Del Mar and William Twining (eds.), *Legal Fictions in Theory and Practice* (Cham: Springer, 2015), 9. *Cf.* Fuller, *Legal Fictions*, 125.

94 Fuller differentiates between "jurisprudential fictions" and "fictions of legal technique." The former "attempt to describe 'the nature of law in general'" and insofar as they tend "to reduce a complex reality to a simple formula," they clearly "represent a precise parallel to the methods of the physical scientist." *Ibid*, 127–128. The latter refer to various concepts (e.g., legal personality, liability), which "are the devices through which we organize and simplify our subject matter." *Ibid*, 130. Kelsen seems to acknowledge only the second category as "fictions of legal theory." For him, they "are true, i.e. epistemological fictions in legal science. They are fictions of the attempt to know the law, fictions of the intellectual mastery of the legal order." Such fictions, as "auxiliary constructs," are, for instance, the "concepts" of a legal subject or of a subjective right. Kelsen, "On the Theory of Juridic Fictions," 5.

95 Interestingly enough, in the latest phase of his work, Kelsen retreated from the position that *Grundnorm* is a presupposition of legal cognition and started openly to speak of it as a "fiction." In one of the late reformulations of his theory, Kelsen explicitly states that the basic norm is "the typical case of a fiction in the sense of Vaihinger's *Philosophie des Als-Ob*." (Hans Kelsen, "On the Pure Theory of Law" (1966) 1 *Israel Law Review* 1: 6) For an analysis of this move in Kelsen's theory, *see, e.g.*, Neil Duxbury, "The Basic Norm: An Unsolved Murder Mystery" (2007) *LSE Law, Society and Economy Working Papers*, 17–2007: 1–10, at www.lse.ac.uk/law/working-paper-series/2007-08/WPS17-2007Duxbury.pdf

some of them, which are at the lower abstraction (e.g., legal subject, delict), are regularly employed by various legal instruments, ranging from statutes to judicial decisions. And yet, no precise line is possible to draw. Certain jurisprudential ideational constructs, even when not explicitly endorsed by legal instruments, function as background pillars of a legal practitioner's reasoning. Such is exactly the case with the "fiction" that "jurisprudence must conceive of the rules of law as forming a unity."[96] At the municipal level, this ideational construct is institutionally supported by the hierarchical structure of the judiciary and, sometimes, by the specially designed power of judicial review, which can be vested in regular courts and/or in a distinctive adjudicative body (e.g., constitutional tribunal). In their functioning, these law-applying institutions resort to interpretative techniques and normative-conflict-resolution tools, such as the *lex specialis* maxim, whose origin and nature are highly contestable,[97] but whose *ratio* is clearly linked to the "fiction" of law's unity. Despite the fact that in reality a number of normative conflicts that disrupt the given ideational construct will never be authoritatively resolved by the adjudicative institutions, the mere presence of this institutional structure gives the pretense that some such unified legal system *exists*.

International legal theory and practice are no exception in that respect. They also count on the same ideational construct of international law's unity. This is, for instance, evidenced in the ILC's remark that "[i]n international law, there is a strong presumption against normative conflict."[98] But, how is international legal practice in its functioning to rely on this "fiction" in the absence of a comparable institutional setting characteristic of municipal law?[99] The ILC's Report concludes by noting

96 This is one of several such constructs, which Ehrlich mentions, arguing that "upon closer inspection they reveal themselves as fictions." Eugene Ehrlich, *Die juristische Logik* (Tübingen: J. C. B. Mohr, 1918), 148–149.

97 The source of putative bindingness of this maxim is a matter of contestation. "According to the mainstream in legal practice and the general theory of law, the *lex specialis* principle is . . . a positive rule whose existence depends on the normative choices of the legal authorities (i.e., legislators and/or legal interpreters). In the eyes of jurists and theoreticians, the *lex specialis* principle is mostly a traditional and implicit rule that is independent by all its expressed formulations in legal texts. In actual fact, its origin and nature are disputed: there is no consensus for instance on its customary nature. But . . . there is wide agreement that it is a historical tool to make laws and legal rules consistent." Zorzetto, "The *Lex Specialis* Principle and its Uses in Legal Argumentation: An Analytical Inquire," 64.

98 ILC, *Fragmentation of International Law*, par. 37.

99 One obvious way to circumvent the so-called institutional problem (Collins) is to argue that even if such an international institutional rearrangement were possible, it would not be desirable. Ulfstein, for instance, argues that reform of this sort may bring more "legal clarity," but only at the expense of "effective" international problem solving. Geir Ulfstein,

that "*no homogenous, hierarchical meta-system is realistically available to do away*" with conflicting rules and overlapping legal regimes. In this regard, international law is destined "to operate within an area where the demands of coherence and reasonable pluralism will point in different directions." In order to perform its task successfully, "*increasing attention will have to be given to the ... rules, methods and techniques for dealing with [normative conflicts and regime] collisions.*"[100] That is, the ILC's ultimate message is – as long as we are in the possession of "a basic professional tool-box that is able to respond in a flexible way to most substantive fragmentation problems," we are fine.[101]

This thesis, however, is decisively dependent upon the unstated assumption that various international adjudicative institutions *(ought to) use* the available interpretative toolbox in a way consistent with the ideational construct of international law's coherence and unity. A crucial element of this construct concerns the very self-portrayal of these institutional actors as officials of a unified international legal order. At the municipal level, such self-portrayal is, normally, taken for granted due to the fact that the law is "not merely a set of guides for court decisions," but also "a political institution of great importance to the working of societies and to their members."[102] Adhering to the ideational construct of law's unity is a specific way for municipal legal officials to express the previously discussed "respect for law,"[103] understood as loyalty to the given political community and identification with it.[104] A reverse implication of this relation is that once the law as a political institution is challenged by some municipal law-applying institutions, this is a clear indicator that the accompanying ideational construct of law's unity is abandoned as well.[105]

"Institutions and Competences," in Klabbers, Peters, and Ulfstein, *The Constitutionalization of International Law*, 70.

100 ILC, *Fragmentation of International Law*, par. 493.

101 *Ibid*, 492.

102 This political aspect of the law implies, for instance, that not every applicable rule will be considered by the court as "the law of the land" (e.g., the applicable rule of foreign law in the private international law cases). Joseph Raz, "Incorporation by Law" (2004) 10 *Legal Theory* 1: 15.

103 *See, supra* pp. 1401–42.

104 As pointed out by Raz, loyalty to one's community may be expressed in different ways, and not necessarily by respecting the law. Raz, "Respect for Law," 260. However, respect for law seems to be a "natural" way for legal officials to display identification with the political community.

105 A more modest form of such a challenge is not uncommon in compound, federal polities. There, the mechanism of constitutional review usually has the function of solving the problem of jurisdictional delimitations and conflicts between federation and federal units. This was, for example, one of the main motives for Jellinek to argue for the establishment of

There are credible signs that international adjudicative bodies, even those of special international legal regimes, *do depict themselves* as officials of a unified international legal order. Take, for instance, the following passage from a ruling of the Tribunal, set up under the *Convention for the Protection of the Marine Environment of the North-East Atlantic* (OSPAR):

> It should go without saying that the first duty of the Tribunal is to apply the OSPAR Convention. An international tribunal, such as this Tribunal, will also apply customary international law and general principles unless and to the extent that the Parties have created a *lex specialis*. Even then, it must defer to a relevant *jus cogens* with which the Parties' *lex specialis* may be inconsistent.[106]

Although being aware of its role – as an institution of a special international legal regime – to proceed from specific treaty rules, the Tribunal also acknowledges that it is "an international tribunal," with the duty to apply general international law, as well as to refuse the application of any special rule that derogates from hierarchically higher jus cogens norms. There is further evidence that various adjudicative institutions, in perceiving themselves as "international tribunals" that operate in a nonhierarchically structured institutional set-up, mutually observe each other's jurisprudence, thereby contributing to the overall *consistency* and *coherence* of international law.[107] Greenwood takes as an example the complex machinery for dispute settlement provided in the 1982 UN Convention on the Law of the Sea. In order to secure some form of compulsory dispute settlement, the Convention offers the choice of recourse to the ICJ, the then-created ITLOS, or arbitration. There were fears that these three institutions might develop very different approaches in the area of maritime delimitation. However, "[t]hose fears now seem unfounded … [because of] a remarkable consistency of approach" between all these adjudicative institutions. What is more, "the judgments and awards given in all three fora have referred extensively to the jurisprudence of other courts and tribunals … The result has been the emergence of a coherent

a constitutional court of Austria. Georg Jellinek, *Ein Verfassungsgericht für Österreich* (Wien: Alfred Hölder, 1885) A full-blown challenge of this sort is raised by secessionist institutions that stop treating the once applicable legal rules as "the law of (their) land."

106 *Dispute Concerning Access to Information under Article 9 of the OSPAR Convention between Ireland and the United Kingdom of Great Britain and Northern Ireland* (Final Award 2 July 2003), par. 84.

107 *See, supra* pp. 181–182.

body of law and practice which is the stronger for having emanated from more than one institution."[108]

To be sure, there are cases in which a tribunal does not follow the earlier established standard of adjudication. Such is, for instance, the well-known case of the ICTY's *Tadić* ruling, which endorses the so-called overall control test for the determination of state responsibility,[109] thereby rejecting the ICJ's earlier established standard of "effective control."[110] In its subsequent *Genocide* judgment,[111] the ICJ, in turn, rejected the ICTY's test.[112] But even when these adjudicative institutions deliberately and consciously depart from what appears to be precedential ruling, they do so with a sense of obligation to refer to the previous decision and to try to provide justification for their move.[113] They operate under what Fischer-Lescano and Teubner call "default deference," that is, under "the rebuttable presumption that the decisions of international . . . courts do have the character of precedent for one another."[114] In so acting, international adjudicative institutions display "the consciousness of the need for a common framework."[115] They do so in spite of the lack of some full-fledged global political community with which they identify and to which they owe allegiance and loyalty. In their case, it seems more reasonable to speak of "a global community of courts"[116] as a potential source and generator of this obligation of "default deference."[117] Despite the fact that such "community" may be characterized as yet another ideational construct of international legal theory, it gives rise to Simma's bold statement that "if there

108 Greenwood, "Unity and Diversity in International Law," 47.

109 *The Prosecutor* v. *Dusko Tadić*, par. 145.

110 *Military and Paramilitary Activities in and against Nicaragua, Merits*, par. 110, 115.

111 *Application of the Convention on the Prevention and Punishment of the Crime of Genocide (Bosnia and Herzegovina* v. *Serbia and Montenegro)*, Judgment, I.C.J. Reports 2007, par. 402.

112 For an analysis, *see, e.g.*, Antonio Cassese, "The Nicaragua and Tadić Tests Revisited in Light of the ICJ Judgment on Genocide in Bosnia" (2007) 18 *European Journal of International Law* 4: 649–668.

113 *The Prosecutor* v. *Dusko Tadić*, par. 115 ("The Grounds on Which the Nicaragua Test Does Not Seem To Be Persuasive"); *Application of the Convention on the Prevention and Punishment of the Crime of Genocide*, par. 403. ("The Court has given careful consideration to the Appeals Chamber's reasoning . . . but finds itself unable to subscribe to the Chamber's view.")

114 Fischer-Lescano and Teubner, "Regime Collisions: The Vain Search for Legal Unity in the Fragmentation of Global Law," 1044.

115 Abi-Saab, "Fragmentation or Unification: Some Concluding Remarks," 929.

116 *See*, Anne-Marie Slaughter, "A Global Community of Courts" (2003) 44 *Harvard International Law Journal* 1: 191–219.

117 For an attempt to elucidate the nature of inter-judicial dialogue through the prism of epistemic authority, *see*, Bojan Spaić, "Epistemic Authority and Legal Interpretation" (2017), available at https://ssrn.com/abstract=3013573

are international institutions that are constantly and painstakingly aware of the necessity to preserve the coherence of international law, it is the international courts and tribunals."[118] In that respect, they seem to assume the role of the last line of defense of international law's unity.[119]

118 Simma, "Fragmentation in a Positive Light," 845.

119 This, in turn, raises the question of their legitimacy and accountability. Drawing from the municipal law experience, Besson notes that "[i]n the absence of other institutions and especially of a legislature with which to interact, and, more generally, of a political community to represent, the judiciary cannot play its interpretive and judicial law-making role. Such a judiciary is neither checked by nor accountable to any institution or community." Samantha Besson, "International Judges as Dispute-Settlers and Law Enforcers: From International Law Without Courts to International Courts Without Law" (2011) 34 *Loyola of Los Angeles International and Comparative Law Review* 1: 49.

# In Lieu of a Conclusion – A Note on (Un)Certainty

The principal claim of this book is that international law possesses all typical features of the central case of law as a "genre." In a distinctive international context, these features display certain specificities. Due to the advanced prototype theory of concepts, this in no way devalues "legality" of international law. And yet, even before coming to the concluding chapter, which raises the question whether "fragmentation" is a unique feature of international law, a careful reader, especially one with classical legal training, might have got the impression that what is an additional specificity of international law is a chronic lack of *certainty*.

And certainty is a highly ranked legal value.[1] Its aspects are closely linked to the realization of justice.[2] Legal certainty can be broken down into the three related, yet distinctive values – knowability, reliability, and calculability. Deficiency in each of them creates respective problems for a legal order. When norm-subjects "do not know exactly which rules are valid, or if they do, they are in doubt as to what the rules require, prohibit or permit," then such rules "are not accessible, comprehensive, comprehensible or sufficiently determinate."[3] Unreliability pertains to the situation when norm-subjects "do not know whether a valid rule will remain valid, or if they do they are not sure whether valid rules will actually be applied to their case."[4] Incalculability exists when norm-subjects "have

[1] In Radbruch's words: "Legal certainty demands the positivity of law: if it cannot be ascertained (*festgestellt*) what is just (*gerecht*), then it must be stipulated (*festgesetzt*) what is lawful (*rechtens*)." Radbruch, *Rechtsphilosophie*, 73.

[2] "That the law be certain and sure, that it not be interpreted and applied one way here and now, another way elsewhere and tomorrow, is also a requirement of justice." Radbruch, "Statutory Lawlessness and Supra-Statutory Law (1946)," 6.

[3] Humberto Ávila, *Certainty in Law* (Basel: Springer, 2016), 21.

[4] *Ibid*, 22.

very little chance of obtaining information about future decisions," that is, when they can hardly anticipate the possible decisions of law-applying institutions.[5]

When it comes to general obstacles to the realization of legal certainty, it is possible to enumerate several of them. A first class of obstacles concerns "the plurality of heterogeneous sources," which are not always hierarchically structured.[6] A second class "arises from the disorder of normative texts." A third class "derives from the (poor) drafting of normative texts," while a fourth stems from inconsistencies in the case law and judicial practice (e.g., a nonuniform interpretation, case-law revisions, and departures from precedent).[7]

When the aforementioned analytical distinctions are taken into account, hardly any international scholar would be ready to argue that international law is not uncertain. Simply put, "[t]o deny uncertainty where it exists ... is one of the gravest failings a scholar can commit."[8] First, there is *uncertainty of sources of law,* that is, what counts as a formal source of international law. The list provided in Art. 38(1) of the ICJ Statute is widely considered as non-exhaustive. There is, then, *uncertainty of determining the content* of an otherwise valid rule of international law. Meta-interpretative rules for the law of treaties, which were incorporated[9] in the VCLT,[10] did not manage to alleviate interpretative conflicts,[11] because there is no consensus as to a possible hierarchy

5 *Ibid.*

6 Ricardo Guastini, "Preface," in Ávila, *Certainty in Law*, vii.

7 *Ibid*, viii

8 Kammerhofer, *Uncertainty in International Law – A Kelsenian Perspective*, 4.

9 Most distinguished members of the ILC were openly suspicious with regard to this initiative. This is also true of Sir Humphrey Waldock, under whose guidance the ILC's final draft was completed. He "was decidedly lukewarm on rules on interpretation, including them more because he thought this was expected of him than out of genuine expectation that rules on interpretation would be of much use." Jan Klabbers, "Virtuous Interpretation," in Malgosia Fitzmaurice et. al. (eds.), *Treaty Interpretation and the Vienna Convention on the Law of Treaties: 30 Years on, Vol. 1* (Leiden: Martinus Nijhoff Publishers, 2010), 18.

10 Art. 31(1) is the general rule of treaty interpretation: "A treaty shall be interpreted in good faith in accordance with the ordinary meaning to be given to the terms of the treaty in their context and in the light of its object and purpose." Article 32 stipulates the recourse to supplementary means of interpretation, including the preparatory work of the treaty (*travaux préparatoires*) and the circumstances of its conclusion.

11 Even commentaries, which are supposed to bring more clarity into the international legal practice, are not always of much help. Take the following opening remark in one such commentary: "Interpretation is the process of *establishing the true meaning* of a treaty." (emphasis in the original) Oliver Dörr, "Article 31," in Oliver Dörr and Kirsten Schmalenbach (eds.), *Vienna Convention on the Law of Treaties – A Commentary* (Heidelberg: Springer, 2012), 522.

of the interpretative techniques.[12] One should add here a linked *uncertainty regarding conflicts between different international legal regimes*, which stems from the fact that "the application of international law rules on interpretation of treaties to identical or similar provisions of different treaties may not yield the same results, having regard to, *inter alia*, differences in the respective contexts, objects and purposes, subsequent practice of parties and *travaux préparatoires*."[13] When it comes to uncertainty of CIL, the situation is even more complex. Since, formally speaking, the external existence of customary rule-content, its materialization,[14] is not provided through the means of language, this "excludes interpretation as a necessary operation" for its application.[15] However, there is a more fundamental, "preliminary question" of ascertaining "whether, at the relevant time, the conditions for its existence are satisfied."[16] Finally, a special sort of uncertainty concerns determining which normative content has the formal quality of a jus cogens norm and/or an *erga omnes* obligation.

Furthermore, there is *uncertainty with respect to the precedential weight of individual rulings*, which is closely related to *uncertainty in the consistent application of valid rules*. Take the so-called unique case argument, which was fostered in the allocative conflict regarding Kosovo's claim to sovereign statehood. According to it, "Kosovo is a unique situation that has required a creative solution. It should not create a precedent for other unresolved conflicts."[17] The "unique case" argument[18] was heavily employed in the subsequent proceeding before the ICJ, and even in the aftermath of the Advisory Opinion, despite the fact that the Court did not explicitly address it. In similar, politically loaded situations, like the suspected usage of chemical weapons in the Syrian town of Douma, or deadly clashes in Gaza, in which

12 "Whereas common lawyers tend to stress the ordinary meaning, continental lawyers tend to stress the object and purpose as teleological method." Anne van Aaken, "Balancing of Human Rights – Constitutional Interpretation in International Law," in Miodrag A. Jovanović and Ivana Krstić (eds.), *Human Rights Today – 60 Years of the Universal Declaration* (Utrecht: Eleven International Publishing, 2010), 61.

13 *MOX Plant (Ireland* v. *United Kingdom), Provisional Measures*, Order of 3 December 2001, ITLOS Reports 2001, par. 51.

14 *See, supra* p. 86.

15 Treves, "Customary International Law," par. 2.

16 *Ibid.*

17 "Kosovo must be independent," *International Herald Tribune*, June 16, 2007.

18 For a refutation of this argument, *see*, Miodrag Jovanović, "Is Kosovo and Metohija Indeed a 'Unique Case'?," in James Summers (ed.), *Kosovo: A Precedent? The Declaration of Independence, the Advisory Opinion and Implications for Statehood, Self-Determination and Minority Rights* (Leiden: Martinus Nijhoff Publishers, 2011), 345–374.

"an independent and transparent investigation" is much needed,[19] there is a lingering *uncertainty of credible fact-finding*. This problem is of particular importance in the area of international human rights law, "where international action seeks to give effective protection to individuals in their daily lives and must therefore be able, in case of doubt or controversy, to ascertain the facts."[20] Since "normative consequences" stipulated in a valid international legal rule can be triggered only if the existence of the requested "operative facts" is ascertained,[21] the lack of credible fact-finding mechanism may trigger *uncertainty regarding compliance with international rulings*. In general, compliance "is the product of an uncertain and at times lengthy process shaped by political and social dynamics." This is particularly noticeable in the international realm, "wherein courts still lack purse and sword, but are more loosely linked to the executive branches and other actors on which they ultimately depend for the efficacy of their judgments."[22]

Does all this somehow undermine the aforementioned claim that international law is an instance of the central case of law as a "genre"? Not at all. First, "'[a]bsolute' [legal] certainty is unattainable" and, hence, it is always "a matter of degree."[23] Moreover, even if there was such a remedy to entirely eliminate uncertainties in a legal order, it would probably produce unintended negative side effects. Hart, thus, explicitly states that "the exclusion of all uncertainty at whatever costs in other values is not a goal which I have ever envisaged for the rule of recognition."[24] Hence, a realistic goal of any legal order is the highest possible level of "uncertainty absorption."[25] Second, "international law is not categorically more uncertain than any other legal system." That is, the

19 These are the words of the UN Secretary General, António Guterres, uttered in the wake of deadly events in Gaza in March 2018. *See*, "Gaza deaths: UN secretary general calls for 'transparent' investigation," at www.theguardian.com/world/2018/mar/31/gaza-clashes-un-secretary-general-calls-for-transparent-investigation

20 Nicolas Valticos, "Foreword to the Original Edition," in Bertrand G. Ramcharan (ed.), *International Law and Fact-Finding in the Field of Human Rights* (revised and edited reprint) (Leiden: Brill Nijhoff, 2014), xv.

21 Legal norm can be recast in the form: "Whenever *OF*, then *NC*," where the former stands for "the specified situation" and the latter for "what has to be done." Neil MacCormick, *Institutions of Law – An Essay in Legal Theory* (Oxford: Oxford University Press, 2007), 25.

22 Alexandra V. Huneeus, "Compliance with International Court Judgments and Decisions," in Karen J. Alter, Cesare Romano, and Yuval Shany (eds.), *The Oxford Handbook of International Adjudication* (Oxford: Oxford University Press, 2014), 437.

23 Guastini, "Preface," vi.

24 Hart, "Postscript," 251.

25 Fisher-Lescano and Teubner unjustifiably speak of this goal as the most realistic option for international law, as if municipal legal orders can realistically expect to realize full legal certainty. Fischer-Lescano and Teubner, "Regime Collisions: The Vain Search for Legal Unity in the Fragmentation of Global Law," 1039.

uncertainty problems at the international level are not of a different conceptual kind than those at the municipal level.[26] This becomes particularly obvious when the traditional distinction between domestic and international law is replaced with "a more important and generative conceptual divide between public law and ordinary domestic law," whereby "public law" stands for "constitutional and international law – legal regimes that both constitute and govern the behavior of states and state actors."[27] What they particularly have in common is that, since aspiring "to stand outside of, and govern, the state, they cannot fully rely on the institutional apparatus of the state itself."[28]

The upshot of this similarity is that, like in international law, there is regularly some level of uncertainty regarding secondary rules of constitutional law[29] and their capacity to resolve first-order uncertainties.[30] And this is so despite the fact that some domestic institutional mechanisms, such as judicial review or centralized enforcement agencies, are of significant help in absorbing uncertainty. Nonetheless, relying only on the constitutional text is hardly ever enough to ascertain the content of the fundamental law of the land;[31] even when the constitutional text specifies what shall count as formal sources of law, this does not necessarily prevent constitutional actors from introducing new ones;[32] in constitutional systems without the institutionalized model of judicial review, constitutional actors (e.g., parliament and the highest courts) are often caught in disputes over the content of constitutional law that are essentially irresolvable on legal grounds;[33] in systems with constitutionalized judicial review, on the other hand, "constitutional lawyers and judges

26 Kammerhofer, *Uncertainty in International Law – A Kelsenian Perspective*, 2.

27 Goldsmith and Levinson, "Law for States: International Law, Constitutional Law, Public Law," 1795.

28 *Ibid*, 1803.

29 Since no institutionalized "tertiary" rules to resolve uncertainties about the secondary rules of constitutional law exist, Waldron even raises the question of their legality, arguing that they may as well be classified as rules of "political morality." Jeremy Waldron, "Are Constitutional Norms Legal Norms?" (2006) 75 *Fordham Law Review* 3: 1697–1713.

30 Goldsmith and Levinson, "Law for States: International Law, Constitutional Law, Public Law," 1802.

31 Probably the most famous example is how judicial review became part of US constitutional law. However, there are numerous examples of "invisible" constitutionalism across the globe. *See*, Rosalind Dixon and Adrienne Stone (eds.), *The Invisible Constitution in Comparative Perspective* (Cambridge: Cambridge University Press, 2018).

32 The Constitutional Court of Serbia, for instance, developed in its jurisprudence the category of "systemic laws," which are of higher normative force than "ordinary laws." It even devised the doctrine of "systemic legal provisions," which can be part of otherwise ordinary laws.

33 Being weaker actors, courts often devise certain techniques for defending the constitutionality of legislation. For a prominent British case, *see*, Neil Duxbury, "Judicial Disapproval as a Constitutional Technique" (2017) 15 *International Journal of Constitutional Law* 3: 649–670.

perpetually disagree on how to go about interpreting constitutional text";[34] and in systems with specialized constitutional courts, these courts often may come in conflict with supreme courts, due to the blurred line between constitutional and ordinary jurisdiction;[35] even under the explicitly or tacitly accepted doctrine of *stare decisis*, uncertainty is unavoidable due to the freedom of the highest courts to overrule constitutional precedents;[36] and the execution of the otherwise final decisions of constitutional tribunals essentially depends on the political will of more powerful state actors, which may be a further source of uncertainty.[37]

Hence, with a slight change in the research perspective it transpires that "[t]he phenomenon of 'uncertainty' is neither confined to international law, nor is it resolvable in most cases."[38] This proves not only that it was never jurisprudentially justified to treat the relationship between municipal law and international law as "a one-way street," where the latter was constantly assessed through the prism of the former,[39] but also that such sort of theoretical testing of international law used to be grounded in rather shaky foundations. Either legal philosophers dared to theorize about the field of law in which "they lack knowledge of its practical applications,"[40] or if they possessed sufficient knowledge, they commonly tested international law against criteria that even the majority of municipal legal orders did not manage to match.[41] While the resulting theoretical misgivings could never seriously hamper the life of international law, they could – and to some extent they did – give a bad name to jurisprudence. The time has come for the philosophy of international law to be placed on more secure foundations. This book is an attempt in that direction.

34 Goldsmith and Levinson, "Law for States: International Law, Constitutional Law, Public Law," 1809.

35 *See, e.g.*, Lech Garlicki, "Constitutional Courts versus Supreme Courts" (2007) 5 *International Journal of Constitutional Law* 1: 44–68.

36 For a case study of the US Supreme Court practice, *see, e.g.*, Christopher J. Peters (ed.), *Precedent in the United States Supreme Court* (Dordrecht: Springer, 2013).

37 On the complexity of the execution of constitutional courts' rulings, *see, e.g.*, Siegfried Bross, "Reflections on the Execution of Constitutional Court Decisions in a Democratic State under the Rule of Law on the Basis of the Constitutional Law Situation in the Federal Republic of Germany" (2009), *European Commission for Democracy through Law*, CDL-JU(2009)001, at www.venice.coe.int/webforms/documents/default.aspx?pdffile=CDL-JU(2009)001-e.

38 Kammerhofer, *Uncertainty in International Law – A Kelsenian Perspective*, 4.

39 Besson and Tasioulas, "Introduction," 7.

40 Brownlie, "The Reality and Efficacy of International Law," 8.

41 For instance, "while Hart does not claim to develop a theory of the law of a specific municipal legal system, his model is designed to fit the modern constitutional state." Payandeh, "The Concept of International Law in the Jurisprudence of H.L.A. Hart," 980.

# Bibliography


Abi-Saab, Georges, "Fragmentation or Unification: Some Concluding Remarks" (1999) 31 *New York University Journal of International Law and Politics* 4: 919–934.

Ackerman, Bruce, "The Rise of World Constitutionalism" (1997) 83 *Virginia Law Review* 4: 771-797.

Ager, Sheila L., "Treaties, Archaic and Classical Greece," in Roger S. Bagnall et al. (eds.), *The Encyclopedia of Ancient History* (1st ed.) (Hoboken: Blackwell Publishing, 2013), 6837–6838.

Ago, Roberto, "The Concept of 'International Community as a Whole': A Guarantee to the Notion of State Crimes," in Joseph H. H. Weiler, Antonio Cassese, and Marina Spinedi (eds.), *International Crimes of State – A Critical Analysis of the ILC's Draft Article 19 on State Responsibility* (Berlin: Walter de Gruyter, 1989), 252–253.

Akande, Dapo, "The Importance of Legal Criteria for Statehood: A Response to Jure Vidmar" (2013) EJIL: *Talk!*, at www.ejiltalk.org/the-importance-of-legal-criteria-for-statehood-a-response-to-jure-vidmar/

Akashi, Kinji, "Hobbes' Relevance to the Modern Law of Nations" (2000) 2 *Journal of the History of International Law*: 199–216.

Akehurst, Michael, "The Hierarchy of the Sources of International Law" (1976) 47 *British Yearbook of International Law*: 273–285.

Alexander, Larry, "Law and Exclusionary Reasons" (1990) 18 *Philosophical Topics* 1: 5–22.

Alexandrov, Stanimir A., "The Compulsory Jurisdiction of the International Court of Justice: How Compulsory Is It?" (2006) 5 *Chinese Journal of International Law* 1: 29–38.

Alexy, Robert, "Hans Kelsens Begriff des Relativen Apriori," in Robert Alexy et al. (eds.), *Neukantianismus und Rechtsphilosophie* (Baden-Baden: Nomos, 2002), 179–202.

Alexy, Robert, "On the Concept and the Nature of Law" (2008) 21 *Ratio Juris* 3: 281–299.

Alexy, Robert, "Law, Morality, and the Existence of Human Rights" (2012) 25 *Ratio Juris* 1: 2–14.

Aljaghoub, Mahasen M., *The Advisory Function of the International Court of Justice: 1946–2005* (Heidelberg: Springer, 2006).

Altman, Amnon, *Tracing the Earliest Recorded Concepts of International Law – The Ancient Near East (2500–330 BCE)* (Leiden: Martinus Nijhoff, 2012).

Alvarez, José E., *International Organizations as Law-makers* (Oxford: Oxford University Press, 2005).

Anaya, S. James, *Indigenous Peoples in International Law* (Oxford: Oxford University Press, 2000).

Andenas, Mads and Bjorge, Eirik, "Introduction: From Fragmentation to Convergence in International Law," in Mads Andenas and Eirik Bjorge (eds.), *A Farewell to Fragmentation – Reassertion and Convergence in International Law* (Cambridge: Cambridge University Press, 2015), 1–34.

Aristotle, *Rhetoric* (translated by John Henry Freese) (London: William Heinemann and G. P. Putnam's Sons, 1926), Book I.

Aristotle, *Politics* (translated, with introduction and notes, by C. D. C. Reeve) (Indianapolis: Hackett Publishing Company, 1998).

Aristotle, *Nicomachean Ethics* (translated, with an interpretative essay, notes, and glossary by Robert C. Bartlett and Susan D. Collins) (Chicago: The University of Chicago Press, 2011), Book V.

Armitage, David R., "Globalizing Jeremy Bentham" (2011) 32 *History of Political Thought* 1: 63–82.

Asamoah, Obed Y., *The Legal Significance of the Declarations of the General Assembly of the United Nations* (The Hague: Martinus Nijhoff, 1966).

Austin, John, *The Province of Jurisprudence Determined* (edited by Wilfrid E. Rumble) (Cambridge: Cambridge University Press, 1995).

Ávila, Humberto, *Certainty in Law* (Basel: Springer, 2016).

Backer, David A., Bhavnani, Ravi and Huth, Paul K. (eds.), *Peace and Conflict 2017* (New York: Routledge, 2018).

Baker, Alan, "The Dangers of UN Security Council Resolution 2334 (2016)" (2016), at http://jcpa.org/dangers-un-security-council-resolution-2334-2016/

Baker, Lynne Rudder, "The Ontology of Artifacts" (2004) 7 *Philosophical Explorations* 2: 99–111.

Baker, Lynne Rudder, "The Metaphysics of Malfunction" (2009) 13 *Techne* 2: 82.

Baltzly, Dirk, "Stoicism," in Edward N. Zalta (ed.), *The Stanford Encyclopedia of Philosophy* (Fall 2010 ed.), at http://plato.stanford.edu/entries/stoicism/

Banaś, Paweł, "The Philosophy of Legal Philosophy: An Introduction," in Paweł Banaś, Adam Dyrda and Tomasz Gizbert-Studnicki (eds.), *Metaphilosophy of Law* (Oxford: Hart Publishing, 2016), 1–8.

Barboza, Julio, "Legal Injury: The Tip of the Iceberg in the Law of State Responsibility," in Maurizio Ragazzi (ed.), *International Responsibility Today – Essays in Memory of Oscar Schachter* (Leiden: Martinus Nijhoff, 2005), 7–22.

Bartha, Paul, "Analogy and Analogical Reasoning," in Edward N. Zalta (ed.), *The Stanford Encyclopedia of Philosophy* (Winter 2016 ed.), at https://plato.stanford.edu/archives/win2016/entries/reasoning-analogy/).

Baxter, Richard R., "International Law in 'Her Infinite Variety'" (1980) 29 *International and Comparative Law Quarterly* 4: 549–566.

Beaney, Michael, "Analysis," in Edward N. Zalta (ed.), *The Stanford Encyclopedia of Philosophy* (Summer 2016 ed.), at https://plato.stanford.edu/archives/sum2016/entries/analysis/

Beaulac, Stéphane, *The Power of Language in the Making of International Law – The Word Sovereignty in Bodin and Vattel and the Myth of Westpahila* (Leiden: Martinus Nijhoff, 2004).

Beckett, Jason A., "The Hartian Tradition in International Law" (2008) *The Journal Jurisprudence*: 51–83.

Bederman, David J., *International Law in Antiquity* (Cambridge: Cambridge University Press, 2001).

Bederman, David J., *Custom as a Source of Law* (Cambridge: Cambridge University Press, 2010).

Bentham, Jeremy, "Anarchical Fallacies," in *The Works of Jeremy Bentham*, Vol. 2 (edited by Sir John Bowring ) (Edinburgh: William Tait, 1843), 483–534.

Bentham, Jeremy, *A Fragment on Government* (with an introduction by F.C. Montague) (Oxford: Clarendon Press, 1891).

Bentham, Jeremy, *An Introduction to the Principles of Morals and Legislation* (1780/1789) (Kitchener: Batoche Books, 2000).

Benvenisti, Eyal, "Customary International Law as a Judicial Tool for Promoting Efficiency," in Eyal Benvenisti and Moshe Hirsh (eds.), *The Impact of International Law on International Cooperation – Theoretical Perspectives* (Cambridge: Cambridge University Press, 2004), 85–116.

Berman, Sir Franklin, "The International Court of Justice as an 'Agent' of Legal Development," in Christian J. Tams and James Sloan (eds.), *The Development of International Law by the International Court of Justice* (Oxford: Oxford University Press, 2013), 7–21.

Besson, Samantha, "The Authority of International Law – Lifting the State Veil" (2009) 31 *Sydney Law Review* 3: 343–380.

Besson, Samantha, "Theorizing the Sources of International Law," in Samantha Besson and John Tasioulas (eds.), *The Philosophy of International Law* (Oxford: Oxford University Press, 2010), 164–185.

Besson, Samantha, "International Judges as Dispute-Settlers and Law Enforcers: From International Law without Courts to International Courts without Law" (2011). 34 *Loyola of Los Angeles International and Comparative Law Review* 1: 33–52.

Besson, Samantha, "International Legality – A Response to Hathaway & Shapiro" (2011), at http://opiniojuris.org/2011/11/15/international-legality-a-response-to-hathaway-shapiro/

Besson, Samantha, "Sovereignty, International Law and Democracy" (2011) 22 *European Journal of International Law* 2: 373–387.

Besson, Samantha, "Sovereignty," in Rüdiger Wolfrum (ed.), *Max Planck Encyclopedia of Public International Law* (Oxford: Oxford University Press, 2013).

Besson, Samantha and d'Aspremont, Jean, "The Sources of International Law – Introduction," in Samantha Besson and Jean D'Aspremont (eds.), *The Oxford Handbook on the Sources of International Law* (Oxford: Oxford University Press, 2017), 1–44.

Besson, Samantha and Tasioulas, John, "Introduction," in Samantha Besson and John Tasioulas (eds.), *The Philosophy of International Law* (Oxford: Oxford University Press, 2010), 1–32.

Bianchi, Andrea, "Human Rights and the Magic of *Jus Cogens*" (2008) 19 *European Journal of International Law* 3: 491–508.

Bix, Brian H., "Ideals, Practices, and Concepts in Legal Theory," in Jordi Ferrer Beltrán, José Juan Moreso, and Diego M. Papayannis (eds.), *Neutrality and Theory of Law* (Dordrecht: Springer, 2013), 33–47.

Bix, Brian, "Kelsen and Normativity Revisited," at ssrn.com/abstract=2287870 (Published in Spanish, Brian H. Bix, "De Nuevo sobre Kelsen y la normatividad," in Carlos Bernal and Marcelo Porciuncula (eds.), *Kelsen para erizos. Ensayos en honor a Stanley L. Paulson* (Bogota: Universidad Externado de Colombia, 2017), 273–296).

Bix, Brian, "The Nature of Legal Obligation," in Kenneth Einar Himma, Miodrag Jovanović, and Bojan Spaić (eds.), *Unpacking Normativity: Conceptual, Normative, and Descriptive Issues* (Oxford: Hart Publishing, 2018).

Bluntschli, Johann Caspar, *Das moderne Volkerrecht der civilisirten Staaten als Rechtsbuch dargestellt* (Nordlingen: Druck und Verlag der C.H. Beck'schen Buckhandlung, 1872).

Bos, Maarten, "The Recognized Manifestations of International Law" (1977) 20 *German Year Book of International Law*, 9–76.

Bos, Maarten, "The Identification of Custom in International Law" (1982) 25 *German Yearbook of International Law*: 9–53.

Bothe, Michael, "Legal and Non-Legal Norms – A Meaningful Distinction in International Relations?" (1980) 11 *Netherlands Yearbook of International Law*: 65–95.

Bowcott, Owen, "Was the War Legal? Leading Lawyers Give Their Verdict" www.theguardian.com/politics/2004/mar/02/uk.internationaleducationnews

Brake, Elizabeth, *Minimizing Marriage – Marriage, Morality, and the Law* (Oxford: Oxford University Press, 2012).

Brockmöller, Annette, *Die Entstehung der Rechtstheorie im 19. Jahrhundert in Deutschland* (Baden-Baden: Nomos, 1997).

Bross, Siegfried, "Reflections on the Execution of Constitutional Court Decisions in a Democratic State under the Rule of Law on the Basis of the Constitutional Law Situation in the Federal Republic of Germany" (2009), European Commission for Democracy through Law, CDL- JU(2009)001, at www.venice.coe.int/webforms/documents/default.aspx?pdffile=CDL-JU(2009)001-e

Brown, Bartram S., "Human Rights, Sovereignty, and the Final Status of Kosovo" (2005) 80 *Chicago-Kent Law Review* 3: 235–272.

Brownlie, Ian, "The Reality and Efficacy of International Law" (1981) 51 *British Yearbook of International Law*: 1–8.

Brownlie, Ian, "International Law at the Fiftieth Anniversary of the United Nations," *The Rule of Law in International Affairs: International Law at the Fiftieth Anniversary of the United Nations* (The Hague: Martinus Nijhoff Publishers, 1998).

Buchanan, Allen, "Reforming the International Law of Humanitarian Intervention," in J. L. Holzgrefe and Robert E. Jeohane (eds.), *Humanitarian Intervention – Ethical, Legal and Political Dilemmas* (Cambridge: Cambridge University Press, 2003), 130–174.

Buchanan, Allen, "The Legitimacy of International Law," in Samantha Besson and John Tasioulas (eds.), *The Philosophy of International Law* (Oxford: Oxford University Press, 2010), 79–96.

Buerganthal, Thomas, "Proliferation of International Courts and Tribunals: Is It Good or Bad?" (2001) 14 *Leiden Journal of International Law* 2: 267–275.

Bulygin, Eugenio, "An Antinomy in Kelsen's Pure Theory of Law," in Stanley L. Paulson and Bonnie Litschewski Paulson (eds.), *Normativity and Norms – Critical Perspectives on Kelsenian Themes* (Oxford: Clarendon Press, 1998), 297–315.

Burazin, Luka, "Can There Be an Artifact Theory of Law?" (2016) 29 *Ratio Juris* 3: 385–401.

Burns, Tony, *Aristotle and Natural Law* (London: Continuum International Publishing, 2011).

Bustamante, Thomas, "Revisiting Dworkin's Philosophy of International Law: Could the Hedgehog Have Done It Any Other Way?" (2017) 30 *Canadian Journal of Law & Jurisprudence* 2: 259–285.

Butt, Daniel, *Rectifying International Injustice – Principles of Compensation and Restitution Between Nations* (Oxford: Oxford University Press, 2009).

Çali, Başak, "On Interpretivism and International Law" (2009) 20 *European Journal of International Law* 3: 805–822.

Çali, Başak, *The Authority of International Law – Obedience, Respect, and Rebuttal* (Oxford: Oxford University Press, 2015).

Cançado Trindade, Judge Antônio A., *The Construction of a Humanized International Law: A Collection of Individual Opinions (1991–2013)*, Vol. 3 (Brill: Leiden, 2017).

Capps, Patrick, *Human Dignity and the Foundations of International Law* (Oxford: Hart Publishing, 2009).

Carnap, Rudolf, Hahn, Hans and Neurath, Otto (eds.) *Logischer Empirismus – der Wiener Kreis. Ausgewählte Texte mit einer Einleitung* (München: Fink, 1975).

Cassese, Antonio, *Self-determination of Peoples: A Legal Reappraisal* (Cambridge: Cambridge University Press, 1995).

Cassese, Antonio, "*Ex iniuria ius oritur*: Are We Moving towards International Legitimation of Forcible Humanitarian Countermeasures in the World Community?" (1999) 10 *European Journal of International Law* 1: 23–30.

Cassese, Antonio, *International Law* (2nd ed.) (Oxford: Oxford University Press, 2005).

Cassese, Antonio, "The Nicaragua and Tadić Tests Revisited in Light of the ICJ Judgment on Genocide in Bosnia" (2007) 18 *European Journal of International Law* 4: 649–668.

Cassese, Antonio, "For an Enhanced Role of *Jus Cogens*," in Antonio Cassese (ed.), *Realizing Utopia – The Future of International Law* (Oxford: Oxford University Press, 2012), 158–171.

Castaneda, Jorge, *Legal Effects of United Nations Resolutions* (New York: Columbia University Press, 1969).

Cheng, Bin, *Studies in International Space Law* (Oxford: Clarendon Press, 1993).

Chesterman, Simon, Johnstone, Ian and Malone, David M., *Law and Practice of the United Nations – Documents and Commentary* (2nd ed.) (Oxford: Oxford University Press, 2016).

Chiassoni, Pierluigi, "Supporting *The Force of Law*: A Few Complementary Arguments Against Essentialist Jurisprudence," in Christoph Bezemek and Nicoletta Ladavac (eds.), *The Force of Law Reaffirmed – Frederick Schauer Meets the Critics* (Cham: Springer, 2016), 61–71.

Chilton, Adam S., "A Reply to Dworkin's New Theory of International Law" (2013) 80 *The University of Chicago Law Review Dialogue*: 105–115.

Chinkin, Christine M., "The Challenge of Soft Law: Development and Change in International Law" (1989) 38 *International and Comparative Law Quarterly* 4: 850–866.

Christiano, Tom, "Authority," in Edward N. Zalta (ed.), *The Stanford Encyclopedia of Philosophy* (Spring 2013 ed.), at http://plato.stanford.edu/archives/spr2013/entries/authority/

Christiano, Thomas, "Ronald Dworkin, State Consent, and Progressive Cosmopolitanism," in Wil Waluchow and Stefan Sciaraffa (eds.), *The Legacy of Ronald Dworkin* (Oxford: Oxford University Press, 2016), 49–70.
Cicero, *On the Commonwealth and On the Laws* (edited by James E. G. Zetzel) (Cambridge: Cambridge University Press, 1999).
Cohen, Harlan G., "Methodology and Misdirection: Custom and the ICJ," *EJIL: Talk!*, 1 December 2015, at www.ejiltalk.org/methodology-and-misdirection-a-response-to-stefan-talmon-on-custom-and-the-icj/
Colish, Marcia, *The Stoic Tradition from Antiquity to the Early Middle Ages: Stoicism in Classical Latin Literature* (Leiden: Brill Publishers, 1985).
Collins, Richard, "Classical Legal Positivism in International Law Revisited," in Jörg Kammerhofer and Jean D'Aspremont (eds.), *International Legal Positivism in a Post-Modern World* (Cambridge: Cambridge University Press, 2014), 23–49.
Collins, Richard, *The Institutional Problem in Modern International Law* (Oxford: Hart Publishing, 2016).
Commager, Henry Steel and Cantor, Milton (eds.), *Documents of American History (since 1898)*, Vol. II (Englewood Cliffs: Prentice Hall, 1988).
Conforti, Benedetto, *The Law and Practice of the United Nations* (3rd revised ed.) (Leiden: Martinus Nijhoff, 2005).
Cottier, Thomas, *Equitable Principles of Maritime Boundary Delimitation: The Quest for Distributive Justice in International Law* (Cambridge: Cambridge University Press, 2015).
Crawford, James R., *The Creation of States in International Law* (2nd ed.) (Oxford: Oxford University Press, 2007).
Crawford, James, *State Responsibility: The General Part* (Cambridge: Cambridge University Press, 2013).
Crawford, James and Nicholson, Rowan, "The Continued Relevance of Established Rules and Institutions Relating to the Use of Force," in Marc Weller, Alexia Solomou, and Jake William Rylatt (eds.), *The Oxford Handbook of the Use of Force in International Law* (Oxford: Oxford University Press, 2015), 96–113.
Culver, Keith and Giudice, Michael, *Legality's Borders: An Essay in General Jurisprudence* (Oxford: Oxford University Press, 2010).
Cumings, Bruce, *Korea's Place in the Sun: A Modern History* (New York: W.W. Norton, 2005).
Dagger, Richard and Lefkowitz, David, "Political Obligation," in Edward N. Zalta (ed.), *The Stanford Encyclopedia of Philosophy* (Fall 2014 ed.), at https://plato.stanford.edu/archives/fall2014/entries/political-obligation
Dahlman, Christian, "The Function of *Opinio Juris* in Customary International Law" (2012) 81 *Nordic Journal of International Law* 3: 327–339.
D'Amato, Anthony, "Does International Law Bind Superpowers?," at http://opiniojuris.org/2005/08/14/does-international-law-bind-superpowers/
D'Amato, Anthony, "The Neo-Positivist Concept of International Law" (1965) 59 *American Journal of International Law*: 321–324.
D'Amato, Anthony, "It's a Bird, It's a Plane, It's a Jus Cogens!" (1990) 6 *Connecticut Journal of International Law* 1: 1–6.
Darcy, Shane, *Judges, Law and War: The Judicial Development of International Humanitarian Law* (Cambridge: Cambridge University Press, 2014).

d'Aspremont, Jean, "Softness in International Law: A Self-Serving Quest for New Legal Materials" (2008) 19 *European Journal of International Law* 5: 1075–1093.

d'Aspremont, Jean, *Formalism and the Sources of International Law – A Theory of the Ascertainment of Legal Rules* (Oxford: Oxford University Press, 2011).

d'Aspremont, Jean and Aalberts, Taanja, "Which Future for the Scholarly Concept of Soft International Law? Editors' Introductory Remarks" (2012) 25 *Leiden Journal of International Law* 2: 309–312.

d'Aspremont, Jean, "Bindingness" (2015) ACIL Research Paper 2015–19, at https://ssrn.com/abstract=2690155, 1. (forthcoming in Jean d'Aspremont and Sahib Singh (eds.), *Concepts for International Law - Contributions to Disciplinary Thought* (London: Edward Elgar, 2019).

d'Aspremont, Jean, "The Decay of Modern Customary International Law in Spite of Scholarly Heroism" (2015) *The Global Community Yearbook of International Law and Jurisprudence*: 9–30.

d'Aspremont, Jean, "The Doctrine of Fundamental Rights of States and the Functions of Anthropomorphic Thinking in International Law" (2015) 4 *Cambridge Journal of International and Comparative Law* 3: 501–520.

Delacroix, Sylvie, *Legal Norms and Normativity – An Essay in Genealogy* (Oxford: Hart Publishing, 2006).

den Heijer, Maarten and van der Wilt, Harmen, "*Jus Cogens* and the Humanization and Fragmentation of International Law" (2015) 46 *Netherlands Yearbook of International Law*: 3–22.

Deplano, Rosanna, *The Strategic Use of International Law by the United Nations Security Council – An Empirical Study* (Cham: Springer, 2015).

Desta, Melaku Geboye, "Soft Law in International Law: An Overview," in Andrea K. Bjorklund and August Reinisch (eds.), *International Investment Law and Soft Law* (Cheltenham: Edward Elgar, 2012), 39–50.

de Vattel, Emmerich, *The Law of Nations; Or Principles of the Law of Nature Applied to the Conduct and Affairs of Nations and Sovereigns* (Philadelphia: T& J. W. Johnson Law Booksellers, 1844).

Dicke, Klaus, "Weltgesetzgeber Sicherheitsrat" (2001) 49 *Vereinte Nationen* 5: 163–168.

Dickson, Julie, *Evaluation and Legal Theory* (Oxford: Hart Publishing, 2001).

Dickson, Julie, "Is Bad Law Still Law? Is Bad Law *Really* Law?," in Maksymilian Del Mar and Zenon Bankowski (eds.), *Law as Institutional Normative Order* (Farnham: Ashgate, 2009), 161–183.

Dickson, Julie, "Ours is a Broad Church: Indirectly Evaluative Legal Philosophy as a Facet of Jurisprudential Inquiry" (2015) 6 *Jurisprudence: An International Journal of Legal and Political Thought* 2: 207–230.

Dickson, Julie, "Interpretation and Coherence in Legal Reasoning," in Edward N. Zalta (ed.), *The Stanford Encyclopedia of Philosophy* (Winter 2016 ed.), at https://plato.stanford.edu/archives/win2016/entries/legal-reas-interpret/

Dinstein, Yoram, "The Thirteenth Waldemar A. Solf Lecture in International Law" (2000) 166 *Military Law Review*: 93–108.

Divac Öberg, Marko, "The Legal Effects of Resolutions of the UN Security Council and General Assembly in the Jurisprudence of the ICJ" (2005) 16 *European Journal of International Law* 5: 879–906.

Dixon, Rosalind and Stone, Adrienne (eds.), *The Invisible Constitution in Comparative Perspective* (Cambridge: Cambridge University Press, 2018).

Dörr, Oliver, "Article 31," in Oliver Dörr and Kirsten Schmalenbach (eds.), *Vienna Convention on the Law of Treaties – A Commentary* (Heidelberg:, Springer, 2012).

Droubi, Sufyan, *Resisting United Nations Security Council Resolutions* (London: Routledge, 2014).

Duarte D'Almeida, Luís, "Legal Statements and Normative Language" (2011) 30 *Law and Philosophy* 2: 167–199.

Dupuy, Pierre-Marie, "International Law: Torn between Coexistence, Cooperation and Globalization. General Conclusions" (1998) 9 *European Journal of International Law* 2: 278–286.

Dupuy, Pierre-Marie, "The Place and Role of Unilateralism in Contemporary International Law" (2000) 11 *European Journal of International Law* 1: 19–30.

Duxbury, Neil, "The Basic Norm: An Unsolved Murder Mystery" (2007) *LSE Law, Society and Economy Working Papers*, 17–2007: 1–10, at www.lse.ac.uk/law/working-paper-series/2007-08/WPS17-2007Duxbury.pdf

Duxbury, Neil, "Judicial Disapproval as a Constitutional Technique" (2017) 15 *International Journal of Constitutional Law* 3: 649–670.

Dworkin, Ronald, Law's Empire (Cambridge, Mass.: Harvard University Press, 1986).

Dworkin, Ronald, "Hart's Postscript and the Character of Legal Philosophy" (2004) 24 *Oxford Journal of Legal Studies* 1: 1–37.

Dworkin, Ronald, *Is Democracy Possible Here? Principles for a New Political Debate* (Princeton: Princeton University Press, 2006).

Dworkin, Ronald, *Justice in Robes* (Cambridge, Mass.: The Belknap Press of Harvard University Press, 2006).

Dworkin, Ronald, *Justice for Hedgehogs* (Cambridge, Mass.: The Belknap Press of Harvard University Press, 2011).

Dworkin, Ronald, "A New Philosophy for International Law" (2013) 41 *Philosophy and Public Affairs* 1: 2–30.

Eagleton, Clyde, "Covenant of the League of Nations and Charter of the United Nations: Points of Difference" (1945) 13 *The Department of State Bulletin* 321: 263–269.

Eaton, Jonah, "An Emerging Norm – Determining the Meaning and Legal Status of the Responsibility to Protect" (2011) 32 *Michigan Journal of International Law* 4: 765–804.

Ehrenberg, Kenneth M., "Defending the Possibility of a Neutral Functional Theory of Law" (2009) 29 *Oxford Journal of Legal Studies* 1: 91–113.

Ehrenberg, Kenneth, "Critical Reception of Raz's Theory of Authority" (2011) 6 *Philosophy Compass* 11: 777–785.

Ehrenberg, Kenneth, "Joseph Raz's Theory of Authority" (2011) 6 *Philosophy Compass* 12: 884–894.

Ehrenberg, Kenneth M., *The Functions of Law* (Oxford: Oxford University Press, 2016).

Ehrlich, Eugene, *Die juristische Logik* (Tübingen: J. C. B. Mohr, 1918).

Eng, Svein, "Fusion of Descriptive and Normative Propositions. The Concepts of 'Descriptive Proposition' and 'Normative Proposition' as Concepts of Degree" (2000) 13 *Ratio Juris* 3: 236–260.

Esakov, Gennady, "International Criminal Law and Russia: From 'Nuremberg' Passion to 'The Hague' Prejudice" (2017) 69 *Europe-Asia Studies* 8: 1184–1200.

Estreicher, Samuel, "Rethinking the Binding Effect of Customary International Law" (2003) 44 *Virginia Journal of International Law* 1: 5–17.

Fassbender, Bardo, *The United Nations Charter as the Constitution of the International Community* (Leiden: Martinus Nijhoff, 2009).

Fischer-Lescano, Andreas and Teubner, Gunther, "Regime Collisions: The Vain Search for Legal Unity in the Fragmentation of Global Law" (2004) 25 *Michigan Journal of International Law* 4: 999–1046.

Focarelli, Carlo, *International Law as Social Construct – The Struggle for Global Justice* (Oxford: Oxford University Press, 2012).

Franck, Thomas M., *Fairness in International Law and Institutions* (Oxford: Clarendon Press, 1995).

Franck, Thomas M., "Lessons of Kosovo" (1999) 93 *American Journal of International Law* 4: 857–860.

Friedmann, Wolfgang, *The Changing Structure of International Law* (New York: Columbia University Press, 1964).

Finnis, John, "Grounds of Law and Legal Theory: A Response" (2007) 13 *Legal Theory* 3–4: 315–344.

Finnis, John, "Marriage: A Basic and Exigent Good" (2008) 91 *Monist* 3–4: 388–406.

Finnis. John, *Natural Law and Natural Rights* (Oxford: Oxford University Press, 2011).

Finnis, John, *Philosophy of Law: Collected Essays Volume IV* (Oxford: Oxford University Press, 2011).

Finnis, John, "Revolutions and Continuity of Law," in *Philosophy of Law: Collected Essays Volume IV* (Oxford: Oxford University Press, 2011), 407–435.

Fitzmaurice, Gerald G., Special Rapporteur, "Second Report on the Law of Treaties" (1957) *Yearbook of the International Law Commission*, Vol. II.

Fitzmaurice, Sir Gerald G., "Some Problems Regarding the Formal Sources of International Law," in Frederick Mari van Asbek (ed.), *Symbolae Verzijl* (The Hague: Martinus Nijhoff, 1958), 153–186.

Frowein, Jochen Abraham, "Jus Cogens," in *Encyclopedia of Public International Law*, Vol. 7 (Amsterdam: Elsevier, 1984).

Fukuyama, Francis, *The Origins of Political Order – From Prehuman Times to the French Revolution* (New York: Farrar, Straus and Giroux, 2011).

Fuller, Lon, *Legal Fictions* (Stanford: Stanford University Press, 1967).

Fuller, Lon L., *The Morality of Law* (revised ed.) (New Haven: Yale University Press, 1969).

Gagarin, Michael and Woodruff, Paul, "Early Greek Legal Thought," in Fred D. Miller, Jr. and Carrie-Ann Biondi (eds.), *A Treatise of Legal Philosophy and General Jurisprudence Vol. 6 – A History of the Philosophy of Law from the Ancient Greeks to the Scholastics* (Heidelberg: Springer, 2007), 7–34.

García-Salmones Rovira, Mónica, *The Project of Positivism in International Law* (Oxford: Oxford University Press, 2013).

Gardner, John, "Legal Positivism: 5½ Myths" (2001) 46 *The American Journal of Jurisprudence* 1: 199–227.

Gardner, John, "Why Study Jurisprudence?" (2006) *The Inner Temple Yearbook 2006/2007*, at www.dropbox.com/s/rz9l4n8nlgzk7yv/whystudyjurisprudence.pdf?dl=0

Gardner, John, *Law as a Leap of Faith* (Oxford: Oxford University Press, 2012).

Gardner, John, "Why Law Might Emerge: Hart's Problematic Fable," in Luís Duarte d'Almeida, James Edwards, and Andrea Dolcetti (eds.), *Reading HLA Hart's 'The Concept of Law'* (Oxford: Hart Publishing, 2013), 81–96.

Garibaldi, Oscar M., "The Legal Status of General Assembly Resolutions: Some Conceptual Observations" (1979) 73 *Proceedings of the Annual Meeting (American Society of International Law)*: 324–327.

Garlicki, Lech, "Constitutional Courts versus Supreme Courts" (2007) 5 *International Journal of Constitutional Law* 1: 44–68.

Gilbert, Paul, *The Philosophy of Nationalism* (Boulder: Westview Press, 1998).

Giudice, Michael, "Hart and Kelsen on International Law," in Leslie Green and Brian Leiter (eds.), *Oxford Studies in Philosophy of Law, Vol. 2* (Oxford: Oxford University Press, 2013), 148–174.

Giudice, Michael, *Understanding the Nature of Law: A Case for Constructive Conceptual Explanation* (Cheltenham: Edward Elgar Publishing, 2015).

Giudice, Michael, "Sources and the Systematicity of International Law – A Philosophical Perspective," in Samantha Besson and Jean D'Aspremont (eds.), *The Oxford Handbook on the Sources of International Law* (Oxford: Oxford University Press, 2017), 583–603.

Glennon, Michael J., "How International Rules Die" (2005) 93 *Georgetown Law Journal* 3: 939–991.

Goldsmith, Jack and Levinson, Daryl, "Law for States: International Law, Constitutional Law, Public Law" (2009) 122 *Harvard Law Review* 7: 1791–1868.

Goldsmith, Jack L. and Posner, Eric A., *The Limits of International Law* (Oxford: Oxford University Press, 2005).

Goodman, Camille, "Acta Sunt Servanda? A Regime for Regulating the Unilateral Acts of States at International Law" (2006) 25 *Australian Year Book of International Law*: 43–74.

Goodrich, Leland M., "From League of Nations to United Nations" (1947) 1 *International Organization* 1: 3–21.

Grabowski, Andrzej, *Juristic Concept of the Validity of Statutory Law – A Critique of Contemporary Legal Nonpositivism* (Heidelberg: Springer, 2013).

Graebner, Norman A. and Bennett, Edward M., *The Versailles Treaty and Its Legacy – The Failure of the Wilsonian Vision* (Cambridge: Cambridge University Press, 2011).

Green, James A., *The Persistent Objector Rule in International Law* (Oxford: Oxford University Press, 2016).

Green, Leslie, "Legal Positivism," in Edward N. Zalta (ed.), *The Stanford Encyclopedia of Philosophy* (Spring 2007 ed.), at https://plato.stanford.edu/archives/spr2018/entries/legal-positivism/

Green, Leslie, "Positivism and the Inseparability of Law and Morals" (2008) 83 *New York University Law Review* 4: 1035–1058.

Green, Leslie, "The Germ of Justice" (2010) Oxford Legal Studies Research Paper, Paper No. 60/2010, at http://ssrn.com/abstract=1703008

Green, Leslie, "The Morality in Law," in Luís Duarte d'Almeida, James Edwards, and Andrea Dolcetti (eds.), *Reading HLA Hart's 'The Concept of Law'* (Oxford: Hart Publishing, 2013), 177–209.

Green, Leslie, "The Forces of Law: Duty, Coercion and Power" (2016) 29 *Ratio Juris* 2: 164–181.

Greenberg, Mark, "How to Explain Things with Force" (2016) 129 *Harvard Law Review* 7: 1932–1979.

Greenwood, Sir Christopher, "Unity and Diversity in International Law," in Mads Andenas and Eirik Bjorge (eds.), *A Farewell to Fragmentation – Reassertion and Convergence in International Law* (Cambridge: Cambridge University Press, 2015), 37–55.

Gross, Leo, "The Peace of Westphalia, 1648–1948" (1948) 42 *American Journal of International Law* 1: 20–41.

Grotius, Hugo, *The Rights of War and Peace* (edited and with an Introduction by Richard Tuck) (Indianapolis: Liberty Fund, 2005), *Prolegomena to the first edition* of De Iure Belli ac Pacis, 1746.

Gruchalla-Wesierski, Tadeusz, "A Framework for Understanding 'Soft Law'" (1984) 30 *McGill Law Journal* 1: 37–88.

Guastini, Riccardo, "A Realistic View on Law and Legal Cognition" (2015) 27 *Revus – Journal for Constitutional Theory and Philosophy of Law*: 45–54.

Guastini, Riccardo, "Preface," in Humberto Ávila, *Certainty in Law* (Basel: Springer, 2016), v–ix.

Guzman, Andrew T., *How International Law Works: A Rational Choice Theory* (Oxford: Oxford University Press, 2008).

Hallpike, Christopher Robert, *On Primitive Society: And Other Forbidden Topics* (Bloomington: Author House, 2011).

Hampton, James A., "The Role of Similarity in Natural Categorization," in Ulrike Hahn and Michael Ramscar (eds.), *Similarity and Categorization* (Oxford: Oxford University Press, 2001), 13–28.

Harnad, Steven, "To Cognize Is to Categorize: Cognition Is Categorization," in Henry Cohen and Claire Lefebvre (eds.), *Handbook of Categorization in Cognitive Science* (Amsterdam: Elsevier, 2005), 20–45.

Harré, Rom, *Social Being* (Oxford: Blackwell, 1979).

Harrison, Ross, "The Equal Extent of Natural and Civil Law," in David Dyzenhaus and Thomas Poole (eds.), *Hobbes and The Law* (Cambridge: Cambridge University Press, 2012), 22–38.

Hart, Herbert L. A., "Are There Any Natural Rights?" (1955) 64 *The Philosophical Review* 2: 175–191.

Hart, Herbert, "Analytical Jurisprudence in Mid-twentieth Century: A Reply to Professor Bodeheimer" (1957) 105 *University of Pennsylvania Law Review*: 953–974.

Hart, Herbert, "Kelsen Visited" (1963) 10 *UCLA Law Review* 4: 709–728.

Hart, Herbert L. A., "Commands and Authoritative Reasons," in *Essays on Bentham* (Oxford: Oxford University Press, 1982), 243–268.

Hart, Herbert L. A., *Essays in Jurisprudence and Philosophy* (Oxford: Clarendon Press, 1983).

Hart, Herbert, *The Concept of Law* (with an Introduction by Leslie Green, 3rd ed.) (Oxford: Clarendon Press, 2012).

Hart, Herbert, "Answers to Eight Questions," in Luís Duarte d'Almeida, James Edwards, and Andrea Dolcetti (eds.), *Reading HLA Hart's 'The Concept of Law'* (Oxford: Hart Publishing, 2013), 279–297.

Hathaway, Oona and Shapiro, Scott J., "Outcasting: Enforcement in Domestic and International Law" (2011) 121 *The Yale Law Journal* 2:252–348.

Hehir, Aidan, *Humanitarian Intervention – An Introduction* (New York: Palgrave Macmillan, 2010).

Heinsch, Robert, *Die Weiterentwicklung des humanitären Völkerrechts durch die Strafgerichtshöfe für das ehemalige Jugoslawien und Ruanda (Zur Bedeutung von internationalen Gerichtsentscheidungen als Rechtsquelle des Völkerstrafrechts)* (Berlin: Berliner Wissenschafts-Verlag, 2007).

Henkin, Louis, *How Nations Behave* (New York: Columbia University Press, 1979).

Henkin, Louis, "Kosovo and the Law of 'Humanitarian Intervention'" (1999) 93 *American Journal of International Law* 4: 824–828.

Herren, Madeleine, "International Organizations, 1865–1945," in Jacob Katz Cogan, Ian Hurd, and Ian Johnstone (eds.), *Oxford Handbook of International Organizations* (Oxford: Oxford University Press, 2016), 91–112.

Hershey, Amos S., "The History of International Relations during Antiquity and the Middle Ages" (1911) 5 *American Journal of International Law* 4: 901–933.

Higgins, Rosalyn, *Problems and Process: International Law and How We Use It* (Oxford: Oxford University Press, 1994).

Higgins, Rosalyn, "The International Court of Justice: Selected Issues of State Responsibility," in Maurizio Ragazzi (ed.), *International Responsibility Today – Essays in Memory of Oscar Schachter* (Leiden: Martinus Nijhoff, 2005), 271–286.

Hillier, Tim, *Sourcebook on Public International Law* (London: Cavendish Publishing Limited, 1998).

Hilpinen, Risto, "Artifact," in Edward N. Zalta (ed.), *The Stanford Encyclopedia of Philosophy* (Winter 2011 Edition), at https://plato.stanford.edu/archives/win2011/entries/artifact/

Hilpold, Peter, "The EU Law and the UN Law in Conflict: The *Kadi* Case" (2009) 13 *Max Planck Yearbook of United Nations Law*: 141–182.

Himma, Kenneth Einar, "Do Philosophy and Sociology Mix? A Non-Essentialist Socio-Legal Positivist Analysis of the Concept of Law" (2004) 24 *Oxford Journal of Legal Studies* 4: 717–738.

Himma, Kenneth Einar, "Final Authority to Bind with Moral Mistakes: On the Explanatory Potential of Inclusive Legal Positivism" (2005) 24 *Law and Philosophy* 1: 1–45.

Himma, Kenneth Einar, "Conceptual Jurisprudence: An Introduction to Conceptual Analysis and Methodology in Legal Theory" (2015) 26 *Revus – Journal for Constitutional Theory and Philosophy of Law*: 65–92.

Himma, Kenneth Einar, "Can There Really Be Law in a Society of Angels?" (2016), at https://ssrn.com/abstract=2839942

Himma, Kenneth Einar, "The Authorization of Coercive Enforcement Mechanisms as a Conceptually Necessary Feature of Law" (2016) 7 *Jurisprudence* 3: 593–626.

Himma, Kenneth Einar, "Authority," in Giorgio Bongiovanni et al. (eds.), *Handbook of Legal Reasoning and Argumentation* (Dordrecht: Springer, 2018), 191–217.

Hobbes, Thomas, Leviathan (London: Andrew Crooke, 1651). Electronic version at socserv.mcmaster.ca/econ/ugcm/3ll3/hobbes/Leviathan.pdf

Hobe, Stephan, "Evolution of the Principle on Permanent Sovereignty over Natural Resources: From Soft Law to a Customary Law Principle?," in Marc Bungenberg and Stephan Hobe (eds.), *Permanent Sovereignty over Natural Resources* (Cham: Springer, 2015).

Hohfeld, Wesley Newcomb, *Fundamental Legal Conceptions as Applied in Judicial Reasoning and Other Legal Essays* (New Haven: Yale University Press, 1919).

Huneeus, Alexandra V., "Compliance with International Court Judgments and Decisions," in Karen J. Alter, Cesare Romano, and Yuval Shany (eds.), *The Oxford Handbook of International Adjudication* (Oxford: Oxford University Press, 2014), 437–463.

Hunt, Alan, *Governance of Consumer Passions: A History of Sumptuary Law* (Basingstoke: Palgrave Macmillan, 1996).

Hurd, Heide M., *Moral Combat* (Cambridge: Cambridge University Press, 1999).

Hurrell, Andrew, "International Law and the Making and Unmaking of Boundaries," in Allen Buchanan and Margaret Moore (eds.), *States, Nations, and Borders: The Ethics of Making Boundaries* (Cambridge: Cambridge University Press, 2003), 275–297.

International Commission on Intervention and State Sovereignty, *The Responsibility to Protect* (Ottawa: International Development Research Centre, 2001).

Itzkowitz, Norman, *Ottoman Empire and Islamic Tradition* (Chicago: Chicago University Press, 1972).

Jabloner, Clemens and Stadler, Friedrich (eds.), *Logischer Empirismus und Reine Rechtslehre –Beziehungen zwischen dem Wiener Kreis und der Hans Kelsen-Schule* (Wien: Springer, 2001).

Jackson, Frank, *From Metaphysics to Ethics – A Defence of Conceptual Analysis* (Oxford: Clarendon Press, 1998).

Janis, M. W., "Jeremy Bentham and the Fashioning of 'International Law'" (1984) 78 *American Journal of International Law* 2: 405–418.

Jellinek, Georg, *Ein Verfassungsgericht für Österreich* (Wien: Alfred Hölder, 1885).

Jellinek, Georg, *Allgemeine Staatslehre* (Berlin: Verlag von Julius Springer, 1929).

Jennings, Robert and Watts, Arthur (eds.), *Oppenheim's International Law: Volume 1 Peace* (9th ed.) (Oxford: Oxford University Press, 2008).

Jeutner, Valentin, *Irresolvable Norm Conflicts in International Law: The Concept of a Legal Dilemma* (Oxford: Oxford University Press, 2017).

Jovanović, Miodrag, *Constitutionalizing Secession in Federalized States: A Procedural Approach* (Utrecht: Eleven Publishing International, 2007).

Jovanović, Miodrag, "Is Kosovo and Metohija Indeed a 'Unique Case'?", in James Summers (ed.), *Kosovo: A Precedent? The Declaration of Independence, the Advisory Opinion and Implications for Statehood, Self-Determination and Minority Rights* (Leiden: Martinus Nijhoff Publishers, 2011), 345–374.

Jovanović, Miodrag, *Collective Rights – A Legal Theory* (Cambridge: Cambridge University Press, 2012).

Jovanović, Miodrag, "Dworkin on International Law: Not Much of a Legacy?" (2015) 28 *Canadian Journal of Law & Jurisprudence* 2: 443–460.

Jovanović, Miodrag, "Is Legal Positivism Tenable Beyond Moral Relativism?" (2015) 9 *Problema – Anuario de Filosofia y Teoría del Derecho*: 193–252.

Jovanović, Miodrag, "Responsibility to Protect and the International Rule of Law" (2015) 14 *Chinese Journal of International Law* 4: 757–776.

Jovanović, Miodrag, "Theorizing 'Unidentified Normative Objects' of Global Regulatory Regimes," in Himma, Jovanović, and Spaić (eds.), *Unpacking Normativity: Conceptual, Normative, and Descriptive Issues* (Oxford: Hart Publishing, 2018), 227–250.

Jovanović, Miodrag, "'Global/Transnational Law' Challenges to Theorizing About Law," in Jorge Luis Fabra-Zamora (ed.), *Jurisprudence in a Globalized World* (Cheltenham: Edward Elgar Publishing, forthcoming 2019).

Joyner, Dan, "Legal Bindingness of Security Council Resolutions Generally, and Resolution 2334 on the Israeli Settlements in Particular" (2017) *EJIL: Talk!*, at www.ejiltalk.org/legal-bindingness-of-security-council-resolutions-generally-and-resolution-2334-on-the-israeli-settlements-in-particular/

Kadelbach, Stefan, "*Jus Cogens*, Obligations *Erga Omnes* and other Rules – The Identification of Fundamental Norms," in Christian Tomuschat and Jean-Marc Thouvenin (eds.), *The Fundamental rules of the International Legal Order – Jus Cogens and Obligations Erga Omnes* (Leiden: Martinus Nijhoff, 2006, 21–40.

Kammerhofer, Jörg, "The Benefits of the Pure Theory of Law for International Lawyers, or: What use is Kelsenian Theory?" (2006) 12 *International Legal Theory*: 5–54.

Kammerhofer, Jörg, *Uncertainty in International Law – A Kelsenian Perspective* (London: Routledge, 2011).

Kammerhofer, Jörg and D'Aspremont, Jean, "Introduction – The Future of International Legal Positivism," in Jörg Kammerhofer and Jean D'Aspremont (eds.), *International Legal Positivism in a Post-Modern World* (Cambridge: Cambridge University Press, 2014), 1–22.

Kant, Immanuel, *Kritik der reinen Vernunft* (Hamburg: Felix Mainer, 1956).

Kant, Immanuel, "Perpetual Peace: A Philosophical Sketch," in *Political Writings* (Cambridge: Cambridge University Press, 1991), 93–131.

Kaufmann, Arthur, "Problemgeschichte der Rechtsphilosophie," in Arthur Kaufmann, Winfried Hassemer, and Ulfried Neumann (eds.), *Einführung in Rechtsphhilosophie und Rechtstheorie der Gegenwart* (Heidelberg: C. F. Müller Verlag, 2004), 26–147.

Kaufmann, Arthur, "Rechtsphilosophie, Rechtstheorie, Rechtsdogmatik," in Arthur Kaufmann, Winfried Hassemer, and Ulfried Neumann (eds.), *Einführung in Rechtsphilosophie und Rechtstheorie der Gegenwart* (Heidelberg: C.F. Müller Verlag, 2004), 1–25.

Kazui, Tashiro, "Foreign Relations during the Edo Period: Sakoku Reexamined" (1982) 8 *Journal of Japanese Studies* 2: 283–306.

Keay, Andrew, "Comply or Explain in Corporate Governance Codes: In Need of Greater Regulatory Oversight?" (2014) 34 *Legal Studies* 2: 279–304.

Kelly, J. Patrick, "The Twilight of Customary International Law" (2000) 40 *Virginia Journal of International Law* 2: 449–543.

Kelsen, Hans, *Das Problem der Souveränität und die Theorie des Völkerrechts* (Tübingen: J. C. B. Mohr [P. Siebeck], 1920).

Kelsen, Hans, "The Pure Theory of Law and Analytical Jurisprudence" (1941) 55 *Harvard Law Review* 1: 44–70.

Kelsen, Hans, *Law and Peace in International Relations, The Oliver Wendell Holmes Lectures, 1940–41* (Cambridge, Mass.: Harvard University Press, 1942).

Kelsen, Hans, *General Theory of Law and State* (Cambridge, Mass.: Harvard University Press, 1949).

Kelsen, Hans, "Science and Politics" (1951) 45 *The American Political Science Review* 3: 641–661.

Kelsen, Hans, *The Law of the United Nations – A Critical Analysis of Its Fundamental Problems (With Supplement)* (London: Stevens & Sons Ltd., 1951).

Kelsen, Hans, *Principles of International Law* (New York: Rinehart & Company Inc., 1952).

Kelsen, Hans, "On the Pure Theory of Law" (1966) 1 *Israel Law Review* 1: 1–7.

Kelsen, Hans, *Pure Theory of Law* (trans. by Max Knight) (Berkeley: University of California Press: 1967).

Kelsen, Hans, *On the Issue of the Continental Shelf – Two Legal Opinions* (Wien: Springer, 1986).

Kelsen, Hans, "Naturrechtslehre und Rechtspositivismus" in Friedrich Koja (ed.), *Hans Kelsen oder Die Reinheit der Rehtslehre* (Vienna: Böhlau Verlag 1988), 231–247.

Kelsen, Hans, *Was ist Gerechtigkeit?* (Stuttgart: Reclam, 2000).

Kelsen, Hans, *General Theory of Law and State* (with a new introduction by A. Javier Treviño) (New Brunswick: Transaction Publishers, 2006).

Kelsen, Hans, "On the Theory of Juridic Fictions. With Special Consideration of Vaihinger's Philosophy of the As-If," in Maksymilian Del Mar and William Twining (eds.), *Legal Fictions in Theory and Practice* (Cham: Springer, 2015), 3–22.

Kelsen, Hans, "Validity and Efficacy of the Law" (1967), in Carlos Bernal et al. (eds.), *Essays in Legal Philosophy – Eugenio Bulygin* (Oxford: Oxford University Press, 2015), 52–68.

Keohane, Robert O., *Power and Governance in a Partially Globalized World* (London: Routledge, 2002).

Kingsbury, Benedict and Straumann, Benjamin, "State of Nature versus Commercial Sociability as the Basis of International Law: Reflections on the Roman Foundations and Current Interpretations of the International Political and Legal Thought of Grotius, Hobbes, and Pufendorf," in Samantha Besson and John Tasioulas (eds.), *The Philosophy of International Law* (Oxford: Oxford University Press, 2010), 33–52.

Klabbers, Jan, "The Redundancy of Soft Law" (1996) 65 *Nordic Journal of International Law* 2: 167–182.

Klabbers, Jan, *An Introduction to International Institutional Law* (Cambridge: Cambridge University Press, 2002).

Klabbers, Jan, "(I Can't Get No) Recognition: Subjects Doctrine and the Emergence of Non-State Actors," in Jarna Petman and Jan Klabbers (eds.), *Nordic Cosmopolitanism – Essays in International Law for Martti Koskenniemi* (Leiden: Martinus Nijhoff, 2003), 351–369.

Klabbers, Jan, "Virtuous Interpretation," in Malgosia Fitzmaurice et. al. (eds.), *Treaty Interpretation and the Vienna Convention on the Law of Treaties: 30 Years on*, Vol. 1 (Leiden: Martinus Nijhoff Publishers, 2010), 15–38.

Klabbers, Jan, "Setting the Scene," in Jan Klabbers, Anne Peters, and Geir Ulfstein, *The Constitutionalization of International Law* (Oxford: Oxford University Press, 2011), 1–44.

Klabbers, Jan, Peters, Anne and Ulfstein, Geir, *The Constitutionalization of International Law* (Oxford: Oxford University Press, 2011).

Klass, Gregory, "Efficient Breach," in Gregory Klass, George Letsas, and Prince Saprai (eds.), *The Philosophical Foundations of Contract Law* (Oxford: Oxford University Press, 2014), 362–387.

Kleingeld, Pauline and Brown, Eric, "Cosmopolitanism," in Edward N. Zalta (ed.), *The Stanford Encyclopedia of Philosophy* (Fall 2013 Edition), at http://plato.stanford.edu/archives/fall2013/entries/cosmopolitanism/

Klinton, Alexander W., "NATO's Intervention in Kosovo: The Legal Case for Violating Yugoslavia's National Sovereignty in the Absence of Security Council Approval" (2000) 22 *Houston Journal of International Law* 3: 403–449.

Klosko, George, *Political Obligations* (Oxford: Oxford University Press, 2005).

Kolb, Robert, *Peremptory International Law – Jus Cogens: A General Inventory* (Oxford: Hart Publishing, 2015).

Koskenniemi, Martti, *The Gentle Civilizer of Nations – The Rise and Fall of International Law* 1870– 1960 (Cambridge: Cambridge University Press, 2001).

Koskenniemi, Martti, *From Apology to Utopia – The Structure of International Legal Argument* (Reissue with a new Epilogue) (Cambridge: Cambridge University Press, 2005).

Koskenniemi, Martti. "Into Positivism: Georg Friedrich von Martens (1756–1821) and Modern International Law" (2008) 15 *Constellations* 2: 189–207.

Koskenniemi, Martti, "'The Lady Doth Protest Too Much': Kosovo, and the Turn to Ethics in International Law," in *The Politics of International Law* (Oxford: Hart Publishing, 2011).

Koskenniemi, Martti, "Methodology of International Law," in Rüdiger Wolfrum (ed.), *Max Planck Encyclopedia of Public International Law* (Oxford: Oxford University Press, 2013).

Kripke, Saul A., *Naming and Necessity* (Cambridge, Mass.: Harvard University Press, 1980).

Krisch, Nico, "Unilateral Enforcement of Collective Will: Kosovo, Iraq, and the Security Council" (1999) 3 *Max Planck Yearbook of International Law*: 59–103.

Krisch, Nico, *Beyond Constitutionalism – The Pluralist Structure of Postnational Law* (Oxford: Oxford University Press, 2010).

Lacey, Nicola, *A Life of H.L.A. Hart: The Nightmare and the Noble Dream* (Oxford: Oxford University Press, 2004).

Lalonde, Suzanne, *Determining Boundaries in a Conflicted World – The Role of Uti Possidetis* (Montreal: McGill-Queen's University Press, 2002).

Lamond, Grant, "Precedent and Analogy in Legal Reasoning," in Edward N. Zalta (ed.), *The Stanford Encyclopedia of Philosophy* (Spring 2016 Edition), at https://plato.stanford.edu/archives/spr2016/entries/legal-reas-prec/

Langford, Peter, Bryan, Ian and McGarry, John, "Introduction: Kelsen, Legal Science and Positive Law," in Peter Langford, Ian Bryan, and John McGarry (eds.), *Kelsenian Legal Science and the Nature of Law* (Cham: Springer, 2017), 1–19.

Lansing, Robert, *The Peace Negotiations – A Personal Narrative* (Orlando: Houghton Mifflin Company, 1921).

Larkins, Jeremy, *From Hierarchy to Anarchy – Territory and Politics before Westphalia* (New York: Palgrave Macmillan, 2010).

Laursen, Andreas, "NATO, the War over Kosovo, and the ICTY Investigation" (2002) 17 *American University International Law Review* 4: 765–814.

Lauterpacht, Hersch, "Westlake and Present Day International Law" (1925) 15 *Economica*: 307–325.

Lauterpacht, Hersch, *Private Law Sources and Analogies of International Law: With Special Reference to International Arbitration* (Hamden: Archon Books, 1927).
Lauterpacht, Hersch, "The Covenant as the Higher Law" (1936) 17 *British Year Book of International Law*: 54–65.
Lauterpacht, Sir Hersch, *The Development of International Law by the International Court* (Cambridge: Cambridge University Press, 1982).
Lauterpacht, Sir Hersch, *The Function of Law in the International Community* (Oxford: Oxford University Press, 2011).
Lauterpacht, Sir Hersch, *Recognition in International Law* (Cambridge: Cambridge University Press, [1947] 2013).
Leben, Charles, "Hans Kelsen and the Advancement of International Law" (1998) 9 *European Journal of International Law* 2: 287–305.
Leiter, Brian, "Beyond the Hart/Dworkin Debate: The Methodology Problem in Jurisprudence" (2003) 48 *American Journal of Jurisprudence* 1: 17–51.
Leiter, Brian, *Naturalizing Jurisprudence: Essays on American Legal Realism and Naturalism in Legal Philosophy* (Oxford: Oxford University Press, 2007).
Leiter, Brian, "Legal Realism and Legal Formalism: What Is the Issue?" (2010) 16 *Legal Theory* 2: 111–133.
Leiter, Brian, "The Demarcation Problem in Jurisprudence: A New Case for Skepticism" (2011) 31 *Oxford Journal of Legal Studies* 4: 663–677.
Lepard, Brian D., *Customary International Law: A New Theory with Practical Applications* (Cambridge: Cambridge University Press, 2010).
Linderfalk, Ulf, "Normative Conflict and the Fuzziness of the International *ius cogens* Regime" (2009) 69 *Zeitschrift für ausländisches öffentliches Recht und Völkerrecht*: 961–977.
Linderfalk, Ulf, "Understanding the Jus Cogens Debate: The Pervasive Influence of Legal Positivism and Legal Idealism" (2015) 46 *Netherlands Yearbook of International Law*: 51–84.
Llano Alonso, *Fernando*, "Cosmopolitanism and Natural Law in Cicero," in Francisco José Contreras (ed.), *The Threads of Natural Law – Unravelling a Philosophical Tradition* (Heidelberg: Springer, 2013), 27–36.
Long, Roderick T., "Hellenistic Philosophers of Law," in Fred D. Miller, Jr. and Carrie-Ann Biondi (eds.), *A Treatise of Legal Philosophy and General Jurisprudence Vol. 6 – A History of the Philosophy of Law from the Ancient Greeks to the Scholastics* (Heidelberg: Springer, 2007), 111–131.
Loquai, Heinz, "Kosovo – A Missed Opportunity for a Peaceful Solution to the Conflict?" (1999) *OSCE Yearbook*: 79–92.
Loquai, Heinz, *Der Kosovo-Konflikt – Wege in einen vermeidbaren Krieg (Die Zeit von Ende November 1997 bis März 1999)* (Baden-Baden: Nomos, 2000).
Luck, Edward C., "Remarks to the General Assembly on the Responsibility to Protect (RtoP)'"(New York, 23 July 2009), at 2, www.ipacademy.org/images/pdfs/luck_ga_statement23july2009.pdf
Luhman, Niklas, *Law as a Social System* (translated by Klaus A. Ziegert) (Oxford: Oxford University Press, 2004).
Luhmann, Niklas, *A Systems Theory of Religion* (translated by David A. Brenner with Adrian Hermann) (Stanford: Stanford University Press, 2013).

Lyons, David, "On Formal Justice" (1973) 58 *Cornell Law Review* 5: 833–861.

MacCormack, Geoffrey, "Anthropology and Legal Theory" (1978) *The Juridical Review*: 216–232.

MacCormick, Neil, *Legal Reasoning and Legal Theory* (with a revised foreword) (Oxford: Clarendon Press, 1994).

MacCormick, Neil, "Institutional Normative Order: A Conception of Law" (1997) 82 *Cornell Law Review* 5: 1051–1070.

MacCormick, Neil, *Institutions of Law – An Essay in Legal Theory* (Oxford: Oxford University Press, 2007).

Machiavelli, Niccolò, *The Prince* (Translated and edited by Peter Bondanella) (Oxford: Oxford University Press, 2005).

Marmor, Andrei, *Law in the Age of Pluralism* (Oxford: Oxford University Press, 2007).

Marmor, Andrei, "The Conventional Foundations of Law," in Stefano Bertea and George Pavlakos (eds.), *New Essays on the Normativity of Law* (Oxford: Hart Publishing, 2011), 143–157.

Marmor, Andrei, "Farewell to Conceptual Analysis (in Jurisprudence)," in Wil Waluchow and Stefan Sciaraffa (eds.), *Philosophical Foundations to the Nature of Law* (Oxford: Oxford University Press, 2013), 209–229.

Martenczuk, Bernd, "The Security Council, the International Court and Judicial Review: What Lessons from Lockerbie?" (1999) 10 *European Journal of International Law* 3: 517–547.

Martens, Georg Friedrich, *Summary of the Law of Nations, Founded on the Treaties and Customs of the Modern Nations of Europe* (translated by William Cobbett) (Philadelphia: Thomas Bradford, 1795).

Martin, Elizabeth A. (ed.), *A Dictionary of Law* (4th ed.) (Oxford: Oxford University Press, 1997).

Martinez, Jenny S., *The Slave Trade and the Origins of International Human Rights Law* (Oxford: Oxford University Press, 2012).

Massa, Anne-Sophie, "NATO's Intervention in Kosovo and the Decision of the Prosecutor of the International Criminal Tribunal for the Former Yugoslavia Not to Investigate: An Abusive Exercise of Prosecutorial Discretion?" (2006) 24 *Berkeley Journal of International Law* 2: 610–649.

McCaffrey, Stephen, "*Lex Lata* or the Continuum of State Responsibility," in Joseph H. H. Weiler, Antonio Cassese, and Marina Spinedi (eds.), *International Crimes of State – A Critical Analysis of the ILC's Draft Article 19 on State Responsibility* (Berlin: Walter de Gruyter, 1989), 242–244.

McCormick, Alison, "From Sovereignty to Responsibility: An Emerging International Norm and Its Call to Action in Burma" (2011) 18 *Indiana Journal of Global Legal Studies* 1: 563–591.

Mégret, Frédéric, "Globalization," in Rüdiger Wolfrum (ed.), *Max Planck Encyclopedia of Public International Law* (Oxford: Oxford University Press, 2013), 493–507.

Merrills, John G., *International Dispute Settlement* (5th ed.) (Cambridge: Cambridge University Press, 2011).

Merrills, John, "The Place of International Litigation in International Law," in Natalie Klein (ed.), *Litigating International Law Disputes – Weighing the Balance* (Cambridge: Cambridge University Press, 2014), 3–23.

Meyerson, Denise, "The Rule of Law and the Separation of Powers" (2004) 4 *Macquarie Law Journal* 1: 1–6.
Michelon, Claudio, "The Public Nature of Private Law?," in Claudio Michelon et al. (eds.), *The Public in Law Representations of the Political in Legal Discourse* (Farnham: Ashgate, 2012), 195–204.
Miller, Fred D. Jr., "Aristotle's Philosophy of Law," in Fred D. Miller, Jr. and Carrie-Ann Biondi (eds.), *A Treatise of Legal Philosophy and General Jurisprudence Vol. 6 – A History of the Philosophy of Law from the Ancient Greeks to the Scholastics* (Heidelberg: Springer, 2007), 79–110.
Miller, Fred D.Jr., "Near Eastern Antecedents of Western Legal Thought," in Fred D. Miller, Jr. and Carrie-Ann Biondi (eds.), *A Treatise of Legal Philosophy and General Jurisprudence Vol. 6 – A History of the Philosophy of Law from the Ancient Greeks to the Scholastics* (Heidelberg: Springer, 2007), 1–5.
Miller, Seumas, "Social Institutions," in Edward N. Zalta (ed.), The Stanford Encyclopedia of Philosophy (Winter 2014 Edition), at.
https://plato.stanford.edu/archives/win2014/entries/social-institutions/
Moral Soiano, Leonor, "A Modest Notion of Coherence in Legal Reasoning. A Model for the European Court of Justice" (2003) 16 *Ratio Juris* 3: 296–323.
Morgenthau, Hans J., *Politics among Nations: The Struggle for Power and Peace* (2nd ed.) (New York: Alfred A. Knopf, 1954).
Morpeth, Neil, "Autarkeia: Notes on its Cultural and Historical Context" (1993) 25 *Prudentia (Supplementary Number: Multarum Artium Scientia)*: 126–130.
Munzer, Stephen, *Legal Validity* (The Hague: Martinus Nijhoff, 1972).
Murphy, Liam, *What Makes Law? An Introduction to the Philosophy of Law* (Cambridge: Cambridge University Press, 2014).
Murphy, Mark C., "Two Unhappy Dilemmas for Natural Law Jurisprudence" (2015) 60 *The American Journal of Jurisprudence* 2: 121–141.
Murphy, Sean D., "Assessing the Legality of Invading Iraq" (2004) 92 *Georgetown Journal of International Law* 2: 173–257.
Murphy, Sean D., "Identification of Customary International Law and other Topics: The Sixty-Seventh Session of the International Law Commission" (2015) 109 *American Journal of International Law* 4: 822–844.
Nader, Laura and Sursock, Andrée, "Anthropology and Justice," in Ronald L. Cohen (ed.), *Justice – Views from the Social Sciences* (New York: Plenum Press, 1986), 205–233.
Neiberg, Michael S., *The Treaty of Versailles – A Concise History* (Oxford: Oxford University Press, 2017).
Newey, Glen, *Routledge Philosophy Guidebook to Hobbes and Leviathan* (London: Routledge, 2008).
O'Connor, Timothy and Sandis, Constantine (eds.), *A Companion to the Philosophy of Action* (Oxford: Wiley-Blackwell, 2010).
Oellers-Frahm, Karin "Lawmaking through Advisory Opinions?" (2011) 12 *German Law Journal* 5: 1033–1056.
Orakhelashvili, Alexander, *Peremptory Norms in International Law* (Oxford: Oxford University Press, 2006).
Orakhelashvili, Alexander, "The Acts of the Security Council: Meaning and Standards of Review" (2007) 11 *Max Planck Yearbook of United Nations Law*: 143–195.

Osherson, Daniel N. and Smith, Edward E., "On the Adequacy of Prototype Theory as the Theory of Concepts" (1981) 9 *Cognition* 1: 35–58.

Palladini, Fiammetta, "Pufendorf Disciple of Hobbes: The Nature of Man and the State of Nature: The Doctrine of *Socialitas*" (2008) 34 *History of European Ideas* 1: 26–60.

Palmeter, David and Mavroidis, Petros C., "The WTO Legal System: Sources of Law" (1998) 92 *American Journal of International Law* 3: 398–413.

Passerin d'Entreves, Alexander, *The Notion of the State – An Introduction to Political Theory* (Oxford: Clarendon Press, 1967).

Pavlakos, George and Rodriguez-Blanco, Veronica (eds.), *Reasons and Intentions in Law and Practical Agency* (Cambridge: Cambridge University Press, 2015).

Pavlakos, George and Rodriguez-Blanco, Veronica, "Introduction," in George Pavlakos and Veronica Rodriguez-Blanco (eds.), *Reasons and Intentions in Law and Practical Agency* (Cambridge: Cambridge University Press, 2015), 1–10.

Payan deh, Mehrdad, *Internationales Gemeinschaftsrecht – Zur Herausbildung gemeinschaftsrechtlicher Strukturen im Völkerrecht der Globalisierung* (Heidelberg: Springer, 2010).

Payandeh, Mehrdad, "The Concept of International Law in the Jurisprudence of H.L.A. Hart" (2010) 21 *European Journal of International Law* 4: 967–995.

Payandeh, Mehrdad, "With Great Power Comes Great Responsibility? The Concept of the Responsibility To Protect Within the Process of International Lawmaking" (2010) 35 *Yale Journal of International Law* 2: 469–516.

Pelc, Krzysztof J., "Eluding Efficiency: Why Do We Not See More Efficient Breach at the WTO?" (2010) 9 *World Trade Review* 4: 629–642.

Pellet, Alain, "Brief Remarks on the Unilateral Use of Force" (2000) 11 *European Journal of International Law* 2: 385–392.

Pellet, Alain, "Article 38," in Andreas Zimmerman, Christian Tomuschat, and Karin Oellers- Frahm (eds.), *The Statute of the International Court of Justice – A Commentary* (2nd ed.) (Oxford: Oxford University Press, 2012), 677–792.

Peristiany, John George, "Law," in Edward Evan Evans-Pritchard et al. (eds.), *The Institutions of Primitive Society* (Oxford: Basil Blackwell, 1954), 39–49.

Perreau-Saussine, Amanda, "Immanuel Kant on International Law," in Samantha Besson and John Tasioulas (eds.), *The Philosophy of International* Law (Oxford: Oxford University Press, 2010), 53–78.

Perry, Stephen, "Second Order Reasons, Uncertainty, and Legal Theory" (1989) 62 *Southern California Law Review*: 913–994.

Perry, Stephen R., "On the Relationship Between Corrective and Distributive Justice," in Jeremy Horder (ed.), *Oxford Essays in Jurisprudence* (Fourth Series) (Oxford: Oxford University Press, 2002), 237–263.

Peters, Anne, "Statehood after 1989: 'Effectivités' between Legality and Virtuality," in James Crawford and Sarah Nouwen (eds.), *Select Proceedings of the European Society of International Law, Vol III* (Oxford: Hart Publishing, 2012), 171–183.

Peters, Anne, *Beyond Human Rights: The Legal Status of the Individual in International Law* (Cambridge: Cambridge University Press, 2016).

Peters, Anne, "International Organizations and International Law," in Jacob Katz Cogan, Ian Hurd, and Ian Johnstone (eds.), *Oxford Handbook of International Organizations* (Oxford: Oxford University Press, 2016), 33–59.

Peters, Anne and Pagotto, Isabella, "Soft Law as a New Mode of Governance: A Legal Perspective" (2006) *New Modes of Governance Project*, Paper n. 04°/D11: 1–35.

Peters, Christopher J. (ed.), *Precedent in the United States Supreme Court* (Dordrecht: Springer, 2013).

Peters, Ronald M., *The Massachusetts Constitution of 1780: A Social Compact* (Amherst: University of Massachusetts Press, 1978).

Pettersson, Therese and Wallensteen, Peter. "Armed Conflicts, 1946–2014" (2015) 52 *Journal of Peace Research* 4: 536–550.

Pitts, Jennifer, *A Turn to Empire: The Rise of Imperial Liberalism in Britain and France* (Princeton: Princeton University Press, 2005).

Posner, Eric and Sykes, Alan O., "Efficient Breach of International Law: Optimal Remedies, Legalized Noncompliance, and Related Issues" (2011) 110 *Michigan Law Review* 2: 243–294.

Pound, Roscoe, "Philosophical Theory and International Law," in *Bibliotheca Visseriana dissertationum ius internationale illustrantium* Vol. 1 (Leiden: E. J. Brill, 1923).

Priel, Dan, "Jurisprudence and Necessity" (2007) 20 *Canadian Journal of Law and Jurisprudence* 1: 173–200.

Priel, Dan, "Jurisprudence and Psychology," in Maksymilian Del Mar (ed.), *New Waves in Philosophy of Law* (Basingstoke: Palgrave Macmillan, 2011), 77–99.

Priel, Dan, "Jurisprudence Between Science and the Humanities" (2012) 4 *Washington University Jurisprudence Review*: 269–323.

Priel, Dan, "The Misguided Search for the Nature of Law" (2015) Osgoode Legal Studies Research Paper No. 34/2015: 41. at https://ssrn.com/abstract=2642461

Primmer, Jennifer W., "Beyond the Law-State: The Adequacy of Raz's Account of Legal Systems in Explaining Intra-State and Supra-State Legality" (2015) 28 *Ratio Juris* 1: 149–158.

Pütter, Johann Stephan and Achenwall, Gottfried, *Anfangsgründe des Naturrechts (Elementa juris naturae)* (edited by Jan Schröder) (Frankfurt: Insel Verlag, 1995).

Radbruch, Gustav, "Statutory Lawlessness and Supra-Statutory Law (1946)" (2006) 26 *Oxford Journal of Legal Studies* 1: 1–11.

Radbruch, Gustav, *Rechtsphilosophie* (Heidelberg: C. F. Müller Verlag, 2011).

Raftopoulos, Evangelos, *The Inadequacy of the Contractual Analogy in the Law of Treaties* (Athens: Publications of the Hellenic Institute of International and Foreign Law, 1990).

Ragazzi, Maurizio, *The Concept of International Obligations Erga Omnes* (Oxford: Clarendon Press, 1997).

Rainioa, J., Lalu, K. and Penttila, A., "Independent Forensic Autopsies in an Armed Conflict: Investigation of the Victims from Racak, Kosovo" (2001) 116 *Forensic Science International* 2: 171–185.

Ralston, Jackson Harvey, *International Arbitration from Athens to Locarno* (Stanford: Stanford University Press, 1929).

Ramsey, William M., "Prototypes and Conceptual Analysis" (1992) 11 *Topoi* 1: 59–70.

Ramsey, William M., *Representation Reconsidered* (Cambridge: Cambridge University Press, 2007).

Ratner, Steven R., *The Thin Justice of International Law: A Moral Reckoning of the Law of Nations* (Oxford: Oxford University Press, 2015).

Rauschning, Dietrich, "Georg Friedrich von Martens (1756–1821) Lehrer des praktischen Europäischen Völkerrechts und der Diplomatie zu Göttingen," in Fritz Loos (ed.), *Rechtswissenschaft in Göttingen: Göttinger Juristen aus 250 Jahren* (Göttingen: Vandenhoeck & Ruprecht, 1987), 123–145.

Rawls, John, *A Theory of Justice* (Cambridge, Mass.: The Belknap Press of Harvard University Press, 1971).

Raz, Joseph, *The Authority of Law – Essays on Law and Morality* (Oxford: Oxford University Press, 1979).

Raz, Joseph, *The Concept of a Legal System: An Introduction to the Theory of Legal System* (2nd ed.) (Oxford: Clarendon Press, 1980).

Raz, Joseph, "Authority, Law, and Morality" (1985) 68 *The Monist* 3: 295–324.

Raz, Joseph, *The Morality of Freedom* (Oxford: Clarendon Press, 1986).

Raz, Joseph, "Facing Up: A Reply" (1989) 62 *Southern California Law Review* 3–4: 1135–1235.

Raz, Joseph, "Rights and Politics" (1995) 71 *Indiana Law Journal* 1: 27–44.

Raz, Joseph, *Ethics in Public Domain – Essays in Morality of Law and Politics* (revised ed.) (Oxford: Clarendon Press, 1995).

Raz, Joseph, "Two Views of the Nature of the Theory of Law: A Partial Comparison" (1998) 4 *Legal Theory* 3: 249–282.

Raz, Joseph, *Engaging Reason – On the Theory of Value and Action* (Oxford: Oxford University Press, 1999).

Raz, Joseph, *Practical Reason and Norms* (2nd ed.) (Oxford: Oxford University Press, 2002).

Raz, Joseph, "Incorporation by Law" (2004) 10 *Legal Theory* 1: 1–17.

Raz, Joseph, "Can There Be a Theory of Law?," in Martin P. Golding and William A. Edmundson (eds.), *The Blackwell Guide to the Philosophy of Law and Legal Theory* (Oxford: Blackwell Publishing, 2005), 324–342.

Raz, Joseph, "Theory and Concepts: Responding to Alexy and Bulygin," in *Una Discusion Sobre la Teoria del Derecho* (Madrid: Marcial Pons, 2007) (in Spanish) English version at josephnraz.googlepages.com/TheoryandConcepts-finalversion .pdf

Raz, Joseph, "Respect for Law," in *The Authority of Law – Essays on Law and Morality* (2nd ed.) (Oxford: Oxford University Press, 2009), 250–261.

Raz, Joseph, "The Purity of the Pure Theory," in *The Authority of Law – Essays on Law and Morality* (2nd ed.) (Oxford: Oxford University Press, 2009), 293–312.

Raz, Joseph, "Reasons: Explanatory and Normative," in Constantine Sandis (ed.), *New Essays on the Explanation of Action* (Basingstoke: Palgrave Macmillan, 2009), 184–202.

Raz, Joseph, "Human Rights in the Emerging World Order" (2010) 1 *Transnational Legal Theory* 1: 31–47.

Raz, Joseph, "Human Rights Without Foundations," in Samantha Besson and John Tasioulas (eds.), *The Philosophy of International Law* (Oxford: Oxford University Press, 2010), 321–337.

Raz, Joseph, "On the Guise of the Good," in Sergio Tenenbaum (ed.), *Desire, Practical Reason and the Good* (Oxford: Oxford University Press, 2010), 111–137.

Raz, Joseph, "Why the State?" (2014) Legal Studies Research Paper Series, Paper No. 2014–38: 1-23. at ssrn.com/abstract=2339522

Regan, Donald H., "Reasons, Authority, and the Meaning of 'Obey': Further Thoughts on Raz and Obedience to Law" (1990) 3 *Canadian Journal of Law and Jurisprudence* 1: 3–28.

Reichler, Paul S. and Parkhomenko, Yuri B., "*Nicaragua* v. *United States* and Matters of Evidence Before the International Court of Justice," in Edgardo Sobenes Obregon and Benjamin Samson (eds.), *Nicaragua Before the International Court of Justice – Impacts on International Law* (Cham: Springer, 2018), 43–56.

Reisman,W. Michael, "Kosovo Antinomies" (1999) 93 *American Journal of International Law* 4: 860–862.

Reisman, W. Michael, "Sanctions and International Law" (2009) 4 *Intercultural Human Rights Law Review* 1: 9–20.

Rigaux, Francois, "Hans Kelsen on International Law" (1998) 9 *European Journal of International Law* 2: 325–343.

Rodriguez-Blanco, Veronica, "Is Finnis Wrong? Understanding Normative Jurisprudence" (2007) 13 *Legal Theory* 3–4: 257–283.

Rodriguez-Blanco, Veronica, *Law and Authority under the Guise of the Good* (Oxford: Hart Publishing, 2014).

Rodriguez-Blanco, Veronica, "Legal Authority and the Paradox of Intention in Action," in George Pavlakos and Veronica Rodriguez-Blanco (eds.), *Reasons and Intentions in Law and Practical Agency* (Cambridge: Cambridge University Press, 2015), 121–139.

Romano, Cesare P. R., "The Proliferation of International Judicial Bodies: The Pieces of the Puzzle" (1999) 31 *New York University Journal of International Law and Politics* 4: 709–751.

Romano, Cesare P. R., "The Shift From the Consensual to the Compulsory Paradigm in International Adjudication: Elements for a Theory of Consent" (2007) 39 *New York University Journal of International Law and Politics* 4: 791–872.

Romano, Cesare P. R., "A Taxonomy of International Rule of Law Institutions" (2011) 2 *Journal of International Dispute Settlement* 1: 241–277.

Romano, Cesare P. R., "Litigating International Law Disputes: Where To?," in Natalie Klein (ed.), *Litigating International Law Disputes – Weighing the Balance* (Cambridge: Cambridge University Press, 2014), 461–471.

Rosch, Eleanor, "Reclaiming Concepts," in Rafael Núñez and Walter J. Freeman (eds.), *Reclaiming Cognition: The Primacy of Action, Intention and Emotion* (Thorverton: Imprint Academic, 1999), 61–76.

Rosch, Eleanor and Mervis, Carolyn B., "Family Resemblances: Studies in the Internal Structure of Categories" (1975) 7 *Cognitive Psychology*: 573–605.

Ross, Alf, *A Textbook of International Law – General Part* (London: Longmans, Green & Co., 1947).

Rüthers, Bernd, *Rechtstheorie (3. Auflage)* (München: Verlag. C.H. Beck, 2007).

Sadat, Leila N. and Drumbl, Mark A., "The United States and the International Criminal Court: A Complicated, Uneasy, Yet at Times Engaging Relationship" (2016) Washington University in St. Louis Legal Studies Research Paper Series, at https://scholarlycommons.law.wlu.edu/cgi/viewcontent.cgi?article=1504&context=wlufac

Sancin, Vasilka (ed.), *Responsibility to Protect: Where Do We Stand Ten Years After?* (Ljubljana: University of Ljubljana Press, 2015).

Sandis, Constantine (ed.), *New Essays on the Explanation of Action* (Basingstoke: Palgrave Macmillan, 2009).

Sandro, Paolo, "An Axiomatic Theory of Law" (2011) 17 *Res Publica* 4: 343–354.
Scarffe, Eric J., "'A New Philosophy for International Law' and Dworkin's Political Realism" (2016) 29 *Canadian Journal of Law & Jurisprudence* 1: 191–213.
Schauer, Frederick, *Playing By the Rules – A Philosophical Examination of Rule-Based Decision-Making in Law and in Life* (Oxford: Clarendon Press, 1991).
Schauer, Frederick, *The Force of Law* (Cambridge, Mass.: Harvard University Press, 2015).
Schermers, Henry G. and Blokker, Niels M., *International Institutional Law – Unity within Diversity* (5th revised ed.) (Leiden: Martinus Nijhoff, 2011).
Schill, Stephan W., "System-Building in Investment Treaty Arbitration and Lawmaking" (2011) 12 *German Law Journal* 5: 1083–1110.
Schlütter, Birgit, *Developments in Customary International Law (Theory and the Practice of the International Court of Justice and the International ad hoc Criminal Tribunals for Rwanda and Yugoslavia)* (Leiden: Martinus Nijhoff Publishers, 2010).
Schrijver, Nico, *Sovereignty over Natural Resources – Balancing Rights and Duties* (Cambridge: Cambridge University Press, 1997).
Searle, John R., "How to Derive 'Ought' From 'Is'" (1964) 73 *The Philosophical Review* 1: 43–58.
Seidler, Michael, "Pufendorf's Moral and Political Philosophy," in Edward N. Zalta (ed.), *The Stanford Encyclopedia of Philosophy* (Winter 2015 Edition), at http://plato.stanford.edu/archives/win2015/entries/pufendorf-moral
Sender, Omri and Wood, Michael, "The International Court of Justice and Customary International Law: A Reply to Stefan Talmon," *EJIL: Talk!*, 30 November 2015, at www.ejiltalk.org/the-international-court-of-justice-and-customary-international-law-a-reply-to-stefan-talmon/
Shahabuddeen, Mohamed, *Precedent in the World Court* (Cambridge: Cambridge University Press, 1996).
Shahabuddeen, Mohamed, *International Criminal Justice at the Yugoslav Tribunal: A Judge's Recollection* (Oxford: Oxford University Press, 2012).
Shapiro, Scott J., *Legality* (Cambridge, Mass.: The Belknap Press of Harvard University Press, 2011).
Shaw, Malcolm, *Title to Territory in Africa – International Legal Issues* (Oxford: Clarendon Press, 1986).
Shaw, Malcolm N., *International Law* (6th ed.) (Cambridge: Cambridge University Press, 2008).
Shea, Nicholas and Bayne, Tim, "The Vegetative State and the Science of Consciousness" (2010) 61 *The British Journal for the Philosophy of Science* 3: 459–484.
Shelton, Dinah, "International Law and 'Relative Normativity,'" in Malcolm D. Evans (ed.), *International Law* (1st ed.) (Oxford: Oxford University Press, 2003), 141–171.
Shelton, Dinah, "Sherlock Holmes and the Mystery of *Jus Cogens*" (2015) 46 *Netherlands Yearbook of International Law*: 23–50.
Shiner, Roger A., "Law and Normativity," in Dennis Patterson (ed.), *A Companion to Philosophy of Law and Legal Theory* (2nd ed.) (Oxford: Wiley-Blackwell, 2010), 417–445.
Simma, Bruno, "Self-contained Regimes" (1985) 16 *Netherlands Yearbook of International Law*: 111–136.
Simma, Bruno, "NATO, the UN and the Use of Force: Legal Aspects" (1999) 10 *European Journal of International Law* 1: 1–22.

Simma, Bruno, "Fragmentation in a Positive Light" (2004) 25 *Michigan Journal of International Law* 4: 845–847.

Simma, Bruno and Alston, Philip "The Sources of Human Rights Law: Custom, *Jus Cogens* and General Principles" (1988–1989) 12 *Australian Yearbook of International Law*: 82–108.

Simma, Bruno and Pulkowski, Dirk, "Of Planets and the Universe: Self-contained Regimes in International Law" (2006) 17 *European Journal of International Law* 3: 483–529.

Skubiszewski, Krzysztof, "Implied Powers of International Organizations," in Yoram Dinstein (ed.), *International Law at a Time of Perplexity – Essays in Honour of Shabatai Rosenne* (Dordrecht: Martinus Nijhoff, 1989), 855–868.

Slaughter, Anne-Marie, "A Global Community of Courts" (2003) 44 *Harvard International Law Journal* 1: 191–219.

Sloan, Blaine, "General Assembly Resolutions Revisited (Forty Years Later)" (1988) 58 *British Yearbook of International Law*: 39–150.

Slocum, Brian G. (ed.), *The Nature of Legal Interpretation: What Jurists Can Learn about Legal Interpretation from Linguistics and Philosophy* (Chicago: University of Chicago Press, 2017).

Solum, Lawrence B., "Procedural Justice" (2004) 78 *Southern California Law Review* 1: 181–321.

Somek, Alexander, "Kelsen Lives" (2007) 18 *European Journal of International Law* 3: 409–451.

Somek, Alexander, "Beyond Kelsen and Hart," in Jörg Kammerhofer and Jean D'Aspremont (eds.), *International Legal Positivism in a Post-Modern World* (Cambridge: Cambridge University Press, 2014), 151–181.

Spaak, Torben, "Schauer's Anti-Essentialism" (2016) 29 *Ratio Juris* 2: 184–214.

Spaak, Torben, "Legal Positivism, Conventionalism, and the Normativity of Law" (2018) 9 *Jurisprudence* 2: 319–344.

Spaić, Bojan, "Epistemic Authority and Legal Interpretation" (2017), at https://ssrn.com/abstract=3013573

Spain, Anna, "Integration Matters: Rethinking the Architecture of International Dispute Resolution" (2010) 32 *University of Pennsylvania Journal of International Law* 1: 1–55.

Spain, Anna, "Examining the International Judicial Function: International Courts as Dispute Resolvers" (2011) 34 *Loyola of Los Angeles International and Comparative Law Review* 1: 5–31.

Spierman, Ole, *International Legal Argument in the Permanent Court of International Justice – The Rise of the International Judiciary* (Cambridge: Cambridge University Press, 2005).

Squires, Judith, "Liberal Constitutionalism, Identity and Difference" (1996) 44 *Political Studies* 3: 620–634.

Stevenson, Drury D., "Kelsen's View of the Addressee of the Law: Primary and Secondary Norms," in D. A. Jeremy Telman (ed.), *Hans Kelsen in America – Selective Affinities and the Mysteries of Academic Influence* (Berlin: Springer, 2016), 297–318.

Striker, Gisela, *Essays on Hellenistic Epistemology and Ethics* (Cambridge: Cambridge University Press, 1996).

Summers, Robert S., "H. L. A. Hart on Justice" (1962) 59 *Journal of Philosophy*: 479–500.

Summers, Robert S., "The *New* Analytical Jurist" (1966) 41 *New York University Law Review* 5: 861–896.

Sweet, Alec Stone, *The Judicial Construction of Europe* (Oxford: Oxford University Press, 2004).

Talmon, Stefan, "The Security Council as World Legislature" (2005) 99 *American Journal of International Law* 1: 175–193.

Talmon, Stefan, "Determining Customary International Law: The ICJ's Methodology between Induction, Deduction and Assertion" (2015) 26 *The European Journal of International Law* 2: 417–443.

Talmon, Stefan, "Determining Customary International Law: The ICJ's Methodology and the Idyllic World of the ILC," *EJIL: Talk!*, 3 December 2015, at www.ejiltalk.org/determining-customary-international-law-the-icjs-methodology-and-the-idyllic-world-of-the-ilc/

Tamanaha, Brian Z., "Understanding Legal Pluralism: Past to Present, Local to Global" (2008) 30 *Sidney Law Review* 3: 375–411.

Tamanaha, Brian, *A Realistic Theory of Law* (Cambridge: Cambridge University Press, 2017).

Tams, Christian J., "Meta-Custom and the Court: A Study in Judicial Law-Making" (2015) 14 *The Law and Practice of International Courts and Tribunals* 1: 51–79.

Tan, Elaine S., "An Empty Shell? Rethinking the Usury Laws in Medieval Europe" (2002) 23 *The Journal of Legal History* 3: 177–196.

Tenenbaum, Sergio (ed.), *Desire, Practical Reason and the Good* (Oxford: Oxford University Press, 2010).

Tesón, Fernando R., "Fake Custom," in Brian D. Lepard (ed.), *Reexamining Customary International Law* (Cambridge: Cambridge University Press, 2017), 86–110.

Teubner, Gunther, "Autopoiesis in Law and Society: A Rejoinder to Blankenburg" (1984) 18 *Law & Society Review* 2: 291–301.

Thirlway, Hugh, *The Sources of International Law* (Oxford: Oxford University Press, 2014).

Tomuschat, Christian, "Reconceptualizing the Debate on *Jus Cogens* and Obligations *Erga Omnes*– Concluding Observations," in Christian Tomuschat and Jean-Marc Thouvenin (eds.), *The Fundamental Rules of the International Legal Order – Jus Cogens and Obligations Erga Omnes* (Leiden: Martinus Nijhoff, 2006), 425–436.

Toohey, Lisa, "Barriers to Universal Membership of the World Trade Organization" (2012) 19 *Australian International Law Journal*: 97–115.

Trachtman, Joel P., "The Growing Obsolescence of Customary International Law," in Curtis A. Bradley (ed.), *Custom's Future – International Law in a Changing World* (Cambridge: Cambridge University Press, 2016), 172–204.

Treves, Tulio, "Customary International Law," in Rüdiger Wolfrum (ed.), *Max Planck Encyclopedia of Public International Law*, (Oxford: Oxford University Press, 2013).

Tuck, Richard, *The Rights of War and Peace – Political Thought and the International Order from Grotius to Kant* (Oxford: Oxford University Press, 1999).

Twining, William, *General Jurisprudence: Understanding Law from a Global Perspective* (Cambridge: Cambridge University Press, 2009).

Twining, William, *Globalisation and Legal Scholarship* (Oisterwijk: Wolf Legal Publishers, 2011).

Ulfstein, Geir, "Institutions and Competences," in Jan Klabbers, Anne Peters, and Geir Ulfstein, *The Constitutionalization of International Law* (Oxford: Oxford University Press, 2011), 45–80.

Ullmann, Walter, *Law and Politics in the Middle Ages – An Introduction to the Sources of Medieval Political Ideas* (Cambridge: Cambridge University Press, 1975).

Vaihinger, Hans, *The Philosophy of 'As if' – A System of Theoretical, Practical and Religious Fictions of Mankind* (translated by C. K. Ogden) (London: Routledge and Kegan Paul, 1925).

Valticos, Nicolas, "Foreword to the Original Edition," in Bertrand G. Ramcharan (ed.), *International Law and Fact-Finding in the Field of Human Rights* (revised and edited reprint) (Leiden: Brill Nijhoff, 2014), xv–xix.

Vamvoukos, Athanassios, *Termination of Treaties in International Law: The Doctrine of Rebus Sic Stantibus and Desuetude* (Oxford: Clarendon Oxford 1985).

van Aaken, Anne, "Balancing of Human Rights – Constitutional Interpretation in International Law," in Miodrag A. Jovanović and Ivana Krstić (eds.), *Human Rights Today – 60 Years of the Universal Declaration* (Utrecht: Eleven International Publishing, 2010), 51–76.

VanLandingham, Rachel E., "Politics or Law? The Dual Nature of the Responsibility to Protect" (2012) 41 *Denver Journal of International Law & Policy* 1: 101–123.

Van Orman Quine, Willard, "Two Dogmas of Empiricism" (1951) 60 *The Philosophical Review* 1: 20–43.

Venzke, Ingo, *How Interpretation Makes International Law – On Semantic Change and Normative Twists* (Oxford: Oxford University Press, 2012).

Verdross, Alfred, *Völkerrecht (unter Mitarbeit von Karl Zemanek)* (4th ed.) (Wien: Springer, 1959).

Verdross, Alfred, "Jus Dispositivum and Jus Cogens in International Law" (1966) 60 *American Journal of International Law* 1: 55–63.

Vernet, Paula María, "Decolonization: Spanish Territories," in Rüdiger Wolfrum (ed.), *Max Planck Encyclopedia of Public International Law* (Oxford: Oxford University Press, 2013).

Vidmar, Jure, *Democratic Statehood in International Law: The Emergence of New States in Post-Cold War Practice* (Oxford: Hart Publishing, 2013).

Vidmar, Jure, "The Importance of Legal Criteria for Statehood: A Rejoinder to Dapo Akande" (2013), at www.ejiltalk.org/the-importance-of-legal-criteria-for-statehood-a-rejoinder-to-dapo-akande/

Vinx, Lars, "Austin, Kelsen, and the Model of Sovereignty: Notes on the History of Modern Legal Positivism," in Michael Freeman and Patricia Mindus (eds.), *The Legacy of John Austin's Jurisprudence* (Dordrecht: Springer, 2013), 51–71.

von Bernstorff, Jochen, *The Public International Law Theory of Hans Kelsen: Believing in Universal Law* (translated by Thomas Dunlap) (Cambridge: Cambridge University Press, 2010).

von Bernstorff, Jochen, "German Intellectual Historical Origins of International Legal Positivism," in Jörg Kammerhofer and Jean D'Aspremont (eds.), *International Legal Positivism in a Post- Modern World* (Cambridge: Cambridge University Press, 2014), 50–80.

von Bogdandy, Armin and Venzke, Ingo, "International Courts as Lawmakers," in Rüdiger Wolfrum and Ina Gätzschmann (eds.), *International Dispute Settlement: Room for Innovations?* (Heidelberg: Springer, 2013), 159–327.

von Pufendorf, Samuel, *Of the Law of Nature and Nations* (translated by Basil Kennett) (London: J. Walthoe et. al., 1729), Book II.

von Verdross, Alfred, "Forbidden Treaties in International Law" (1937) 31 *American Journal of International Law* 4: 571–577.

von Verdross, Alfred, "On the Concept of International Law" (1949) 43 *American Journal of International Law* 3: 435–440.

Waldron, Jeremy, "Does Law Promise Justice?" (2001) 17 *Georgia State University Law Review* 3: 759–788.

Waldron, Jeremy, "Authority for Officials," in Lukas H. Meyer, Stanley L. Paulson, and Thomas W. Pogge (eds.), *Rights, Culture and the Law – Themes from the Legal and Political Philosophy of Joseph Raz* (Oxford: Oxford University Press, 2003), 45–69.

Waldron, Jeremy, "Are Constitutional Norms *Legal* Norms?" (2006) 75 *Fordham Law Review* 3: 1697–1713.

Waldron, Jeremy, "Hart and the Principle of Legality," in Matthew H. Kramer et. al. (eds.), *The Legacy of H.L.A. Hart: Legal, Political, and Moral Philosophy* (Oxford: Oxford University Press, 2008), 67–84.

Waldron, Jeremy, "Are Sovereigns Entitled to the Benefit of the International Rule of Law?" (2011) 22 *European Journal of International Law* 2: 315–343.

Waldron, Jeremy, "International Law: 'A Relatively Small and Unimportant' Part of Jurisprudence?," in Luís Duarte d'Almeida, James Edwards, and Andrea Dolcetti (eds.), *Reading HLA Hart's 'The Concept of Law'* (Oxford: Hart Publishing, 2013), 209–227.

Waldron, Jeremy, "Ronald Dworkin: An Appreciation" (2013) Public Law and Legal Theory Research Paper Series – Working Paper No. 13–39: 1–8.

Wall, Andru E., "Was the 2003 Invasion of Iraq Legal?" (2003) 86 *International Law Studies*: 69–80.

Wallace, Jay R., "Practical Reason," in Edward N. Zalta (ed.), The Stanford Encyclopedia of Philosophy (Spring 2018 Edition), at https://plato.stanford.edu/archives/spr2018/entries/practical-reason

Walzer, Michael, *Spheres of Justice – A Defense of Pluralism and Equality* (New York: Basic Books, 1983).

Weatherall, Thomas, *Jus Cogens – International Law and Social Contract* (Cambridge: Cambridge University Press, 2015).

Webber, Grégoire, "Asking Why in the Study of Human Affairs" (2015) 60 *The American Journal of Jurisprudence* 1: 51–78.

Weber, Max, *Economy and Society – An Outline of Interpretative Sociology* (edited by Guenther Roth and Claus Wittich) (Berkeley: University of California Press, 1978), Vol. 1.

Weil, Prosper, "Towards Relative Normativity in International Law?" (1983) 77 *American Journal of International Law* 3: 413–442.

Weisburd, A. Mark, *Failings of the International Court of Justice* (Oxford: Oxford University Press, 2016).

Weller, Marc, "The Rambouillet Conference on Kosovo" (1999) 75 *International Affairs* 2: 211–251.

Weller, Marc, "Settling Self-determination Conflicts: Recent Developments" (2009) 20 *European Journal of International Law* 1: 111–165.

Williamson, Timothy, "How Did We Get Here From There? The Transformation of Analytic Philosophy" (2014) 27 *Belgrade Philosophical Annual*: 7–37.

Winston, Kenneth I., "On Treating Like Cases Alike" (1974) 62 *California Law Review* 1: 1–39.

Wittgenstein, Ludwig, *Tractatus Logico-Philosophicus* (London: Kegan Paul, Trench, Trubner & Co., 1922).

Wittgenstein, Ludwig, *Philosophical Investigations* (Oxford: Basil Blackwell, 1958 [1953]).

Wolff, Christian, *Jus Gentium Methodo Scientifica Pertractatum, Vol. II* (translated by Joseph H. Drake) (Oxford: Clarendon Press, 1934).

Wolfrum, Rüdiger, "Sources of International Law," in Rüdiger Wolfrum (ed.), *Max Planck Encyclopedia of Public International Law* (Oxford: Oxford University Press, 2013).

Wood, Michael C., "The Interpretation of Security Council Resolutions" (1998) 2 *Max Planck Yearbook of United Nations Law*: 73–95.

Wood, Sir Michael, "Formation and Evidence of Customary International Law, Address to the International Law Commission, Geneva, 30. July 2012" (2013) 12 *The Law and Practice of International Courts and Tribunals* 2: 273–280.

Wood, Michael C., "The Interpretation of Security Council Resolutions, Revisited" (2017) 20 *Max Planck Yearbook of United Nations Law*: 1–35.

Wouters, Jan and Verhoeven, Sten, "Desuetudo," in Rüdiger Wolfrum (ed.), *Max Planck Encyclopedia of Public International Law* (Oxford: Oxford University Press, 2013).

Yavuz, M. Hakan and Sluglett, Peter (eds.), *War and Diplomacy: The Russo-Turkish War of 1877–1878 and the Treaty of Berlin* (Salt Lake City: The University of Utah Press, 2011).

Young, James O., "The Coherence Theory of Truth," in Edward N. Zalta (ed.), *The Stanford Encyclopedia of Philosophy* (Fall 2018 Edition), https://plato.stanford.edu/archives/fall2018/entries/truth-coherence/

Young, Margaret A., "Introduction: The Productive Friction between Regimes," in Margaret A. Young (ed.), *Regime Interaction in International Law – Facing Fragmentation* (Cambridge: Cambridge University Press, 2012), 1–19.

Zimmern, Alfred, *The League of Nations and the Rule of Law* (London: MacMillan and Co., 1936).

Zoller, Elisabeth, "Institutional Aspects of International Governance" (1995) 3 *Indiana Journal of Global Legal Studies* 1: 121–131.

Zolo, Danilo, "Hans Kelsen: International Peace through International Law" (1998) 9 *European Journal of International Law* 2: 306–324.

Zorzetto, Silvia, "The *Lex Specialis* Principle and Its Uses in Legal Argumentation: An Analytical Inquiry" (2012–2013) 3 *Eunomía. Revista en Cultura de la Legalidad*: 61–88.

# Index

For EU product safety concerns, contact us at Calle de José Abascal, 56–1°,
28003 Madrid, Spain or eugpsr@cambridge.org.

www.ingramcontent.com/pod-product-compliance
Ingram Content Group UK Ltd.
Pitfield, Milton Keynes, MK11 3LW, UK
UKHW020650180726
473384UK00011B/532
* 9 7 8 1 1 0 8 4 6 1 3 8 2 *